Case Studies for Advances in Paleoimaging and Other Non-Clinical Applications

Case Studies for Advances in Paleoimaging and Other Non-Clinical Applications

Ronald G. Beckett, Gerald J. Conlogue,
and Andrew J. Nelson

CRC Press is an imprint of the
Taylor & Francis Group, an **informa** business

CRC Press
Taylor & Francis Group
6000 Broken Sound Parkway NW, Suite 300
Boca Raton, FL 33487-2742

CRC Press is an imprint of Taylor & Francis Group, an Informa business

International Standard Book Number-13: 978-0-367-25166-6 (Hardback)

Visit the Taylor & Francis Web site at
http://www.taylorandfrancis.com

and the CRC Press Web site at
http://www.crcpress.com

Dedication

Unlike the previous volume that presented facts supporting the science behind the modalities, the following requires taking those basic tenants and applying them to specific nontraditional applications. In order to be successful, these types of efforts required not only support and encouragement from colleagues, friends, and loved ones, but also from those individuals that control access to material to be willing to take a chance and provide the necessary opportunity. To that end, I'd like to dedicate this work to the many professionals and colleagues who have made this research possible:

- *To Roy Sagram, Jeanne Hoadley, and Barbara Ann Little for their assistance and Drs. D. Gordon Potts and Philip Partington for their backing to accept the challenge to develop a contrast media that would not only be radiopaque but also remain in vessels following dissection.*
- *To Drs. E. Leon Kier and William E. Allen III for their willingness to allow the incorporation of that contrast media into the research protocol.*
- *To Dr. John Ogden for establishing the Yale Marine Mammal Stranding Center and providing the opportunity to learn the art of marine mammal and reptile necropsy and incorporating radiography into the study protocol.*
- *To James Mead, Charley Potter, and Bob Schoelkopf for providing access to stranded animals.*
- *To Gretchen Worden, who rejected the assertion that it is not possible to acquire diagnostic quality images in a museum without moving the mummified to an imaging facility with the most sophisticated equipment.*
- *To Andrew Nelson and Sonia Guillén, who ignored claims that a functional mobile field radiographic facility using film as an image receptor could not be established in a remote area.*
- *To Larry Engle, Engle Brothers Media, and the National Geographic Channel for their faith that for 40 episodes of the* Mummy Road Show *all challenges would be accepted and every effort made to produce valid scientific results.*

Without access to materials in collections and confidence in our abilities to acquire images, none of the studies would have been possible; therefore, this book is also dedicated to the following:

- *To Terry Dagradi, Laura Lindgren, Paul Lincoln, Kathy Maher, Adrienne Saint-Pierre, Anna Dhody, Maria Patricia Ordoñez, Jelena Bekvalac, and Dario Piombino-Mascali.*
- *To Jason Kreitner, who permitted access to a clinical facility to carry out a multiple modality study of the mummified remains of an individual that died of smallpox in the mid-nineteenth century.*
- *For providing access to the most recent advances in digital radiographic equipment, I dedicate this work to everyone at Kubtec including Vikram Butani, Chester Lowe, Robert Velasco, and Tim Ely.*

Since I did not work in isolation:

- *To the radiographers Natalie Pelletier, Tania Grgurich, Jiazi Li, Mark Farmer, Deborah Gulliver, and Kim Hutchings, and the student radiographers Aniello Catapano, Jennifer Curry, and Annamaria DiCesare, who have helped ensure that studies were successfully completed.*

For field studies to be successful, there is much more required than just image acquisition; an understanding and acceptance of cultural differences and differing viewpoints are necessary to create a positive environment. To that end, this work is dedicated to Ed Claycomb, Gloria Lizcano, Alfe Lester Hanson, and Segundo Quesquen.

Last but certainly not least, I dedicate this book to my son, Byron, and daughter, Keanau, who endured assisting in necropsies of sharks in the Panama City Beach landfill. And to my other son, Michael, who, along with the other two, never complained about the dermestid beetle colony in the back yard. And finally to Shar Walbaum, who not only tolerated all the work while encouraging me to continue, but also totally supported my first trip to Peru to establish a field radiographic facility. – Gerald Conlogue

In addition to the many names listed above, I would like to further dedicate this book to my sons, Matthew and Paul, my daughter, Julie, and to my other son, James, who have tolerated and participated in the active mummification of various roadkill specimens. And to my wife, Katherine, who has always been more than supportive, understanding, and empathetic and who has also been an able member of our research team efforts. – Ronald Beckett

The two dedications outlined above emphasize that paleoimaging is an inherently interdisciplinary and hugely collaborative undertaking. Over the years, I have been fortunate to work with many clinicians, imaging physicists, archaeologists, museum curators and conservators, students, and many others. However, to keep this short, I will dedicate this volume to the memory of my late wife, Christine Nelson, who was a big part of many of these imaging adventures, and to these two amazing friends and colleagues, Ron and Jerry. – Andrew Nelson

Contents

Preface

With a thorough understanding of the scientific basis for each of the modalities found in *Advances in Paleoimaging*, it is possible to discuss specific examples that have been divided into eight categories. The latter were arbitrarily organized and there may be a bit of overlap. However, because of the wide range of topics that will be considered, it was necessary to create some type of groupings.

For each category, the narrative develops in a linear fashion taking into account the specific objects for each study and the imaging approach based on available resources. There is an emphasis on implementing and adapting well-documented medical imaging protocols and procedures to each unique situation. In addition, there is a common theme on the problem-solving process necessary to attain the study objectives. Included are comments related to the frequent recalibrations and adjustments required of methods and procedures when faced with challenges as the imaging study progressed. The incorporation of the successful elements of these novel approaches to study design are then woven into future studies. Over time, when possible, as the technology evolved, the approaches were modified and comparisons are made regarding the productivity of each methodology. For example, the mummified remains from Guanajuato, Mexico, were radiographed on five separate occasions over a span of 15 years. During that period, the technology evolved, including the type of image receptors available: four studies were recorded with either radiographic film or Polaroid photographic film, and the fifth was recorded with a digital imaging system. The data demonstrated that going from film to a digital system more than doubled the number of images that could be acquired per day.

Although the case studies go back over 50 years, the principles are still applicable today. In fact, although in the United States film has been completely replaced by primarily direct digital radiography (DR) technology which eliminates the need for "wet" processing of physical film, there are many other countries where film is still the recording media most frequently used.

Website support:

Paleoimaging is a visual science and in order to demonstrate its full potential the authors have provided a website where you can view the chapter/case figures referenced as [WS] in the text. There are, of course, figures here in the text, but the website allows you to better visualize the concepts described in the various cases. As you will see, in some of the case presentations there are "call outs" to [WS] figures that do not appear in the text but are housed on the website where these color figures can be viewed. While this may be a novel approach, as authors, we want to assure that you have access to as much visual support for the text as possible.

To access the website, go to: https://briq.squarespace.com. Open the menu bars on the upper right and select the "Advances in Paleoimaging: Image Gallery" item. Then select Book 2 and the chapter/case number to view the additional figures associated with that case. You may review them as often as you like.

We hope that you find the additional figures instructive as you explore *Case Studies for Advances in Paleoimaging and Other Non-Clinical Applications.*

Acknowledgments

Karen Garrick Craft
Jason Kritner
Jaizi Li
Michael (Mike) Schlenk
Frank Cerrone
Ann Marie Lombardo
Lisa Schwappach
Richard (Dick) Horn
James Taylor
Hilary Lester
Susan Steiger-Vanegas, Dr. Med. Vet., PhD, DECVDI
Jason Wiest
Mike Zohn
Evan Michelson
Adrienne Saint Pierre
Kathleen (Kathy) Maher
Anna Dhody
Hanna Polasky
George Grigonis
Carol Snow
Gary Aronsen
Nicholas (Nick) Bellantoni
Rob Greenburg
Chester Lowe
Laura Lindgren
Paul Etienne Lincoln
Roger Colten
Gary Double
Deborah Gulliver
Mark Farmer
Dick Horn
David Hunt
Chester Lowe
Roberto Velasco
Edward Meyer
Andrew Gernon
Vivian Zoë
David Bugg
Robert Kowaski
Robert French

Editors

Ronald G. Beckett is Professor Emeritus in the Department of Biomedical Sciences at Quinnipiac University. **Gerald J. Conlogue** is Co-Director of the Bioanthropology Research Institute at Quinnipiac College. In 1999, Beckett and Conologue cofounded the Bioanthropology Research Institute at Quinnipiac University. Their work with mummified remains has been featured in television documentaries on paleoimaging, including on the Discovery, Learning, and National Geographic channels. For National Geographic, they travelled to over 13 countries where they served as cohosts for a three-year, 40-episode documentary series called *The Mummy Road Show*. In 2010, CRC Press published their book *Paleoimaging: Field Applications for Cultural Remains and Artifacts*. In addition to conducting paleoimaging research, they continue to speak at various scientific symposia, museums, and civic organizations around the world. **Andrew J. Nelson** is Professor in the Departments of Anthropology and Chemistry and member of the Bone and Joint Institute at Western University in London, Ontario, Canada. He is widely published in the field and his research interests include the use of nondestructive imaging in human skeletal remains and artifacts, Peruvian bioarchaelogy, and hominin growth and development.

Contributors

Yvette Bailey
Diagnostic Radiologist
Diagnostic Radiology
Avon, Connecticut

Jelena Bekvalac
Curator of Human Osteology
Centre for Human Bioarchaeology
Museum of London
London, UK

Alicia Giaimo
Clinical Associate Professor, Diagnostic Imaging
Program Director, Radiologic Sciences Program
Department of Diagnostic Imaging, Quinnipiac University
Hamden, Connecticut

Sonia Guillen
Minister of Culture
National Museum of Archeology, Anthropology, and History of Peru
Lima, Peru

Emad Hamid
Attending Radiologist
Diagnostic Imaging Associates
Tulsa, Oklahoma

Stan Kogon
Emeritus, Schulich School of Medicine and Dentistry
The University of Western Ontario
London, Ontario, Canada

Roberto Lombardo
Adjunct Faculty
Diagnostic Imaging Program, Quinnipiac University
Hamden, Connecticut and
Forensic Imaging Consultant
Office of the Chief Medical Examiner for the State of Connecticut
Farmington, Connecticut

Alan G. Lurie
Department of Oral Health and Diagnostic Sciences
School of Dental Medicine
University of Connecticut
Farmington, Connecticut

Bernadette Mele
Clinical Associate Professor of Diagnostic Imaging
Director of Clinical Education, Magnetic Resonance Imaging
Quinnipiac University
Hamden, Connecticut

Maria Patricia Ordóñez
Lecturer, Forensic Anthropologist and Archaeologist
Universidad San Francisco de Quito
Quito, Ecuador

Natalie Pelletier
Mammography Manager, Central Region
MidState Radiology Associates
Meriden, Connecticut

John Posh
Director of Education, MRI Safety Officer
Metrasens
Lisle, Illinois

Mark Viner
Cranfield Forensic Institute
Defence Academy of the United Kingdom
Shrivenham, United Kingdom
and
Barts and The London School of Medicine and Dentistry
Queen Mary University
London, United Kingdom

Scott C. Warnasch
Forensic Archaeologist
Principal Consultant at SC Warnasch L.L.C.
Bloomfield, New Jersey

Bruce Young
Department of Anatomy
Kirksville College of Osteopathic Medicine
Kirksville, Missouri

Large Objects

1

GERALD J. CONLOGUE

Objective: Radiograph objects that are larger than the largest film holder or cassette available.

In 1934, Arthur W. Fuchs published an image of a full body in high heels in what looked like a pearl necklace (Figure 1.1). The image appeared in an article that he titled "Radiography of entire body employing one film and a single exposure" in the journal *Radiography and Clinical Photography*, which he edited for Kodak. There was great interest in capturing images of entire objects beyond the limitation of conventional size cassettes, that is, 14 × 17 inches (36 × 43 cm).

Due to beam divergence, multiple individual radiographs of a large object, changing the position of the X-ray source between exposures, will result in images that cannot be perfectly matched to create a single large image. This case study is comprised of multiple cases that span 40 years and demonstrate the evolution of imaging receptors in an attempt to repeat Fuchs's work over eight decades ago.

After seeing the image, I really wanted to X-ray large objects, but the opportunity did not come until 1993 with a request from Andrew Nelson, a physical anthropology graduate student at UCLA, who wanted images of skeletons with acromegaly to be included in a study that he was conducting. Nelson identified two skeletons with the condition: one at the Mütter Museum, in the College of Physicians in Philadelphia, Pennyslvania, and the other in the anatomy department at the Yale School of Medicine in New Haven, Connecticut. Although both skeletons demonstrated the disease and were hanging in display cases, from an imaging prospective each had to be approached differently.

The skeletal remains of an individual at Yale were associated with Harvey Cushing, who first described the condition resulting from a tumor of the anterior pituitary gland, located at the base of the brain. The mass caused excess growth hormone to be secreted and resulted in the gigantic outward appearance of the individual. The skeleton was approximately 80 inches (203 cm) high and located in a corridor that would be unoccupied after 6 PM each evening. A 1940s vintage Picker Army Field unit, acquired from a veterinarian in eastern Connecticut, was donated to the diagnostic imaging program at Quinnipiac University to enable mobile radiography. Because it disassembled into five sections—a column with crank mechanism, X-ray tube with cables, the control unit, the transformer, and a base with wheels—it was considered a portable unit. The heaviest component, the transformer, weighted almost 100 pounds. However, because the X-ray tube could be rotated, it would be possible to direct a horizontal beam toward the skeleton.

Although it was a functional X-ray source the unit presented several problems for the Yale study. The first obstacle was that the unit lacked a collimator light to indicate the distance required to cover the entire skeleton. The solution: back at the Quinnipiac diagnostic imaging laboratory, an assortment of various-sized cassettes were taped to the wall to achieve the 80-inch (203-cm) height required to expose the entire skeleton (Figure 1.2). Once it was determined that a 105-inch (267-cm) SID was the minimum distance required, the necessary exposure factors were established. A skeleton in the imaging lab was used with a nonscreen film holder to simulate the conditions at Yale. In order to reduce wear on the 50-year-old X-ray tube, a 50-inch (127-cm) SID was used to determine the optimal exposure factors: 48 kVp, 14 mA, and 14 separate 13 second exposures with a 30-second delay between exposures to permit the X-ray tube to cool. Using the inverse square law, it was calculated that 62 exposures were necessary at a 105-inch (267-cm) SID.

The next problem was the image receptor. Two sheets of foam core were fastened together to create a 25 × 80-inch (64 × 203-cm) rigid support. The foam core was taken into the university's large photographic darkroom and laid on the floor, and 14 × 17-inch (36 × 43-cm) sheets of X-ray film were thumb-tacked to the rigid support. In order to ensure that there would be no gaps between films, care was taken to have at least an inch overlap of adjacent films. The *loaded film holder* was then wrapped with three layers of black gardening plastic with the ends folded over and sealed with duct tape. The mounted skeleton was removed from the display case, the anterior surface placed against the film holder, and a cloth strap was fastened across the back to secure it in place (Figure 1.3). Because of the 30-second delays between exposures, the total exposure time was approximately 45 minutes. Following the completion of the study, the film holder was brought back to the photographic darkroom at Quinnipiac and, unwrapped, the sheets of X-ray film were transferred into a light-tight

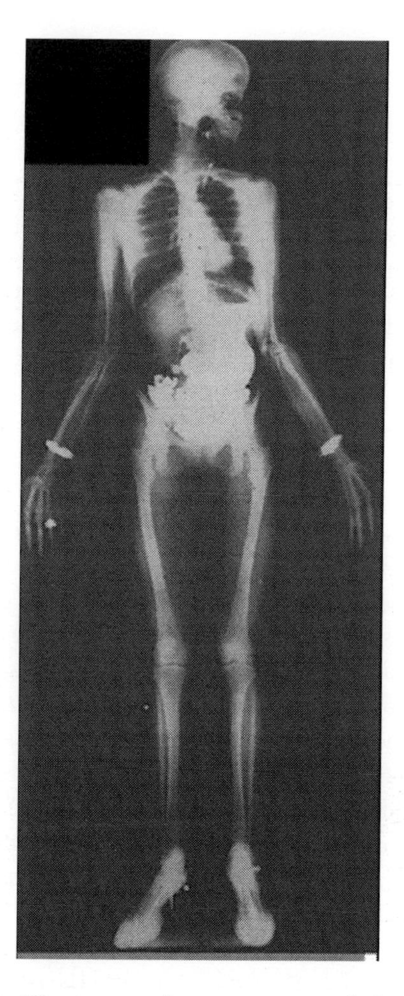

Figure 1.1. The image of a woman recorded on a single sheet of film that Arthur W. Fuchs published in 1934.

Figure 1.2. The assortment of various-sized cassettes taped to the wall in the Quinnipiac diagnostic imaging laboratory used to determine the minimum distance required to cover the 80-inch (203-cm) vertical height requirement. Two Quinnipiac diagnostic imaging students, Karen Garrick (Craft) and Jason Kreitner, worked on the study. Note the 1940s vintage Picker Army Field unit X-ray tube (arrow).

film transport box, and finally were developed with the automatic processing unit in the X-ray lab. The processed films were trimmed to remove the regions of overlap and taped onto a specially constructed viewbox (Figure 1.4). In 2010, the X-ray films were digitized and stitched together to produce a single image.

The 7-foot 6-inch (229-cm) skeleton at the Mütter Museum has somewhat mysterious origins. Most of what is known is based on an article published by Guy Hinsdale in 1898. According to Hinsdale, the remains arrived at the museum in 1877 from Kentucky with the stipulation "no questions asked." It was skeletonized and mounted for display and became known as the *Kentucky* or *American Giant*. The 1898 article discussed the connection between the pituitary gland and gigantism and a comparison to other skeletons in the collection.

The circumstances at the Mütter Museum presented a different set of problems. First, not only was the acromegalic skeleton was in a display case with two other skeletons, but it could not be removed from the exhibit **[WS 1.5]**. In addition, it was not possible to get more than a 94-inch (239-cm) SID, meaning that the X-ray could not cover an area larger than 40 inches (101 cm). Three 40 × 28-inch (101 × 71-cm) foam core–backed film holders were created as described in the previous Yale study **[WS 1.6]** and the skeleton was radiographed in three sections **[WS 1.7]**. The shorter SID reduced the necessary exposures to a total of 50 at 13 seconds each with a 30-second delay between successive exposures, or about 40 minutes total time. However, because there were three radiographs necessary to cover the entire skeleton, a total of two hours was required to complete the study. Instead of having to drive back to Connecticut to process the radiographs, all of the X-rays were developed at Graduate Hospital on South Street in Philadelphia, only a few miles from the museum. Unfortunately, the first set of radiographs was not acceptable due to blurred images. After much pondering, it was realized that during the nearly 40-minute exposure required for each section of the skeleton vibration was created by the

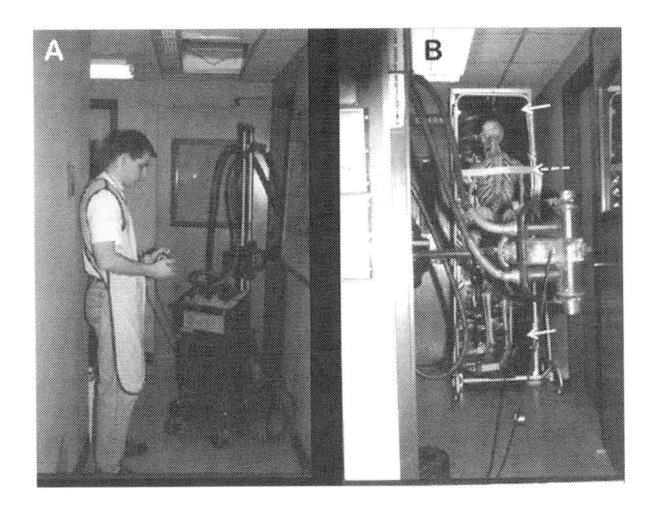

Figure 1.3. (A) Jason Kreitner taking one of the exposures using the spring timer. (B) The horizontally directed X-ray tube directed toward the skeleton and nonscreen film holder covered in layers of gardening plastic (solid arrows). Note the cloth strap (dashed arrow) fastened across the back of the skeleton for stabilization.

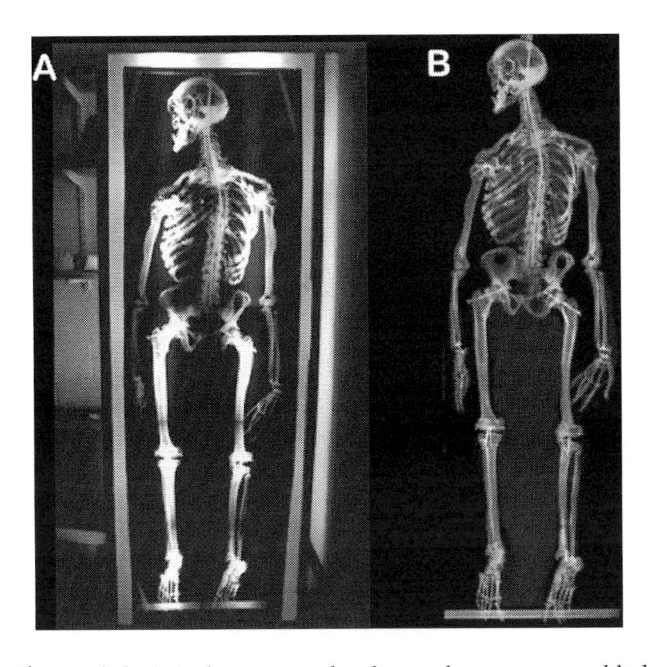

Figure 1.4. (A) The trimmed radiographs were assembled and taped onto the opal plexiglass of the specially built viewbox. (B) In 2010, the original radiographs were scanned using a flatbed scanner with a transparency adapter. All of the images were stitched together to produce a single image.

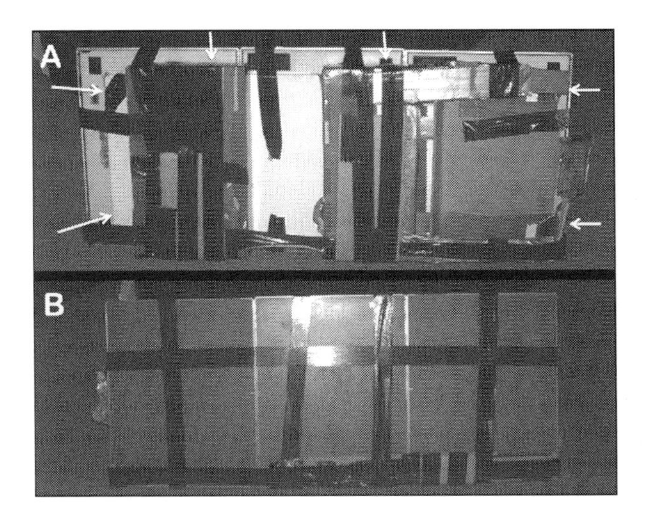

Figure 1.5. (A) The backing created by a combination of foam core and cardboard (arrows) taped together. (B) The face of the three cassettes taped together.

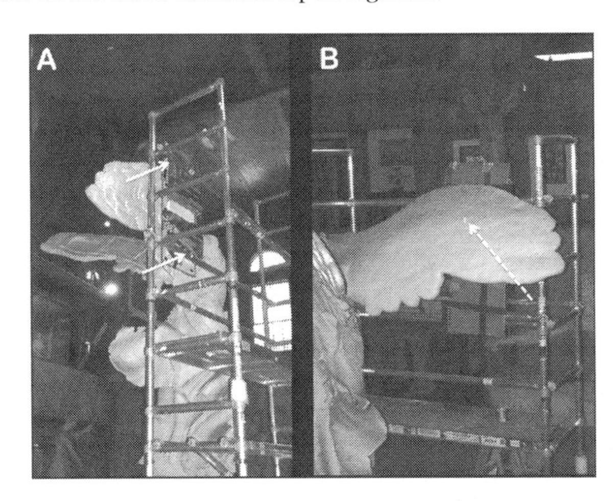

Figure 1.6. (A) The 42×17-inches (107×42-cm) film holder taped (solid arrows) to the aluminum frame of the scaffold. (B) The laser dot (dashed arrow) projected by the X-ray source to indicate the center of the X-ray field for the first of three setups to image the entire right wing.

air conditioning system periodically cycling on. It was necessary to reschedule another imaging session and coordinate the exposure times to avoid the vibrations. In addition to the AP set of radiographs, the final procedure included a lateral projection **[WS 1.8]**.

Another opportunity to X-ray a large object came in August 2006 when the Slater Museum in Norwich, Connecticut, requested a radiographic examination of a statue of the Winged Victory of Samothrace. Complete details of the project are described in "Case Study 5: Manufactured or Created Objects." However, the important considerations here were the long SID, 40 feet (12 m), the stature was on a pedestal approximately 15 feet (4.6 m) off the floor and the composition of plaster with iron rods employed for reinforcement. Therefore, higher kVp settings were necessary to penetrate the object and intensifying screens to reduce the exposure time were necessary. Three 14×17-inch (36×43-cm) cassettes were held together by creating a rigid foam core and cardboard backing to produce a *single image receptor* that covered a 42×17-inch (107×43-cm) area (Figure 1.5). In order to place the modified film holder against the wing, a scaffold needed to be erected and a cassette taped to the aluminum frame (Figure 1.6).

The X-ray source was place on cart and positioned on the balcony facing each wing (Figure 1.7A). The 40-foot (12-m) SID required a total of 143 exposures at 90 kVp and 40 mAs over approximately a 90-minute period to complete one set of X-rays. Because the X-ray source was not equipped with a fan for cooling, an ice pack was taped to each side of the X-ray tube in order to facilitate cooling (Figure 1.7B). Following the exposures, the cassettes were unloaded and reloaded in a makeshift darkroom constructed in the back of a Dodge van (Figure 1.8). It required three sets of exposures, or about five and a half hours, to cover the entire right wing. All nine exposed films were transported 65 miles back to the X-ray lab at Quinnipiac for processing. Because of the thickness of the edges of the cassettes, the final images were not seamlessly matched (Figure 1.9). For the left wing, on the second visit to the museum, the repositioned X-ray source had a 20-foot (6.1-m) SID and required only 30 exposures at 90 kVp at 40 mAs. Once again, a total of three sets of images were necessary to demonstrate the internal structure of the wing (Figure 1.10). On the third trip, a single 42×17-inch (107×42-cm) image receptor was employed to visualize the *chest* region and base of the wings (Figure 1.11). For this last image, the X-ray source was positioned with a 15-foot (4.6-m) SID, resulting in a total of 15 exposures at 90 kVp at 40 mAs. Due to the great differences in thickness in the *chest* region and base of the wings, it was not possible to clearly demonstrate the internal structures in that area (Figure 1.12).

It was at this time that Bob Lombardo, an applications specialist at FUJIFILM NDT (industrial radiology division), provided accessibility to Computed Radiography (CR) and the use of Fuji digital imaging plates, ST-VI. These plates, placed in a cardboard envelope, are unique because they do not need to be in a plate holder or cassette. The plates can be cleared or prepared for X-ray exposure by exposing them to fluorescent light for approximately one-half hour. A 34×28-inch (86×71-cm) plate holder was constructed using a foam core back, and pockets were created using processed X-ray film and duct tape (Figure 1.13). The four plates were placed into the pockets and secured in place with duct tape (Figure 1.14) and positioned for an image of the chest region of the statue. Because the system had not been tested prior to this study, an approximation of the technical factors was made, resulting in 75 exposures at 90 kVp at 40 mAs. In order to process the plates, it was necessary to drive 96 miles from Norwich to the Fuji facility in Stamford, Connecticut. Unfortunately, as expected, the resulting images were very underexposed but demonstrated the increased latitude not available with film as a recording media (Figure 1.15).

An opportunity to explore the unique nature of the Fuji CR system came in 2009 with a radiographic study of the *Soap Lady* at the Mütter Museum of the College of Physicians in Philadelphia. The imaging study of the mummified remains began in 1986 (Conlogue, 1988; Conlogue, Schlenk, Cerrone, & Ogden, 1989) and, up to this point, film was the sole image receptor employed. (There is more information regarding the *Soap Lady* in "Case Study 4: Mummified Remains.") Because the plates could be used outside a cassette, it provided a mechanism to create an image receptor for large objects. Four 14×17-inch (36×43-cm) Fuji CR ST-VI plates were cleared in the museum basement by exposing them to fluorescent light for 30 minutes. The cleared plates were placed on a 18×64×0.125-inch (48×162×0.3-cm) sheet of chipboard in a specific sequence: the first plate

Figure 1.7. (A) Ron Beckett positioning the X-ray source to radiograph the right wing of the statue of the Winged Victory of Samothrace. (B) Position of the X-ray source to radiograph the left wing (solid arrow). Note the position of the cassette (dashed arrow) for the base of the wing and the ice packs (dotted arrows) used to cool the X-ray tube during the multiple exposures.

Figure 1.8. A makeshift darkroom was constructed in the back of a Dodge van using a 0.5-inch (1.3-cm) PVC tubing frame (dashed arrow) over which three layers of black gardening plastic were place to create light-tight space to unload and load cassettes. Note the foam padding (solid arrows) taped to the floor to produce a cushioned surface to kneel.

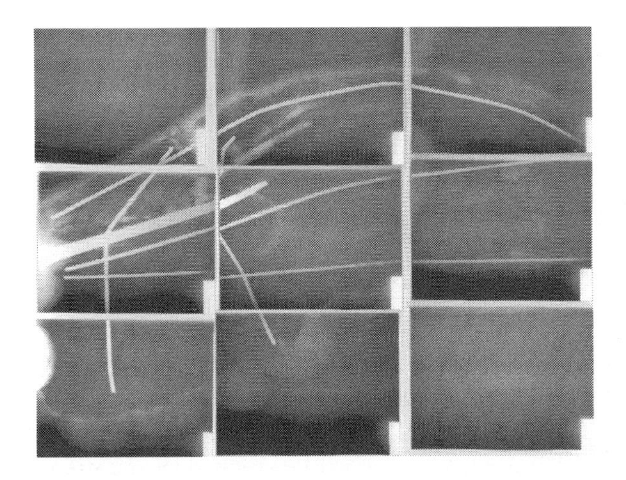

Figure 1.9. The nine radiographs required to cover the entire right wing demonstrating the iron rod support framing within the structure.

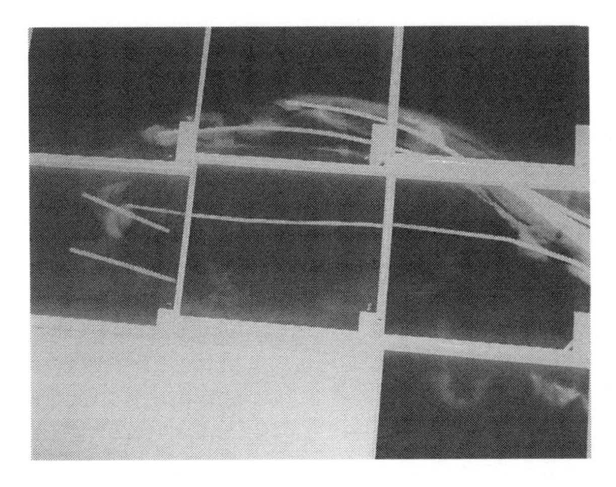

Figure 1.10. The left wing required seven radiographs to demonstrate the internal iron frame support structure.

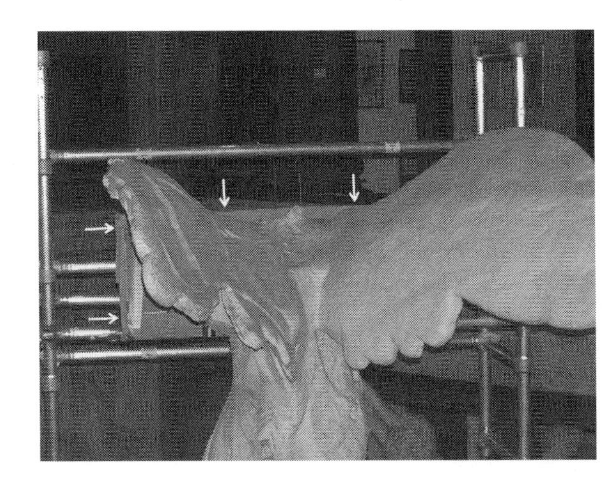

Figure 1.11. Position of the 42×17-inches (107×42-cm) cassette (arrows) to reveal the internal structure of the *chest* region and base of the wings.

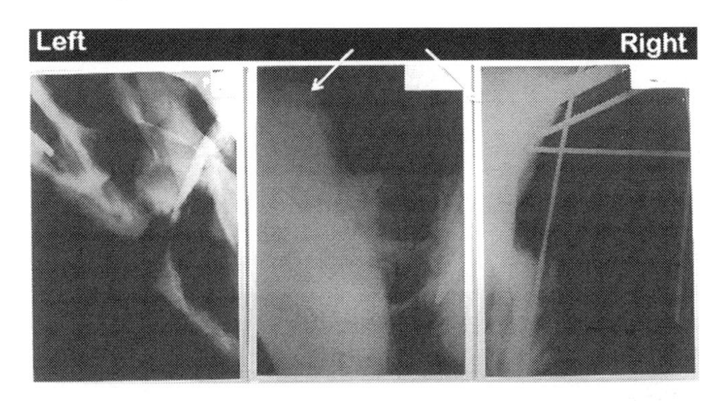

Figure 1.12. The set of radiographs of the *chest* region, but due to the very dense regions (arrows) near the base of the wings, it was not possible to visualize the ends of the iron stabilization rods.

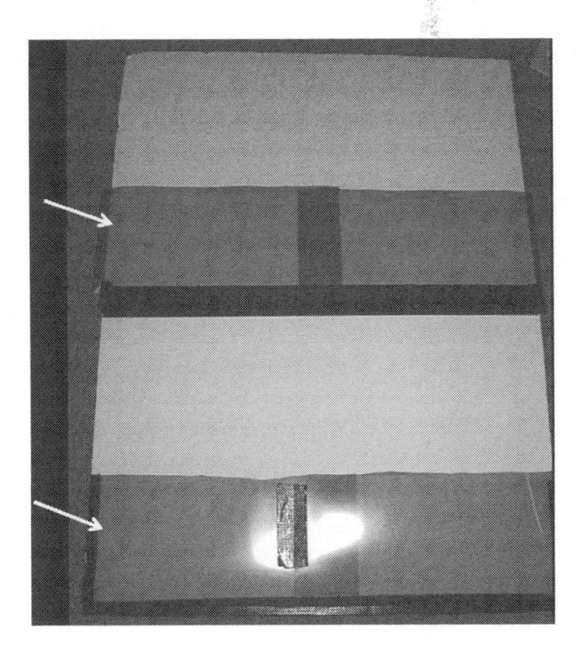

Figure 1.13. A 34×28-inch (86×71-cm) plate holder was made using a foam core back with pockets created with exposed X-ray film (arrows) and duct tape.

Figure 1.14. The four Fuji CR plates held in place with duct tape.

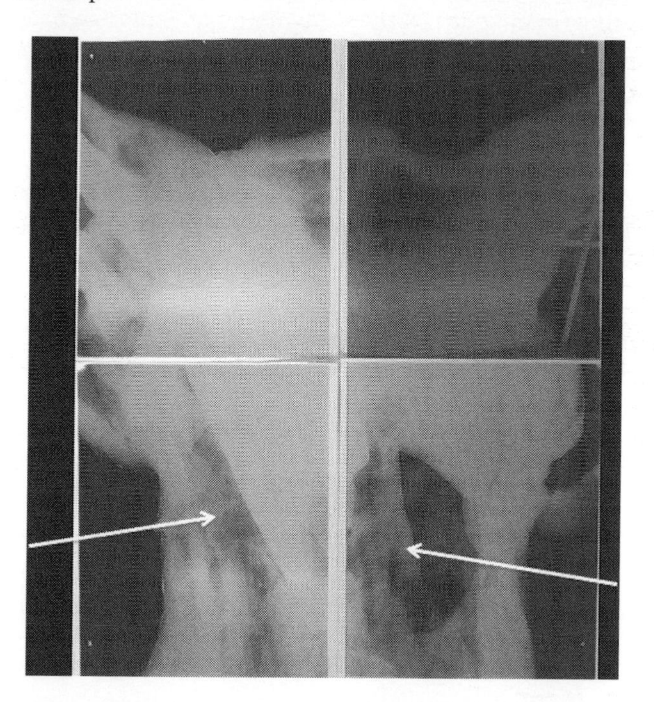

Figure 1.15. The processed FUJI CR ST-VI plates were underexposed but demonstrated the increased number of shades of gray available (arrows) with the CR system compared to the film.

was lengthwise, the next two crosswise and the last lengthwise. The plates were held in place by strips of duct tape (Figure 1.16). Once mounted onto the board, the new image receptor was wrapped in three layers of black gardening plastic to make it light-tight.

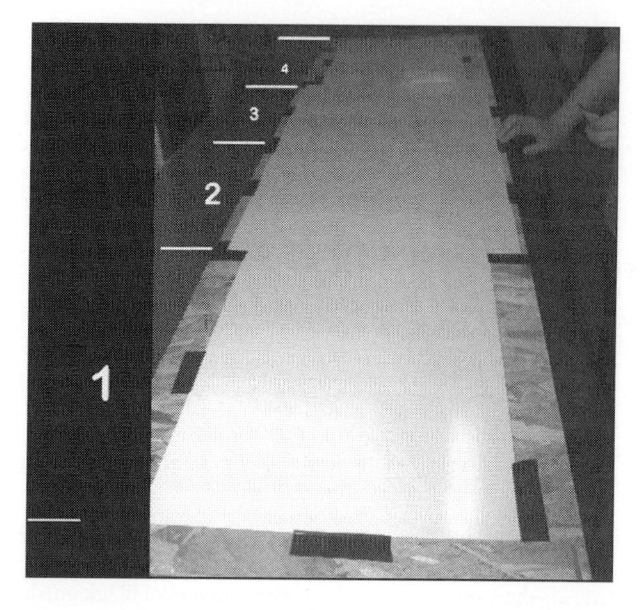

Figure 1.16. The four cleared Fuji CR ST-VI plates taped onto the surface of the sheet of chipboard.

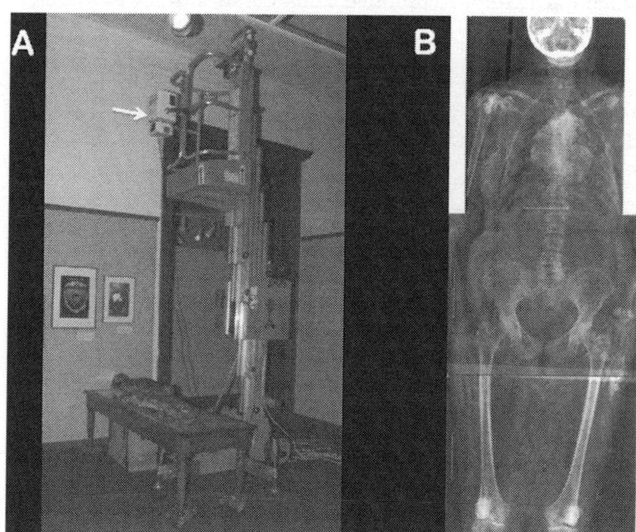

Figure 1.17. (A) The X-ray source taped to the bucket of the SkyJack™ to produce a 124-inch (315-cm) SID. (B) The assembled processed CR images stitched together.

The X-ray source was taped to the bucket of the SkyJack™ and elevated to the maximum height of the ceiling enabled a 124-inch (315-cm) SID (Figure 1.17A). The black plastic–wrapped image receptor was placed under the table on which the *Soap Lady* was resting. A total of 12 exposures were made at 86 kVp at 12 mAs with a 30-second pause between exposures to permit the X-ray tube to cool. Because the CR reader was not in Philadelphia, the exposed image receptor was transported back to the Fuji facility in Stamford, Connecticut, a total of 150 miles, about a 3.5-hour drive. Due to the restricted height of the ceiling, the X-ray beam covered only three of the four CR plates. In addition, as the mummy's head was at the top of the table, at least

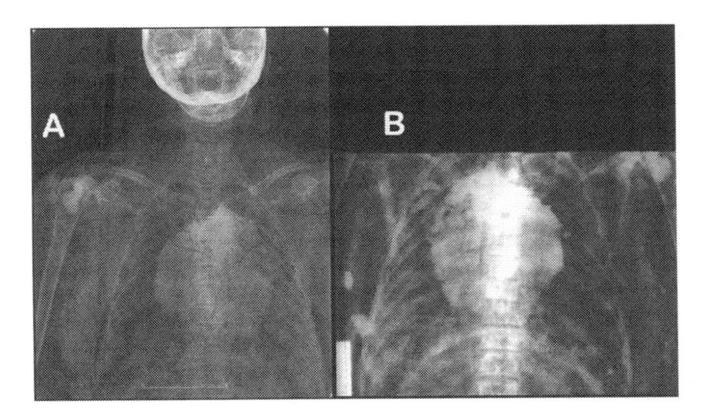

Figure 1.18. (A) Fuji CR image processed with a rubber algorithm has wider latitude and higher resolution than the (B) radiograph acquired in 1986 using film and intensifying screens.

a third of the skull was projected off the image receptor (Figure 1.17B). Comparing the CR image, processed at the Fuji facility, using an industrial algorithm for rubber provided a wider latitude image with higher resolution than the images acquired on film in 1986 (Figure 1.18). As discussed in Chapter 4, Plane Radiography, Digital Radiography, Mammography, Tomosyntheses, and Fluroscopy (*Advances in Paleoimaging: Applications for Paleoanthropology, Bioarchaeology, Forensics, and Cultural Artefacts, 1st Edition*, Conlogue and Beckett (eds.) CRC Press, 2020), although any radiograph acquired without the use of intensifying screen has greater latitude and increased resolution, the resulting CR image had the added benefit that it could be postprocessed, or the contrast and density could be manipulated.

Without the CR reader, large-scale studies still relied on film as a recording media. An example was a 2009 study of a group of mummies from Guanajuato, Mexico, on loan to the Detroit Science Museum in Detroit, Michigan, for an exhibit, *Accidental Mummies*. The objective was to acquire AP and lateral images of each entire mummy that could be stitched together. The X-ray source was fixed to the tines of a forklift truck [**WS 1.23**]. The height of the ceiling permitted a 144-inch (366-cm) SID that allowed the X-ray beam to cover the entire mummy in the AP position [**WS 1.23**]. Due to the height of the X-ray tube, the attached exposure cord minimized the distance that the person taking the exposure could get away from the exposure field, and a protected lead shielding area needed to be established [**WS 1.24**].

All exposures were taken using a 14×36-inch (36×91-cm) cassette loaded with three 11×14-inch (28×36-cm) Fuji Medical NHD films. Because the appropriate size film was not available, using the three sheets of smaller size film resulted in a 3-inch (8-cm) space without film at the base of the cassette. Because the exposed film were going to all be processed at the end of the day and three films were in each cassette, three sets of lead numbers had to be put on the cassette to ensure all the films would be marked [**WS 1.25**]. The cassette was either slid in from the top or from the bottom of the table that the mummy was resting on [**WS 1.26**]. All films were taken with seven exposures at 55 kVp at 50 mAs with a 30-second delay between exposures.

After all of the AP projects were acquired, the X-ray source was removed from the forklift truck and placed on a table. To create a 72-inch (183-cm) SID, each mummy was placed on a board elevated by approximately 2 inches (5 cm) and then positioned on a table [**WS 1.27**]. Due to superimposition of structures from the hips to feet, only a single 14×17-inch (36×43-cm) lateral project was acquired of the head to pelvis. The reduced distance enabled the total exposures to be decreased to two sets of 55 kVp at 50 mAs. Follow completion of the study, arrangements had been previously made to process all the films at the VCA Animal Hospital in Royal Oak, Michigan. After driving the approximately 15 miles to the vet clinic, a total of 108 films were put through the automatic processor. Because it takes approximately 60 seconds to feed each film into the unit, it took more than 90 minutes to process all of the films.

In 2010, the diagnostic imaging program at Quinnipiac University purchased a Kubtec KUBSCAN® 3600 CR system and made it available to the bioanthropology research institute, bringing large object imaging into the twenty-first century. The only component required was an adjustable frame that could hold multiple CR plates. When Bob Lombardo originally planed the PVC pipe frame device, it was only going to consist of a short section of tubing for the base. The cassette frame was planned to have an equally long section of tubing that fit into the base. The idea was to drill holes in both receiver and frame columns so that they would be able to telescope upward and would be pinned for the desired height. Preliminary work demonstrated the inability to get low enough, so the columns were shortened, which left little availability to raise the frame. Bob then had the revelation to add threaded fittings onto the receiver base. Once we had a threaded frame base, various lengths of PVC pipe were then cut, and threaded fittings were added to all of the lengths [**WS 1.28**]. With this idea, we were able to just screw in the desired height of the base columns and place the cassette frame to the required height. This approach allowed large and small height adjustments by using various lengths and combining them for the height that was needed.

The first real test of the imaging system was the mounted skeleton of a lowland gorilla from the Yale Peabody Museum of Natural History in New Haven, Connecticut. According to the museum website (peabody.yale.edu/exhibits/gargantua-great), the month-old orphaned infant lived with missionaries in the Belgian Congo until obtained by a sea captain and brought to Boston in 1931. Unfortunately, in a vengeful act against the captain, a sailor disfigured the primate with nitric acid. Shortly thereafter, the gorilla was purchased by Gertrude Davies Lintz, who named him Buddha, or "Buddy" for short. Despite her care, the animal's face was "permanently disfigured and his mouth twisted into a fierce snarl." In 1937 she offered the estimated 450-pound (205-kg) great ape to the *Ringling Brothers and Barnum & Bailey Circus*. Henry Ringling North, a 1933 Yale graduate, renamed him *Gargantua the Great* after one of the giants in *The Life of Gargantua and of Panagruel*, a series of novels written in the sixteenth century by François Rabelais. The gorilla became "the most famous circus animal of the twentieth century." After 12 years of touring the country, the animal died in 1949 and North donated the skeleton to the Yale Peabody Museum in 1950.

Other than acquiring radiographs of the entire skeleton that could be stitched together, there were several additional challenges that had to be addressed. First, the skeleton could not be removed from the large base on which it was mounted **[WS 1.29]**. Second, the rays' source position needed to be far enough to permit the beam to cover the entire gorilla while taking into account the projected position of the near extremities and skull **[WS 1.30]**. However, with the central ray of the X-ray beam passing through the center of the skeleton, the near extremities would be projected well below the surface of the base. Although seemingly counterintuitive, with the central portion of the X-ray bean directed through the feet, the interference of base with the feet would be minimized **[WS 1.31]**.

Both AP and lateral radiographs were obtained and, as the base was on wheels, it permitted establishing a single setup for the X-ray source and rotating the skeleton and base for each projection. The base did make it easier to acquire the lowest row of images. The PVC pipe image receptor support system was secured to the floor with duct tape to prevent the frame from moving **[WS 1.32]**. For the second level of plates, with the increased height of the image receptor support system, strips of duct tape were required to provide addition stabilization. Because only two 14 × 17-inch (36 × 43-cm) CR plates were available, each was positioned to allow a space smaller than the size of the image receptor between them. On the next set of exposures, a plate was positioned in the previous space to capture the image of the structures in that location **[WS 1.33]**. The collimator light was also useful in projecting the location of the object on the plate **[WS 1.34]**.

Because the lateral projection provided the most esthetic image of Gargantua, it was decided to *stitch together* the total of 15 CR radiographs comprising the lateral. However, mere stitching did not provide a satisfactory image **[WS 1.35]**. Additional manipulation of the assembled radiographs by Ann Marie Lombardo, graphic artist, was required to produce the desired results **[WS 1.35]**.

The success of the Gargantua study led to even more complex challenges with an imaging project at the Barnum Museum in Bridgeport, Connecticut. The museum opened on Main Street in that city in 1893 as The Barnum Institute of Science and History. P. T. Barnum, possibly the greatest showman of all time, purchased the land and paid for the construction of the building, which was completed two years after his death **[WS 1.36]**. His intention was to have a place that would not only showcase the history of the city but also serve as a resource library, lecture hall, and a general educational resource for children. Unfortunately, in June 2010 a tornado damaged the building and closed it to the public until structural repairs could be made. In March 2014, almost 21 years to the day of the giant study at Yale, work began on radiographing the skeleton of a *centaur* in a small portion of the Museum that was still open to the public. The articulated remains, measuring approximately 8 × 6 feet (2.4 × 1.8 m), were created in 1980 by Bill Willers, an artist and biology professor from the University of Wisconsin-Oshkosh. He constructed the centaur from the skull, torso, and upper extremities of a human and, with the exception of the skull and neck, the bones of a Shetland pony. Keeping with the spirit of the master (P.T. Barnum), a press release went out describing it as an "inexplicable specimen and was going to be revealed to the public on April 1, 2014, April Fools' Day."

The first step was to determine the exposure factors for the skeleton. At a 40-inch (100-cm) SID, 56 kVP at 4 mAs provided an acceptable lateral skull radiograph **[WS 1.37]**. A greater challenge was to find a position to place the X-ray tube that would eliminate superimposition of the cabinet frame over the skeleton. A sheet of white paper was attached to the back of the frame and, using the light from the X-ray source collimator, the X-ray tube was moved until the shadow of the centaur was unobstructed by the case **[WS 1.38]**. With the final position of the X-ray source at 18 feet (5.5 m), using the direct square rule described in Chapter 4, Plane Radiography, Digital Radiography, Mammography, Tomosyntheses, and Fluroscopy (*Advances in Paleoimaging*), it was necessary to use 56 kVp and three exposures of 40 mAs to produce satisfactory images. In order to provide a stable support for the X-ray source, the X-ray tube was placed on the transport case, a milk crate, and several books. Once in position, a strip of duct tape secured everything **[WS 1.39]**. In addition, a second X-ray tube was brought for the study in case the repeated exposures overheat the first X-ray source. The remains were so large that the single PVC pipe CR plate support system would not cover the entire skeleton. In order to cover the entire centaur, the system had to be positioned twice. To ensure that all of the plates would be in the same plane, the position of each base had to be taped in place before the first exposure was taken **[WS 1.40]**. Due to the height requirement, the PVC support system had to be stabilized with duct tape **[WS 1.41]**. In order to ensure that no one would be exposed to radiation, the study was conducted before the museum opened for visitors.

The study began with a single radiograph at the highest level of the CR plate support system. Beginning on the second level, a sheet of white cardboard was used to see the shadow cast on the CR plate and to help with positioning the plate **[WS 1.42]**. Because only two CR plates were available, it was important to remember which areas of the skeleton had been radiographed and which had not in order to not forget to image any region **[WS 1.43]**. A total of 32 images was required to cover the entire skeleton and the final composite image was assembled once again by Ann Marie Lombardo using PhotoShop® **[WS 1.44]**.

The success of the centaur project resulted in Kathy Maher, Executive Director of the Barnum Museum, to request an even larger and more historic object be radiographed: *Baby Bridgeport*. The 6-foot 8-inch (2.0-m) elephant was born in 1882 in Bridgeport, Connecticut, at the winter quarters for P. T. Barnum's *Greatest Show on Earth and Great London Circus*. This was only the second elephant to be born in the United States. Unfortunately, the animal died at age four in Bridgeport on April 12, 1886. Barnum shipped the remains to Professor Henry Ward at the Ward Scientific Institute of Rochester, New York, for taxidermy. Always the entrepreneur, Barnum had called upon Ward when, in 1885, his most famous animal attraction, *Jumbo the Elephant*, was killed by a train in St. Thomas, Ontario, Canada. Ward traveled to Canada and articulated the skeleton, which was then gifted to the American Museum of Natural History in New York. In addition, he prepared a taxidermy mount of the hide that was later given to the Barnum Museum at Tufts University, outside Boston. The mounted Baby Bridgeport was first given to the Bridgeport Scientific Society in 1886 and later became one of the first exhibits when the Barnum Institute of Science and History opened in 1893.

According to Adrienne Saint Pierre, Curator at the Barnum Museum (personal communication, September 16, 2017), the first cosmetic restoration of Baby Bridgeport occurred locally in the 1930s. However, as the local news clippings of the time made reference to the disappointing results, the individual assuming the task was apparently unskilled in the appropriate methodology. In 1993, another restoration was undertaken by the Schoepfer Studios in Manhattan, New York, where restoration experts attempted to recapture her nineteenth-century appearance. Unfortunately, due to the compromised state of Baby Bridgeport, the New York studio may have done their best with what they were given. Following damage created by a tornado in 2010, the Barnum Museum closed for repairs and provided an opportunity to assess the condition of a number of objects in the collection, including the mounted pachyderm.

The image receptor plate holding system utilized for the centaur was the basis for the Baby Bridgeport study. However, because of the size of the elephant, the approach had to be modified. First, in order for the X-ray beam to cover the entire animal, a 37-foot (11.3-m) SID was required (Figure 1.19). Because it was a little more

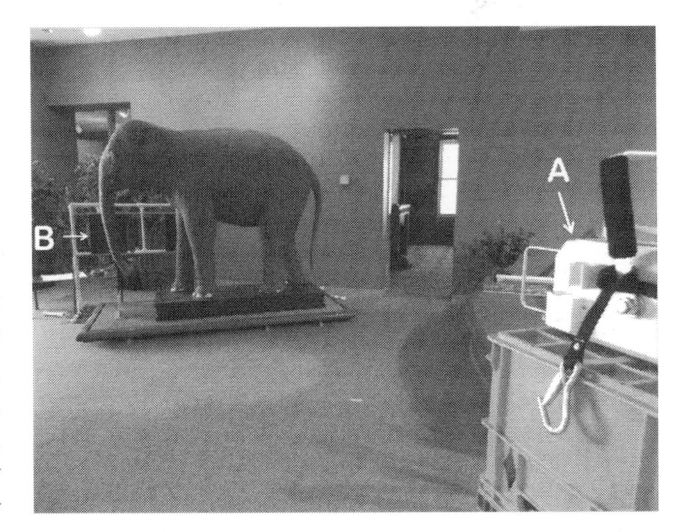

Figure 1.19. In order to cover the entire elephant with the X-ray beam, a distance of 37 feet (11.3 m) was required between (A) the Kubtec XTEND® 100HF X-ray source and (B) the image receptor.

Figure 1.20. The cross-hair (arrow) generated by the X-ray collimator, indicating the center of the X-ray beam.

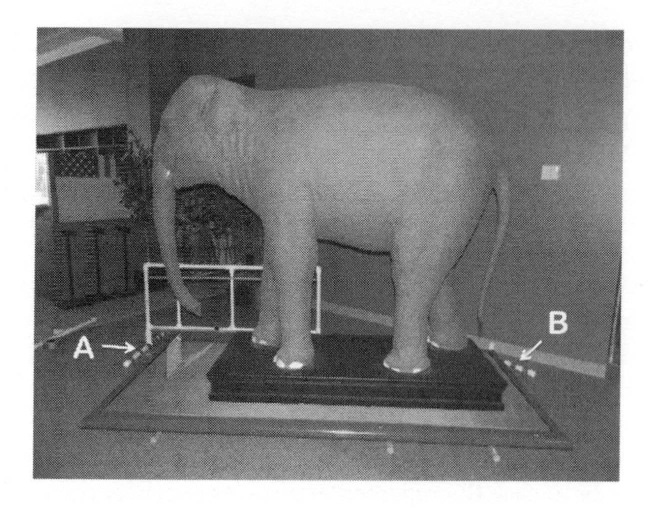

Figure 1.21. During the first imaging session, the base was taped to the floor (A) for the imaging plate support system to acquire all of the radiographs of the anterior half of the taxidermy mount. Because nothing would be moved between sessions, the base for the frame to image the posterior half was taped in place (B).

than twice the SID required for the centaur, it necessitated four times the amount of X-ray intensity or 12 exposures at 56 kVp and 40 mAs. With a 30-second delay between successive exposures to permit the X-ray tube to cool, each set of X-rays took approximately eight minutes. Similar to Gargantua, the elephant was on a large base, so the center of the X-ray beam had to be positioned to minimize the shadow of the base and not project the top of the head and spine too high (Figure 1.20). The base could be easily subtracted off the final image and the intent was to keep the number of imaging levels to five.

With the imaging plate support frame requiring five levels of adjustment, approximately 64 total images were required to cover the entire elephant. Because only two CR plates were available and a minimum of eight minutes was necessary to acquire each set of X-rays, it was decided to take two days to complete the study. Because the mounted specimen was in the closed portion of the museum, this ensured that the setup would not be disturbed between imaging sessions. The isolated nature of the location also eliminated radiation protection considerations for the museum staff. During the first session, the base for each PVC pipe frame was taped in place and the entire anterior portion of the elephant completed (Figure 1.21). By levels four (Figure 1.22A) and five (Figure 1.22B), the frame had to be stabilized for the long exposures.

The final composite image was stitched together by Ann Marie Lombardo from the total of 64 radiographs using PhotoShop® (Figure 23). Unlike taxidermy today, the skin of the four-year-old elephant was not stretched over a fiberglass frame. A metal frame and wooden support system demonstrated the nineteenth century approach

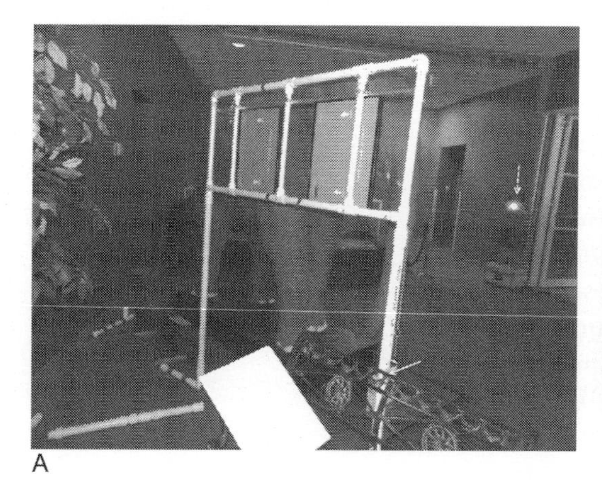

A

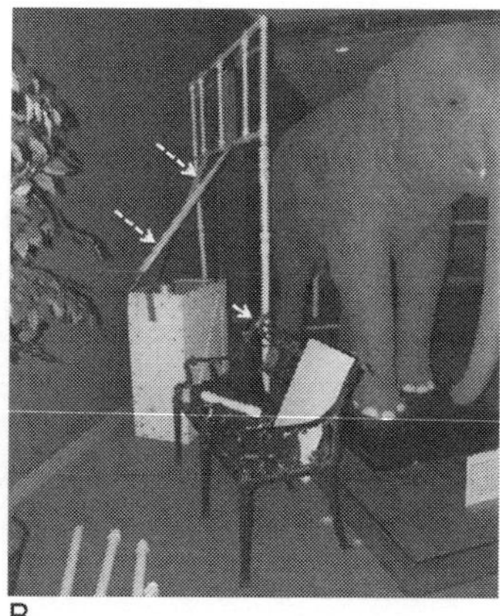

B

Figure 1.22. (A) By level four, during the first session, it was necessary to incorporate a metal bench (solid arrow) to stabilize the image receptor support frame. Note the position of the X-ray tube (dashed arrow). (B) Level five of the posterior half required not only the metal bench to be duct taped (solid arrow) to the frame but also long strips of duct tape (dashed arrows) to be anchored to the large wooden chest.

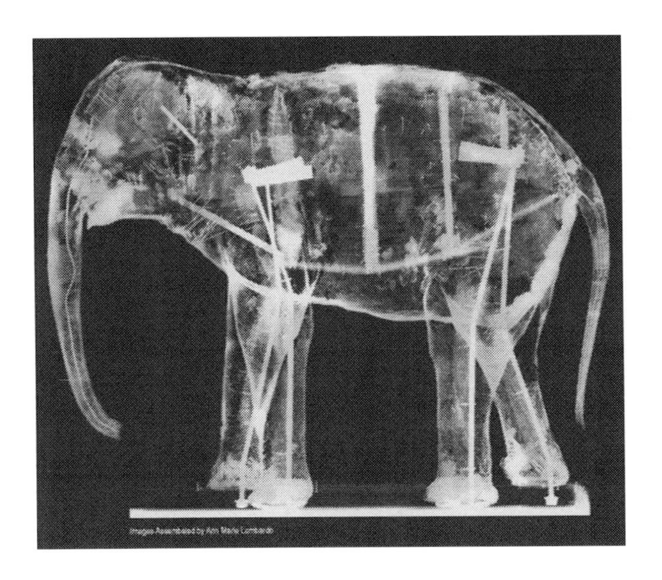

Figure 1.23. The composite image composed from the 64 radiographs clearly demonstrated the internal frame of the taxidermy full mount from 1886.

to taxidermy. Both Barnum Museum studies confirmed the ability of a CR system and a 100 kVp X-ray source to image large objects of relatively low density.

References

Conlogue, GJ. (June 1988). *Dr. Leidy's Soap Lady.* Presentation at the annual meeting of the Connecticut Society of Radiologic Technologists, Waterbury, CT.

Conlogue, GJ, M Schlenk, F Cerrone & JA Ogden. (1989). Dr. Liedy's Soap Lady: Imaging the Past. *Radiologic Technology.* 60:411–415.

http://strangeremains.com/2014/07/26/the-skeletal-anatomy-of-the-centaur-of-volos/

Zoological Specimens

2

GERALD J. CONLOGUE AND JOHN POSH

Contents

Marine Mammal Flippers—Gerald Conlogue and John Posh

In the 1970s, John Ogden, the Chairman of Department of Orthopedics at the Yale University School of Medicine and a member of the Human Growth and Development Study Unit at Yale, in New Haven, Connecticut, was interested in comparative skeletal development. His interests in the unique characteristic of marine mammal skeletal development led to his founding the Yale Marine Mammal Recovery Center in 1979. A responsibility of the center was to perform necropsies on cetaceans, pinnipeds, and marine turtles that stranded primarily along the coast in Connecticut and assist in strandings in Massachusetts, Rhode Island, and New Jersey. Among the marine reptiles that strand in the area, was the leatherback turtle, *Dermochelys coriacea*, the largest known extant reptile, reaching weights exceeding 1499 lbs (680 kg). Necropsies on large stranded cetaceans were massive, complex procedures that could take several days to complete. Logistically, strandings presented challenges because they occasionally occurred in unusual places **[WS 2.1]** or isolated locations (Figure 2.1). In addition, large equipment such as a crane was sometimes required to lift a carcass out of the water (Figure 2.2) or to remove huge chunks of tissue **[WS 2.4]**. Although the primary intent of the necropsies was to aid in determining the factors that contribute to strandings (Figure 2.3), Ogden included in the protocol the removal of the flippers, a structure analogous to the human upper extremity. The appendages were transported back to the Yale University School of Medicine for a radiographic study prior to dissection and histological examination (Figure 2.4). Ogden theorized that with the examination of sufficient flippers, it would be possible to determine the animal's age through an assessment of skeletal development, similar to radiographic studies of the human hand and wrist (Grulich and Pyle, 1950).

Objective: Therefore, the objective of the planned study was to radiograph entire flippers and document the skeletal development of all the components from the head of the humerus to the tips of the phalanges. Because the assessments were undertaken for targeted regions, such as the carpus, it was not necessary to include the entire flipper on a single image. Had we planned to assess the entire flipper it would have been included in Case Study 1: Large Objects. From the radiographs, a single line drawing representing the spatial relationship and skeletal development was produced for each flipper. Because histological sections were the final step in the protocol, high-resolution radiographs were not required. For smaller animals, such as a pygmy sperm whale, *Kogia breviceps* (Figure 2.5), and a harbor seal, *Phoca vitulina* (Figure 2.6), the former flipper easily fit on a 14 × 17-inch (36 × 43 cm) and the latter on a 10 × 12-inch (25 × 30 cm) cassette.

However, for large cetaceans, such as a sperm whale, *Physeter macrocephalus*, even when using a 14 × 36 inch (36 × 91 cm) cassette, multiple exposures were necessary to include the entire appendage. But a more serious concern was related with the larger cetaceans: the rather unpleasant odor particularly associated with marine animals that may have died more than a week before being recovered. The smell precluded bringing the specimens into any clinical medical facility at the university. Fortunately, space was provided in the Medical School Anatomy Department, where medical students dissected cadavers. A 300 mA Picker portable X-ray unit was donated to the Human Growth and Development Study Unit and moved into a room in the Anatomy Department. Unfortunately, with the X-ray tube fixed

Figure 2.1. Early stages of a necropsy on a sperm whale stranded during February 1979 on a beach in Scituate, Massachusetts.

Figure 2.2. Once straps had been placed around the carcass of a fin whale, a crane was required to lift this fin whale out of the water (A) and onto a flatbed tractor-trailer truck (B). The stranding occurred on the New Jersey side of the Walt Whitman Bridge at Gloucester City.

Figure 2.3. Examining the stomach contents of a fin whale that stranded on the New Jersey side under the Walt Whitman Bridge in February 1980. The necropsy took place in a landfill in Gloucester, New Jersey.

Figure 2.4. A sperm whale flipper from the Scituate, Massachusetts, stranding unloaded onto a hand truck near the morgue entrance at Yale University School of Medicine.

to a vertical column, the maximum SID obtainable was 72 inches (183 cm), sufficient to cover the 14×36 inch (36×91 cm) cassette, but in some cases not the entire flipper (Figure 2.7). On occasions where the flippers exceeded the size of the cassette, it was necessary to reposition the appendage to acquire a complete set of radiographs. In order to create a single line drawing of the skeletal components, due to the misalignment, the approximate position of the bones was only possible (Figure 2.8).

In the case of a humpback whale, *Megaptera novaeanglie*, with a 14-foot (4.3-m) flipper, it was possible to transport only one flipper back to the university. In addition, due to the extreme length, it was not possible to enter the building with the appendage intact. Instead, it had to be cut into sections in the morgue parking lot and brought into the Anatomy Department in sections (Figure 2.9). The obvious problem with this situation was the limitation of the vertical distance obtainable with the X-ray source fixed to the support column of the portable units.

Once the radiographic study was completed, the flippers were first dissected down to the bone, removing all the muscles, tendons, and ligaments but leaving the joint capsule intact (Figure 2.10). The humerus

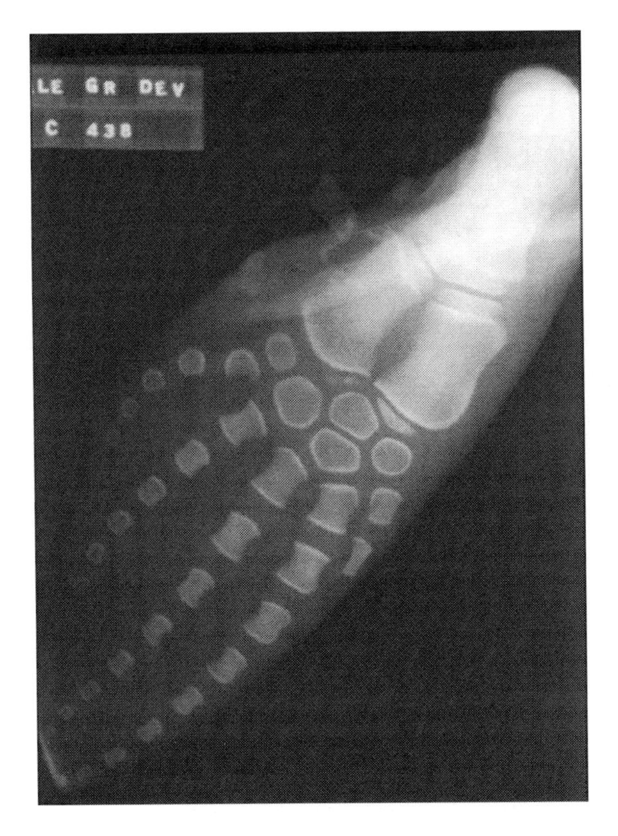

Figure 2.5. Smaller flippers, such as the pigmy sperm whale, *Kogia breviceps*, fit diagonally on a 14×17-inch (36×43 cm) cassette.

Figure 2.6. The skeletally immature harbor seal, *Phoca vitulina*, was placed on a 10×12-inch (25×30 cm) cassette lengthwise.

was then separated from the rest of the appendage and radiographed. Unfortunately, with the larger cetaceans, such as the sperm whale, the radiograph of the entire humerus was not satisfactory. Due to the thickness and rounded surfaces, superimposition in areas such as the physeal region lacked detail (Figure 2.11). The solution

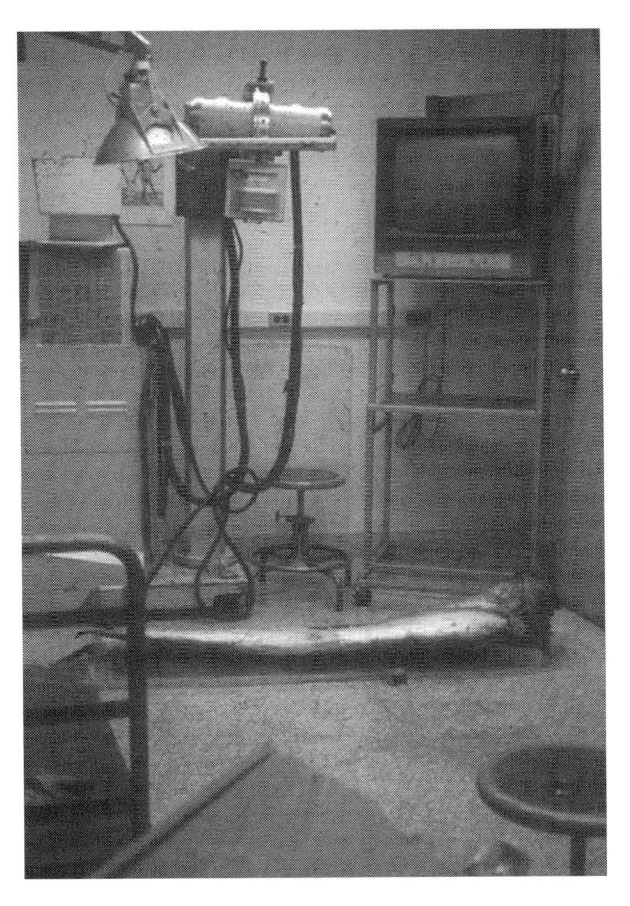

Figure 2.7. The setup at the Yale Medical School Anatomy Department to radiograph the flippers. The fin whale flipper from Gloucester, New Jersey, was too large to fit on a single 14×36-inch (36×91 cm) cassette.

was to cut a mid-coronal section of not only the humerus but also the entire extremity using a handsaw. The sections were photographed (Figure 2.12) and radiographed. Sectioning eliminated some of the superimposition that obscured osteological features required to document the bone development. In addition, the intensifying screens provided sufficient resolution on the sectioned specimens to reveal structures, such as longitudinally oriented endochondral-derived bone and growth slowdown regions in at least the endochondral regions. Unfortunately, with the largest humeri from the humpback whale, the radiographs of the sections did not clearly defined margins (Figure 2.13).

Unfortunately, due to small samples sizes for each species, it was only possible to accomplish a generalization of the radiographic indicators of skeletal maturity in cetaceans (Ogden et al., 1981a, 1981d). Similarly, although a number of species of stranded marine turtles were examined, the sample sizes permitted more generalized observations (Rhodin et al., 1980, 1981). Nevertheless, aside from documenting the anatomic structure, an example of pathology was noted in a leatherback turtle, weighing approximately 551 lbs (250 kg), stranded near

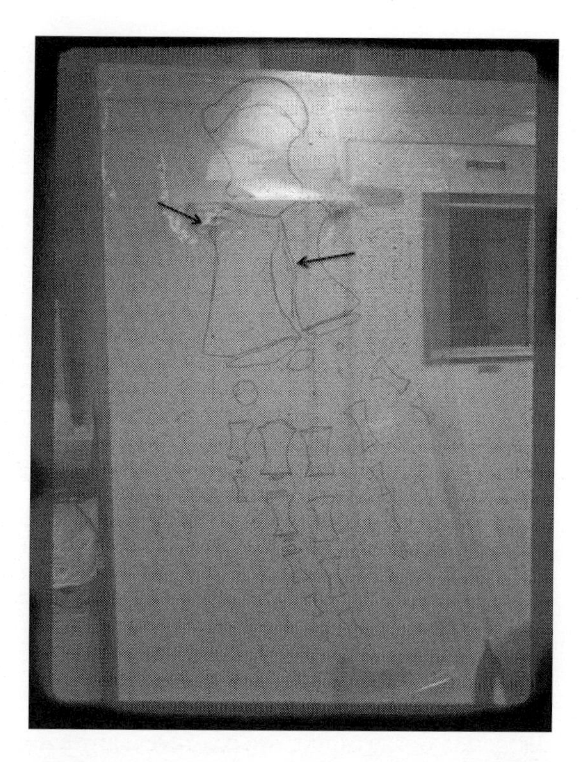

Figure 2.8. A tracing onto a sheet of acetate of the radiographs of the sperm whale, *Physeter macrocephalus*, flipper recovered from Scituate, Massachusetts. Note the lines (arrows) that indicates multiple images with differing margins.

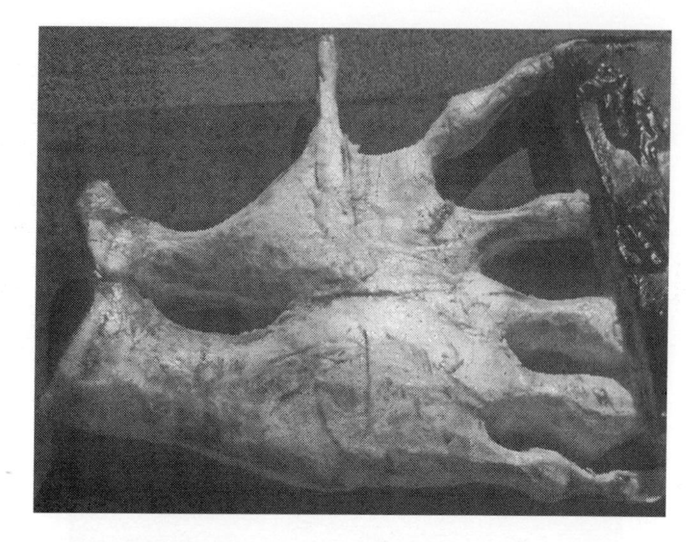

Figure 2.10. One of the sperm whale flippers from the Scituate, Massachusetts stranding. The humerus has been removed along with all the muscles, tendons, and ligaments covering the radius, ulna, carpus, and proximal metacarpals.

Figure 2.9. The humpback whale flipper, extended across two stretchers in the morgue parking lot. Each stretcher had to be tied off to prevent them rolling away during the process of dividing the appendage into sections before it could be brought into the building to be radiographed. At the time that the photograph was taken, the humerus had been removed, exposing the articular surface of the ulna (U) and the radius (R).

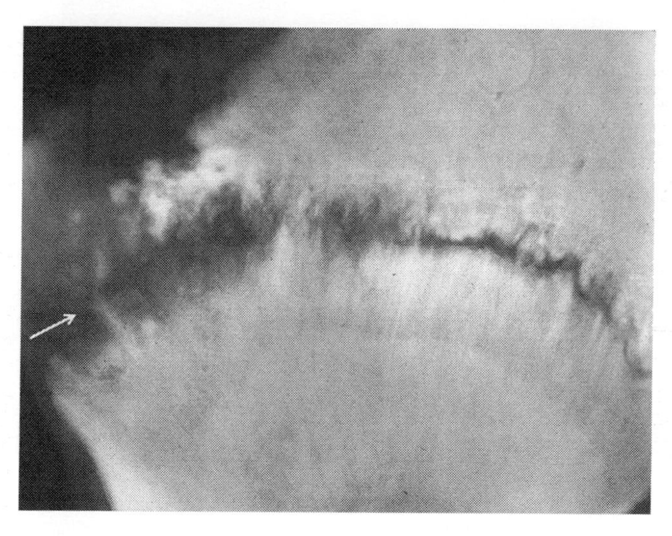

Figure 2.11. The radiograph of the proximal end of the intact humerus. The lack of resolution in the physeal area (arrow) was due to superimposition and the rounded surface.

Atlantic City, New Jersey, after apparently being hit in the head by a boat propeller. The external examination of both the pectoral and pelvic limbs showed no evidence of recent or old trauma. However, during the dissection of the right pectoral flipper, extensive scar formation and an abnormal layer of fibrovascular tissue or pannus completely replaced the elbow joint. The humerus, radius, and ulna were split longitudinally, visually inspected, radiographed, and prepared for histological examination. Visual examination of the sections failed to reveal any active infection or pockets of purulent material. Radiographs of the distal right humerus demonstrated extension of the infection into the metaphyseal bone. In addition, the infected radius and ulna showed longitudinal overgrowth of the distal ends. The histological findings were most revealing and confirmed the condition was septic arthritis and contiguous osteomyelitis

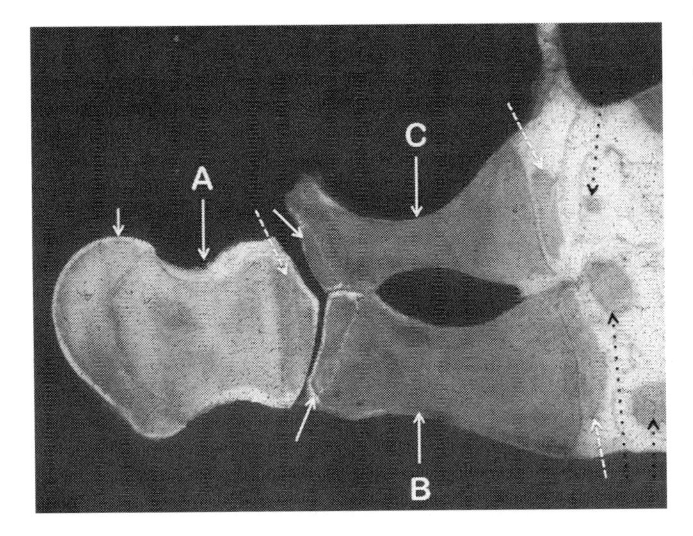

Figure 2.12. A coronal section cut through (A) the humerus, (B) the radius and (C) the ulna with the proximal epiphysis of each bone indicated by solid arrows and the distal epiphyses designated with dashed arrows. Note that three of the five epiphyses have begun to ossify in the carpus (dotted arrow).

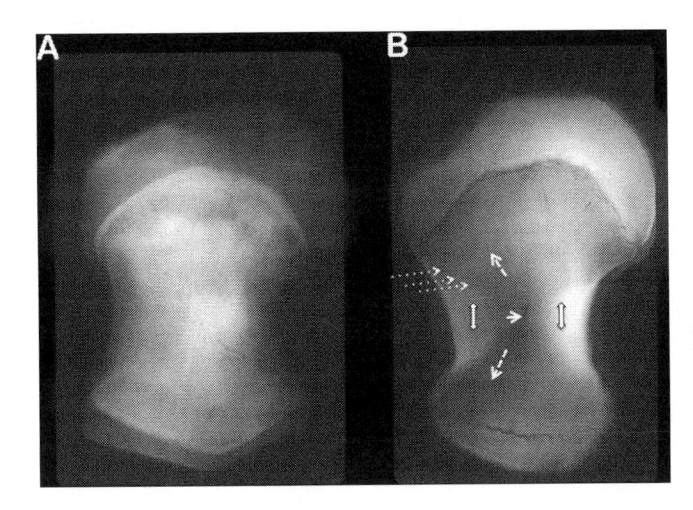

Figure 2.13. Radiographs of two of the coronal sectioned humeri from sperm whales. (A) The proximal and distal epiphyses have not yet ossified. (B) A much more skeletally developed individual: the endochondral-derived bone (dashed arrows) is longitudinally oriented toward each physis; it is clearly demarcated from the membranous bone formed by the periostium (double-headed arrows); growth slowdown regions (dotted arrows) are more prominent in the endochondral bone; and juxtaposition of the apices of the two endochondral cones (solid arrow).

involving the elbow, distal humerus, and proximal radius and ulna (Ogden et al., 1981b).

A traumatic injury was discovered in the fin whale, *Balaenoptera physalus*, that stranded in Gloucester, New Jersey, and possibly was a contributing factor in the death of the animal (Ogden et al., 1981c). The only evidence of trauma noted on the carcass, measuring 45 feet (14 m), was the missing tail or flukes, presumably cut off by a ship's propeller. The cetacean was loaded onto a flatbed truck and transported to the Gloucester landfill for the necropsy. During the procedure, both flippers were removed and transported back to New Haven, Connecticut, for the radiographic examination. Both flippers appeared to have normal contours and neither had evidence of external trauma.

The X-ray evaluation of both flippers revealed a skeletally immature individual. However, the right flipper demonstrated a complete fracture of the distal radius and ulna at the metaphyseal/diaphyseal junction **[WS 2.16]**. The fracture appeared to widen on the dorsal aspect consistent with tension failure and cortical fragmentation on the volar side consistent with compression failure. Sclerotic areas and growth arrest lines were noted on both the radius and ulna, suggesting that the fractures were several weeks to several months old. Small additional propagation fractures substantiated the chronic nature of the defect.

Dissection of the flipper did not reveal any evidence of hemorrhage in the interosseous musculature on either aspect of the appendage over the fracture site that might be expected with an acute injury. At the microscopic level, additional evidence that this had been a chronic condition was an intact periosteum with areas of hyperemia and proliferation of small blood vessels.

The chronic nature of this injury potentially limited the whale's use of the flipper for stabilization and subsequent maneuverability. Continued use of the appendage, with constant external water pressure and drag on the dorsal surface, further exacerbated the problem, as seen by the additional propagation fracture. Therefore, the animal eventually was probably unable to avoid a subsequent collision with a large vessel.

Fast forward to 2009: a veterinarian, Paul Nader, wanted several whale flippers examined. Unlike the late 1970s when film radiography was the only option, advanced imaging modalities, including MDCT and MR, were now available in a non-clinical environment. Dr. Nader transported a single sperm whale flipper on the roof of his car to the Quinnipiac Diagnostic Imaging Laboratory in North Haven, Connecticut **[WS 2.17]**.

A minimal number of modifications to the MDCT protocol were necessary. Instead of setting the slice thickness to 0.5 mm and employing all 64 detectors, the slice thickness was increased to 1.0 mm and the detectors were coupled together to produce 32 rows. Next, in order to maintain isotropic voxels, a 500 mm FOV was selected. From Chapter 7: Computed Tomography in *Advances in Paleoimaging* (CRC Press, 2020), recall that the matrix size of the CT image, along the X–Y axis, is 512 × 512 pixels and that pixel size is calculated by

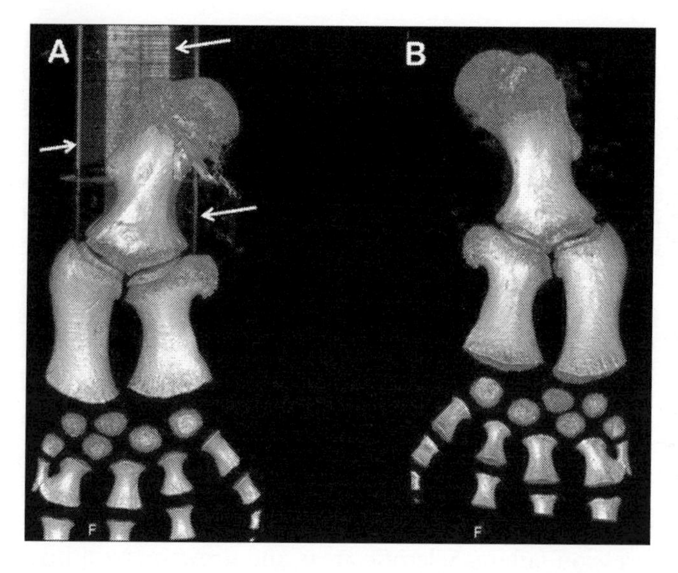

Figure 2.14. Within 10 minutes of the data acquisition, it was possible to reconstruct a 3-D image of the flipper (A), utilize the segmentation tool to eliminate the support under the appendage (arrows), and rotate the extremity 180° (B).

dividing the FOV by 512 (FOV÷512) or approximately 0.98 mm. With the slice thickness, representing the Z-axia, set at 1.0 mm, the voxels is virtually isometric. The kV was set to 120 and the mAs at 150.

In less than 10 minutes after the data had been acquired, it was possible to reconstruct the 3D image of the flipper on the display console, utilize the segmentation tool, further discussed in Chapter 7 in *Advances in Paleoimaging* (CRC Press, 2020), to eliminate the support under the appendage, and rotated the flipper 180° (Figure 2.14). Other tools also facilitated the examination of the anatomic structure. Because the flipper was wedge-shaped and the distal aspects curled, the curved multiplanar reformat (MPR) made it easy to create coronal sections (Figure 2.15). A similar section, created approximately 30 years ago, required about 20 hours of dissection to remove all the soft tissue, muscles, ligament, and tendons, separate the humerus from the radius and ulna, and finally use a handsaw to cut through the entire appendage (Figure 2.16). Three decades ago, it was necessary to destroy all the tissue covering the skeletal elements, losing the relation between the tendons and ligaments and the underlying bone. Using the oblique MPR, it was possible to examine those structures on the dorsal surface without cutting into the specimen (Figure 2.17). Similarly, the curved MPR clearly visualized the structures on the ventral surface (Figure 2.18). In addition, once the data set was collected it could be reexamined by changing parameters such as slice thickness (Figure 2.19) or downloaded to another platform, such as an independent work station, and reexamined employing other software and algorithms (Figure 2.20).

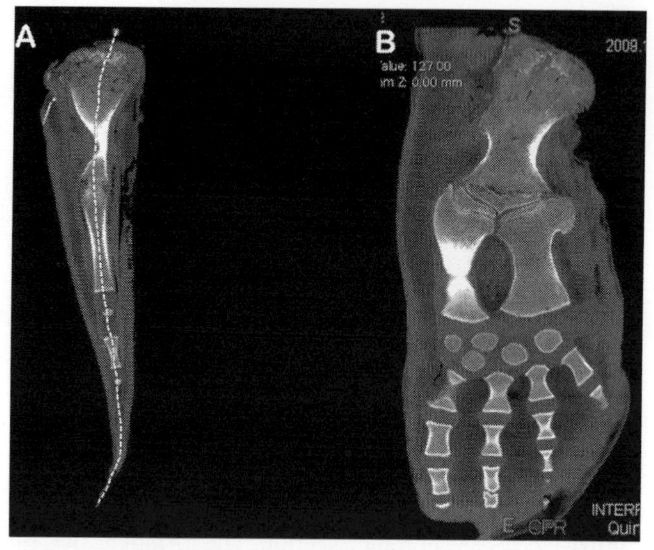

Figure 2.15. (A) Using curved multiplanar reconstruction (MPR), a line was traced along the central portion of each of the bones within the selected sagittal section (dashed line). (B) When the line is complete, the computer reconstructed the coronal plane designated by the line.

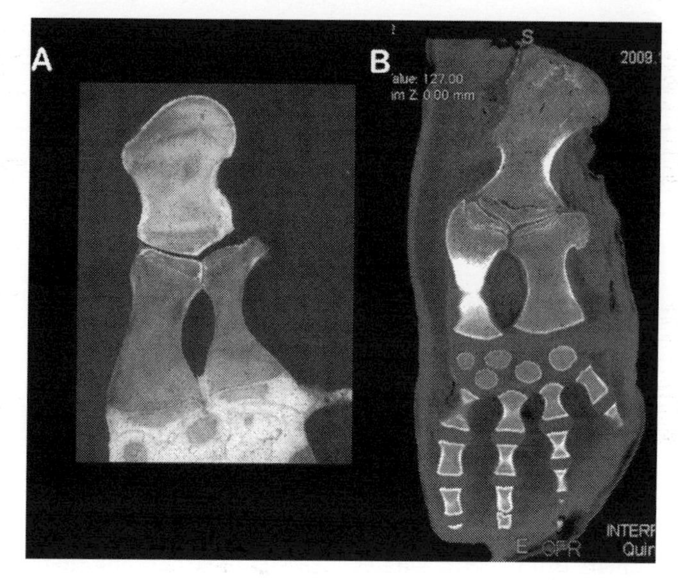

Figure 2.16. (A) Approximately 30 years earlier, it required about 20 hours of dissection and employing a handsaw to cut a coronal section of a sperm whale flipper. (B) With the MDCT scanner the entire process took less than 15 minutes.

Significance

It took John Ogden many hours of work in the late 1970s and 1980s to demonstrate the internal structure of the sperm whale humerus, but with MDCT it required less than one half-hour without the need for and destruction of the appendage (Figure 2.21). However, that was before the flipper was examined with MR, a procedure that was unavailable in Ogden's day.

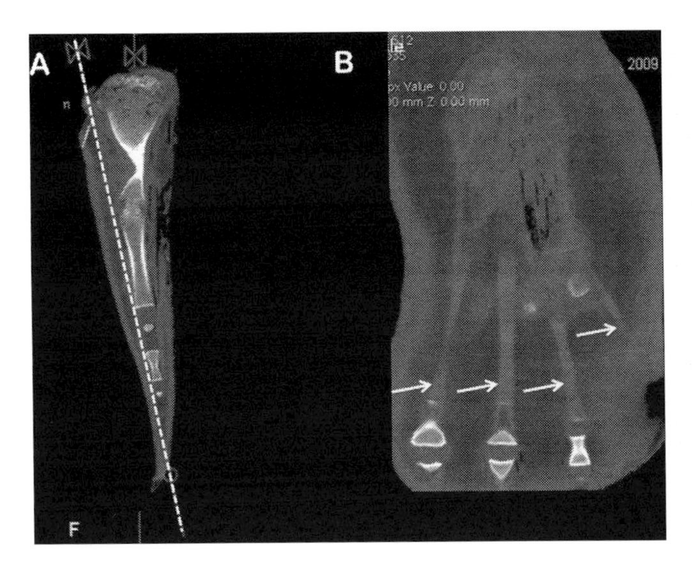

Figure 2.17. (A) A sagittal section was used to determine the placement of the oblique MPR (dashed line). (B) The oblique coronal section demonstrating the extensor tendons on the dorsal surface to the flipper (arrows).

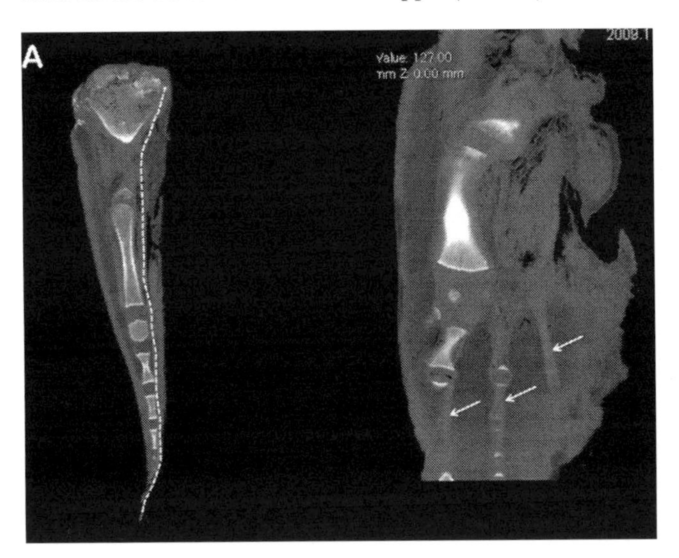

Figure 2.18. (A) The sagittal section used to determine the path of the curved MPR on the ventral surface (dashed line). (B) The relation of the flexor tendons to the boney structures of the appendages were clearly demonstrated.

Elephant Foot—John Posh and Gerald Conlogue

In the spring of 2010, the Bioanthropology Research Institute at Quinnipiac University received an unusual request to conduct a magnetic resonance imaging examination on the foot of an African elephant, *Loxodonta Africana*. The 52-year-old animal died in a zoo and a complete necropsy was planned. It was decided to freeze a front foot or manus with the intention of locating a site where a detailed imaging study could be completed. A study was published in 2006 that included CT and MR examinations of two hind feet or pedes: a 6.5-year-old juvenile and a 26-year-old adult (Weissengruber et al., 2006).

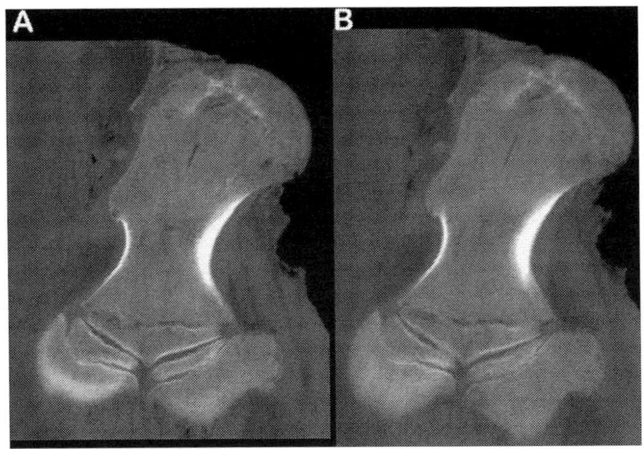

Figure 2.19. Once saved, the MDCT data can be reexamined by changing parameters such as slice thickness: (A) 1.0 mm; (B) 20 mm.

Specific Objective

The foot of the elephant has unique features to accommodate the weight of the largest terrestrial animal. The role of a large subcutaneous cushion has been reported in the literature, including a study employing computer tomography and magnetic resonance imaging (ibid, 2006). Therefore, orthopedic problems in elephants can be devastating, and an MR of the manus might provide an insight into how to better assist elephants with podiatric problems in the future. In addition, it was decided to complement the MR study with a MDCT study.

The Study

The 90 lb. (41 kg) specimen was frozen solid and the ambient room temperature thawing process began four days prior to the arrival of the manus at the Quinnipiac Diagnostic Imaging Laboratory in North Haven, Connecticut. The series of imaging studies were planned to begin with the MR examination. Unfortunately, the manus was not completely thawed and was indicated on the MR scan by an area of low signal [**WS 2.26**]. Recall that one of the principles of the modality is based on the mobility of the hydrogen ions is the tissues. Hydrogen in the water molecules is highly mobile unless the liquid is frozen. After looking at the images, it was determined that another 24 hours was required for the specimen to completely thaw. The delay provided the opportunity to complete the MDCT aspect of the study.

Although the MR would provide excellent resolution of soft tissue, such as the position of tendons and

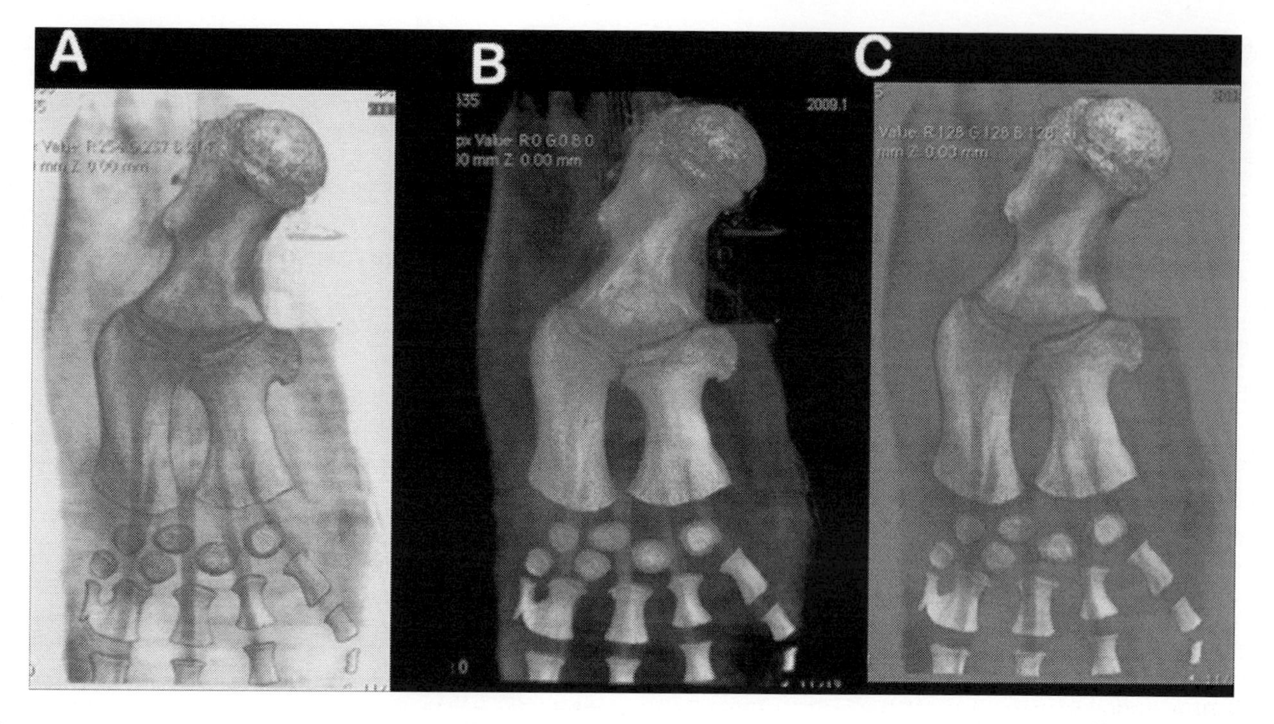

Figure 2.20. The sperm whale flipper data was downloaded onto an independent console loaded with Vitrea™ software and the 3-D images altered by using various background colors (A–C).

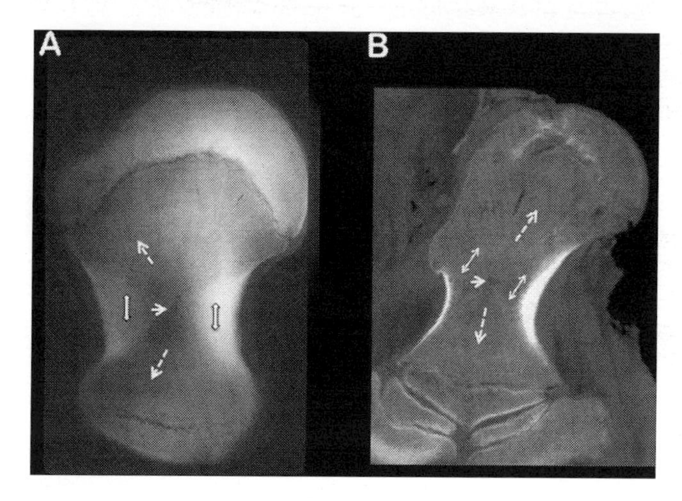

Figure 2.21. (A) The internal structure of the sperm whale flipper demonstrated 30 years ago and requiring many hours of work, and (B) the same internal structure visualized in less than one half-hour.

ligaments relative to the skeletal elements, the MDCT would afford a volume that could later be sectioned in any plane to correspond with the location of specific MR slices. Remember that MR acquisition is in a designated thickness in a specified plane. In addition, the volume data cannot be used to create a 3-D reconstruction. Unlike the clinical setting, where MDCT protocols were developed in order to make a diagnosis with the minimal radiation dose, in this situation resolution is the primary objective, disregarding dose. A 240-mm field of view (FOV), was selected and with 0.5-mm thick sections would produce isotropic voxels (see Chapter 7: Computed Tomography in *Advances in Paleoimaging* (CRC Press, 2020)). On the volume reconstructions, instead of prescribing contiguous slices to create the 3-D image, the slices were overlapped by 0.3 mm. The latter operation increased the total number of sections from 1353 to 2254, resulting in a file size of 3607 total sections to be saved. The final important factor to be included in the protocol was the reconstruction algorithm or filter convolution. A high-resolution bone algorithm was selected that would maximize the edge enhancement.

In order to demonstrate the flexibility of the saved MDCT data, eight years later the DICOM data set was downloaded from the university's PACS and uploaded to a MAC desktop computer with OsiriX MD® software. The 2254 slice scan was brought up and displayed as 3-D MPRs, and the slice thickness was increased to 25.85 mm. On the axial image, the axis of the sagittal plane was rotated to enable a sagittal section through one of the digits **[WS 2.27]**. The result was a comparison of a tendon on a sagittal T1 MR section and the off-axis or oblique MDCT reconstruction **[WS 2.28]**.

Significance

This case demonstrates several important imaging considerations. Unfortunately, the parameters cited in the publication for the 2006 CT scans were wanting. The penetrating power, indicated by the kV and the quantity of the X-ray utilized, designated by the mAs were provided along with the slice thickness. However, the FOV was not stipulated for either scan. The FOV is important because it determines the dimensions of the pixels and, in combination with the slice thickness, the ultimate resolution of the reformatted coronal and sagittal reconstructions. The matrix dimension cited in the publication, 512×512 pixels, is actually irrelevant because that is the standard for most CT scanners.

Similarly, the published MR parameters were also lacking. No specific pulse sequences for the axial, sagittal, or coronal acquisitions were included in the methods citations only the specific slice thicknesses and slice spaces were provided. Because these parameters determine the appearance of the image and cannot be reformatted or altered following acquisition, exclusion of that information minimizes reproducibility. This is even more significant when the specimen may not be frequently available. In addition, the choice of a 10 mm interslice gap to improve sign-to-noise ratio (SNR) reflects a lack of understanding of the principles of image quality.

Once the initial study was completed in 2010, the MR and MDCT DICOM data was burned onto a DVD and sent back to the veterinarian along with the elephant foot. To the best of our knowledge, the individual never published the data. It has been the policy of the institute not to publish any information regarding a particular study until after the principle investigator has had an opportunity to do so. If the data had been collected in a clinical setting, it may only have existed on the CPU of unit for a month or so before it is copied over. Generally, non-clinical cases would not be sent to the PACS to be archived. The institute is unusual in that it retains all imaging studies including MDCT, MR, and CR studies acquired at the university or in the field. In this case, the MR and MDCT studies were recently downloaded onto a DVD and later uploaded to a desktop computer with a DICOM reader, OsiriX MD®.

Possibly the most important factor was in the data acquisition phase, particularly with the selection of MR sequences. Unless the optimal parameters are chosen, including the slice thickness, the resulting images would be less than satisfactory. In addition, depending on the size of the specimen, it may require 15 to 30 minutes to complete. Because this study was based on 14 MR pulse sequences, the entire study required over three hours. By contrast, the MDCT volume acquisition was competed in a total of 15 minutes.

Although the MDCT scan required less time and data set could be manipulated eight-years later, if a clinical protocol had been employed, the resulting images would have been less than satisfactory.

What To Do With A Less Than Satisfactory Specimen?—Gerald Conlogue

Objective: Animals that were preserved possibly many decades ago in museum collections represent a potentially important source of radiographic data for these species. Even if initial radiographs were taken, for example, 20 years ago, they may need to be reexamined with the current advanced technologies that were not available at the time. The following example describes a specimen that was not included in a cerebral vascular study but still has potentially great value demonstrated by utilizing software with a multidetector computed tomography data set.

In 1972, as part of a comparative neuroradiology examination of cerebral circulation, discussed more thoroughly in Case Study 7: Contrast Media Injections, a slow loris, *Nycticebus sp*, was injected. Following the injection and cooling period, the general practice was to skin the animals and produce at least one burr hole made over the junction of the parietal/frontal bones before it was placed into a tank with 10% buffered formalin solution. However, because this was the only slow loris in the study, the skin was not removed, nor were the cerebral hemispheres exposed. The preliminary CR image was acquired with the body of the animal in a ventral-dorsal (VD) position, but the skull was rotated **[WS 2.29]**. From that perspective, there was a suggestion of a radiolucent area inside the skull. A second CR image was taken with the skull rotated into a more lateral position **[WS 2.30]**. Within the skull there appeared to be a large radiolucent area suggesting cavitation of the brain due to poor fixation. The impression as later confirmed on sagittal reconstructions of the multidetector computed tomography data set **[WS 2.31]**. However, because the Toshiba *Aquilion*™ that was used to acquire the data had software capable of curvilinear reconstructions, it was possible to isolate individual extremities. The process required the selection of images in a particular plane, in this case the coronal. After choosing the curvilinear function, the structure of interest, for example, the elements of the upper extremity as they appear, had to be traced while scrolling through the stack of images **[WS 2.32]**. Employing this approach, it was possible to isolate the humerus, ulna, and carpus **[WS 2.33]**; the humerus, radius, and carpus **[WS 2.34]**; and the hind leg **[WS 2.35]**.

Significance: Although this was a time-consuming process and required an individual skilled in manipulation of the software, it was possible to visualize the upper and lower extremities without the need to dissect this specimen preserved over 45 years ago. However, it must be kept in mind that the scanner used in this example was designed for clinical use and not intended to image small structures. Higher resolution on smaller specimens would require a microCT unit. Finally, the nondestructive approach also preserved the intact specimen, making it available to imaging technologies that may be developed decades in the future.

References

Grulich, WW and SI Pyle. *Radiographic Atlas of Skeletal Development of the Hand and Wrist*. Stanford University Press, Stanford, CA. 1950.

Ogden, JA, GJ Conlogue and TR Light. Fractures of the Radius and Ulna in a Skeletally Immature Fin Whale. *Journal of Wildlife Disease*. 17:111–116. 1981c.

Ogden, JA, GJ Conlogue, MJ Murphy and JS Barnett. Prenatal and Postnatal Skeletal Development of the Spine in the Short Finned Pilot Whale, *Globicephala macrorhyncha*. *The Anatomical Record*. 200:83–94. 1981d.

Ogden, JA, GJ Conlogue and AGJ Rhodin. Roentgenographic Indicators of Skeletal Maturity in Marine Mammals (Cetacea). *Skeletal Radiology*. 7:119–123. 1981a.

Ogden, JA, AGJ Rhodin, GJ Conlogue and TR Light. Pathology of Septic Arthritis and Contiguous Osteomylitis in the Leatherback Turtle, *Dermachelys coriacea*. *Journal of Wildlife Disease*. 17:277–287. 1981b.

Rhodin, AGJ, JA Ogden and GJ Conlogue. Preliminary Studies on Skeletal Morphology of the Leatherback Turtle. *Marine Turtle Newsletter*. 16:7–9. 1980.

Rhodin, AGJ, JA Ogden and GJ Conlogue. Chondro-osseous Morphology of *Dermochelys coriacea*, a Marine Reptile with Mammalian Skeletal Features. *Nature*. 290:244–246. 1981.

Weissengruber, GE, GF Egger, JR Hutchinson, HB Groenewald, L Elsässer, D Famini and G Forstenpointer. The Structure of the Cushions in the Feet of African Elephants (*Loxodonta Africana*). *Journal of Anatomy*. 209(6):781–792. 2006.

Skeletal Remains

3

GERALD J. CONLOGUE, ANDREW J. NELSON,
MARK VINER, ALAN LURIE, AND ALICIA GIAIMO

Contents

Objective: To demonstrate the internal structure of skeletal elements.

The discussion of imaging skeletal remains has been separated from consideration of mummified material for several reasons. First, because the elements are disarticulated, each can be radiographed separately and visually placed into very specific anatomic positions. Second, they can generally be more easily packaged for transportation to an imaging facility than mummified remains.

Chepén, Peru—Moche Culture (1997)

In the spring of 1997, Andrew Nelson, a physical anthropologist from the University of Western Ontario, in London, Ontario, Canada, wanted to include radiography as part of the bioarchaeological study of skeletal remains recovered from the archaeological site of San José de Moro on the north coast of Peru. At the same time, Jerry Conlogue, director of the Diagnostic Imaging Program at Quinnipiac University, was looking for an interesting challenge for his radiologic technology students. The solution was to join forces.

Nelson was one of three codirectors of the Archaeological Field Project "El Complejo de San José de Moro," Peru. The other directors were Luis Jaime Castillo of the Pontifica Universidad Católica del Peru in Lima, and Carol Mackey, of California State University, Northridge. Excavation at the site from 1995 to 1997 yielded 52 human skeletons of men, women, and children from the Middle and Late Moche (ca. 450–750 AD), Transitional (ca. 750–900), and Lambayeque (ca. 900–1100AD) time periods.

In collaboration with what would become the Bioanthropology Research Institute at Quinnipiac University, in July 1997 the first field radiographic facility was set up by the future Institute in Chepén, Peru, to work with the archaeological project. Chepén is only about 4 miles (6.3 km) from the archeological site of San José de Moro, but is still 432 miles (696 km) from Lima, Peru, on the Pan American Highway.

Objective: The research goals of the imaging component were to document patterns of artificial cranial modification, demonstrate pathological lesions on the skeletal material, and to assist with the assessment of age of subadult individuals. An additional objective, added

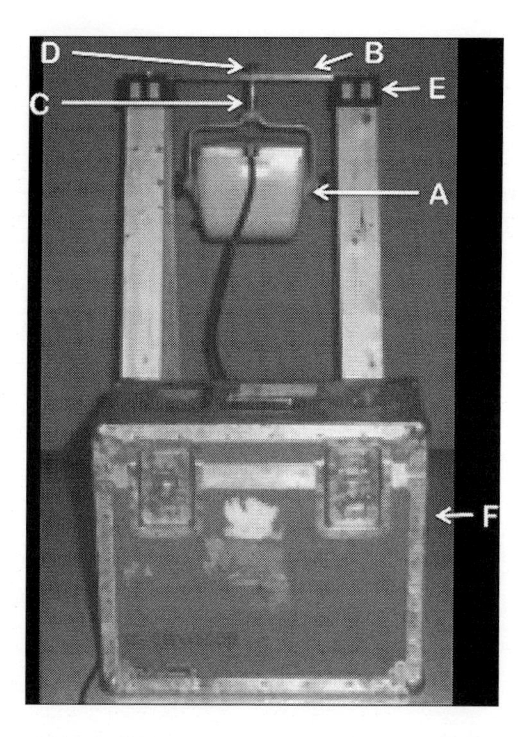

Figure 3.1. The assembled X-ray system system transport to Chepén, Peru: (A) 1960s vintage Profex Ray dental X-ray tube; (B) 20×3×0.5 inch (60×51×1.8 cm) steel plate; (C) a 5/16×5 inch carriage bolt attached the X-ray tube to the steel plate; (D) 5/16 inch wing nut securing the carriage bolt; (E) polystyrene sawhorse brackets; and (F) the 30×56×48 cm aluminum and plywood transport case that all but the wooden sawhorse legs were shipped in.

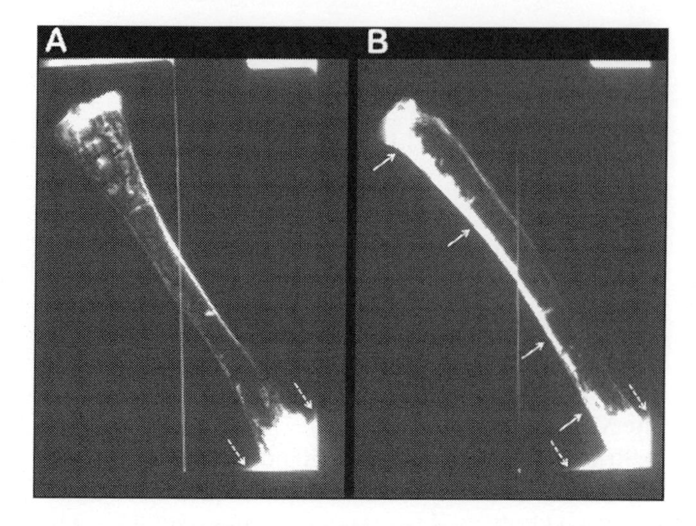

Figure 3.2. An AP (A) and lateral (B) radiographs of a tibia recorder on two sheets of Konica MG/SR 7×17 inch (18×43 cm) film loaded into a single Konica KF 100 speed 14×17 inch (36×43 cm) cassette. Both radiographs were taken at a 43 inch (110 cm) using 55 kVp, 5 mA, 2 seconds. Note: Because there was no collimator, the edge of the X-ray beam (dashed arrows) was circular due to the shape of the X-ray tube window; the dense material (solid arrows) represents mud that was caked inside of the bone.

on site, was to explore the use of radiography to understand the construction of ceramic, metal, and other archaeological artifacts.

Because there was no funding available for the imaging aspect of the project, it was necessary to minimize costs as much as possible.

X-Ray Source and Tube Stand

Because skeletal remains require 55 kVp for optimal penetration and contrast, it was decided that an old dental unit would meet that requirement. Dental units also had the transformer, required to step-up the voltage to kilovoltage or kV, mounted within the tube head. The X-ray tube was easily removed from an extendable tube stand. Finally, the control portion of the unit was small and easily detachable. An obsolete 1960s vintage Profex Ray dental unit was located and removed from the original tube stand. In order to reduce the shipping weight, the tube stand was discarded and replaced by a simple steel plate, 20×3×0.5 inch (60×51×1.8 cm), that could be mounted onto a sawhorse. With the X-ray tube bolted to the sawhorse by means of the steel plate, the 40-inch (100-cm) required X-ray source – to image receptor – distance (SID) to cover a 14×17 inch (36×43 cm) cassette was achieved. Again, to minimize the volume of material shipped to Peru, only the polystyrene sawhorse brackets were packed. The wood for the sawhorse legs was cut in Peru. When packed into the 30×56×48 cm (11.8 x 22 x 18.9 inch) aluminum and plywood container, the A-ray tube, control unit, hand switch with timer, electrical cables, sawhorse mounts, and steel plate weighed less than the maximum 77 pounds (35 kg) allowed for shipping (Figure 3.1).

Image Receptor and Processing

Konica Corporation donated 300 sheets of outdated 7×17 inch (18×43 cm) and 100 sheets of 14×17 inch (36×43 cm) MG/SR film and a total of three KF cassettes, one 14×17 inch (36×43 cm) and two 7×17 (18×43 cm) cassettes. All of the cassettes had a relative speed of 100, excellent for bone detail. Although the outdated film could not be used in a clinical facility, it would certainly be acceptable for this project. With only 100 sheets of 14×17 inch (36×43 cm) film available, two sheets of the donated 7×17 inch (18×43 cm) cassettes were placed into the larger film holder (Figure 3.2). In addition, as skeletal remains were the focus of the project, most of the bones would fit on a single 7×17 inch (18×43 cm) cassette.

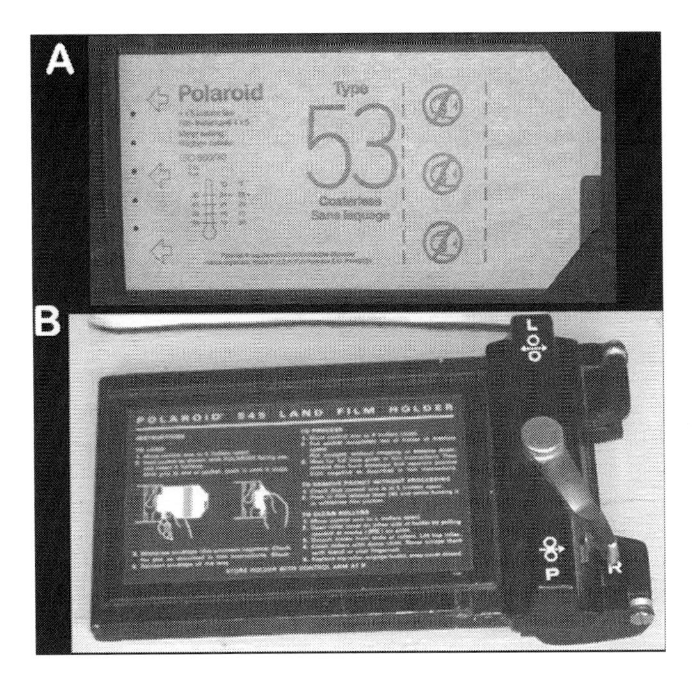

Figure 3.3. (A) Polaroid Type 53 photographic 4×5 inch film; (B) 4×5 inch Polaroid Type 545 film processor.

Polaroid Corporation donated a Model 545 photographic film holder/processing system and 200 sheets of the 4×5 inch (10×13 cm) Type 53 photographic film intended for use in a view camera (Figure 3.3). Although the film was small, because it lacked on intensifying screen, it would provide greater detail than the 100-speed Konica cassettes for demonstrating trabecular pattern in the femoral neck and calcaneus of adults, and teeth within the mandibles particularly of subadults (Figure 3.4). Because the film would be exposed solely by the interaction of X-ray photons and not light emitted by an intensifying screen, the exposure time had to be increased by a factor of 130. In order to reduce the quantity of X-ray mAs required, the SID was reduced to 31 inches (97 cm) or 24 inches (61 cm). The use of Polaroid film in the archaeological field context was published in Conlogue and Nelson (1999).

Fortunately, Chepén is a fairly large city with a population of around 40,000 and therefore has a regional hospital, the Hospital Apoyo de Chepén, approximately 1 km from the hostel where the X-ray facility was established [**WS 3.5**]. Access to film processing was generously provided; however, the X-ray facility lacked an automatic processer, instead relying on manual processing, and access would be limited until after 4 PM each day. Therefore, it was necessary to construct a film-changing darkroom for the site where exposed films were placed into a light-tight transport case before daily processing at the hospital. A 35×47×60 inch (0.9×1.2×1.5 m) portable darkroom was constructed using a ¾ inch (1.8 cm) polyvinylchloride (PVC) pipe frame (Figure 3.5A) covered with 0.6-mm-thick black gardening plastic (Frost King-Thermwell). Eight layers of the plastic material were required to before the structure was sufficiently light-tight to prevent light fogging of the X-ray film (Figure 3.5B–C).

The X-Ray Facility

Although the pretravel preparations were thought to be fairly comprehensive, a number of problems had to be resolved once everyone arrived at the location chosen for the actual X-ray examination, the *Hostal Quinta Sonia*. The motel was to serve not only as the location of the X-ray laboratory but also as lodging for the team including anthropologists, radiographer, undergraduate radiography students, and graduate anthropology

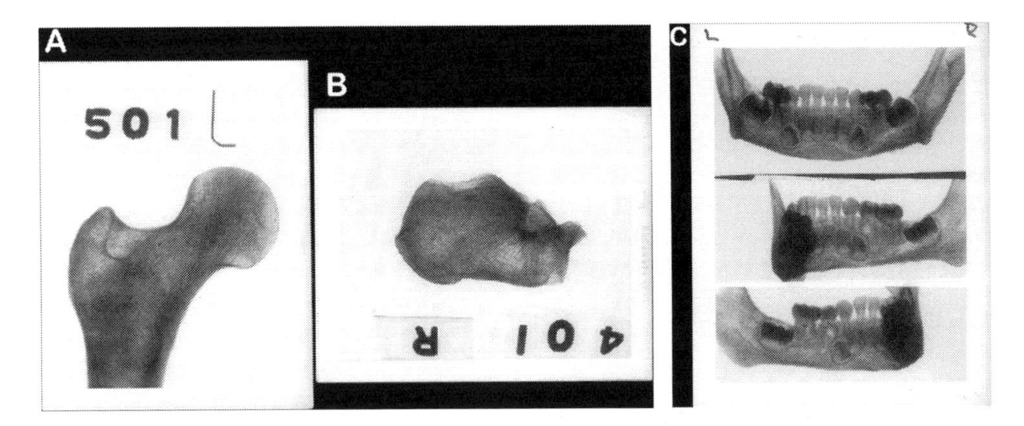

Figure 3.4. (A) A lateral femur taken using 14 exposures at 55 kVp; 5 mA; and 10 seconds, totaling 700 mAs. (B) A lateral calcaneus acquired by 20 exposures at 55 kVp; 4 mA; and 10 seconds, totaling 800 mAs. Both radiographs were taken at a 43 inch (110 cm) SID on the Polaroid Type 53 photographic film to provide the highest resolution for evaluation of the trabecular pattern within the bone. (C) In order to reduce the total number of exposures required, the SID was reduced to 24 inches (61 cm).

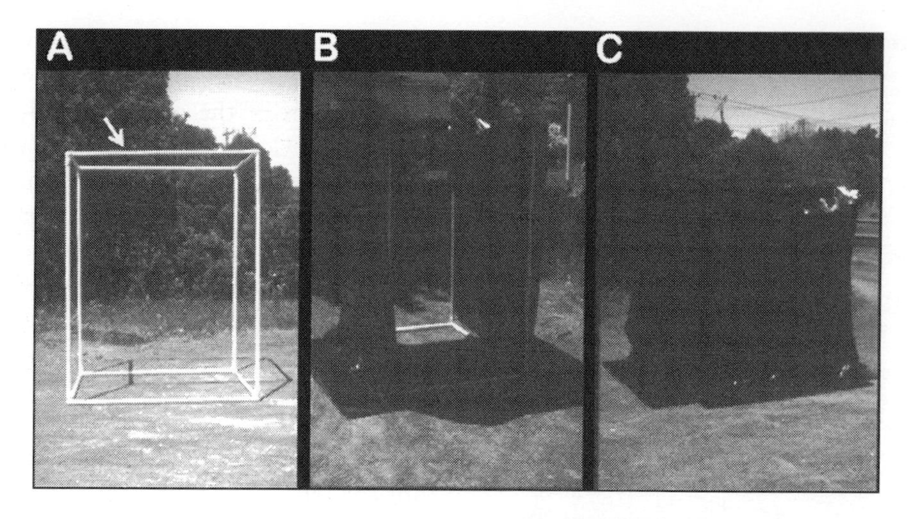

Figure 3.5. (A) The ¾ inch (1.8 cm) polyvinylchoride (PVC) pipe frame (arrow) of the 35×47×60 inch (0.9×1.2×1.5 m) portable darkroom. (B) The first eight layers of 0.6 mm-thick (0.0236 inch) black gardening plastic (Frost King-Thermwell) laid across the frame. (C) The second eight layers of 0.6 mm-thick black gardening plastic laid perpendicular across first layer to create a light tight enclosure.

students. Unfortunately, the electrical supply for the establishment was less than consistent or stable current. In addition, the X-ray tube was rated at 110 VAC and 8 amps, but the current in Peru was 220 VAC. Regrettably, a step-down transformer was not included in the equipment shipped to the site and the local hardware store, *ferretería*, had none available. After nearly a day of local inquiries, an old transformer for a Betamax video magnetic tape player was found for a small fee, but it only provided 2.5 amps or 31.25% of the current necessary for the x-ray output (Figure 3.6). Therefore, the transformer permitted a maximum of 5 of the 30 mAs the X-ray tube was designed to deliver. Combine with the inconsistent current available from the street, X-ray exposures were far from dependable and resulted in a large number of repeat exposures.

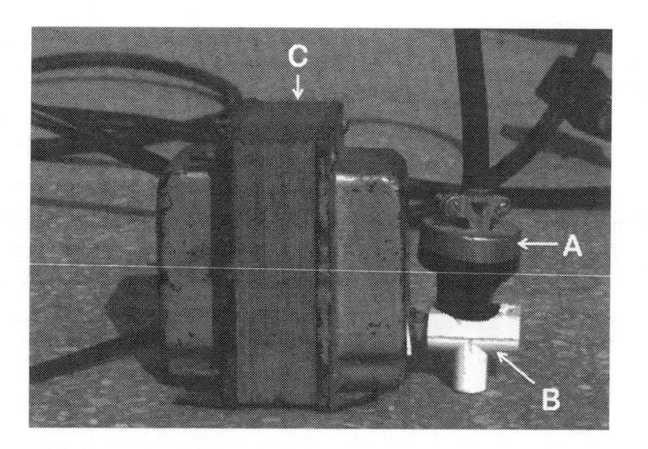

Figure 3.6. The plug from the X-ray unit (A) inserted into an adapter (B) plugged into the old step-down transformer (C) that was used with a Betamax video magnetic tape player.

The *ferretería* did provide the location where the wood was cut for the sawhorse. Abundant cedar was available, but the longest pieces created an SID of only 31.5 inches (80 cm). Therefore, at that distance, the area covered by the X-ray beam would not be sufficient to cover the 7×17 inch (18×43 cm) cassette. It was necessary to elevate the sawhorse/tube stand onto the two transport shipping containers (Figure 3.7).

Once the X-ray equipment was in place, the next step was to consider radiation safety for everyone working on the project and hostel staff that might have been in the area. Because the room had concrete block walls on three sides, the walls served as a barrier for scatter radiation. A safety zone was established approximately 20 feet (3 m) in the open area in front and away from the X-ray source. Prior to taking an X-ray, there was verbal notification of the impending exposure and only once everyone had reached the safe zone was the film exposed.

In order to repay the hospital for the use of their darkroom, five 200-speed 14×17 inch (36×43 cm) and four 200-speed 10×12 inch (25×30 cm) cassettes along with an 8:1 snap on grid were brought from Connecticut as gifts and presented to the Xray department's radiographer, Segundo Quesquen. Although used, the equipment was well received and he was more than willing to assist the team. He explained the hospital processed an average of 100 radiographs per month, or about three films per day. It was noted that the film drier was also located within the darkroom (Figure 3.8). Although this was an unusual location, with the low volume of films processed, the drier, which was set for around 100° F (38° C), never had the opportunity to significantly heat up the darkroom while films were being processed.

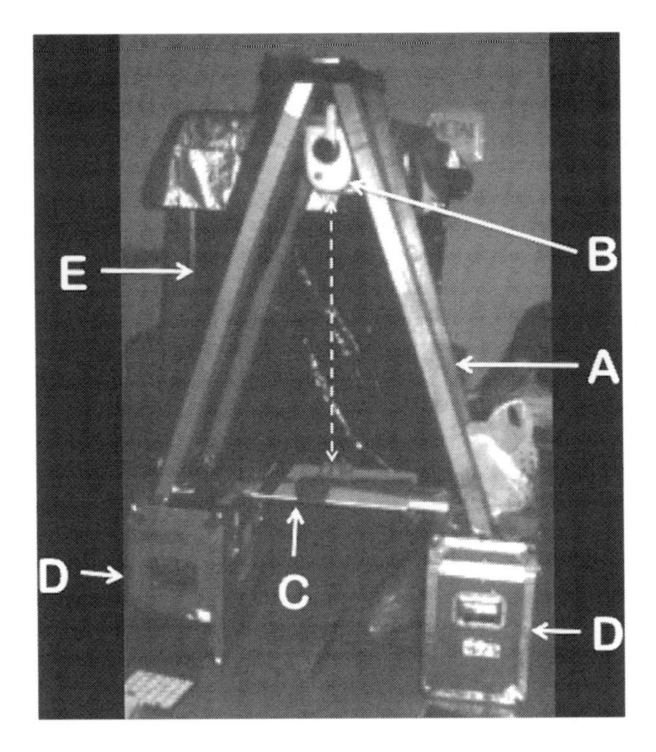

Figure 3.7. The radiography facility set-up in Chepén, Peru: (A) the short cedar legs on the saw horse resulted in a 31.5 inch (80 cm) SID (dashed arrow); between the X-ray tube (B) and the foam core table (C) stretched between the two transport cases (D). With the saw horse resting on the transport cases and an object placed on the floor, a 43 inch (110 cm) SID was achieved. Note the black plastic covered darkroom (E) in the background.

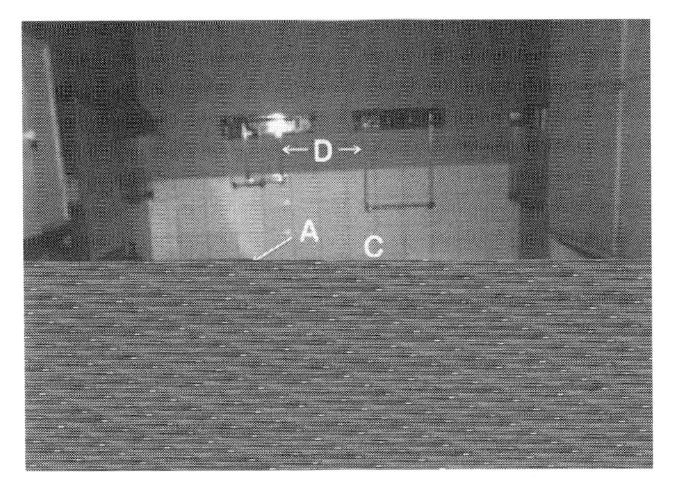

Figure 3.8. The darkroom at the hospital in Chepén: (A) the location of the developer and fixer tanks; (B) the large wash tank; (C) the film drier; and (D) the film hangers on the wall.

Segundo suggesting developing for three minutes, wash and fix for three minutes, wash for another five minutes, and dry for about 30 minutes.

Before the processing could begin, the film needed to be removed from the light-tight transport case and the four corners clipped into a film hanger. The procedure, although straightforward, would be usually accomplished in a darkroom where there was a safelight. Unfortunately, this darkroom lacked a functioning safelight, so the Quinnipiac radiography students had to practice the procedure with several sheets of film before actually attempting it on an exposed radiograph. The film hanging procedure added another 30 seconds to the entire developing process. If two students were both working in the darkroom together, it would facilitate the procedure and 40 films could be developed in about two hours. Unfortunately, with the drier operating, the darkroom temperature easily reached 100°F (38°C) during the period the students were in there. Because of the length of time required for the films to properly dry, ten films were left in the dryer to be picked up the following day.

The quantity of radiographs processed in just two days was almost equivalent to the number of films developed by the hospital in one month. Within several days, the developer was almost completely oxidized and new chemistry had to be prepared. Unfortunately, the hospital did not have the fresh chemistry on the premises, so fresh developer had to be ordered, which necessitated a wait of several days for delivery. The additional cost had to be provided by the project.

Once the X-ray unit was operational and other possible applications realized, the study was expanded to include not only skeletal material **[WS 3.10]** but also intact and fragments of pottery **[WS 3.11]** and beads **[WS 3.12]** recovered from the excavation. Imaging of the artifacts proved valuable in determining how they were manufactured.

Significance: The project extended for 33 days with a total of 18 days of radiography and 412 X-rays processed, or approximately 23 radiographs per day. It was the first attempt by the team to establish a field radiographic facility and a number of lessons were learned. The logistical problems related to moving three groups of radiography students to and from Chepén partially accounted for only 54% of the days involving radiography. The other reason for the low productivity was the need to wait for quantities of developer to be delivered to the hospital. The latter could be easily remedied by ensuring that a sufficient amount of developer and fixer were included with the supplies transported to the site. In addition, including a more compatible transformer would increase the efficiency of the X-ray output.

The results of the radiographic study of X-rays from the San Jose de Moro were published in two journal articles, the previously indicated Conlogue and Nelson (1999) and Conlogue, Nelson, and Guillén (2004), five conference presentations (Nelson & Conlogue, 1997; Conlogue & Nelson, 1998; Nelson, Conlogue,

Hennessy, & Gauld, 1999; Nelson, Lichtenfeld, Conlogue, Toyne, & Pool, 2000; Boston, Short, Nelson, & Conlogue, 2008) and one Master's thesis (Lichtenfeld, 2001). The radiographs have also been included in numerous public presentation and classroom lectures. The collection of radiographs is housed in the Department of Anthropology at the University of Western Ontario.

St. Brides Church, London, England—2010

In summer 2010, the Bioanthropology Research Institute (BRIQ), Inforce Foundation, Cranfield Forensic Institute at Cranfield University, and the Centre for Human Bioarchaeology (CHB) at the Museum of London began a multiyear project to radiograph the skeletal remains in the crypts under St. Bride's Church, Fleet Street, London, England. The church has long and storied history including being destroyed in the Great Fire of 1666, rebuilt by Christopher Wren and then gutted by a German incendiary bomb during the Blitz on 27 December 1940. In 1952, prior to the long process of reconstruction, a mandated architectural survey uncovered evidence demonstrating that the site had been occupied since the Roman occupation of *Londinium*. In addition to charnel house, nearly 300 lead-lined coffins were discovered in long forgotten crypts from the 18th and 19th centuries below the rubble of the burned-out church. What made the find even more incredible was the discovery that attached to each coffin was a metallic plate that included the occupant's name, age at the time of death, and date of death. A 1995 report (Scheuer & Black, 1995) documented the history of the remains beginning with the discovery until the time when the skeletons of a total of 227 individuals were examined and reboxed. In addition, when available, the report assembled parish documents to create a catalogue with biographical details such as name, age, dates of birth, death and burial, abode, and cause of death. Today, the CHB based at the Museum of London assists the church to curate the skeletal assemblage and oversee applications for research. Data has been recorded onto the electronic Oracle database, Wellcome Osteological Research Database (WORD).

Objective: The technical goal of the project was to determine the feasibility of establishing a functional, highly productive radiographic facility within the crypt. Once established, one of the scholarly objectives of the project was to create a more robust WORD database by adding radiographic images to the photographs of the skeletal elements. Because the radiographs were acquired within the crypt, there was no need to transport the skeletal remains to an imaging facility, thereby reducing the possibility of damaging the collection. The ability to X-ray in situ made it possible to greatly reduce the total time required to complete the study. Finally, the initial phase of this project served as a triage mechanism to select the most stable skeletal components that demonstrated particularly interesting pathology as candidate for advanced modality studies, such as MDCT.

In order to minimize the transport costs of shipping equipment from the United States to England, the X-ray source and DR images receptor system were rented from Xograph Healthcare Limited near London. The mobile radiographic unit was equipped with a Sedecal SP-HF® X-ray source mounted on a *flexible* support stand **[WS 3.13]**. The X-ray tube was equipped with a collimator to restrict the area irradiated and a laser light to aid with positioning and directing the central beam while minimizing the scatter radiation and reducing the radiation risks to the equipment operator. The image recording system consisted of a Canon Lanmix™ CXDI—50C DR plate (Figure 3.9) connected by a 21-foot (7-m) cable to a Dell laptop Latitude 510 Celeron™ M 350 computer. The latter operated at 1.30 GHz with 512 MB, 400 MHz DDR2 SDRAM memory and 40 GB hard drive that operated on a Windows XP PRO® operating system (Figure 3.10). The imaging data were saved in Digital Imaging and Communication in Medicine (DICOM) files. When downloaded from the system onto external media, such as a CD or DVD, a DICOM reader was also included

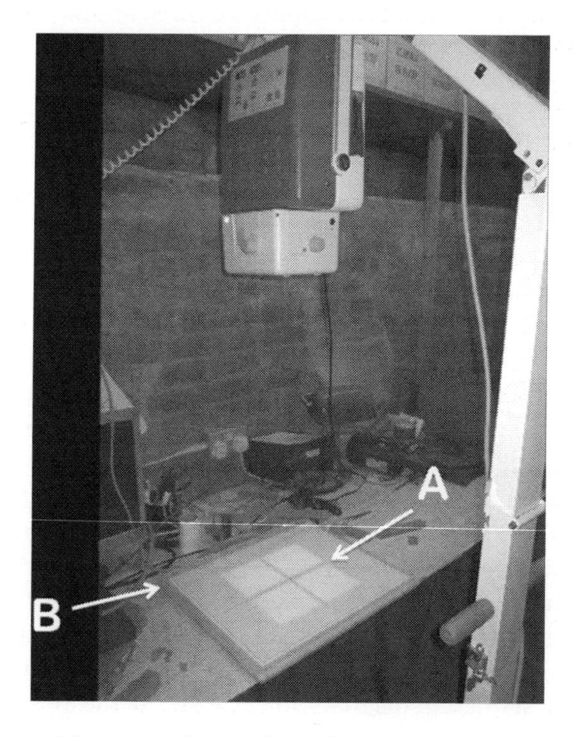

Figure 3.9. The collimated area forming a square with the laser light indicating the center of the X-ray field (A) on Canon Lanmix™ CXDI—50C DR plate (B).

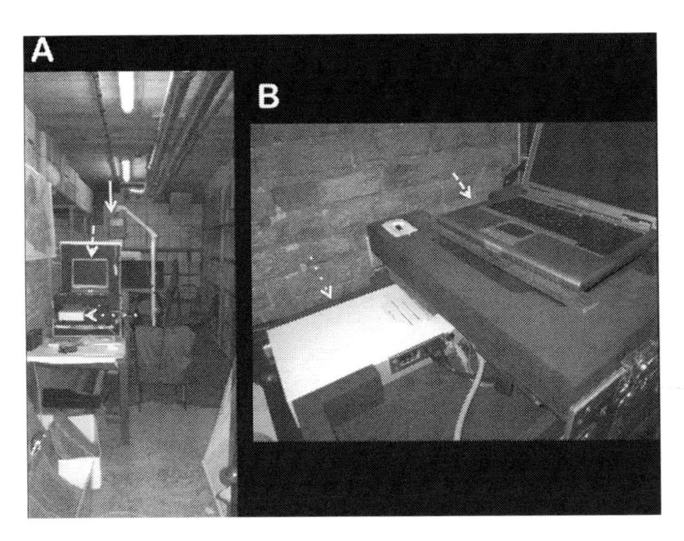

Figure 3.10. (A) The proximity of the X-ray source (solid arrow) to the Dell laptop Latitude 510 Celeron™ M 350 computer (dashed arrow) and (B) the router (dotted arrow). The latter connects the DR plate to the computer.

with the files to enable viewing on a PC-based computer system (Conlogue et al., 2011).

When creating a field radiographic facility and before taking any exposures, radiation safety is always considered as was the case in this example. With only one door into the crypt, consisting of a thick ceiling and walls, the primary factor was establishing a safe distance based on the inverse square law. With the exposure hand switch cord stretching approximately 12 feet (3.7 m), it was possible to extend the cord beyond the door that could be partially closed while taking the exposure. Referring back to Figure 3.9, the DR plate was placed on a table and the beam collimated, restricting the beam reduced scatter radiation. In addition, referring to Figure 3.10, the case for the laptop and the DR router were placed on a table in between the X-ray exposure area and the radiographer taking the exposure, serving as a barrier to scatter radiation.

During the total of seven days, 748 images or an average of 107 radiographs per day, were acquired of the complete skeletal remains of 14 subadults and the skulls and mandibles of 70 adults. Although the daily average appears impressive, due to problems with the computer system, there were several days spent waiting for the computer to be serviced during which no images were acquired. However, more notable was a single day when 195 images were recorded, a number that could never be achieved with film as an image receptor. In addition, the exceptional quality of the images at least matched, if not generally surpassed, the detail available with a standard film/screen system. The stabilized power supply ensured that consistently accurate output of the X-ray source was achieved. Because the image appearance could be manipulated, for example, changing the scale of contrast or the number of shades of gray demonstrated, the system proved extremely successful with the all subadult material, eliminating the need to repeat any exposures.

At the end of the study, only two disadvantages of the entire system were noted. The first was with the X-ray tube support. At a weight of 58 lbs. (26.5 kg), it was not only heavy but also proved to be unwieldy to transport into the crypt. In addition, it was not easy to assemble and the vertical support component prevented easy access to the specimens on the imaging plate.

The second shortcoming was the number of problems experienced with the computer system, specifically the interface between the Canon processing unit and the Dell software. Although Xograph provided assistance whenever problems were encountered, the result was an equivalent of at least two days downtime, or about 25% of the entire study period. Following the completion of the project, Xograph representatives indicated that changes would be made to increase the efficiency of the system.

Significance: Probably the most important aspect of this project was the lessons learned regarding DR during the acquisition of over 700 images. As briefly mentioned in the plane radiograph Chapter 4 in *Advances in Paleoimaging* (CRC Press, 2020), in the clinical facility, the X-ray beam would be restricted or collimated to the size of the body part under examination, such as the cervical spine, and not all of the 14×17 inch (36×43 cm) or 17×17 inch (43×43 cm) plate would be utilized. The radiograph of the smaller body part would fill the entire monitor screen. However, if the bones that comprise the cervical spine were assembled and the entire plate utilized, the full area of the large plate would now fill the monitor screen with the spine occupying only a portion of the image. In order to view the smaller spine, that section of the radiograph would need to be magnified and the resulting image appeared pixilated (see Figures 4.99–4.101, Chapter 4 Plane Radiography, *Advances in Paleoimaging* (CRC Press, 2020)). When using film as an image receptor, the entire cassette would be covered by skeletal elements **[WS 3.16]**. Because film is an analog media, magnification of the image would be dependent on factors such as focal-spot size at the anode within the X-ray tube and whether nonscreen or screen film was utilized. Therefore, with DR, individual skeletal elements had to be radiographed resulting in lengthening the time required to complete an entire skeleton. In order to compensate for this delay, the assistance of an additional person trained as a radiographer familiar with positioning and/or anthropology would reduce acquisition time. Using the positioning aids described in Chapter 4: Plane Radiography in *Advances in Paleoimaging* (CRC Press, 2020) (Figures 4.117–4.119), an assistant would position complicated skeletal elements, such as the cervical spine, before the radiograph is acquired.

For 8.5 days in January and February 2011, the X-ray facility was reestablished in the crypt with the focus on the remaining 135 adult skulls and mandibles. The X-ray tube support was not changed but a new computer system, Panasonic Toughbook®, was linked to the Cannon DR system. With the computer replacement, the system was only down for one day. The total number of images for the second study was 1192 images, for an average of 140 images per day. The 31% increase in efficiency over the first study was attributed to a number of factors. First and most important was the improved computer interface with the DR receptor. Second, familiarity was the system and limiting the study to adult skulls and mandibles and not the more complex positioning required for the complete subadult individuals. Finally, an additional radiographer was available to help with the positioning. The value of the latter was evident dating back to the 1997 radiographic study in Chepén. However, when computer manipulation is a component of the process, the additional person, particularly a radiographer, is imperative to reduce the time required to complete the project.

On a third trip over a total of five days in June 2012, the equipment was returned to the crypt with the target being documenting pathologic changes in the adult skeletal remains. In addition, a group of skulls were radiographed to compare direct measurements to measurements taken from the radiographs. Another difference was in the method used to keep track of the time spent to acquire the radiographs. In the clinical setting, an important concept is *through-put* or the number of patient examinations completed per unit time. Because the X-ray equipment was rented, it was important to maximize the number of images acquired during the rental period in order to justify the cost. If the cost per radiograph could be reduced, it would provide an incentive for more radiographic studies. Therefore, an effort was made to record the *start* and *stop* times for each exposure (Table 3.1). During the five-day period, at total of 23 hours and 41 minutes (23:41) were required to acquire 488 images or averaging 2.9 minutes per image. Referring back to the study in Chepén. Peru where only an average of 23 radiographs were acquired per day, in the crypt at St. Bride's that was a little more that the number of images acquired in one hour.

Table 3.1. The log of the DR images taken in the crypt at St. Bride's Church during 2012

Day	Hours (Min)	Images	Time (min)/Image
1	2:00 (120)	44	2.7
2	7:50 (470)	112	4.2
3	5:36 (336)	143	2.3
4	4:30 (270)	79	3.4
5	3:45 (225)	110*	2.0
Total	23:41 (1421)	488	Average 2.9

*Two individuals assisted in acquiring the material and positioning

Table 3.2. The cost per image calculation for the three-year study at St. Bride's Church

Year	Cost ($)	# Days	# Images	Cost ($)/Image
2010	2400	7	748	3.20
2011	2570	9	1192	2.16
2012	1600	5	488	3.30

Because the study continued over a three-year period, it was possible to examine the charges for equipment rental and calculate the cost per image (Table 3.2). The latter is particularly important if someone is preparing a budget for an imaging study. If the approximate number of objects to be radiographed is known and highest cost per image is used for calculation, a fairly confident estimate for that phase of the study can be determined. The factors that contributed to the lower cost per image during the second year of the study was discussed earlier. Two of those elements—familiarity with the equipment, particularly the software, and including an addition radiographer to assist in the positioning—should be considered. The initial cost of the second radiographer can easily be offset by the increased throughput.

All the images were stored in three locations: on the hard drive of the DR system in a DICOM format, and downloaded onto two 2-terabyte (TB) external hard drives. Of the latter, one went, as TIFF files, to the Centre for Human Bioanthropology at the Museum of London (MOL), the organization that oversees the St. Bride's remains, and the other as DICOM images was returned to the BRIQ. TIFF files have the potential to be directly downloaded to the WORD database and easily viewed without the need for DICOM viewer software. However, because BRIQ will share the images with radiologists for interpretation, the DICOM format was preferred.

Museum of London, London, England (2013)

The studies at St. Bride's Church not only provided an excellent test of a field DR approach to imaging skeletal remains but also furnished material for presentations at professional meetings (Conlogue et al., 2011; Gonzalez, Conlogue, Viner, & Bekvalac, 2014) and a publication (Conlogue et al., 2016). Jelena Bekvalac, Curator of Human Osteology at the

Centre for Human Bioanthropology at the Museum of London, suggested expanding the project to include selected skeletal remains at the museum. The Museum of London, only a short distance from St. Bride's, maintains a collection of over 20,000 archaeologically derived human skeletal remains many with documented pathologies. This expanded project in London provided an opportunity to determine the value of using a field CR system, while the DR facility would be simultaneously located at St. Bride's. Kubtec Medical Imaging in Stratford, Connecticut, agreed to ship their Kubtec Kubscan® CR system and X-ray source, Xtend® 100HF, to the Museum of London. Two rolling cases were sent: the first, measuring 33.25 × 24.25 × 21.75 inches (85 × 62 × 56 cm), contained the X-ray tube, computer keyboard, monitor, and mouse, two CR 14 × 17 inch (36 × 43 cm) plates, cables, and extension cords weighing 110 pound (50 kg); and the second case, measuring 49.25 × 34.5 × 19.5 inches (126 × 88 × 50 cm), with the CR reader, weighed 173 pounds (79 kg).

The X-ray facility was established in the basement of the Museum away from areas of activity. Because the X-ray source was intended for use with 110-volt, 60-cycle current a step-down transformer was required adjust the 220-volt, 50-cycle current employed in England [**WS**]. In order to reduce the weight of the equipment shipped from the United States, the heavy manufacturer X-ray tube support was replaced by the bathtub seat base described in Chapter 4 Plane Radiography, Figure 4.42 (*Advances in Paleoimaging*). The X-ray tube was bolted to the legs of the bathtub seat. Two legs of the latter were taped to a stepladder while support poles were inserted into the other two legs [**WS 3.17**]. The CR plate was placed on a footstool under the X-ray tube to create a 40-inch (100-cm) SID [**WS 3.17B**]. The CR reader was place on top of the shipping case along the same concrete wall as the X-ray tube support [**WS 3.17B, C**].

In order to reduce radiation exposure to the radiographer, the computer keyboard, mouse, monitor, and exposure switch were placed on the other shipping case around the corner from the wall with the X-ray tube [**WS 3.17D, E**]. Radiation exposure monitors were positioned hanging from the over pipes behind the area where the radiographer took the exposures [**WS 3.18**].

A preparation area was established in the radiation safe exposure zone so that undergraduate radiologic science students from University College Dublin could assemble skeletal elements for radiography, reducing the time required to complete each set of skeletal remains [**WS 3.19**]. Because multiple exposures could be taken on a single CR plate prior to processing, several collimated images of skeletal elements, such as assembled vertebrae, were acquired reducing the total number of plates required for the study [**WS 3.20**]. Because it took approximately 1.5 to 2 minutes for the CR plate to be processed, multiple images increased the efficient use of the imaging plates. In addition, when possible, to have two images on a single plate facilitates accessibility and viewing [**WS 3.21**]. To further reduce the through-put time, two plates were available for the study. As one plate was being exposed, another skeletal element, such as a pelvis, was being positioned, using foam pieces, on the second plate. When the first exposure was completed, the plates were exchanged and the process repeated [**WS 3.22**]. The exposure for all skeletal elements was the same: 55 kVp at 2.5 mAs.

In order to monitor through-put during the 13 days of the project, start and stop times were recorded each day so that the total number of hour involved in radiography could be calculated. Because the CR system permits multiple images on a single plate, the log included the number of exposures and the number of plates (Table 3.3). In all, a total of 687 images on 566 plates were taken on the skeletal remains of 179 individuals. Therefore, the throughput averaged 5.7 minutes per exposure. In 2012, with the DR system at St. Bride's, the average was 2.9 minutes per exposure or nearly double the through-put at the Museum of London. However, at the latter, the 566 plates, requiring approximately 90 seconds to process each plate, accounted for 849 minutes or over 14 hours. Over the 13-day period of the study, an average of five hours per day were spent radiographing specimens. Taking into account the time spend processing the plates, if a DR system had been used, the same number of images could have been done in 10 or 11 days.

Table 3.3. The log of the CR images taken at the Museum of London in 2013

Day	Hours (Min)	Exposures	Plates	Min/Exposure
1	3:40 (220)	24	24	9.2
2	6:00 (360)	61	50	5.9
3	5:45 (345)	46	39	7.5
4	5:00 (300)	86	66	3.5
5	1:00 (60)	18	13	3.3
6	5:00 (300)	78	54	3.8
7	6:30 (390)	64	54	6.1
8	5:00 (300)	41	35	7.3
9	6:10 (370)	82	61	4.5
10	1:45 (105)	12	12	8.8
11	6:30 (390)	63	58	6.2
12	7:40 (460)	81	72	5.7
13	5:15 (315)	31	28	10.2
Total	65:25 (3,925)	687	566	Average 5.7

Dry Fetal Skull, Cushing Center, Cushing/Whitney Medial Library, Yale University, Hew Haven, Connecticut (2016)

Thus far, the discussion has only considered acquiring images of skeletal remains in a field situation. Over the past several decades, tremendous changes have taken place in medical imaging and the applications for each modality have been somewhat defined without considering possible non-clinical uses. The following discussion explores expanding applications and determining limitations.

During the mid- to late 1970s, Robert Shapiro, the Chief of Radiology and Franklin Robinson, a neurosurgeon, both at the Hospital of St. Raphael, in New Haven, Connecticut, began collecting material for a book, *The Embryogenesis of the Human Skull, An Anatomic and Radiographic Atlas*, which was published in 1980. The collection eventually consisted of dry skulls, alizarin stained/cleared skulls, and coronal and sagittal histological sections of decalcified skulls. In 1984, Dr. Shapiro moved from New Haven, Connecticut, to Miami, Florida, to become the Residency Program Director and Professor of Radiology at the University of Miami. After the death of Dr. Shapiro in 1992, Dr. Robinson donated the entire collection to Dr. E. Leon Kier, Chief of Neuroradiology at Yale University Medical School. Dr. Robinson died in 2003. Additional dry skulls were obtained by Kier from biological supply companies, a common practice in the 1960s and 1970s when such specimens were readily available. Eventually the entire Shapiro/Robinson collection was incorporated into the larger Kier/Conlogue anatomic collection. In 2010, items from the Shapiro/Robinson materials, including the dry fetal skulls were among the specimens displayed in the newly opened Cushing Center at the Cushing/Whitney Medical Library on the Yale Medical School campus.

Objectives: At the time of the Shapiro/Robinson book, the only high resolution imaging modality available was plain radiography using single emulsion film. In the summer of 2016, the Bioanthropology Research Institute at Quinnipiac University and collaborators began a project to reexamine the dry skulls. The study had two principle goals: to demonstrate the value of maintaining accessibility to specimens in anatomic collections; and to utilize imaging technologies not available at the time the original research was conducted. The multimodality approach involved several Universities: Quinnipiac University in North Haven, Connecticut, for plain film and computed radiography (CR), multi-detector computed tomography (MDCT), and a direct digital radiography (DR) equipped mammography unit; the University of Connecticut School of Dental

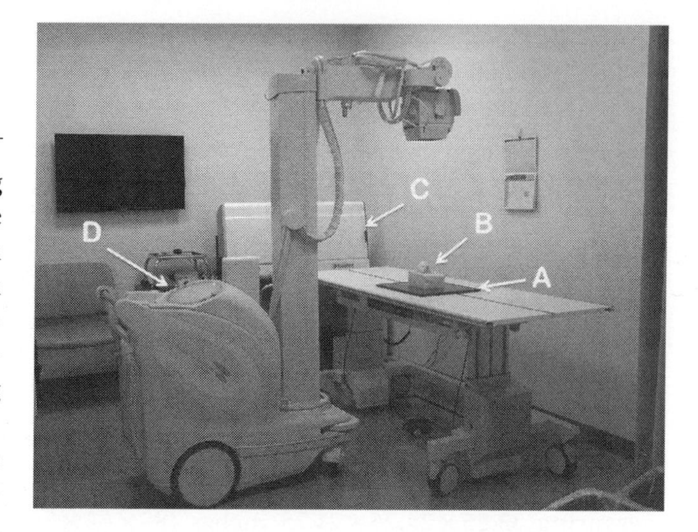

Figure 3.11. (A) KUBSCAN® CR imaging plate; (B) Skull #2 supported in at foam positioning device; (C) KUBSCAN™ CR plate reader; (D) Shimadzu Mobile Art Evolution® portable radiographic unit.

Medicine in Farmington, Connecticut, made available their cone-beam computed tomography (CBCT) dental unit; and the University of Western Ontario in London, Ontario, Canada, provided access to their micro-CT unit. In addition, a private company, Kubtec Medical Imaging in Stratford, Connecticut provided use of several digital imaging systems including a cabinet tomosynthesis unit.

Plain Radiography—Film/CR

A Shimadzu Mobile Art Evolution® radiographic unit with a 0.7 mm focal spot was used for all the CR images. Radiograph exposure were taken at 40 kVp, the lowest setting possible on the unit, and 1.6 mAs at a 100 cm Source-to Image receptor-Distance (SID) and the CR plates were processed with a Kubscan® CR reader (Figure 3.11), the same system used at the Museum of London. A positioning aid was created from scooping out a section from a block of foam (Figure 3.12). For all skulls, anterior-posterior (AP), right lateral, both oblique projections to demonstrate the mandible/maxilla, and a submento vertical projection (Figure 3.13) were acquired. For all images, because dental development was focus, the center of the X-ray beam was directed to the teeth, in order to minimize distortion (Figure 3.14).

Both film and CR exposures were also taken with a 1970s vintage Faxitron® (Hewlett-Packard), a self-contained X-ray cabinet system (Figure 3.15). With a 0.5 mm focal spot, the unit was designed for microradiography. In addition, it was equipped with a 0.03-inch (0.8 mm) thick beryllium window, to permit the lower

Figure 3.12. Shapiro/Robinson Skull #5 placed within a foam positioning device created by scooping out an area for the skull.

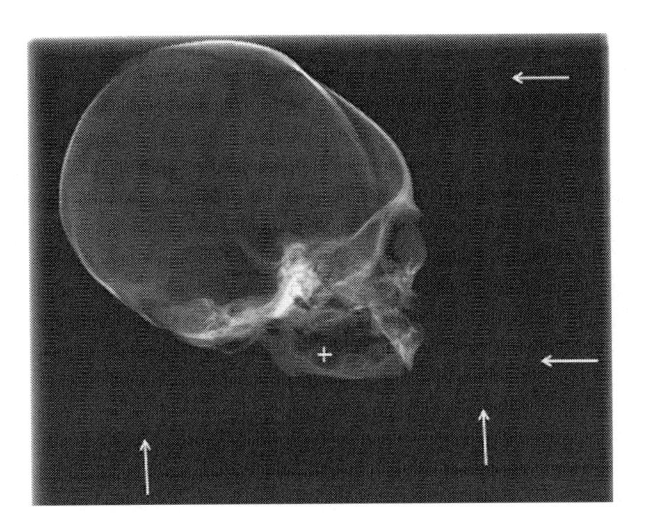

Figure 3.14. Because to focus of the study was dental development, the center of the X-ray beam was directed to the teeth (cross): Note the margins of the foam sponge positioning device (arrows).

energy photons, soft X-ray, generated by lower kV, to interact with the object. Both non-screen film, Fuji industrial 100 IX film, and FujiFilm Super HR-U screen film loaded into a non-screen holder were used. The exposures for the industrial film were 30 kVp, 2 mA for 6 minutes (720 mAs) and had to be hand-processed in photographic trays (Figure 3.16A). For the screen-film in the nonscreen holder, the exposures were reduced to 30kVp, 2 mA for 10 seconds (20 mAs) and developed with a Konica SRX-101A automatic processing unit (Figure 3.16B).

Mammography Unit

A Hologic Selenia Dimensions digital mammographic unit was used to obtain images of the fetal skulls. Images were obtained in the PA, both laterals, both oblique projections to demonstrate the mandible/maxilla, as well as the submento vertical projection with the compression paddle removed. Because the dental development and the auditory canal were the focus centering was directed to these areas.

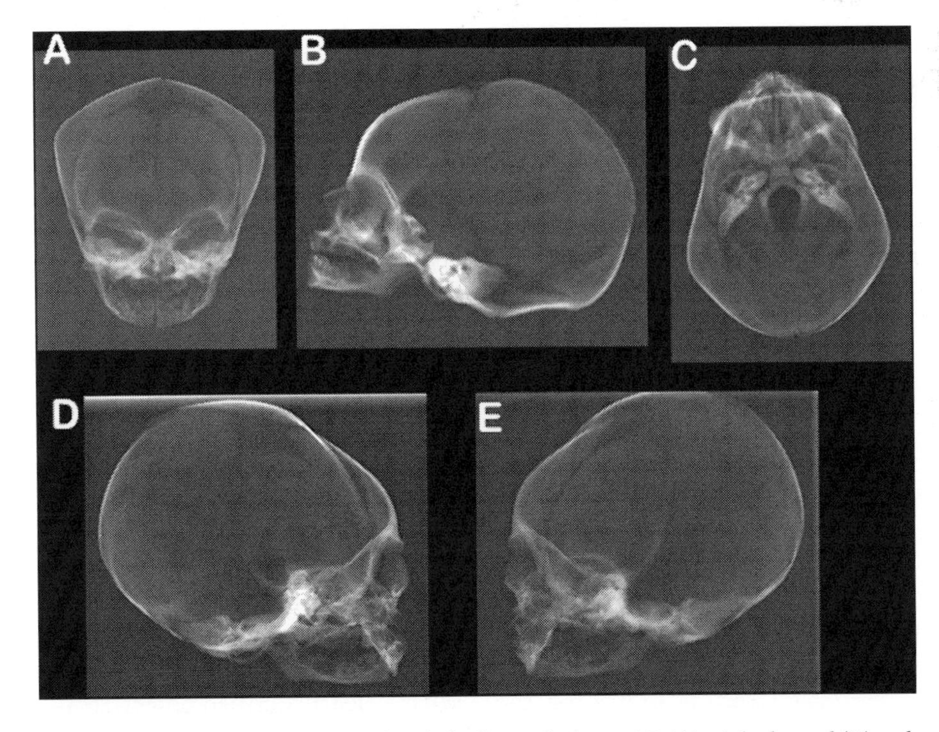

Figure 13.13. The routine radiographs for the dry fetal skulls include an AP (A), right lateral (B), sub-mento vertical (C), a left (D) and right (E) oblique projections.

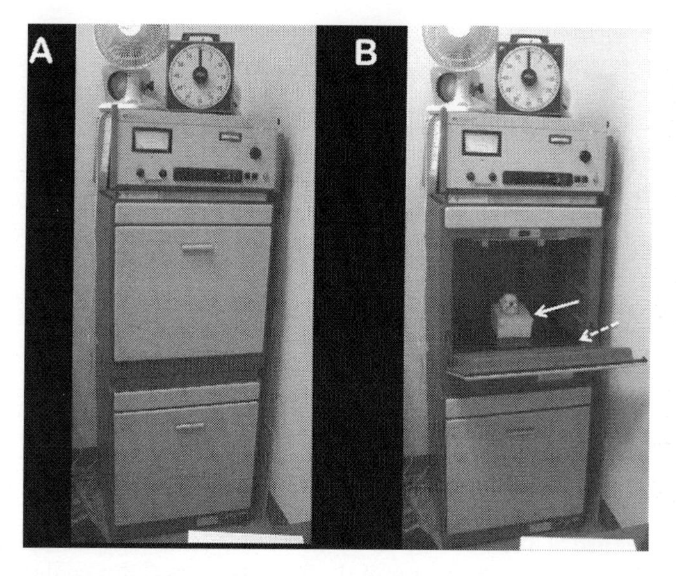

Figure 3.15. (A) Faxitron™ (Hewlett-Packard) self-contained X-ray cabinet system. (B) Door open to the top cabinet revealing the dry skull #2 supported in at foam positioning device (solid arrow) and set on top of a non-screen film holder (dashed arrow).

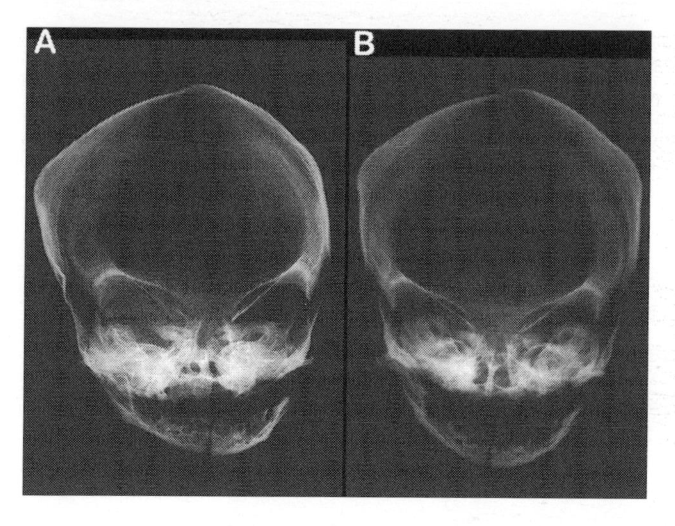

Figure 3.16. The AP projection of dry fetal skull #5 recorded on (A) Fuji Industrial 100 IX film manually processed and (B) FujiFilm Super HR screen film processed with a Konica SRX-101A automatic processor.

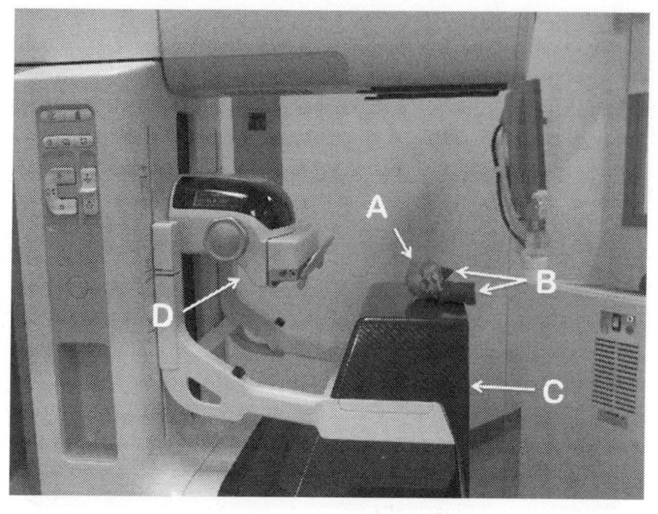

Figure 3.17. Fetal skull #2 (A) placed in a right lateral position supported by small radiolucent foam wedges (B) on top of the 1.8 magnification stand and the compression device (D) at the lowest setting.

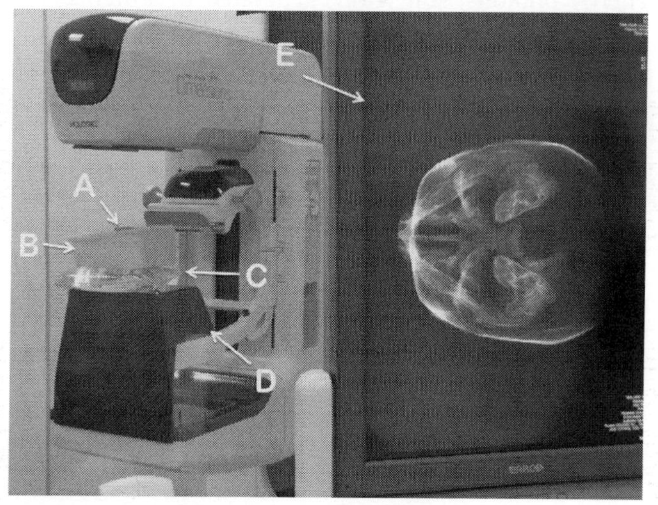

Figure 3.18. Fetal skull #5 (A) positioned in a foam cradle (B) resting on the saline bag (C) on top of the 1.8 magnification stand (D). Because it was a DR system, the image appeared on the monitor (E) seconds following the termination of the exposure.

Manipulation of the equipment was necessary to obtain images of diagnostic quality. Multiple attempts were made using various settings on the equipment. It was determined that the Auto kV setting provided the best detail of the skulls. Due to the size of the skulls the 1.8 magnification stand was used to enhance visualization of the anatomy. Of note was the thickness recorded by the machine. The images were improved when the compression paddle was removed and the mechanism was at the lowest setting indicating the smallest thickness (Figure 3.17). Despite not having actually recorded force this made a dramatic difference in the exposure. In addition, we also utilized a saline bag to add thickness to the skulls (Figures 3.18 and 3.19). This helped with the two larger skulls but not the smallest. In addition to the IV bag, small radiolucent foam wedges were used to hold the skulls in the desired position.

Although the mammography unit was not designed to image skeletal material, with a radiographer manipulating the hardware and software, diagnostic quality images were acquired (Figure 3.20). With a clearly defined objective, in this case the demonstration of dental development, and a small sample size, the mammography unit would not necessarily

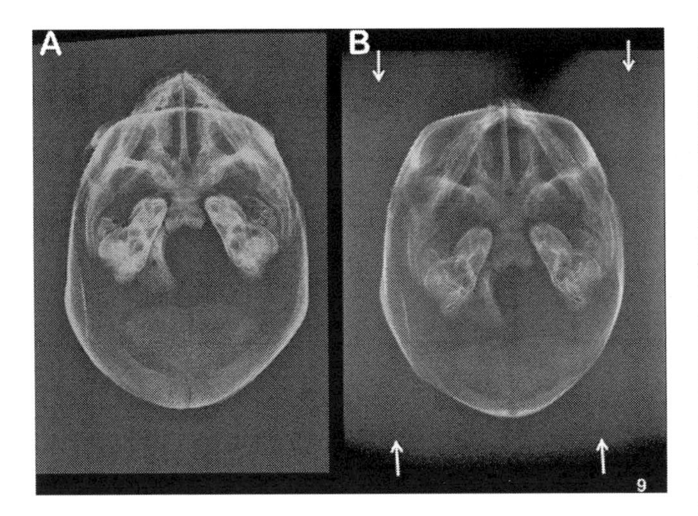

Figure 3.19. Two submento vertical projections of skull #5: (A) positioned only in a foam cradle and (B) in the foam cradle placed on a saline bag. The margins of the bag are indicated by the arrows.

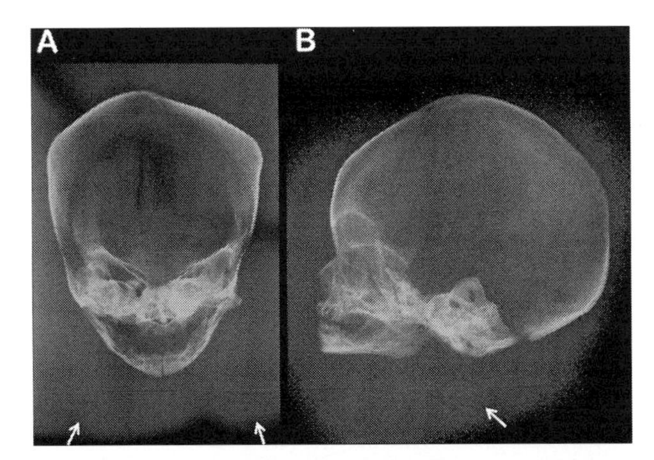

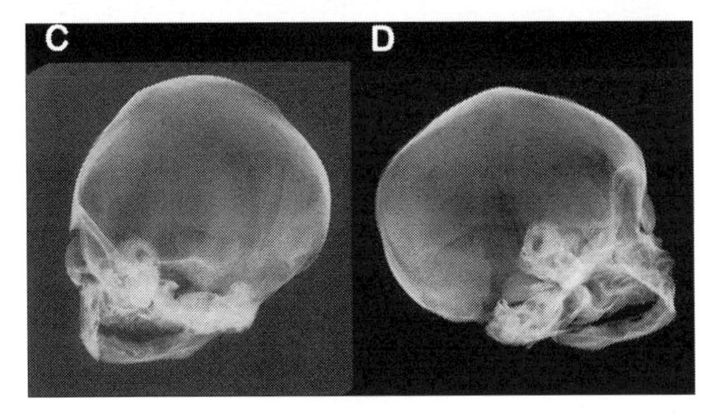

Figure 3.20. (A) Sample of multiple images of dry fetal skull #5: (A) A PA and (B) right later projects both utilizing the saline bag. (C) a right and (D) left oblique projections demonstrating dental development in the mandible and maxillae.

have been the first choice but proved successful. Because there are numerous mammography units available at imaging facilities, it might be easier to get access to this modality, at least for a preliminary study.

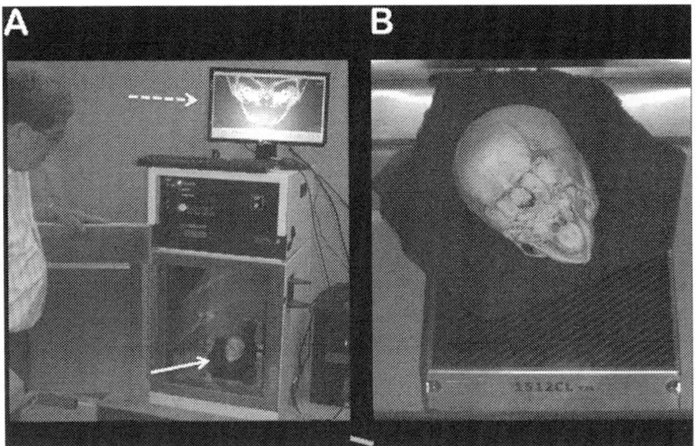

Figure 3.21. (A) Chester Lowe, Ph.D. FACR, Chief Technology Office, Kubtec Medical Imaging ready to remove dry skull #5 positioned on the detector (solid arrow) from the XPERT® 80 cabinet system. Note the recently acquired PA image of the skull on the monitor (dashed arrow). (B) Dry skull #5 positioned on the detector for a left oblique mandible.

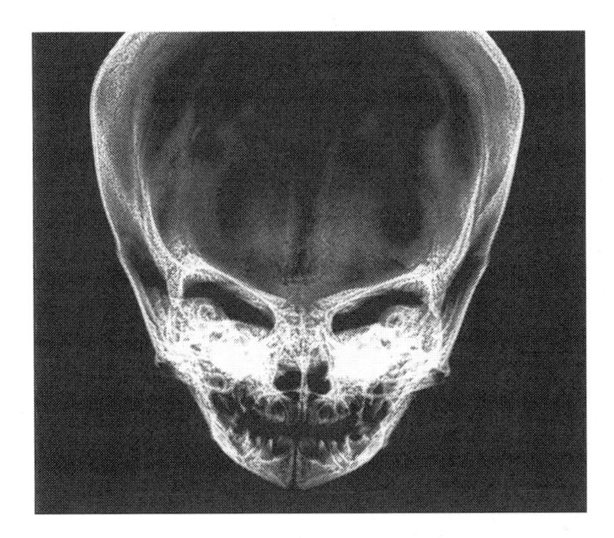

Figure 3.22. The AP projection of dry fetal skull #2 acquired with the XPERT® 80 Specimen Radiography System.

Digital Radiography and Tomosysntheis

Kubtec Medical Imaging in Stratford, Connecticut provided access to the XPERT® 80 Specimen Radiography System and the PARAMETER® 3D Tomosynthesis Radiography System. Both units, developed for examining pathology specimens, are self-contained and lead lined, therefore, with no possible radiation leakage, they can be placed without restriction in any location. The XPERT® 80 System is the twenty-first-century digital version of the 1970s era Faxitron® (Figure 3.21), however, with a 5 μm focal spot size and 48 μm pixel size on plate, the resolution capabilities far exceed the older film based system (Figure 3.22).

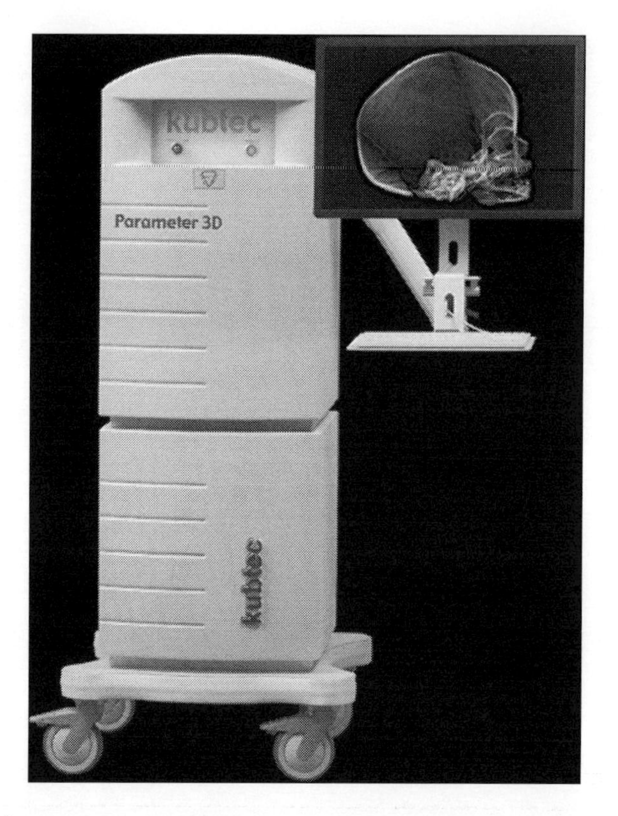

Figure 3.23. The Kubtec Parameter® 3D tomosynthesis unit with the composite image of dry fetal skull #5 on the monitor.

The PARAMETER® 3D Tomosynthesis System was initially developed to examine breast tissue removed during surgery for a pathological assessment and comparison to the preoperative mammogram (Figure 3.23). However, the unit, equipped with a 50 μm focal spot size, offers both 3D and 2D image capabilities have found other applications in science and research, forensics and nondestructive testing (NDT). The tomosynthesis function created 1.0 mm thick digital slices parallel to the 5 × 6 inch (12 × 15 cm) detector. Therefore, to demonstrate the dental development each dry fetal skull was placed into a lateral positioned and scanned (Figure 3.24).

Multidetector Computed Tomography (MDCT)

All of the MDCT images were acquired with the Toshiba *Aquilion* 64 slice unit at the Quinnipiac University Diagnostic Imaging Laboratory. The following protocol was employed: 100 kVp; 300 mA; 0.5 mm detector width (slice thickness); 64 detectors; 240 mm CFOV; HP (helical pitch) 41; PF (pitch factor) 0.6; FC81 (high resolution bone-maximum edge enhancement). Once the data was collected, the curve-linear reconstruction was the most useful to demonstrate dental development [**WS 3.37**].

Cone Beam Computed Tomography

Craniofacial and dentoalveolar imaging of dried fetal skulls from the Kier-Conlogue Collection, ranging from 11 to 38 weeks' gestation, was accomplished using Cone Beam CT imaging, performed on a J. Morita 3D Accuitomo® 170 CBCT unit at the University of Connecticut Dental School. The fetal skulls were held in place with Play-Doh® (Hasbro) and the multiplanar laser guides were used to ensure proper positioning of the skull (Figure 3.25). The smallest FOV that would acquire the entire skull was used, and included 40 mm × 40 mm, 60 mm × 60 mm 100 mm × 100 mm or 140 mm × 100 mm. Ideal acquisition techniques were 70kVp, 3mAs and the smallest voxel size preset available. Multiplanar views, various 3-D and panoramic emulations were performed using InVivo5® software by Anatomage on normal (Figure 3.26) and abnormal skulls [**WS 3.40**]. Panoramic reconstructions of the mandible [**WS 3.41**] and maxilla [**WS 3.42**] clearly demonstrated the dental development. In addition, cross-sectional reconstructions from the panoramic reconstruction enabled visualization of the development of individual teeth [**WS 3.43**]. Small skulls as

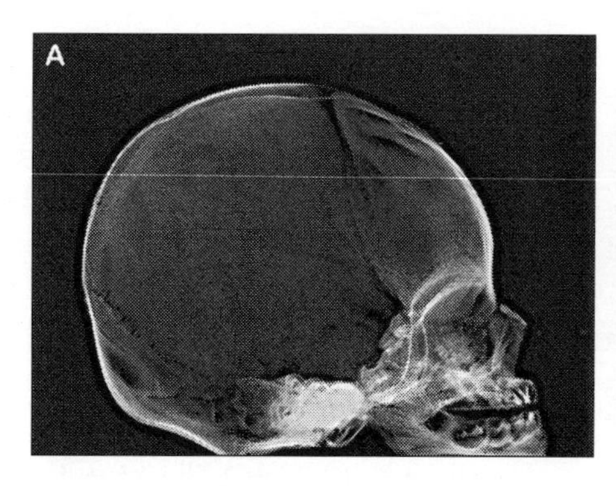

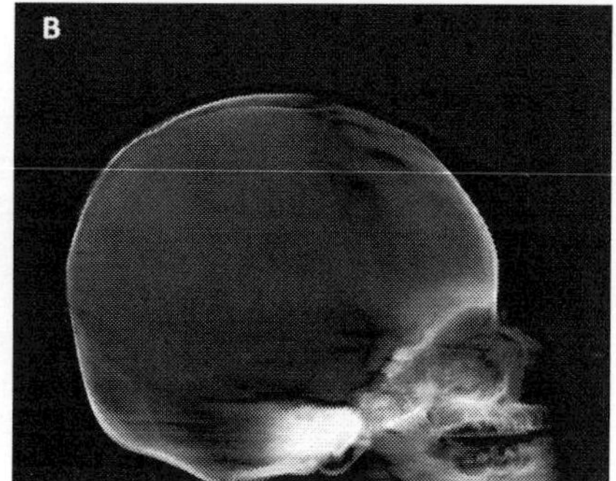

Figure 3.24. (A) Composite 3D tomosynthesis of dry fetal skull #2. (B) A 1.0 mm thick slice of the right mandible and maxilla of dry fetal skull #2.

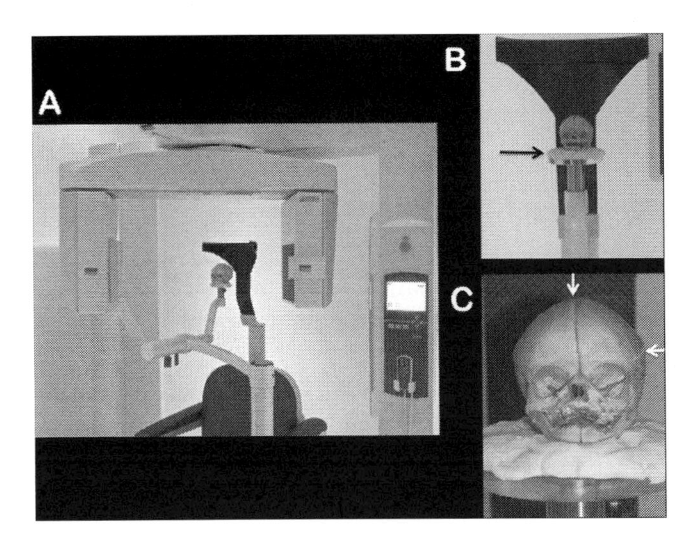

Figure 3.25. (A) Dry fetal skull positioned in the Accuitomo™ 170 CBCT Unit. (B) The specimen secured on the stand (arrow) with Play-Doh® (Hasbro). (C) The multi-planar laser guide (arrows) was employed to ensure proper positioning.

well as other small mineralized structures are best visualized using CBCT because of its superior spatial resolution. Imaging of these skulls revealed great detail of dental development, cranial base development (including ossicles), and also demonstrated several skulls with severe craniofacial and dental developmental abnormalities.

Arch Street Cemetery Coffins, Burlington, New Jersey (2017)

The most challenging and complex skeletal imaging project involved a group of skeletal remains within coffins. In March 2017 while excavation at a site for a future apartment complex at Arch and 2nd Street in Philadelphia, Pennsylvania, the old First Baptist Church burial ground was uncovered. Founded around 1707 the graves were supposedly exhumed around 1860 and moved to the Mount Moriah Cemetery in the southwest section of the city. Over 40 coffins were recovered and the team of anthropologists, including George Leader and Jared Beatrice from the College of New Jersey in Ewing, New Jersey, Kimberlee Moran from Rutgers University-Camden, and Anna Dhody from the Mütter Museum, the College of Physicians in Philadelphia, wanted to document the content of the coffins before each was opened.

X-Ray Tube Support

Before actually seeing the coffins, a list of the measurements of all the coffins was sent to the Bioanthropology Research Institute. A support was constructed that not only permitted vertical radiographs but also would enable horizontal beam images to be acquired. In the

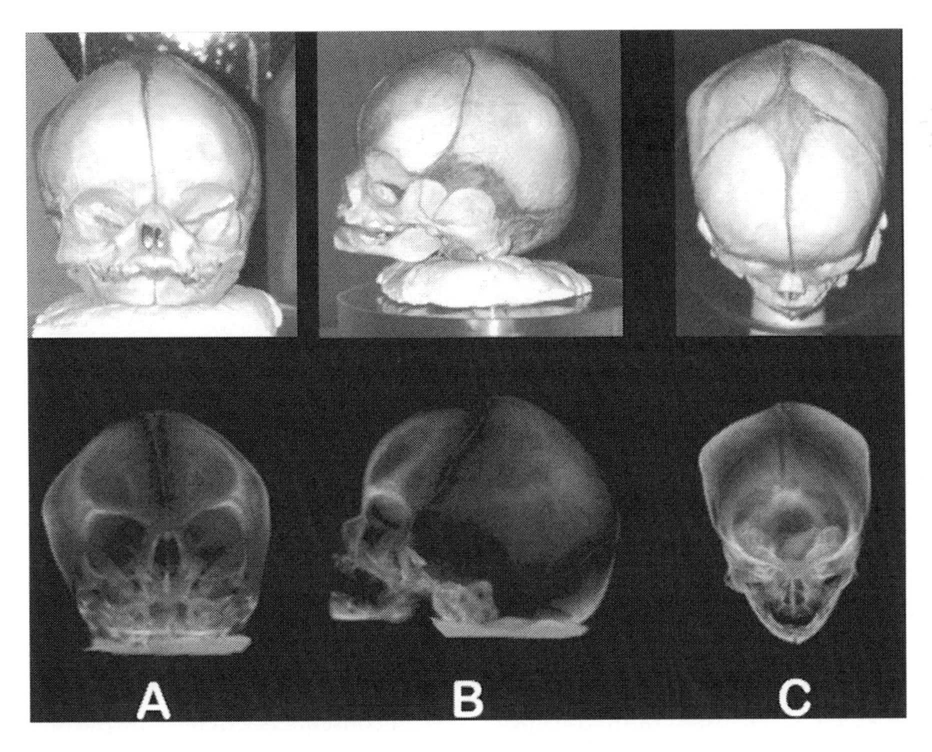

Figure 3.26. Skull #5 was 20- to 28-weeks' gestation. The top row presents the position of the dry fetal skull and the bottom row provides the 3D emulations for the similar CBCT projections: Coronal (A); Sagittal (B); and Axial (C). The images are 3-D emulations generated with InVivo5 Software by Anatomage.

initial design, the frame of the X-ray tube support was built with 1×3-inch (2.5×7.5 cm) pine [**WS 3.44**]. A 60-inch (152 cm)-long sheet of bakelite that was going to be used as the table top had been recovered from a 1950s vintage upright cassette holder from a chiropractors office. However, because some of the coffins were longer than 60 inches, another table was constructed using another sheet of recovered bakelite that measured 72 inches (183 cm) long.

Image Receptor Systems

Unlike previous studies, both a CR and DR system were transported to Burlington, New Jersey. The plan was to use the Kubtec KUBSCAN® CR system for all the vertical images and the Kubtec DIGIVIEW™ 430 DR system for all the horizontally directed X-rays. The latter is identical to the wireless DIGIVIEW® 395, except that it is tethered to the router by a 21-foot (6.4 m) cable. In addition, two Kubtec XTEND® 100HF X-ray tubes were transported to the site. The two complete imaging systems, X-ray sources and image receptors, would permit biplanar radiography without moving the coffin. Because either system could be used for the horizontal and vertical images, the systems were interchangeable and also served as a backup if an X-ray source or image receptor failed.

Transporting the Equipment

Because the Kubtec KUBSCAN® CR system had two large transport cases, it was possible to fit the DR components, the plate, cables, router, and laptop into one of those cases. The second X-ray source was packed into a cardboard box. The vertical X-ray tube support was disassembled. A small dolly was constructed to support the X-ray tube for the horizontal beam. A small stepladder was included to permit the X-ray source to be bolted to the top of the horizontal frame. Finally, a folding chair was added and everything fit into a 2010 Ford Transit Connect [**WS 3.45**].

Modifications on Site

It took approximately one hour to assemble the mobile imaging facility. Because the site lacked available tables or other surfaces that could be used, both transport cases, a milk crate used to store extension cords, and the folding chair were pulled into service [**WS 3.46**]. The frame to support the vertically oriented X-ray beam had only a single modification. Because the coffins were on plywood, there was no need for the bakelite table [**WS 3.47**]. Another modification was implemented for the horizontal; the tracks designed to allow the plate to be slid into position was determined not to be necessary and therefore removed. Without the track, the DR plate rested against the frame [**WS 3.48**].

Although all coffin measurements were sent in order to determine the dimensions of the X-ray source support system, no mention was made that the coffins were filled with soil. The adult coffins weighed as much as 600 pounds (273 kg) and could not be easily moved and lifted onto the bakelite table under the vertically directed X-ray beam. A horizontal X-ray beam approach would be the only possible method to acquire radiographs of the adult coffins [**WS 3.49**]. The initial lateral projection, exposed at 90 kVp and 10.0 mAs at a 59-inch (150 cm) SID, was grossly under penetrated [**WS 3.50**]. A second X-ray was taken increasing the kVp to the maximum output of 100 and quadrupling the mAs to 40, but the resulting image was still underpenetrated. Although the second image clearly had increased penetration, it was insufficient to reveal the skeletal remains with the coffin [**WS 3.51**]. The only possible solution would be an industrial X-ray source with a much higher kV output, but until that type of unit was available there was no point in attempting to radiograph more adult coffins.

Therefore, efforts were refocused on the coffins of the children. For the latter, partially filled with dirt, AP radiographs [**WS 3.52**] provided sufficient information to document the orientation of the child within the coffin and the hardware associated with the construction [**WS 3.53**]. However, with a coffin containing less dirt, the findings were more revealing. As initially planned, three AP projections including the top, middle, and bottom sections of the child's coffin were taken using the CR system and revealed round headed pins associated with the body and not the construction of the coffin [**WS 3.54**]. The pins were significant for three reasons: that type of pin was first manufactured around 1830, establishing temporal context for the remains; they were possibly employed to secure a shroud wrapped around the body; and finally raise the awareness of the existence and number of pins present in this section of the coffin before the contents of the coffin was removed. Because the pins and even the nails could have been corroded or oxidize, if they were located in hard-packed soil, many could have been overlooked or destroyed while breaking up a chunk of dirt [**WS 3.45C**].

A consequence of moving the object under examination between exposures was clearly demonstrated in the relative placement of a pin and two nails seen in the mid- and bottom sections of the coffin AP images [**WS 3.55**].

However, on any two dimensional radiograph, such as an AP projection, determining spatial orientation is limited. In order better assess the positions of the pins within the coffin, a lateral projection was necessary and acquired using the DR system. Unexpectedly, the pins appeared to be located on the posterior or lateral aspects of the remains **[WS 3.56]**. Because the horizontally directed X-ray was utilized and the coffin wasn't moved, the relative position of specific pins could be determined **[WS 3.57]**.

With the materials available, supplementary applications other the coffin radiography we carried out at the site without equipment modifications. The DR system was used for radiographic assessment of dental development on the skeletally immature individuals removed from the coffins. Because the light at the site could not be adjusted, it was difficult to collimate the X-ray beam tightly around the mandibles that were radiographed **[WS 3.58]**. As stated in the plane radiography chapter, the smaller the area irradiated on the DR plate the higher the resolution. Another consideration, as soon as the exposure is taken, it is processed and appears on the computer monitor. Therefore, multiple images cannot be taken on the DR plate and a complete examination of the mandible required three exposures: a right oblique; PA; and left oblique **[WS 3.59]**. The DR system was selected over the CR for the study, because the plate did not need to be move for processing and the mandible remained in position until the image was viewed. As only a slight adjust was require to achieve a better position to view the dental development, the correction could be made and another DR exposure taken.

Other radiographs taken included an adult lateral skull with residual brain tissue **[WS 3.60]**; a tibia with possible pathologic changes **[WS 3.61]**; coffin hardware enclosed in a chunk of dirt **[WS 3.62]**; and hardware revealing areas of oxidation **[WS 3.63]**. Although the skeletal and artifact radiography were not in the initial plan, because the adult coffins were filled with dirt, the plan had to be modified.

Recommendations

- The radiographic field facility should be completely self-contained
- If possible, have a backup X-ray source and image receptors
- A wooden frame can be developed for a particular application and only the metallic components shipped with the equipment. The actual wooden parts would be cut at the field site.
- The frame should have sufficient height to ensure the X-ray beam covers the entire object. If this factor is not taken into consideration, moving the object between exposures will change the relative position of internal structures on subsequent images
- Be prepared for major modifications of the planned protocol
- Be sure to overlap images by at least several inches, centimeters, to prevent missing and objects that might be present

References

Boston, C.E., Short, L., Nelson, A.J. & Conlogue, G. (October, 2008). *Changes in the Growth and Development of the Face as Related to Artificial Cranial Modification: A Cephalometric Analysis.* Poster presented at the 36th Canadian Association for Physical Anthropologists, Hamilton, ON, Canada.

Conlogue, G. & Nelson, A. (1999). Polaroid Imaging at an Archaeological Site in Peru. *Radiologic Technology.* 70(3), 244–250.

Conlogue, G. & Nelson, A.J. (April, 1998). *The Use of Polaroid Photographic Imagery Systems to Produce Radiographic Images at a Field Site in Perú.* Poster presented at the 25th annual meeting of the Paleopathology Association, Salt Lake City, UT, USA.

Conlogue, G., Nelson, A. & Guillén, S. (2004). The Application of Radiography to Field Studies in Physical Anthropology. *JACR.* 55(4), 254–257.

Conlogue, G., Viner, M., Beckett, R., Bekvalac, J., Gonzalez, R., Sharkey, M., Kramer, K., Koverman, B. (2016). A Post-Mortem Evaluation of the Degree of Mobility in an Individual with Severe Kyphoscoliosis Using Direct Digital Radiography (DR) and Multi-Detector Computed Tomography (MDCT). In L. Tilley and A.A. Schrenk (Ed.), *New Developments in the Bioarchaeology of Care Further Case Studies and Expanded Theory.* Springer International Publishing Switzerland AG.

Conlogue, G., Viner, M., Farmer, M., Gulliver, D., Bekvalac, J. & Eggleton, K. (April, 2011). *Tales from the Crypt: Preliminary Findings of a Digital Radiographic Study of Skeletal Remains Under St Bride's Church in London, England.* Poster presented at 38th Annual North American Paleopathology Association Meeting. Minneapolis, MN, USA.

Gonzalez, R., Conlogue, G., Viner, M. & Bekvalac, J. (April, 2014). *A Mutli-Modality Imaging Study of a Skeleton Diagnosed with von Recklinhause's Neurofibromatosis.* Poster presented at the 41st Annual Meeting of the Paleopathology Association, Calgary, AB, Canada.

Lichtenfeld, M. (2001). *Artificial Cranial Modification in the Jequetepeque Valley, Peru.* Unpublished MA thesis, Faculty of Graduate Studies, The University of Western Ontario, London, ON, Canada.

Nelson, A.J. & Conlogue, G. (October, 1997). *Field Radiology in Archaeology: Penetrating the Problems and Illuminating Research in Osteology.* Paper presented at the 25th Annual Meeting of the Canadian Association for Physical Anthropology, London, ON, Canada.

Nelson, A.J., Conlogue, G., Hennessy, W. & Gauld, S.A. (April, 1999). *Preliminary Study to Determine the Most Suitable Radiographic Projection to Document Intentional Cranial Deformation*. Poster presented at the 26th Annual Meeting of the Paleopathology Association, Columbus, OH, USA.

Nelson, A.J., Lichtenfeld, M.J., Conlogue, G., Toyne, J.M. & Pool, S. (October, 2000). *Cranial Modification in the Jequetepeque Valley*. Paper presented at the 19th Annual NE Andean Archaeology and Ethnohistory Conference, Hanover, NH, USA.

Scheuer, L. & Black, S. 1995. *The St. Bride's Documented Skeletal Collection*. Unpublished archive held at the Calvin Wells Laboratory at the Department of Archaeological Sciences, University of Bradford.

Mummified Remains

4

GERALD J. CONLOGUE, RONALD G. BECKETT,
JOHN POSH, MARK VINER, AND ALAN LURIE

Contents

Imaging mummified remains presents some of the most challenging experiences. Because the dehydrated soft tissue attenuates very little radiation compared to the surrounding skeletal components, the greatest challenge has been to demonstrate these vastly different tissues. With regard to preserved internal organs, the relative sizes and locations of these structures may vary greatly compared to the living individual. In addition, the remains can be in either extended or flexed positions. The latter, contributes to the associated imaging problems due to the added superimposition of the extremities over the trunk.

The optimal approach would be to initially radiograph the remains where they are stored generally requiring the creation of a field imaging facility at the site. These preliminary radiographs will establish the presence of pathologic conditions or other interesting features that might suggest additional imaging or even the need of an advanced modality, such as MDCT. In addition, images acquired on site will ascertain the condition of the mummy and used to determine if it can be safely moved to an imaging facility.

Because of the difference in approach to the imaging objectives, the following discussion will be divided into the study of individual mummies and groups of mummified remains.

Individual Mummies

Soap Lady: Mütter Museum, Philadelphia, Pennsylvania—Gerald Conlogue, Ron Beckett

Objective: Provide a radiographic assessment in order to determine age at the time of death and possibly reveal pathologies.

In 1986, Gretchen Worden, director of Mütter Museum, College of Physicians in Philadelphia, Pennsylvania, wanted a radiographic study on one of the museum's most well-known specimens, known as *The Soap Lady*. According to records at the museum, the specimen was donated on November 18, 1875 by Dr. Joseph Leidy, a renowned paleontologist and professor of anatomy at the University of Pennsylvania. According to description in the museum records, "The woman named Ellenbogen, died in Philadelphia of yellow fever in 1792 and was buried near Fourth and Race Streets." In 1942, Joseph McFarland, the museum director, published a paper that questioned the exact name, cause and date of death and location of exhumation of the adipocere mummy (McFarland, 1942). His archival research found: no individuals named Ellenbogen were listed in Philadelphia records or city directories until 1836; no yellow fever in Philadelphia in 1792; nor ever a cemetery at Fourth and Race Streets. In addition, anecdotally, at the time Leidy was notified of the discovery of the unusual remains of a male and female, he was conducting an anatomy lecture of the upper extremity and decided to identify the female remains as Ellenbogen, German for elbow and the male, Wilhelm von Ellenbogen. The former was transferred to the Mütter while the latter first to the Wistar and Homer Museum of the Medical Department of the University of Pennsylvania and now located at the Smithsonian Institution in Washington, DC. Worden wondered if a radiographic examination might provide additional information to answer the questions put forth by McFarland over four decades earlier.

Due to the fragile condition of the Mütter mummy, it had not been moved from the 73×25.5 inch (185×65 cm) glass covered case where it was first placed in 1875 and therefore could not be transported to an imaging facility. A 1950s vintage Profex™ mobile radiographic unit that had been donated to Thomas Jefferson University was transported to the museum. The first obstacle concerned the maximum output of the unit that was only 40 kVp at 20 mA and 12 seconds exposure time. With the limited exposure settings, nonscreen film was not even a consideration; rather, eight 14×17 inch (35×43 cm) cassettes equipped with either par- or high-speed intensifying screens were brought from the Radiologic Sciences Program at the university. The par-speed intensifying screens have a relative speed index (RSI) of 200, while the high-speed screens were rated at 400. Therefore, the latter would require half the mAs as the former.

The second challenge was that the museum lacked a darkroom. Because the X-ray unit was probably 30 years old and only provided low output, it might require a number of exposures to establish the technical factors. Fortunately, an old Polaroid Radiographic System was found in the Radiology Department storage area at Jefferson University Hospital. Because the Polaroid was equipped with two 10×12 inch (25×30 cm) cassettes equivalent of a par-speed intensifying screen, it provided a means to establish the optimal radiographic exposure for the larger conventional radiographic film.

A third impediment to the study was that the remains could not be moved on the table and the radiographs had to be taken through the table. In addition, two 1×2.5 inch (2.5×6 cm) support structures traversed the underside of the table: the first at a level approximately 2 inches (5 cm) inferior to the top of the skull, and the second at the level of the hips. Because of the placement of the supports under the table, the least object-image receptor-distance (OID) was 8 inches (20 cm) for all anterior-posterior (AP) projections. The increase OID resulted in magnification of the object and a reduction in detail. That related to the fourth problem: a maximum of 43.5 inches (110 cm) source-image receptor-distance, SID, was possible for AP projections with the X-ray unit. Referring back to the Chapter 4: Plane Radiography in *Advances in Paleoimaging* (CRC Press, 2020) for the formula to calculate the percent magnification, the minimum magnification for objects close to the tabletop would be 23%.

In order to avoid initially dealing with the complexities associated with the AP radiographs, it was decided to start with horizontal beam lateral projections of the skull using the Polaroid system with Polaroid TXL film. The cassette was inserted into a vertical cassette holder (Cone Instruments) and when placed at the edge of the table afforded a 9.5 inch OID (24 cm). With the X-ray beam directed across the table, it easy to achieve a 80 inch (152 cm) SID (Figure 4.1). Even though OID was increased, the longer SID reduced the percent magnification to 13% and correspondingly improved the resolution. Three

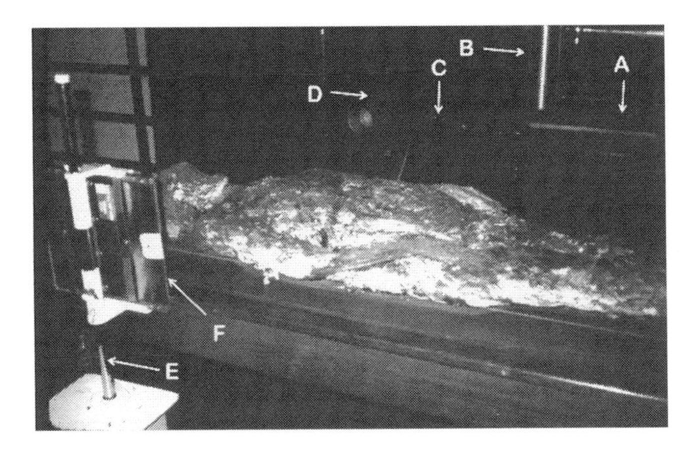

Figure 4.1. The set-up for the horizontal beam lateral projection: (A) The main compartment of the Profex™ mobile X-ray unit containing the transformer; (B) the vertical column supporting the (C) extension arm and (D) the X-ray tube. On the other side of the mummified remains: (E) the vertical cassette holder; and (F) the Polaroid cassette loaded with Polaroid Type TXL film.

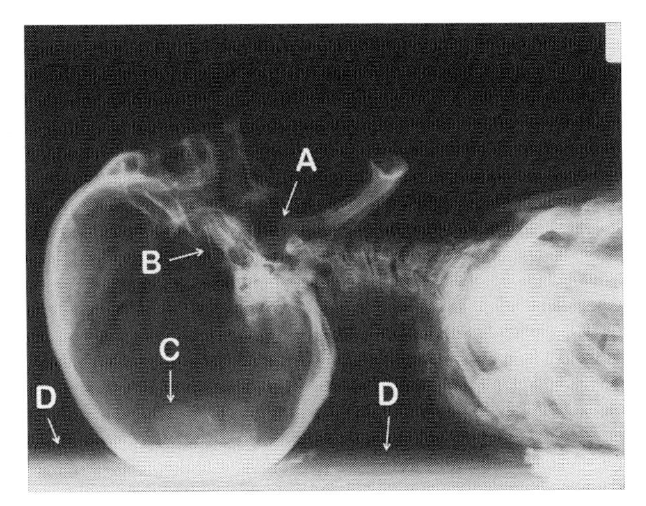

Figure 4.3. The lateral skull taken using the 14×17 cassette loaded with X-ray film was taken at 40 kVp at 20 mA for one second was processed back at the Radiologic Sciences Program at Thomas Jefferson University: Note the fractured mandible (A); brain remnants in the posterior portion of the skull (B); and the round-headed pin (C). Because the head is resting on the tabletop in combination with the divergent X-ray beam, the margin of the table (D) was superimposed over the base of the skull.

exposures were taken at 40 kVp and 20 mA, but exposure times were varied: 1 second (Figure 4.2A), 3 seconds (Figure 4.2B), and 1 second (Figure 4.2C). The first was underexposed, the second overexposed, and the third provided an acceptable exposure. Because the Polaroid system was rated as a par-speed and the 14×17 inch (35×43 cm) cassette selected for the lateral skull was rated as high-speed, the exposure time was reduced to 1 second, but the other settings, kVp and mA, were unchanged (Figure 4.3). With only the lateral radiograph of the skull, important information in the form of an artifact previously unknown was revealed: a pin. Analysis of the pin would be used later to help establish temporal context.

Due to superimposition by the upper extremities over the lateral aspects of the chest (Figure 4.4), the lateral projection was of limited value only providing the location of artifacts. In addition, because the remains rested directly on the table combined with the effect of the divergent X-ray beam, the posterior portion of the mummy were obscured by the *shadow* of the table (Figures 4.3 and 4.4).

A total of seven AP radiographs were taken with the cassettes positioned under the table from slightly above the top of the skull to just below the feet. In an attempt to prevent gaps of anatomy, each succeeding cassette was overlapped at least several inches (Figure 4.5A, B, and D). Overlapping is important so as not to exclude any structures or abnormalities, such as a gallstone in the abdomen or a bone cyst in the diaphysis of a femur. With the exception of the skull, when the cassette was positioned lengthwise, the remaining initial AP radiographs had the film holders oriented crosswise. The latter was to include as much of both sides of the mummy as possible.

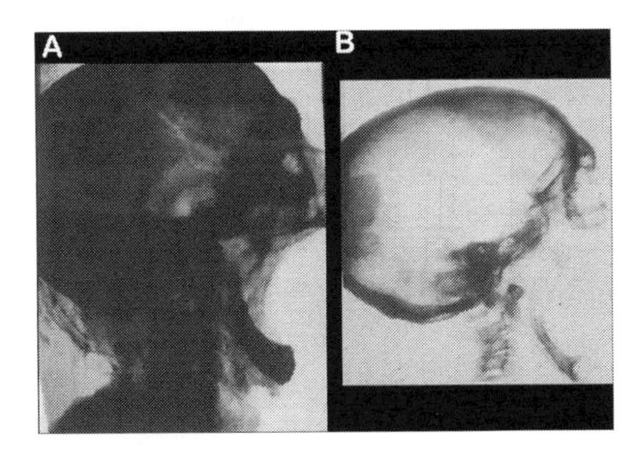

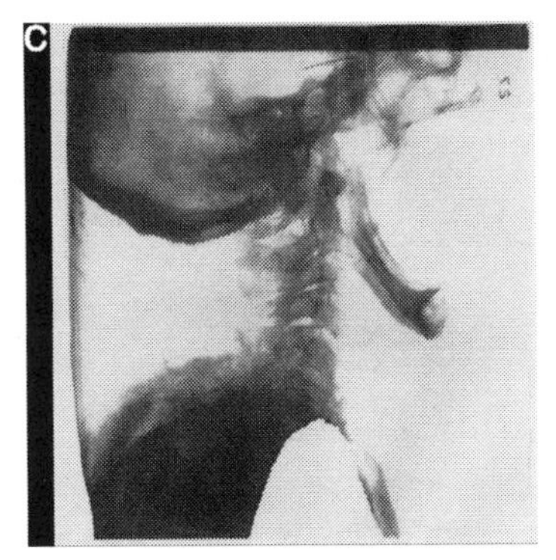

Figure 4.2. Three exposures taken on Polaroid TXL film with par-speed intensifying screens: (A) 40 kVp at 20 mA for 1 second was underexposed; (B) 40 kVp at 20 mA for 3 seconds was overexposed; Figure 4.2(C) 40 kVp at 20 mA for 3 seconds producing a correctly exposed image.

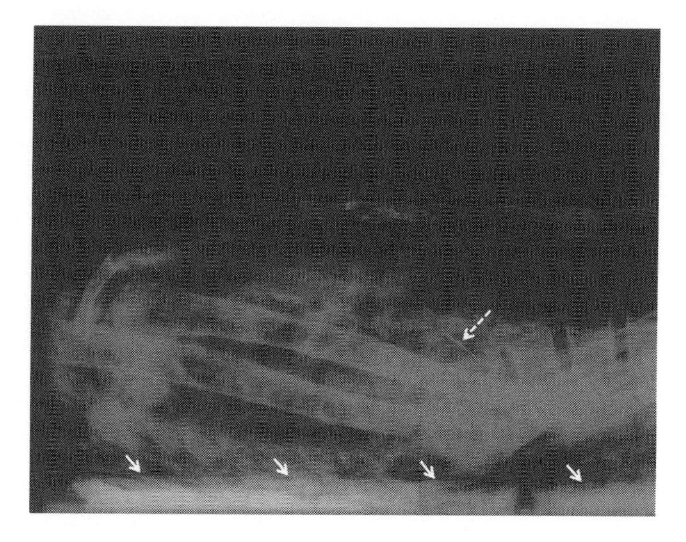

Figure 4.4. The lateral projection of the chest provided little additional information except the location of the straight pin (dashed arrow). Note the superimposition created by the table (solid arrows).

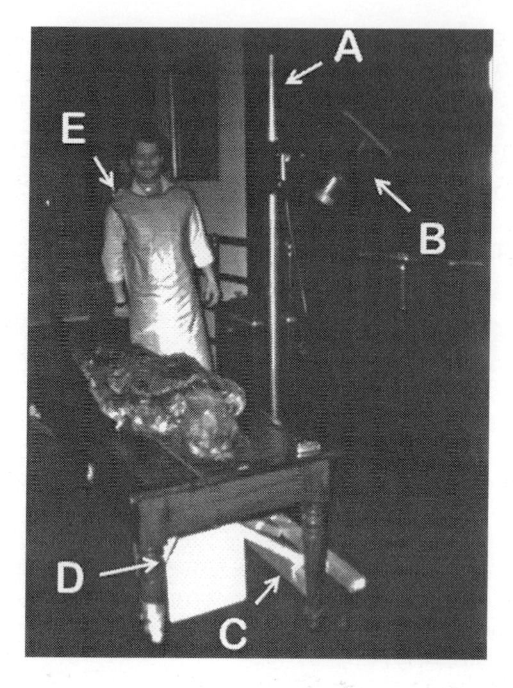

Figure 4.6. Mounted on the X-ray unit tube stand (A), it was possible to rotate the X-ray tube (B) about 45° corresponding to the angulation of the image receptor support device created with a wooden frame (C) resting on a box (D). Frank Cerrone (E), a student radiographer at Thomas Jefferson University wearing a lead apron to minimize radiation dose preparing to take the exposure.

With the hands positioned by the sides of the pelvis, both were excluded from the AP radiograph of that area. Therefore, two additional radiographs required with the cassette placed lengthwise under the table **[WS 4.6]**. All of the vertically directed radiographs did provide a great deal of information, such as the locations of additional pins and two buttons, they also revealed a lack of degenerative changes in the knees and hips. However, with all the superimposition to deal with on the lateral radiographs another projection was required to provide a more accurate assessment.

Because the mummy could not be moved, an alternate approach was to angle the X-ray beam and image receptor to acquire oblique radiographs (Figure 4.6). The 45° oblique projections provided clarification of observations revealed on the AP radiographs. On the oblique chest image, the mass of material noted on the AP chest X-ray was projected outside of the rib margin indicated that it was against the mummy's back and not inside the remains. Similarly, the two pieces of packed dirt seen on the same X-ray were also projected in the away from the remains confirming they were also behind the mummy (Figure 4.7A). The oblique demonstrated

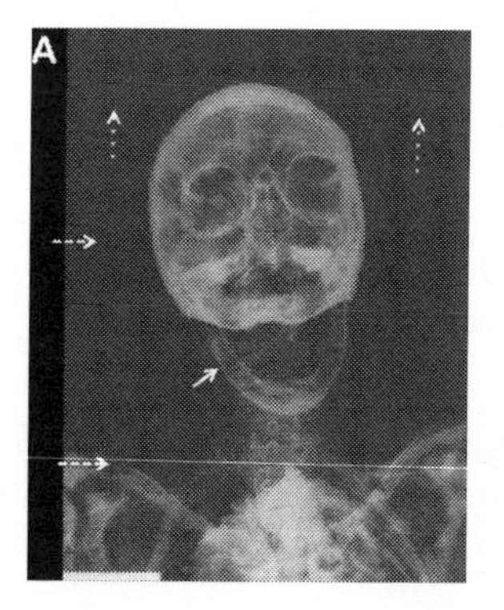

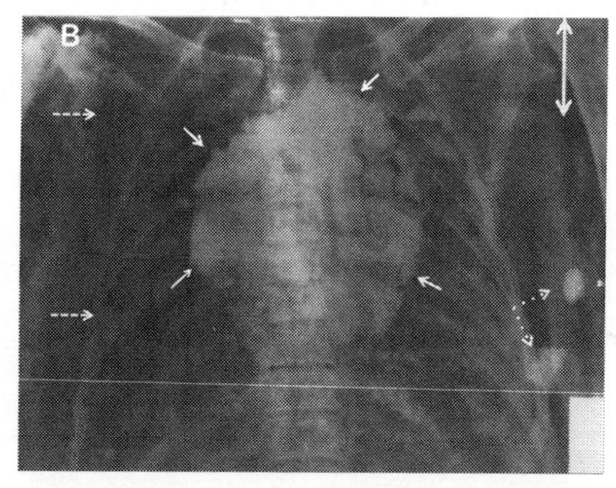

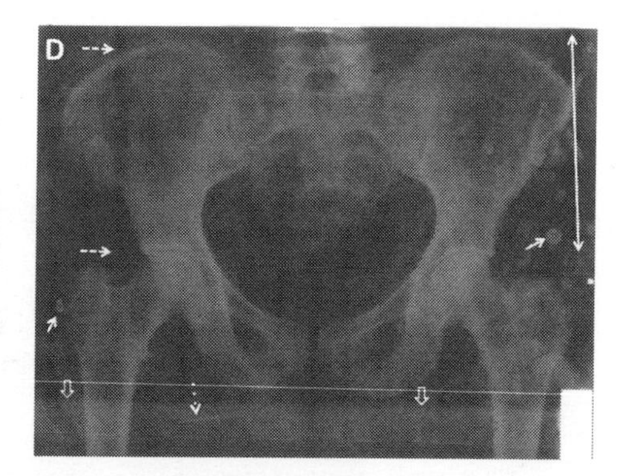

Figure 4.5. (A) A somewhat AP projection of the skull, neck and upper chest region: Note the wooden support under the table (dotted arrows); the edentulous mandible (solid arrow); and the long, linear radiolucent structure (dashed arrows) representing the crack in the oak table. (B) AP projection of the chest: Note the area of overlap with the X-ray of the skull (white double headed arrow) and the crack in the table (dashed arrows); the mass of material in the center of the chest (solid arrows); and the dense objects (dotted arrows) that appear to be packed dirt; (D) The AP of the pelvis: Note the large area of overlap (double headed white arrow); crack in the table (dashed arrows); the support under the table (open arrows); an addition straight pin (dotted arrow); and a total of two buttons (solid arrows).

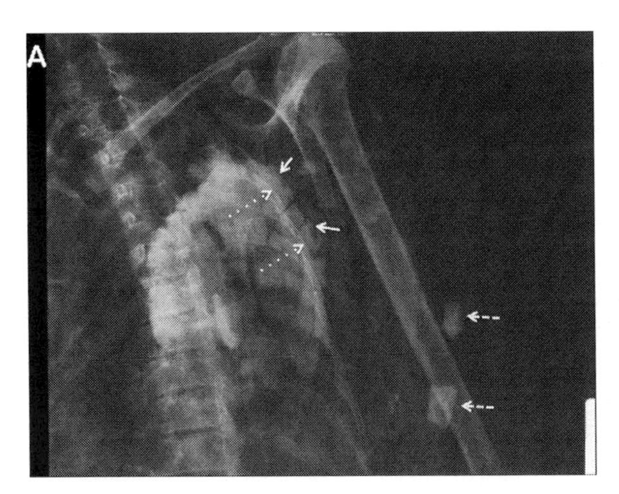

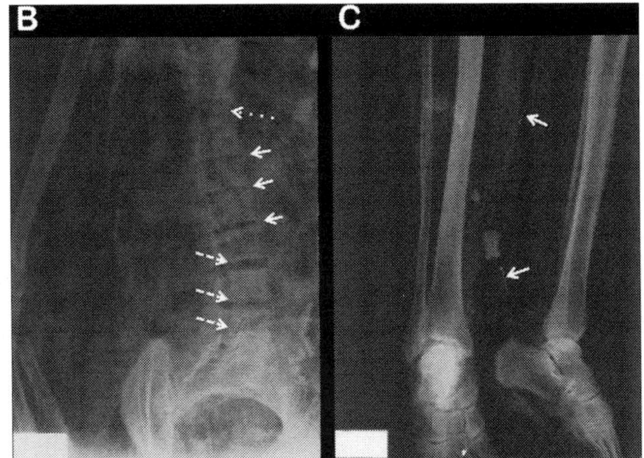

Figure 4.7. (A) The oblique chest radiograph: Note the edge of the massive of material (solid arrows) was projected outside of the margin of the ribs (dotted arrows) and the two pieces of packed dirt (dashed arrows) shifted in the same direction indicating they were also behind the mummy. (B) The oblique abdomen demonstrated decreased vertebral body bone density, implying osteopenia, minimal osteophyte formation (solid arrows) on the margins of the lumber vertebral interspaces and a Schmorl's node (dotted arrow) on the body of the 11th thoracic vertebrae suggesting degenerative changes. However, the lumbar facet spaces appeared free of any indications of degeneration (dashed arrows). (C) The oblique radiograph of the lower leg resulted in an AP of the right ankle and a lateral projection of the left ankle and foot. There was no evidence of degenerative changes in any of the joints visualized. Note both straight pins (arrows) clearly have rounded heads.

only minimal degenerative changes in the lumber spine (Figure 4.7B) suggesting that the remains were not those of an *old lady* as described by McFarland in 1942. On the oblique of the lower legs and ankle demonstrated ankle joints free of degenerative changes and two straight pins with clearly rounded heads. The ends of the pins provided the temporal context: they were not manufactured until the 1830s.

The radiographs were also valuable in localizing a pin and button for recovery and analysis. Of the eight pins seen on the radiographs, pin #2 on the left lateral aspect of the skull was retrieved and sent to the Smithsonian Institution in Washington, DC, for identification. According to experts at the Institution, it was a machine headed pin first manufactured in England in 1824 and in the United States in 1838. Of the two buttons, the one located on the medial aspect of the wrist at a level between the novicular and the greater multangular was removed for examination. Unfortunately, due to corrosion, the surface details of the button were obscured. Therefore, it was taken to Thomas Jefferson University, where it was radiographed using a Faxitron microradiography unit (Figure 4.8). The radiograph revealed that the four holes in the center had been punched out, but slightly off center suggesting it was machine made. In addition, a pattern of eight small flowers was apparent around the margin of the metal button. Although a button collector was not able to provide a specific date, she was certain that it was characteristic of the nineteenth century.

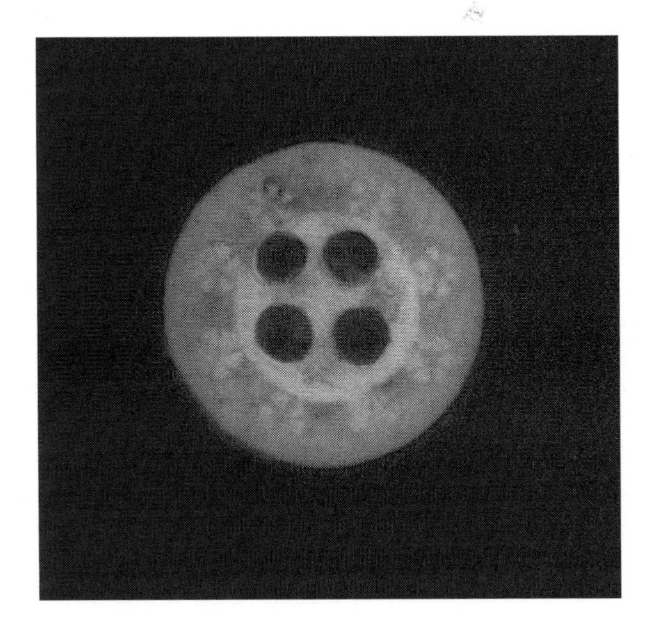

Figure 4.8. The microradiograph acquired with the Faxitron unit at a 23-inch (58 cm) SID using 30 kVp at 2.5 mA and 425 seconds. According to the button collector, the four slightly off-center centrally punched holes suggested the button was machine made. In addition, the embossed floral pattern around the outer margin also intimates the button was not hand-made.

Study Significance

This study demonstrated several important findings regarding the radiographic examination of mummified remains. The mummy did not need to be transported to an imaging facility with advanced modalities. A few plane radiographs have the potential to reveal much more than just the presence of pathological changes but also employed to assist in ascertaining age at the time of death and establish temporal context. Instead of moving the remains, a clinical radiography approach was employed equating the mummy to a patient from the emergency department who cannot be moved so that all of the radiographs must be done with the patient on the stretcher.

However, besides ensuring the safety of the mummy, there were facets of the study that suggested abandoning the constraints of the clinic methodology and return to basic X-ray fundamentals in order to optimize the radiographs. The short SID, due to the height restriction of the mobile unit, was responsible for image magnification that degraded the resolution. The solution was to devolve the mobile unit to make it more portable and separate the X-ray source from the restrictive X-ray tube support system. An X-ray source with the transformer included in the X-ray tube would eliminate the bulky component along with the support system.

Knowledge of radiographic history and fundamentals made it possible to incorporate the Polaroid system into the study to determine the required exposure setting and produce diagnostic quality radiographs. Familiarity with alternative methods of positioning permitted the acquisition of the oblique radiographs when the lateral projections were not adequate to provide the required information.

In 2001 the *Soap Lady* was revisited for a more in-depth radiographic examination for an episode of the National Geographic series, *The Mummy Road Show (Soap Lady, 2001).* For this study, a Philips Tomoscan M™ mobile CT unit was provided courtesy of Philips Medical System in cooperation with Georgetown University Medical Center. Although the unit was considered mobile, the donut-shaped structure, the *gantry*, weighed approximately 1,000 pounds (450 kg), and the table an additional 300 pounds (135 kg) making it a difficult, time-consuming operation to get it first into the museum and then set up in the banquet hall.

Before and after a ⅛ inch (3 mm) thick sheet of plexiglass was slid under the remains, a radiograph was taken with the Polaroid system to ensure that there were minimal changes to the neck region supporting the head. Once on the plexiglass, the entire table the mummy had been displayed on was carried into the banquet hall and placed next to the CT table. From here, the plexiglass supported *Soap Lady* was carefully transferred on the examination table. David Lindisch, the CT manager from the Georgetown University Medical Center selected the protocol and began the scanning process that entailed an eight-hour wait before we could examine the images (Figure 4.9). Unfortunately, it was nearly two decades later that the Bioanthropology Research Institute was able to get the hard copies of the CT study for review by Ramon Gonzalez, MD, a radiologist and one of the founders of the Radiology Assistant Program at Quinnipiac University.

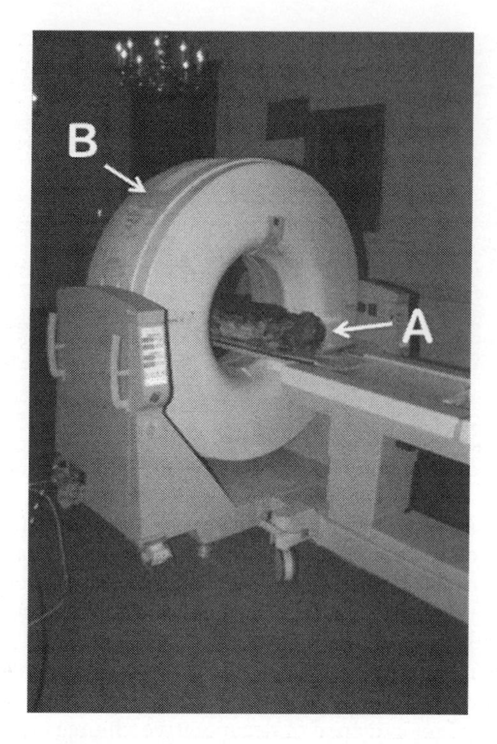

Figure 4.9. The Soap Lady (A) moving through the gantry (B) of the Philips Tomoscan M™ mobile CT unit the was set up in the banquet hall of the Mütter Museum.

Several of the findings, such as the remnants of the brain within the skull not visualized on the films acquired in 1987, were clearly demonstrated on the CT scan without the disadvantage of superimposition (Figure 4.10). However, the ability of CT to demonstrate soft tissue not visualized with plane radiography was spectacularly revealed in the thoracic (Figure 4.11) and abdominal (Figure 4.12) cavities. Obviously, the CT scans provided information that could not be acquired with plane radiography. However, if the scan could not have been accomplished in the museum, it would not have been possible to transport the mummy to an imaging facility with the advanced imaging modality. Unfortunately, after all these years the protocol to acquire the CT data was either never recorded or lost. The reason: during this period clinical protocols were employed even with dehydrated remains.

Another opportunity to radiograph the *Soap Lady* was presented in 2008, due to a plan to upgrade it and other exhibits under the direction of Anna Dhody, who succeeded Worden after her death in 2004. Eventually, the radiographic reexamination of the mummified

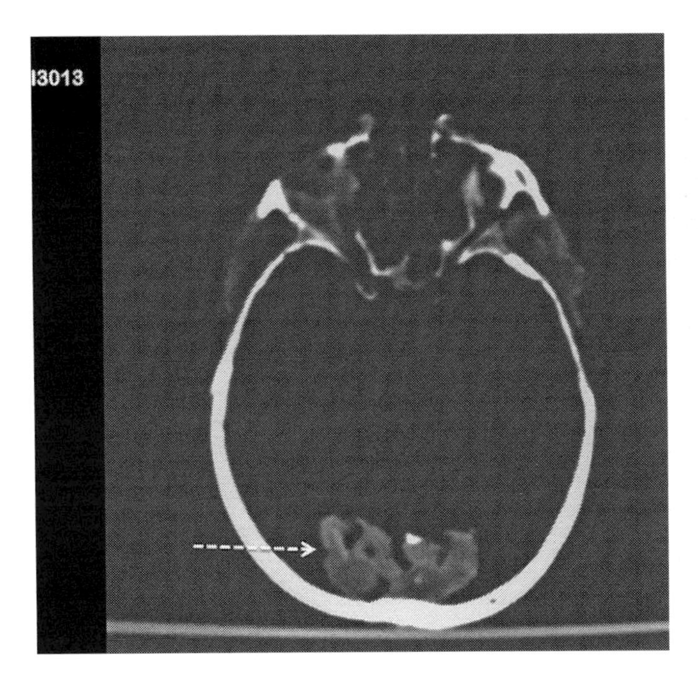

Figure 4.10. An axial image of the skull of the *Soap Lady* revealing the brain remnants in the posterior portion of the cranium.

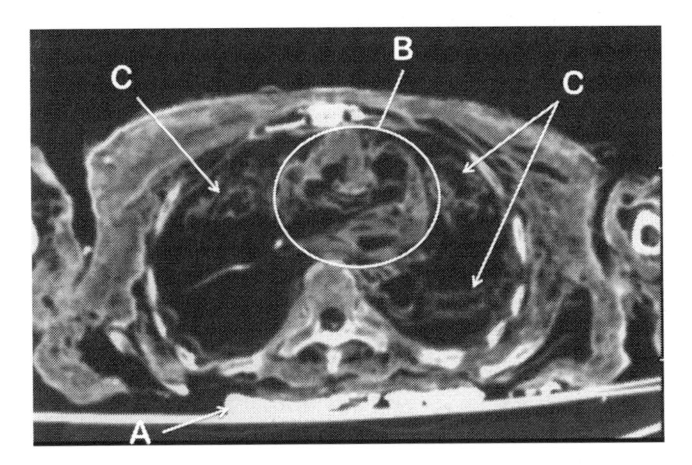

Figure 4.11. As expected, the axial section of the chest demonstrated the large piece of material (A), probably packed dirt seen on the AP chest radiograph from 1987, see Figure 4.5B. However, a large portion of the heart (B) and sections of the lungs, not visualized on the chest radiograph were clearly present.

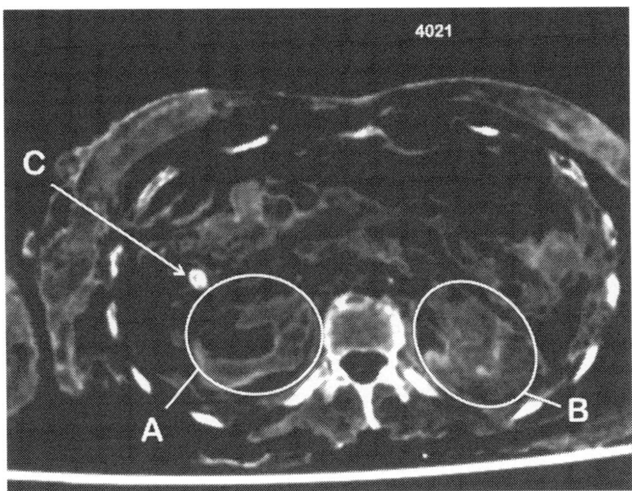

Figure 4.12. In an axial section of the abdomen it was a bit more difficult to identify specific structures, however, the right (A) and left (B) kidneys were clearly delineated. The round radiopaque mass (C) was in the general location to suggest a gall stone.

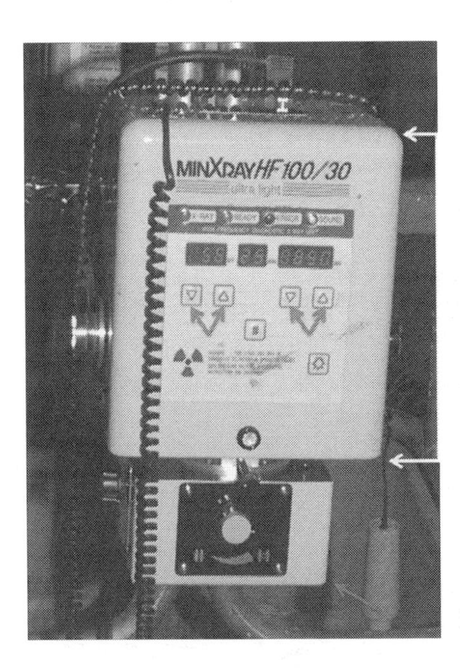

Figure 4.13. The tube head (white arrows) of the MinXray™ HF 100/30 contained not only the X-ray source and high frequency generator, but also the exposure controls (arrows on front of unit). In addition, the collimator (shaded arrow at bottom) was attached to the tube head to restrict the area irradiated by the X-ray beam.

remains took place over two visits to the museum and demonstrated technical advances since the initial study. The first major development was the replacement of the Profex™ 1950's vintage mobile X-ray unit that presented a number of constraints, with a very portable MinXRay™ HF 100/30 unit. Because the tube head contained not only the X-ray source and high frequency generator but also the exposure controls while weighing only 45 pounds (20 kg), the unit provided maneuverability not available nearly 20 years earlier. In addition, the unit was equipped with a collimator to enable accurate restriction of the X-ray beam and reduction of scattered X-ray, increasing the radiation safety factor significantly (Figure 4.13).

The museum still lacked a darkroom; however, as the team was now based at Quinnipiac University in Hamden, Connecticut, a temporary, light-tight film changing area was created in the museum basement. The door to a windowless storage room was covered with two layers of black felt secured to the frame over the door with Duct Tape™. A light-tight film transport case (see Chapter 4: Plane Radiography, Figure 4.94, *Advances in Paleoimaging* (CRC Press, 2020)) was used to transport exposed films back to the university for processing with a Konica SRX-101A processing unit. The primary image receptor was a 14×36 inch (35×91 cm) Spectroline™ cassette equipped with RareX Blue™ III intensifying screens. Because the film for that size cassette was no longer manufactured, the film holder was loaded with three sheets of 11×14 inch (30×35 cm) Fuji Medical NHD film, resulting in 33 of the 36 inches of screens utilized. The area of the cassette without film was marked with tape on the tube side of the film holder.

The other key variation from the study completed two decades earlier, by the mid-1990s the film was no longer produced for the Polaroid medical system. Instead, Polaroid produced a new product that was primarily employed by groups like bomb disposal units to determine the content of a suspected attaché case or suitcase. It consisted of a cassette with a single screen that used Polaroid Type 803™, 8×10 inch (20×25 cm) photographic film (Figure 4.14).

The first images obtained were horizontal beam lateral projections with the X-ray source placed on a table across from the mummy. Using the light from the collimator

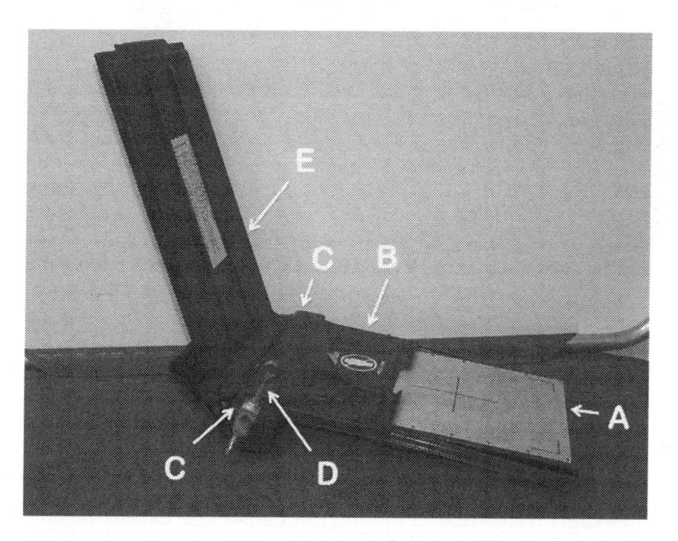

Figure 4.14. The 8×10 inch (20×25 cm) Polaroid cassette (A) was loaded into the processing unit (B). The Polaroid Type 803 film was drawn through the roller system located at the end of the section (C) the cassette was inserted into. Turning the crank (D) pulled the film between the rollers, rupturing the pod containing the process chemicals and evenly spreading the paste between the exposed film and the receiving sheet. The two sheets undergoing processing were advanced into the receiving chamber of the unit (E). During processing the latter would have been in a horizontal position. After approximately a minute, the two sheets were separated, the original film discarded and the receiving sheet saved and coated with a plastic solution.

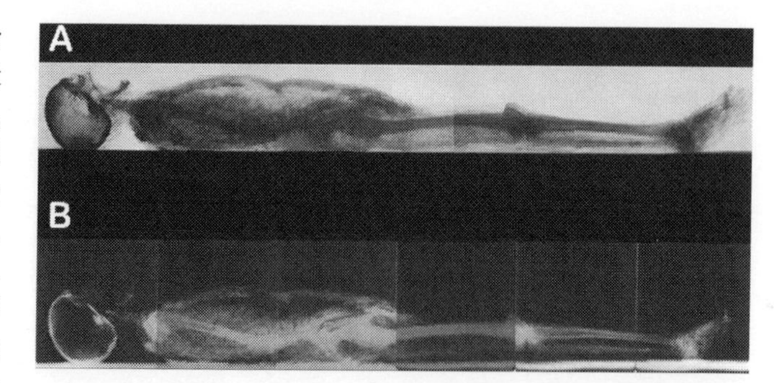

Figure 4.15. The lateral radiographs acquired with the Polaroid system (A) and the conventional film/X-ray cassette combination (B).

attached to the X-ray tube, it was determined that a 144-inch (366 cm) SID would produce an X-ray beam that would cover the entire remains. From past experience (Conlogue and Hennessy, 1997; Nelson and Conlogue, 1997; Conlogue, 1999; Conlogue et al., 1999), it was determined that 50–55 kVp was optimum for the penetration of bone. A satisfactory test exposure was taken with a 40-inch (100 cm) SID at 50 kVp and 2.5 mAs with the Polaroid system. Expanding the SID to 144-inch (366 cm) and applying the direct square law (see Chapter 4: Plane Radiography, in *Advances in Paleoimaging*), 32.5 mAs would be required to produce an equivalent density on the radiograph at that distance. Since the X-ray unit did not have a cooling system built into the tube head, 10 exposures were taken at 50 kVp and 3.3 mAs with a 30-second delay between exposures to permit the tube to cool.

Following acquisition of all the Polaroid radiographs and confirmation of the optimal exposure setting, it was time to obtain the images with the long cassette and conventional X-ray film. In tests back at the university's imaging laboratory, it was determined that the latter required four times the exposure necessary with the Polaroid system. Therefore, each cassette required 40 exposures. Because the long cassette covered three times the length of the Polaroid film holder, the cassette need to be loaded only twice, in the temporary darkroom, the exposed films placed into the transport case and later returned to Connecticut for processing (Figure 4.15).

For the AP projection, the flexibility provided by the MinXRay™ unit was clearly demonstrated. In order to get the maximum height for the project, the tube head was attached to a Sky Jack™ (Figure 4.16). Unfortunately, due to the height of the ceiling, only a 124-inch (315 cm) SID was possible, providing sufficient distance for the X-ray beam to cover from mid-skull to slightly below the hips. Once again using the direct square law, the total number of exposures was reduced from 40 to 28. As previously indicated, the exposed films were transported back to the university for processing **[WS 4.18]**.

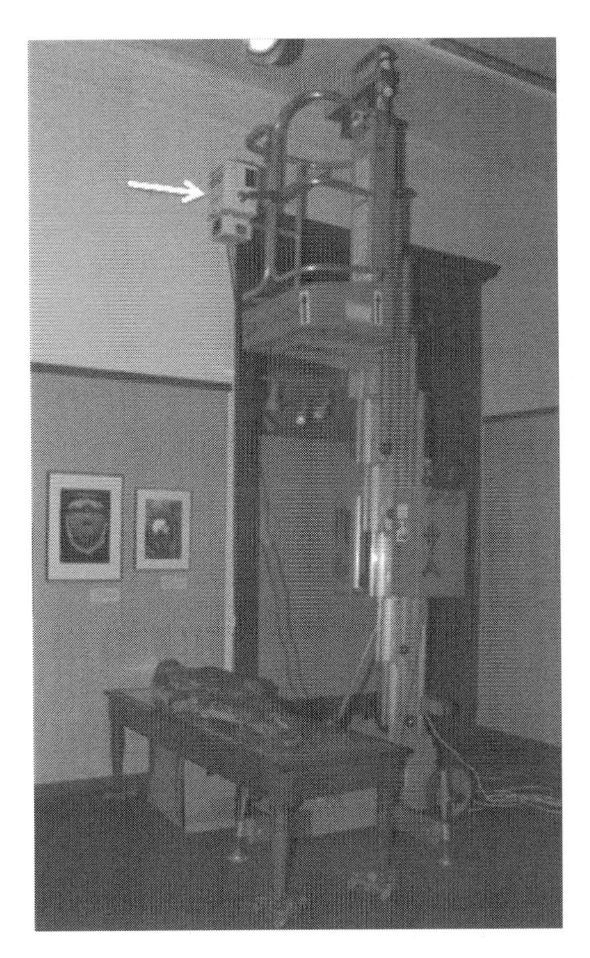

Figure 4.16. The tube head (arrow) attached to the front of the Sky Jack™ permitted a124 inch (315 cm) SID.

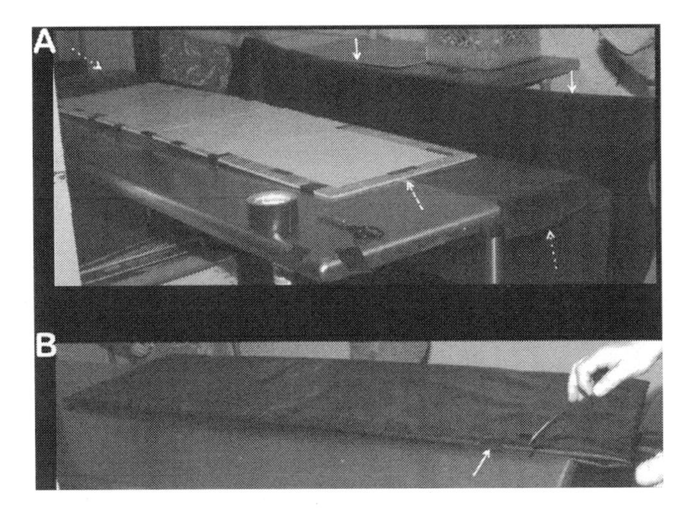

Figure 4.17. (A) Pool liner (solid arrows) was placed under the chipboard support with the attached CR plates (dashed arrow). Approximately 12 inches (30 cm) of the pool liner extended beyond the top and bottom of the chipboard (dotted arrow) to create flaps when the process was completed. (B) Following to complete wraps of the pool liner around the plate holder, the flaps were secured with Duct tape. One taped flap is visible (arrow).

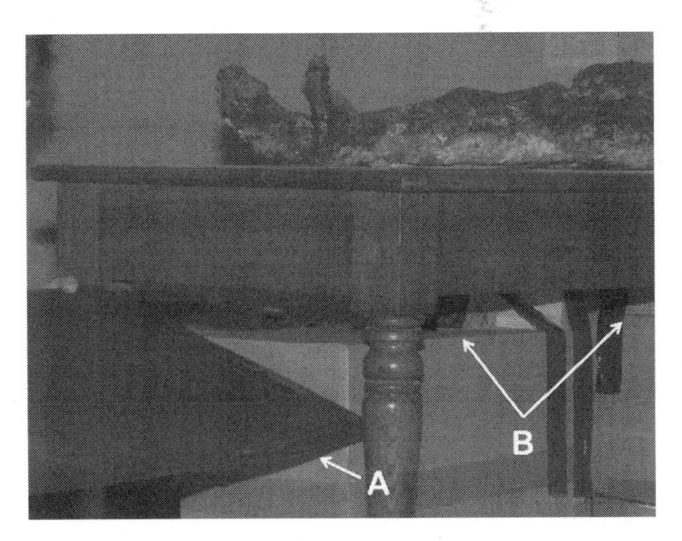

Figure 4.18. The loaded pool liner covered CR image receptor (A) being placed under the table to eventually rest on the cardboard boxes (B) awaiting exposure.

However, as a result of technological innovations available a year later, a return trip to the museum was necessary so that images would be recorded with a digital image receptor instead of film. The Fuji Medical and NDT Systems facility in Stamford, Connecticut provide four, 14×17 inch (35×43 cm) FujiFilm™CR-ST (Standard) imaging plates that were in cardboard holders. Because the plate reader remained in Stamford, the exposed plates had to be returned to that facility to be processed. Once at the Mütter Museum, the plates were prepared for X-ray exposure by removing them for the cardboard envelopes and exposing them to fluorescent light, a process known as *clearing*, for 30 minutes. Because the plates were not confined to a cassette-like holder, they could be arranged end-to-end, forming a 17×64 inch (43×162 cm) image receptor that would fit under the table supporting the remains. A sheet of ⅛ inch (0.3 cm) *chipboard* was cut to the desired dimensions to serve as a substrate for the imaging plates and transported to the museum with the rest of the equipment necessary for the study. In the museum basement, the chipboard was place on a table and the CR plates fixed in place accordingly: the first plate was placed on the board lengthwise, the next two crosswise and the forth lengthwise all secured using Duct Tape™ **[WS 4.19]**. With the CR plates securely in position, the chipboard image receptor was made light-tight by wrapping it with two layers of pool liner. The latter extended beyond the top and bottom of the chipboard to create flaps that here held in place with Duct Tape™ (Figure 4.17). The light-tight plate holder was slid under the table and on top of cardboard boxes (Figure 4.18) to await exposure.

As on the previous trip MinXRay™ HF 100/30 tube head was attached to the Sky Jack™ for a124 inch (315 cm) SID (see Figure 4.16). Because extensive tests had

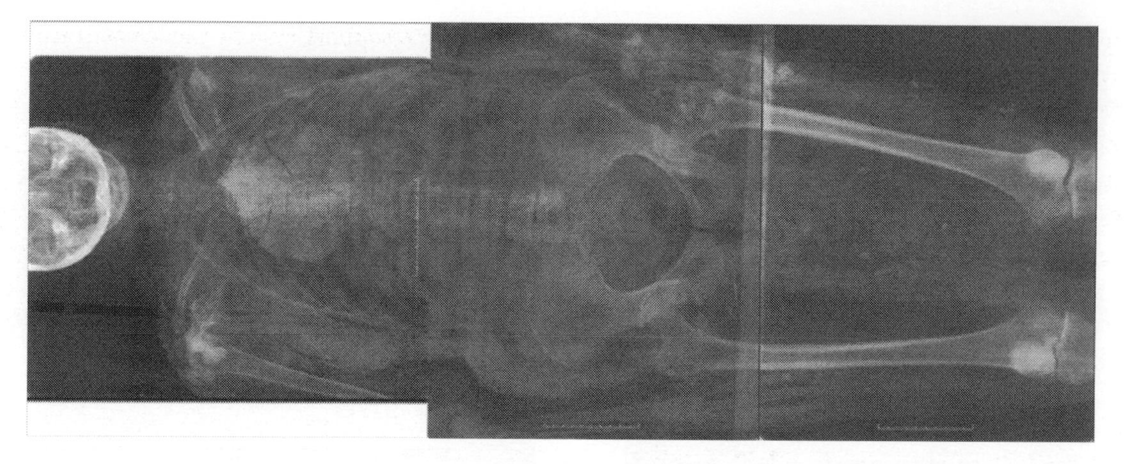

Figure 4.19. The processed FujiFilm™CR-ST (Standard) plates taken using 12 exposures at 86 kVp and 12 mAs.

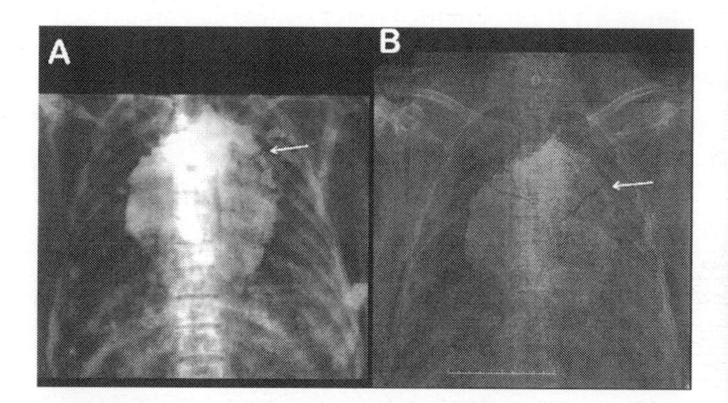

Figure 4.20. On the radiograph, recorded with a cassette and film (A), the crack in the mass behind the back (arrow) cannot be traced more than a few centimeters. However, on the CR image (B) the same crack and others can be easily traced. In addition, the greater latitude, more shades of gray are visible on the digital radiograph.

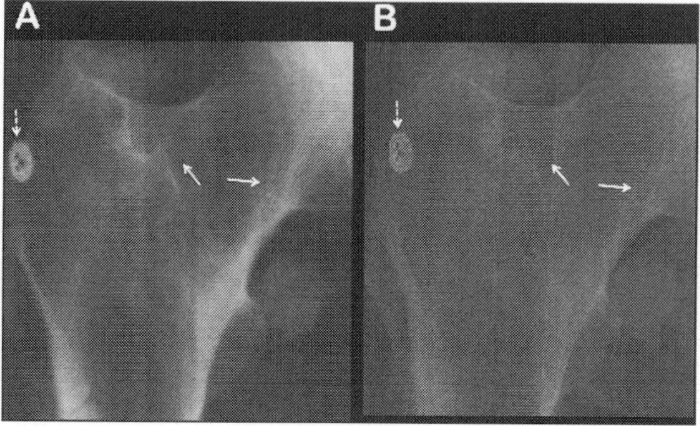

Figure 4.21. A comparison of the magnified images of the right hip recorded on film (A) and with the digital media (B) clearly demonstrates differences. Two regions of trabeculae (solid arrows) can be seen in both images but more clearly delineated, due to the edge enhancement function of the algorithm processing the digital data. Because the image is so magnified, the margins of the cuff button on the digital image is pixilated while just less sharply defined on the analog film (dashed arrow).

not been conducted on the CR system, it was suggested to overexpose the plates, so 12 exposures were taken at 86 kVp and 12 mAs with a 30-second delay between exposures to allow the X-ray tube to cool. The exposed plated were transported back to Stamford, Connecticut, and processed using a rubber algorithm (Figure 4.19).

Study Significance

The compact, lightweight X-ray source certainly opened the possibilities by creating a truly portable X-ray unit. In the urban environment of the Mütter Museum in Philadelphia, with an abundance of ancillary equipment available, such as the Sky Jack™, it was possible to fashion an X-ray tube support system that provided a124 inch (315 cm) SID for AP radiographs. However, the more revolutionary technical advancement, digital image acquisition, undoubtedly changed field radiography. With a CR reader on site, not only would it completely eliminate the need for a darkroom to load and unload films, but it also would exclude the film processor and associated chemistry. In addition, the resolution of the CR over film was clearly demonstrated in the comparison of the chest radiographs (Figure 4.20) and the magnified images of the cuff button by the right hip (Figure 4.21). In addition, the Fuji facility in Stamford, Connecticut, provided the opportunity to break out from the constraints of medical imaging into the broader realm of industrial radiography. The latter not only provided image receptors with higher resolution, but also a broader spectrum of algorithms, such as rubber, to process dehydrated tissues.

***Sylvester*: Ye Olde Curiosity Shop, Seattle, Washington**—Gerald Conlogue, Ron Beckett and John Posh

The *Soap Lady* examinations were an excellent example of a longitudinal study of an individual mummy, providing a comparison of the evolving imaging modalities and illustrating the advantages and disadvantage of each imaging approach. Several other multimodality mummies provide similar illustrations. *Sylvester* at *Ye Olde Curiosity Shop* in Seattle, Washington represents a unique group of mummified remains that can be classified as *Side Show Mummies.* Unlike the *Soap Lady, Sylvester* was embalmed and ended up as an attraction at the shop in the Pacific Northwest United States in the 1950s. Similar to all mummies that were exhibited in this way, *Sylvester* had a fantastic story to encourage customers to relinquish the admissions fee. The legend associated with this mummy: he was a tough cowboy with a gunshot wound to the abdomen, the perfectly round hole with red coloring around it was visible on the body and presumably, without an exit wound, the bullet was still inside him. After being shot, the story goes, he rode off, dying in the dessert where he was naturally mummified by the hot sun in Arizona. However, there was also controversy connected with the remains. Unlike the darkened skin frequently present and fragile state observed with most mummies, his flesh had a yellowish tint and he appeared extremely solid not at all fragile. In addition, the remains weighted approximately 125 pounds (57 kg). Since a human consists of approximately 65% water, this weight appeared a bit heavy for a dehydrated naturally preserved mummy. Therefore, a number of visitors challenged the authenticity.

In 2001, an episode of the National Geographic Channel series, *The Mummy Road Show* (*One Tough Cowboy*, 2001), conducted the first examination of this mummified individual. As with any study developed for broadcast media, there were a number of limitations. Although the production team permitted a great deal of flexibility, without forcing the research into predetermined conclusions, there were time constraints based on a tight two- or three-day taping schedule. Certainly the greatest advantage was the funding available to correlative studies, such as chemical analysis of skin, and access to imaging facilities. The latter was demonstrated by access to the mobile CT unit for the second investigation of the *Soap Lady.* However, there was a previous radiographic examination of the mummy in Philadelphia to offer some direction with the advanced modality. With the remains in Seattle, this was going to be an initial, limited investigation.

Over the entire course of the National Geographic series, a total of 40 episodes, a single X-ray source, a 1950s vintage Picker Army Field Unit (see Figure 4.35, Chapter 4: Plane Radiography in *Advances in Paleoimaging*) was used. It had the advantage of having both the transformer and X-ray tube enclosed in the tube head and a separate control unit. The principle disadvantage, the combined weight of the components was 80 pounds (36 kg). An X-ray source support system was created using electromechanical tubing, EMT (see Figure 4.39A, Chapter 4: Plane Radiography in *Advances in Paleoimaging*) to enable a vertically directed beam. Because a CT scan was scheduled for the following day, it was predetermined that only AP images would be required to verify if it was a mummified individual and document the effects of the gunshot wound to the abdomen. This initial phase of the study was planned for the area of *Ye Olde Curiosity Shop* in front of the vertically displayed mummy. A 9-foot (3 m) parameter was established and marked off to provide a safe distance for the Shop patrons from the radiation exposure. Once the camera and sound recording equipment were in place, the mummy was removed from the display case and placed on a sheet on the floor **[WS 4.25]**. The hole, supposedly the result of a gunshot wound, was clearly visible and marked the draw the attention of visitors **[WS 4.26]**. Possibly the most striking feature of the mummy was the superb preservation of the facial features including his mustache **[WS 4.27]**. The only noticeable blemishes were small raised areas measuring several millimeters on the right side of his face **[WS 4.28]**.

The first radiograph employed the Polaroid Type 803™, 8 × 10 inch (20 × 25 cm) photographic film. It not only provided a quick method to establish the authenticity of the mummy and determine the exposure factors for the radiographic film, but also an opportunity to provide the assembled Shop visitor the opportunity to be included in the study. Everyone anxiously waited for the image, an AP of the upper central portion of the abdomen, to be processed. They were all allowed to watch and be videotaped at the precise moment the positive receiving sheet was separated from film to disclose the presence of a very dense liver and spleen, revealing the remains were in fact human **[WS 4.29]**. The dense liver also helped to explain the unexpected heavy weight of the mummy. A second radiograph was acquired in the same areas in an attempt to visualize the possible effects of a gunshot wound and, since no exit wound was apparent, the projectile that produced the hole. A paper clip was straightened, a loop created at the end and placed over the opening prior to the exposure. The resulting image provided no evidence of any underlying damage nor a metallic foreign body **[WS 4.30]**.

With the technical factors established, AP radiographs were taken on 14 × 17 inch (35 × 43 cm) and 14 × 36 inch (35 × 91 cm) cassettes loaded with X-ray film that were latter developed at Virginia Mason Medical Center. However, before the exposed films were transported to the hospital, the X-ray support system was dismantled. With the X-ray tube, now free, it was decided to take one lateral skull Polaroid exposure in an attempt to possibly visualize the raised areas on the right side of the skull. Not only did the radiograph reveal a well-preserved cerebrum and cerebellum, but totally surprising to all, including the shop visitors, what appeared to be multiple shotgun pellets imbedded in the side of the face **[WS 4.31]**. Dr. Lucy Glenn, a radiologist at the medical center, reviewed the plane radiographs developed at the facility and the only finding of interest, aside for the shotgun pellets **[WS 4.32]**, was a metallic object located at the level of the second rib on the right **[WS 4.33]**.

The following day, in order to demonstrate respect for the dead, the production company arranged for transportation of the remains by ambulance, to the University of Washington Medical Center for a CT scan. Once again, the protocol employed for the study, was determined by the staff at the facility and set for 5.0 mm thick sections resulting in a total of 604 slices. Dr. Stacy Mars, a radiologist, directed the CT and confirmed that the metallic objected appeared to be shotgun pellets. In addition, there appeared to be no evidence to support the gunshot wound to the abdomen. Dr. Udo Schmiedel, another radiologist at the UW Medical Center, reviewed the impressive 3-D surface rendering of the CT data of the head and focusing not only on the shotgun pellets on the right side of the face **[WS 4.34]**, but also precisely located the metal fragment between the first and second ribs **[WS 4.35]**.

Regrettably, no plans were made to get hard copies of the CT images. The only images saved were the ones used by the production company for the episode. During this period, the routine method to store images was to make hard copies with multiple images printed into 14×17 inch (36×43 cm) film. As considered in the Computed Tomography Chapter of *Advances in Paleoimaging* (Chapter 7), there is limited space on the CT unit's CPU. The file will only remain on the computer until the system reaches capacity then the oldest case is deleted to make more space available. Generally, that is several weeks to a month or so depending on the volume of studies performed on that unit. The Polaroid and conventional film images were the only radiographs that were taken away for further analysis.

Before leaving Seattle one of the pellets was removed and a skin sample collected and sent by the production company for analysis. There was confirmation that it was a shotgun pellet, but unfortunately it was lost and further analysis, such as a metallurgical study to determine the precise composition, was not possible. Analysis of the skin sample indicated that high levels of arsenic were present and probably used as the principle embalming agent.

Findings

The most significant finding was that the mummy was not only real but also in an incredible state of preservation as demonstrated, even on the plane radiographs, by the liver and brains. Arsenic had been used as in embalming in the United States since the Civil War. However, because of the toxicity and potential danger to the embalmer, it was used infrequently by the beginning of the twentieth century.

Everyone quickly focused on the shotgun pellets embedded in the right side of the face. Seen both on the plane radiographs and the CT scans, the dense areas around each pellet were granulation tissue indicating a long-term reactive response to the foreign bodies and suggesting the shotgun blast had occurred several years before his death. The wounds were not deeply penetrating, implying low projectile velocity. However, the latter indicated the pellets noted in the pharynx could only have reached that position if the mouth was open at the time of the blast.

Finally, particularly based on the CT images, there was no evidence of underlying disruption of internal organs and structures, including skeletal elements, that would have resulted from a gunshot wound to the abdomen. In addition, the hole on the surface of the abdomen was perfectly round but surrounded by the wrinkled flesh. Theoretically, the margins of a premortem hole would have been subjected to or incorporated in the same folding or wrinkling process as the remaining surface of the abdomen.

Study Significance

There definitely were mixed consequences associated with the study of *Sylvester.* Without the influence of the National Geographic brand, this and all the rest of the studies forming the basis of *Mummy Road Show* episodes would not have been possible. A tremendous amount of work was compressed into a few days. However, with everything moving so rapidly, there was little time for reflection as results began to materialize. With over a decade since the events, it is easy to reflect back and identify the shortcomings. The first was the inability to establish a non-clinical CT protocol. Every effort was made to achieve the best resolution on the scans and it was certainly appropriate for when it was done, but it was still a clinical protocol. Second, and more important, there were no hard copies of the CT study to take away. First impressions are important, but a reexamination of images and the ability to reformat the CT data into various planes after that initial set of observation would have been very helpful in answering new questions.

In fact, a number of new questions did develop following that initial examination. Once the Mummy Road Show ended in 2003, it was determined to attempt to reexamine a number of mummies studied during the series and address the unanswered questions created by each episode. *Sylvester* was near the top of the list, with very specific goals based on the 2001 findings: a focus on the hole in the abdomen; more detailed imaging of the shotgun wound; to the face why was the mummy so heavy; and why was there shiny material on the surface in certain areas. There would be no need to employ plane radiography again, but another CT scan would be beneficial to address the new questions. In addition, it could provide an opportunity to determine the value of MR imaging to contribute information.

In 2005, without the influence of a cable network, it was up to an individual to make contact with a local imaging facility and persuade them to participate in a non-clinical investigation. John Posh, a research fellow with the Bioanthropology Research Institute at Quinnipiac University, BRIQ, since its founding and a resident of Pennsylvania, made arrangement with Inland Pacific Imaging in Seattle, Washington, to provide access to not only CT but also to MR units. Arrangements for print and broadcast media coverage, for the one-day imaging study, was made by the management of *Ye Olde Curiosity Shop* and Inland Pacific Imaging. The latter agreed to waive any fees in lieu of the media interests. Similarly, a local funeral home provided transportation free of charge.

With about two months to lead time, BRIQ organized a team that also included Gary Double, a mortician and former embalming instructor, and Mary Catherine Sonntag, a photographer from the Connecticut Office of the Chief Medical Examiner. The former would offer his expertise in the embalming process while the latter would document the study. After trying to establish photo-documentation of past studies it was noted that few photographs documented the procedural aspects of each projects.

Once again, a clinical CT protocol was used to acquire the data on the Siemens Sensation 16 slice scanner. For scans of the head, 9.0 mm thick sections were collected while those of the chest, abdomen and pelvis were 10.0 mm thick. All scans were accomplished with 140 kVp and a 400 mm Field-of-View (FOV).

Axial and sagittal reconstructed CT images of the abdomen failed to reveal any projectile damage beneath the hole in the abdomen **[WS 4.36]**. Using the same axial image and taking advantage of the measurement function, the exterior and interior diameter of the hole was calculated **[WS 4.37]**. Both measurements equaled 0.26 inches (0.656 cm) or a little more than .25 inch. Taking into account that there was no underlying structural damage, no exit wound and no projectile anywhere in the abdominal region combined with the diameter of the opening, it suggests that a .25-inch drill was used to produce the hole well after the individual was embalmed.

Regarding the shotgun wound on the right side of the face, the pellets were clearly seen on the scout or preliminary CT images used to confirm the region to be scanned **[WS 4.38]**. Once the data was acquired, each pellet could be localized on the multiplanar reconstructions **[WS 4.39]**. The latter also demonstrated the incredible preservation of the brain to the extent that a number of anatomic structures were easily identified **[WS 4.40]**. With little evidence of decomposition, it confirmed that the embalming must have taken place short after death in a location that not only had someone skilled with the practice but also access to the necessary chemicals.

Possibly the most exciting outcome of this study was the MR imaging. John Posh was able to direct the investigation using the Siemens Magnetom Symphony Maestro Class 1.5 T (Tesla) unit. Due to his past experience, Posh realized that the unit would not function unless there was water present somewhere associated with the mummy. Therefore, to provide the needed impetus, he placed a filled plastic water bottle next to the remains and was able to begin imaging. In addition, in order to amplify the signal received from the tissues, 5.0 mm thick sections were needed. On the T1 images, high signal was acquired not from water but fats and there appeared to be a considerable amount of the material in various locations of the body **[WS 4.41]**. By aligning the MR and CT images from approximately the same location, it was possible to identify the anatomic structures with the fat deposits **[WS 4.42]**. The identification of the presents of fats or lipids by MR imaging provided several possible explanations for a number of the initial observations regarding *Sylvester*: his weight and the shiny appearance over certain areas of the body. Embalming does not affect fat within the body. Over time, solid fat deposits can liquefy and, with the assistance of gravity, migrate to the surface.

The findings resulted in several publications (Beckett et al., 2006; Posh et al., 2006, 2007; Conlogue, 2010) and hard copies of the CT and MR studies were provided for future review. Posh was able to control the MR scanning process, but, unfortunately, Conlogue was unable to modify the clinical protocol for the CT scans. The hope was that a future study might be possible where the local imaging facility would permit a non-clinical protocol to be used to acquire the CT data. In 2006, Apartment 11 Productions out of Montreal, Canada, indicated that they wanted technical assistance to conduct another imaging investigation of *Sylvester* for a series, *Mystery Hunters III*, for the Discovery Channel. Unfortunately, once again a CT study was conducted but using a clinical protocol. The episode (*Monster Museums*, 2007), intended for a younger audience, basically reviewed the previous findings with a new CT scan.

In 2009, the Diagnostic Imaging Program at Quinnipiac University acquire a Toshiba Aquilion™ 64-slice Multi-Detector Computed Tomography (MDCT) unit and a Toshiba 1.5 T MR unit that was dedicated to research and training student radiographers with state-of-the-art advanced imaging modality equipment. Because the equipment was not used to image a patient, entire days were spent optimizing protocols for different object, for example, watermelons in MR unit and a mummy in the MDCT unit. By employing non-clinical objects, students and instructors could take their time, manipulating individual settings and observing the effects on the resulting images. Using this approach, it was determined that the creation of isotopic voxels, not a major consideration in clinical imaging, were one of the most important factors in optimizing resolution. The more complete discussion of isotropic voxels is found in the Computed Tomography Chapter 7 in *Advances in Paleoimaging.*

Since the last examination of *Sylvester,* the more technically advanced multidetector or multislice computed tomography units became more common place.

Finally, the opportunity to reexamine *Sylvester* and control data CT data acquisition materialized in 2014 when Saloon Media in Toronto, Canada and Impossible Factual in London, United Kingdom wanted a high-quality CT scan data that could be animated. The production company made arrangements with Via Radiology—Meridian Pavilion in Seattle Washington for the MDCT. After discussions with Robert Moya, a radiographer and operations manager at the imaging facility, he agreed to cooperate with the technical aspects of the study and instructed the MDCT radiographer, Ken Manalo, to incorporate the required modifications into the protocol for the Siemens Biograph 16 PET/CT unit. The final protocol was set at: 100 kVp; 200 mA; 1 second rotation time; 0.75 × 16; 380 mm FOV; and Pitch of 0.45. The acquired data set was processed using three separate algorithms: the first—hi-resolution bone; the second—standard bone; and finally—lung. The resulting 2082 image data set clearly demonstrated the difference in resolution between the clinical protocol and the one developed for mummified remains **[WS 4.43–4.44]**. We were also able to use XRF elemental analysis of both the embalming chemistry as well as the shotgun pellet make-up. These findings are discussed in Case Study 8 of this volume.

Study Significance

As with the *Soap Lady, Sylvester* demonstrated the changes in specific imaging modalities over time. The *Soap Lady* studies began with film and ended, thus far, with computed radiography. Although a mobile CT unit was brought to the Mütter Museum to scan the *Soap Lady,* it was *Sylvester* that demonstrated the evolution of computed tomography over a decade. In addition, the last study in Seattle proved the value of employing a protocol specific for mummified remains to optimize resolution. Both cases also emphasized the importance of reexamining the remains as the imaging technology changed. Because both individuals are located in large urban areas this might easily accomplished, however, for large groups of mummified remains in more isolated locations, more than one imaging study may not be likely.

Egyptian Child Mummy: Yale Peabody Museum, New Haven, Connecticut—

Gerald Conlogue and Ron Beckett

Another individual mummy subjected to multiple radiographic examinations over an extended period of time was an Egyptian child mummy at Yale's Peabody Museum in New Haven, Connecticut. The first series of plane radiographs were taken in 2000 when the Bioanthropology Research Institute was conducting extensive X-ray studies of at the Peabody with the assistance of Roger Colten, Senor Collections Manager in the Division of Anthropology. Known as the *Little Girl from Thebes,* Roger indicated the mummy's arrival at the museum was cataloged (6942) in1919, originating at the archaeological site of Deir el-Bahri and was probably at some point in time exhibited. Deir El-Bahri was a complex of mortuary temple and tombs near ancient Thebes. However, perhaps because the remains were not in pristine condition, the mummy was relegated to a basement storage area **[WS 4.45]**.

The remains were transported from the museum to the old Diagnostic Imaging Program radiography laboratory on the Quinnipiac University campus in Hamden, Connecticut. The Philips Medico 5500™ radiographic unit in the laboratory was used to acquire all the images. Because the mummy was less than 36 inches (91 cm) long, a Halsey 14 × 36 inch (36 × 91 cm) cassette loaded with XMA medical radiographic blue sensitive film was utilized to record the AP radiograph. A 72-inch (183 cm) SID was required for the X-ray beam to cover the entire cassette that was exposed using 58 kVp, 100 mA, and .5 second **[WS 4.46]**. However, in order to increase the resolution and better visualize structures, a series of exposures were acquired with mammography cassettes and film and Polaroid film at an SID reduced to 40 inches (100 cm). There was clearly a fracture of the right forearm noted on the radiograph of the abdominal region **[WS 4.47]**, while an image of the upper chest revealed an apparent missing humeral head on the right humerus and partial disarticulation of the ribs and skull **[WS 4.48]**. In fact, the skull was so dissociated on both vertically and horizontally directed beam projections provided little information [**WS 4.49**].

The Polaroid image of the abdomen clearly demonstrated fractures inferior to the left redial head and left first metacarpal [**WS 4.50**]. In addition, the same projection revealed Harris' growth arrest lines on both iliac crests and an absence of femoral heads [**WS 4.51**]. Based on the plane radiographs, Joseph F. Slade III, MD, a Professor of Orthopaedics and Rehabilitation at Yale University (March 2000, Personal Communication), suggested a blood-borne infection might have been responsible for malformation and dislocation of the femoral and humeral heads. Tony Bravo, a retired radiologist and consultant to the Bioanthropology Research Institute, believed the most striking radiographic finding were the flattened, sclerotic, and irregular appearance of the femoral epiphyses. He felt the findings were consistent with severe Lagg Calves Perthes disease (March 2000, Personal Communication). However, the causes of the fractures were more difficult to decipher from the plane radiographs, with even a suggestion of possible child abuse.

The remains were transported to the Middlesex Hospital Outpatient Clinic in Middletown, Connecticut, for a computed tomography study with a Siemens Somatom 4 unit. As with the experiences with the *Soap Lady* and *Sylvester*, the technical factors were selected based on clinical experience with patients: 120 kVp at 240 mAs with 3.0 mm thick sections. Even with 3.0 mm thick sections, the axial images of the right forearm suggested the fracture was postmortem [**WS 4.52**]. The fractured through the ulna aligned with a tear in the wrappings implying mishandling of the remains as the probable cause of the damage and not premortem abuse. The appearance of the skull collaborated the theory that at some point in time there was little regards for the fragile nature of the remains.

In 2003, the Egyptian child mummy was revisited as an episode of the Mummy Road Show (*Mystery of the Masks, 2003*). A major focus of the episode, as suggested by the title, was the death mask or cartonnage. John Darnell, director of the Yale Egyptological Institute, described the complex portrait painted as being highly symbolic and indicated she died between CE 220 and 270 during the Roman occupation of Egypt. Although the enclosed remains where definitely those of a child, the painted face was that of an adult. The stylized rouge on the cheeks, painted lips, and outlining of the eyes represented the woman that the child would become in the afterlife. John also pointed out that she had a three-strand necklace around her neck and was holding a goblet in her left hand. Background information for the episode revealed that there were 26 mummies collected from four locations that had a similar look: one located at the Metropolitan Museum of Art in New York City and the British Museum in London. Only the funerary mask, acquired in 1895 survived, without the accompanied mummified remains. With the assistance of John Darnell and visits to both museums, the link between the three masks was established. They may not have been manufactured at precisely the same time, but the similarities in style indicated they were definitely from the same group of embalmers and artisans.

According the to the radiographs acquired in 2000 and interpreted by an orthopaedic surgeon and a radiologist, this was not a healthy child. Why would a sick child have been in Thebes? According to John Darnell, Deir el-Bahri had served for several centuries as a place of worship. Many people traveled there looking for healing and perhaps that is how this little girl ended up being buried there.

However, that was not the end of the story for this Peabody mummy. By 2010, several of the faculty of the Diagnostic Imaging Program at Quinnipiac University were focused on the development and optimization of protocols for clinical and non-clinical applications with the Toshiba *Aquilion*™ MDCT unit acquired in 2009. That year, a protocol was developed for mummified remains with the most important factors: the formation of isotropic voxels and a high-resolution algorithm (see CT Chapter 7 in *Advances in Paleoimaging*). Using a 240 mm Field of View, FOV, and a 0.5 mm thick sections, nearly isotropic voxel data were collected to provide optimal multiplanar reformate, MPR, images. In addition, processing the data with an algorithm used for the temporal bone, FC81 – temporal bone, this provided the maximum edge enhancement and enabled better visualization of bone structures. With this level of resolution, it was possible to determine the age at the time of death by several parameters. The first approach was to demonstrate the development of the wrist. Because the remains were scrambled within the wrappings, the wrist would not be found aligned in conventional planes, such as axial, coronal, or sagittal. Off-axis or oblique reformatting was required to reveal the wrist in a plane to evaluate the carpal development [**WS 4.53**]. According to Scheuer and Black (2000), the appearance of ossification of the capitate and hamate, but lack of a distal epiphysis on the distal radius indicated an age of approximately 2.5 years.

The second metric employed to determine age at the time of death was diaphyseal length, also facilitated by using oblique sectioning [**WS 4.54**]. Because magnification is not a factor in CT, measurement can be taken directly off the image (see CT Chapter 7 in *Advances in Paleoimaging*). Although there is a subjective component to selecting the location to create the oblique section and then to actually collect a measurement, it provided an approximation that would be more accurate that one acquired from plane radiographs. The right tibial diaphysis measured 120 mm while the left was determined to be 119 mm. Once again, referring to Scheuer and Black (2000) the age estimate was 1 year old.

Finally, employing another reconstruction algorithm, curve-linear, it was possible to determine the age at the time of death by evaluating dental development. Even with the disarticulated condition of the skull, using a coronal section to reveal the broken sections of the mandible, a line was drawn over the fragments and the algorithm applied **[WS 4.55]**. The reconstruction clearly demonstrated the developing teeth within the mandible. The data set was burned onto a DVD and set to Alan G. Lurie, DDS, PhD, Professor, Department of Oral Health and Diagnostic Sciences and Chair, Section of Oral and Maxillofacial Radiology at the University of Connecticut School of Dental Medicine. Using the OsiriX® DICOM reader on his Mac® computer, Alan performed the same operation and completed his analysis to arrive at an age of between 2 and 4 years **[WS 4.56]**.

Isotropic voxels provided additional information regarding the fractures. A fragment of the right ulna, not reported from the plane radiographs in 2000, was visualized not only on the coronal reconstruction but also on the 3D images **[WS 4.57]**. Once the presence of the fragment was realized, going back and reexamining a plane radiograph from 2000 it suddenly was very apparent **[WS 4.58]**. In addition, a fracture was for the first time revealed on the left ulna, but contrary to the previous report, no fracture was seen on the radius **[WS 4.59]**.

With the success of visualizing structures for age estimation and fracture evaluation, the final phase was to demonstrate the humeral and femoral heads to confirm the diagnoses by Drs. Slatter and Bravo. Unfortunately, by 2010, both had died, but in their memory it seemed important to follow up and acquire images that were not possible when they made their assessments. In 2017, Ramon Gonzalez, a radiologist at Quinnipiac University, reviewed the most recent reconstructions (personal communication, October 2017). On a 3-D reconstruction of the right proximal humerus, he noted the joint capsule appeared not to be intact, but the epiphysis did not appear present **[WS 4.60]**. An area inferior and medial to the joint capsule was examined in an attempt to locate a loose epiphysis, but nothing was found **[WS 4.61]**. At the suggestion of Dr. Gonzalez, the knees were reexamined and on coronal section views where Harris' lines were noted **[WS 4.62]** reinforcing the findings of the growth arrest lines noted on the iliac crests.

Significance

Plane radiographs are extremely helpful in forming first impressions regarding the condition and preliminary findings, such as age at the time of death and presence of skeletal pathologies. However, when the remains are disarticulated and scrambled those initial radiographs can be misleading and MDCT utilizing a protocol with isotropic voxels and a maximum edge enhancement algorithm can clarify or refute initial impressions. In addition, the study demonstrated the importance of maintaining the data to permit re-examination even years following the scan.

Pa Ib: PT Barnum Museum, Bridgeport, Connecticut—Gerald Conlogue and Ron Beckett

The Barnum Museum in Bridgeport, Connecticut, was introduced and described in Case Study 3 of this volume: Skeletal Remains, but there was also a single Egyptian mummy that merits inclusion in the discussion of mummified remains. According to Saxon (1989), a few weeks after the death of her husband, P.T. Barnum, in 1891, his widow, Nancy, traveled abroad including visits to Europe, Scandinavia, and Egypt. While in Cairo, Egypt, the American Consul introduced her to Dimitri Callias Bey, a Greek from Constantinople (Friday, August 9, 1895 Williamsport, Pennsylvania Daily Gazette and Bulletin). As a gift, he presented her "with a mummy for the city historical society". The mummy was shipped back to Bridgeport. In 1895 Nancy married Callias Bey at the Agia Trias Greek Church on West 53rd street in New York City following a civil service. However, prior to the wedding, on August 16, 1894, the Bridgeport Science Society, Fairfield County Historical Society, and the Bridgeport Medical Association presided over the *unpacking* of the mummy (August 16, 1894). The paper reported, "The mummy, when unwound was found to be that of a man, 5 feet 1½ inches tall and from all indicators one who died at an advanced age."

In 2006, the Bioanthropology Research Institute entered into an agreement with Kathy Maher, Executive Director of the Barnum Museum, to conduct radiographic studies of a number of objects in the Museum including the mummy known as Pa Ib **[WS 4.63]**. Unfortunately, PaIb suffered a fate similar to King Tutankhamun in that during the unwrapping, the head separated from the body. The head and body were transported less than 5 miles (8 km) to Advanced Radiology Consultants in Fairfield, Connecticut, for an MDCT scan. Once again, as with other freestanding imaging facilities, clinical scanning parameters were used for data acquisition. The Toshiba *Aquilion*™ 32-slice unit was set for 3.0 mm thick sections at 100 kVp and 75 mA, but unfortunately the FOV was not recorded or imprinted on the hard copies of the images **[WS 4.64]**.

The multiplanar reconstructions revealed the head [WS 4.65] chest, abdomen, and pelvic cavities were filled with resin [WS 4.66]. Following the acquisition, data was downloaded to an independent console loaded with Vitrea® DICOM reader software. After extensive data manipulation at the independent console, the radiographer reconstructed a superb 3D image indicating the location where the brain was removed [WS 4.67]. The image demonstrated the level of quality available when a skilled radiographer familiar with the software was provided the opportunity and time required to manipulate the data.

A consequence of conducting research today with little or no funding is the need to ensure that scheduled studies have optimized the potential for media coverage. The later certainly provided positive publicity for the Museum and University. In addition, in the existing competitive environment, for the freestanding imaging facility, it provided an opportunity for them to demonstrate the superior quality of their imaging equipment. The mummy was transported with a police escort to the imaging facility where the media had already gathered. By the time the images started to appear, a radiologist, who shall remain un-named, declared a truly remarkable finding, there was the mummy of a bird inside the abdomen of PaIb [WS 4.68]. Not only did he consider it was the right size and shape, but the opening was visible on the lower left side of the mummy [WS 4.69], and he noted one another axial section [WS 4.70] thtat provided what he considered to be a route to deposit the bird. Unfortunately, the unnamed radiologist knew nothing about Egyptian mummification practices and the use of organ packets. It does serve to emphasize the need for an anthropologist present during the diagnostic phase of image interpretation. Although the radiologist revelation made national news, neither members of the Bioanthropology Research Institute nor any anthropologist really believed his finding. However, in the spirit of P.T. Barnum, the idea of a mummy within a mummy generated a tremendous amount of interest and made it possible to reexamine Pa Ib in 2010.

Once again, the 2009 opening of Diagnostic Imaging Program Laboratory at Quinnipiac University provided the opportunity to control the imaging acquisition parameters and, unlike a clinical facility, permanently store the data at the university. A 240 mm FOV was selected and the data processed with an algorithm that provided maximum edge enhancement. In true Barnum fashion, the study once again became a media event promoting the museum and the new imaging laboratory. The first objective was to disprove the presents of a bird mummy within Pa Ib. Not only were no bird bones revealed in the packet [WS 4.71], but Ron Beckett also demonstrated the packets with a video-endoscope [WS 4.72]. In addition to the packet that was the focus of attention, there were at least two other packets found within the resin [WS 4.73–4.74]. Once the attention of the media was captured, it was possible to demonstrate the potential to use MDCT to reveal information regarding the embalming technique and the pre-mortem condition of the individual.

The 3D image of the interior of the skull prepared by the radiographer in 2006 provided a great starting point to investigate the embalming procedure. The axial and sagittal sections of the skull clearly revealed layering of the resin within the posterior calvarium first noted on the original scan [WS 4.75]. Regions-Of-Interest, ROI, sampled in each layer of resin substantiated the visible finding that the superficial layer was less dense. In addition, the interface between the surface layer of the resin and the bone on the interior of the skull looked rounded. A 3D reconstruction of the head with the left side removed provided another prospective of the rounded edge interface between the resin and the skull [WS 4.76]. Ron was able to use the video-endoscope to locate the opening from the base of the nasal cavity through the cribiform plate to provide access to the brain (see also Case 8 of this volume). By inserting the endoscope under fluoroscopy, it was possible to verify the position of the camera (Chapter 2: Endoscopy in anthropological and archaeological applications; Figure 2.10, *Advances in Paleoimaging*). The latter has the advantage to directly visualizing an opening, whereas a 3-D reconstruction is exactly that, a reconstruction subjected to edge enhancement [WS 4.77]. An unexpected finding in the thorax was what appeared to be remnants of the pericardium but absence of the heart [WS 4.78], a finding also not noted by the radiologist in the previous study.

After Ron located the opening for removal of the brain, he moved the endoscope to the mouth to examine the teeth. He documented extensive tooth wear probably due to abrasive material, such as sand, incorporated into the food, such as bread, in the diet [WS 4.79–4.80]. The endoscopic findings were corroborated by the multiplanar reconstructions [WS 4.81]. The data set was downloaded and sent, once again, to Dr. Alan Lurie, the dental radiologist from the University of Connecticut who completed the dental interpretation for the Egyptian child.

Alan reported, "Dentoalveolar analysis of Pa-Ib was accomplished by creating curved-surface tomograms through the dental arches using the DICOM data from the MDCT and Cone Beam CT software [WS 4.82]. Curves were made through the maxillary and mandibular arches, respectively, and each arch was separately analyzed. This young individual had extraordinary wear of the incisal and occlusal surfaces of the anterior and premolar maxillary teeth, likely reflective of the grinding of wheat on stone to make breads and resulting in a pumice-like dough that she consumed daily. People of today who consume stone-ground grains frequently experience similar tooth wear. In Pa-Ib's case, the wear extended into the pulp, resulting in pulpal necrosis and infection spreading into the bone at the root apices. The infections at the root apices of the maxillary canines could possibly have led to her death through spread into the cavernous sinus and then into the brain." None of this was presented following the 2006 study primarily because the data lacked review by a dental radiologist familiar with the specialized software required for the reconstruction and interpretative expertise.

Now that a possible cause or contributing factor that brought about the death of the individual was brought to light and before other pathologies were sought, the focus moved to determining the age at the time of death. On the coronal reconstruction of the sternoclavicular articulation **[WS 4.83]**, it was noted that the joints were fused indicating the individual was at least in their mid-20s when they died. There were a lack of degenerative changes in the upper extremities including the shoulders and elbows **[WS 4.84]**. Similarly, degenerative changes were not seen in the lower extremity including the knees **[WS 4.85]** and the feet **[WS 4.86]** and ankles **[WS 4.87]**. Although the spine lacked evidence of arthritic changes, minor degenerative changes in the form of Schmorl's nodes were noted **[WS 4.88]**. While examining the pelvis, also free of degenerative changes, it was noted the subpubic angle measure 45°, suggesting the individual was a male **[WS 4.89]**. However, an axial section at the level of the greater trochanter revealed a vagina and the surface reconstruction confirmed the individual to be a female **[WS 4.90]**. It was now clarified that the remains were those of a female who, due to the lack of degenerative changes, and she probably died between 30 and 40 years old.

Significance

Even when less than optimal protocols were employed to acquire the data, a radiographer experienced with the software and provided sufficient time can create amazing 3D-images to provide significant feature documentation. When the optimal protocol has been utilized, the skilled radiographer can manipulate applications, such as oblique or curve-linear reformats, to more clearly reveal structures necessary to draw conclusions related to age at the time of death and presences of pathologies. In addition, more accurate conclusions or diagnoses require not only individuals skilled in the interpretation of radiographs but also an anthropologist to put the image findings into a cultural and temporal context.

The Woman in the Iron Coffin—Scott Warnasch, Gerald Conlogue, and John Posh

Objectives: From an imaging prospective, the following discussion represents a multimodality approach to document smallpox in an incredibly well preserved individual. Since the last victim of a natural case of smallpox died in 1977 (https://io9.gizmodo.com/the-horrifying-story-of-the-last-death-by-smallpox-1161664590), prior to the advent of magnetic resonance imaging and in an area where computed tomography was not available, this provided an incredible opportunity. However, it is not the intention here to present all the pathologic finding but rather to discuss the imaging approaches.

Another objective for inclusion in the case studies was to demonstrate the ability, years later, to re-examine the data using a DICOM reader loaded onto a laptop computer. It is important to remember that the data will not be achieved on the MDCT system that acquired the data. The storage capacity is limited and once that capacity has been reached, the oldest case is written over. Generally, depending on how busy the facility may be, the data may only be stored on the unit for several weeks or a month before it is written over. Imaging facilities have a Picture Archive and Communication System, PACS, where image data for all the imaging equipment is stored. However, non-clinical cases are rarely sent to the clinical PACS.

On 4 October 2011, a backhoe operator at a construction site in Elmhurst, Queens, New York, unexpectedly unearthed the body of an African American woman. It was originally believed that the body was a buried homicide victim. Work was stopped, the authorities notified, the site secured and next day Scott Warnasch, a forensic archaeologist at the Office of the Chief Medical Examiner (OCME), led a small recovery team to investigate the remains **[WS 4.91]**. Once on site, Warnasch found pieces of rusted metal that he recognized from past experience as being parts of an iron coffin dating to the early 1850s. After surveying the scene, it became clear that the backhoe had shattered the thin iron coffin and dragged the body from its grave.

The iron coffin was invented and manufactured in Queens by Almond Dunbar Fisk and was sold by the company Fisk & Raymond between 1848 and 1854. The coffins were specifically designed to naturally preserve bodies as a means for the sanitary transportation and storage of the dead in the years before embalming was widely practiced. The airtight coffins were form-fitting, which reduced the amount of oxygen inside, thus creating an anaerobic environment, which naturally preserved the body. Costing between $25 and $60 at the time, the coffins were pricy but also very practical during the early years of long-distance steam travel. They were also valued as a way to quarantine the body of a contagion victim, while safely allowing for a proper funeral. Warnasch's archival research suggests that the woman had access to such an expensive coffin because she was the domestic servant of William Raymond—the business partner, brother-in-law and next-door neighbor of Fisk, the coffin inventor.

The coffin indicated that instead of a potential crime scene, the site was, in fact, an abandoned burial ground. It was later confirmed that the property had been purchased in 1828 by the United African Society, an organization formed by free blacks following full emancipation in New York state. A humble church was erected in 1837. Although the discovery was determined not to be of forensic significance, it was processed as if it was a crime scene, and therefore, the body, context and recovery were well documented. The body was covered with a thin layer of soil and coffin fragments, which once removed, revealed that the woman was dressed in a white nightgown and thick knee-length stockings. It was while the team was removing the last of the residual soil from the woman's face and upper chest area that they discovered that she was covered in lesions suggestive of smallpox. Immediately, the morgue and body transport team were notified of the potentially hazardous situation and the Centers for Disease Control and Prevention, CDC, were notified. The body was then transported to the OCME morgue in Queens for examination. A CDC team traveled to New York and prior to the limited autopsy, X-rays recorded on film were acquired **[WS 4.92]**. During the autopsy, the CDC team took samples from several external and internal lesion and were able to determine that the virus was inactive **[WS 4.93]**. This was possibly the first time the interior of a smallpox victim has been observed.

The original plan was to transport the body to the Smithsonian Institution in Washington, DC, for an MDCT study. However, a law prevented transporting the remains of the victim of a contagious disease, even though with the virus was deemed inactive into the district.

A Smithsonian anthropologist, David Hunt, contacted the Bioanthropology Research Institute at Quinnipiac University to explore an alternative site for at least a MDCT examination. Unfortunately, transporting the remains that were then being held at a funeral home in New Jersey was cost-prohibitive. However, Jason Kreitner, a 1994 graduate of the Quinnipiac Diagnostic Imaging Program, was now the Administrator of Clinical Services at the Hackensack University Medical Center, only a few miles from the New Jersey funeral home. With this site secured, it was possible to not only obtain a MDCT study, but also plane radiography and magnetic resonance imaging. It was necessary to obtain permission from the group that claimed custody of the remains before any analysis could be conducted. Since no living descendants were known at the time of discovery, custody was granted to the congregation of Saint Mark's African Methodist Episcopal, A.M.E., Church, in Flushing, Queens. Saint Mark's had formerly owned the property but had relocated in the late 1920s. After several conversations with Reverend Kim Detherage, the pastor of Saint Mark's, assuring that the remains would be handled with the same respect afforded a living patient, permission was given to move forward. The study was set for a Saturday in May 2012 when there were no patients in the outpatient imaging facility.

Several weeks prior to the study, knowing that a Siemens Somatom Sensation 64-slice scanner was going to be used for the MDCT study, a suggested protocol was sent to the Medical Center. Because the Siemens' detector width was 0.625 mm, indicating the smallest slice that would be reconstructed, and a 320 mm Field-of-View, FOV, was recommended. With that combination of slice thickness and FOV, the highest resolution multi-planar reconstructions would be available for interpretation. A detailed description of the protocol factors affecting resolution can be found in Chapter 7 of *Advances in Paleoimaging*: Computed Tomography.

The study at the Medical Center began with a direct digital radiography, DR, study using a Siemens Aristos FX™ unit with the remains still in a body bag **[WS 4.94]**. There were several reasons for completing the plane radiography of the entire individual without opening the body bag. First, following discussions with representatives of the church, it was decided the most respectful approach was not to uncover the individual. Because the remains could not be visually examined for artifacts, such as fragments of the iron coffin, the plane radiographs provided a mechanism to visualize the location of any foreign bodies within the body bag. Even though radiographs were taken at the OCME, artifacts within the bag most probably shifted during transport. Because a magnetic resonance imaging study was planned, this was particularly important because the presents of ferromagnetic material would not only pose a potential safety issue but also possibly damage the MR unit. In addition, metallic items would also create a streak artifact on the CT images from that area. Finally, the plane radiographs, although rendering two-dimensional images, provided information regarding the presence and relative location of structures within the body such as remnants of brain and liver.

Because specific regions of the body, such as the head, could not be directly seen for positioning purposes, it required two attempts to completing visualize the entire skull [**WS 4.95A, B**]. Although the skull was somewhat rotated, the radiograph included the dense object, first seen on the OCME chest X-ray, was now located posterior to the mandible. This was an important finding because, as indicated, ferromagnetic material could damage the MRI unit. In addition, because of the wider latitude, more shades of gray visualized on the DR image compared to the X-rays recorded on film, the area anterior to the remnants of the brain was not portrayed as an empty space. The remnants of the desiccated brain were noted in the same position in both images suggesting it was fixed in position and attesting to the level of preservation of the brain and spinal cord.

Following procedures employed in forensic radiography, the remainder of the body was radiographed in regions rather than specific body parts, such as the chest. Furthermore, each region was overlapped by several inches on the succeeding X-rays to ensure that no artifacts or structures would be missed. The neck and upper chest image once again revealed the dense object seen on the previous DR images [**WS 4.96**]. The X-ray of the lower chest appeared to demonstrate the liver and what appears to be the shape of the heart shadow; however, the position of the heart appeared inferior of where it should have been located [**WS 4.97**]. Other artifacts or debris that was removed with the body were less dense suggesting gravel or clumps of dirt and not metallic. Another radiograph was taken over the left side of the lower chest to better assess the artifacts viewed on the previous image [**WS 4.98**]. Unlike the film images acquired at the OCME, the contrast and density of the digital image, or more correctly termed *window* and *level*, were adjusted for a better assessment of two artifacts determining that both were clumps of compact soil.

The DR images of the pelvis revealed the position of the hips were at different levels, suggesting possible pelvis fractures and apparent separation of the left sacral-iliac joint [**WS 4.99**]. Because of superimposition, there were no apparent fractures of the femurs nor tibiae and fibulae; however, the disparity of the levels at the knees were clearly noted [**WS 4.100**]. The only obvious fracture was noted on the images of the distal left tibia and fibula [**WS 4.101**].

Following the DR images, the body was moved down the hall to the to the Siemens Somatom Sensation 64-slice MDCT scanner. The initial scan was of the head; however, the suggested protocol was not followed. Although the head was scanned with a detector width of 0.625 mm and all 64 detectors activated, the actual FOV selected was not known nor the analog used to process the data. After the head scan was completed the entire body was scanned as one data set coupling two detectors to produce a detector width of 1.2 mm with 24 sets of detectors activated. The disadvantage of the latter protocol was that the smallest object that could be sharply delineated was 1.2 mm. Once the data has been collected, it was not possible to reconstruct slices thinner than the acquisition width.

A week after the study was completed, two DVDs containing the DR, MDCT, and MR DICOM data were sent to BRIQ in Connecticut. The data sets were viewed using an independent workstation loaded with Vitrea® viewer and years later on a MacBook Pro™ with an OsiriX MD™ DICOM reader. The former is an elaborate image manipulation system that is frequently loaded onto independent workstations in imaging facilities. Because image manipulation, such as multi-planar reformats, MPR, 3D reconstruction and subsequent operations including segmentation are time-consuming, an independent workstation placed in a different location than the MDCT unit provides a place to concentrate on the task at hand without interruptions.

The stack of 549 axial MDCT slices of the head were the first to be loaded onto the independent workstation. Because this was the first CT examination of a smallpox victim, there were no anticipated findings. However, visualizing lesions on the dura mater covering the brain were certainly unexpected [**WS 4.102**]. When the window and level were adjusted, there was a suggestion that the lesions were not only on the covering of the brain but also on the surface of the organ [**WS 4.103**].

An advantage of the Vitrea® viewer is the variety of 3- D reconstruction algorithms available. One of the first applied to the data set highlighted the densities that the algorithm identified as metallic. Once applied, the skull and lower densities, based on CT numbers or Hounsfield Units (HU), appeared somewhat transparent while the HU values of the dense objects were colored a bright blue, making them stand out [**WS 4.104**]. Another 3D-algorithm was selected that rendered a surface color that was closer to a skin tone. The numerous smallpox lesions were well demonstrated, however, since her head was resting on the right back portion, that area appeared flatten and concealed the underlying structures [**WS 4.105**]. Remaining with that algorithm, the lower density structures, such as the skin were removed from the reconstruction beginning an operation commonly termed a *virtual autopsy*. However, since the lesions were much more dense than the skin, they appeared to be suspended above the surface of the skull [**WS 4.106**]. Because CT is based on the quantitative attenuation of the X-ray beam, it is possible to measure the density of the smallpox lesions. Two of the lesions were measure utilizing the Region-Of-Interest, ROI, function on a coronal section of the skull [**WS 4.107**]. Since the HU values for bone ranges from 700 to 3000 (radclass.mudr.org/content/hounsfield-units-scale-hu-ct-numbers) it accounts for the appearance of the lesions with the skull. Returning back to the 3-D reconstruction of the skull, it was possible using the Vitrea® viewer *clipping* and *cutting* tools to remove the entire skull and isolate the comb **[WS 4.108]**. Unfortunately, because there was dense material adhering to the hair ornament, it was not possible to completely isolate it.

The MDCT body scan data consisted of 2130 1.2 mm thick slices. Among the objectives was to visualize each of the bones to assess the stage of skeletal development for an age assessment, detect the presence of pathology, and document pre- and postmortem trauma. An example of was the left upper extremity **[WS 4.109A–D]**. The epiphyses of the humerus, ulna, and radius were closed, the cortex of all three skeletal components appeared normal in thickness and not pathologic changes were noted. A similar procedure was carried out to evaluate the left hand and wrist and everything that was visualized appeared normal **[WS 4.110]**.

The findings were certainly different for the lower extremities. There were extensive postmortem fractures of the legs resulting from the backhoe. An illustration was the fractures associated with the right distal femur and tibia **[WS 4.111A–D]**. Applying a 3-D reconstruction of the area with a bone-weighted algorithm clearly demonstrated the fracture **[WS 4.112]**. Differentiating organs within the body was more of a challenge. The liver was easily discernible by shape and location **[WS 4.113]**, however, the left chest appeared to be empty and what was thought to be the heart primarily in the right chest **[WS 4.114]**. A sagittal section to the right of mid-line through the chest more clearly demonstrated a structure suggestive of the heart **[WS 4.115]**. Due to the thick sections it was not possible to delineate smallpox lesions on the organs that were seem by the CDC autopsy team. Because of that inability, more time was not spent examining the chest and abdomen. However, in the pelvis region, what appeared to be the uterus was identified **[WS 4.116]**. Finally, once again the thicker slice acquisition affected the 3D-reconstruction of the surface of the mummy resulting in more ill-defined lesions **[WS 4.117]**.

Because both MDCT and MR studies were completed on the remains, it provided the obvious opportunity to compare images at relatively the same location in both modalities. However, because the MR sections needed to be thick in order to provide sufficient signal, there was not an exact location match **[WS 4.118]**. Because MR is based on the content of mobile hydrogen, primarily water molecules, found it tissue, it is more sensitive to slight changes that could be detected using MDCT. This was demonstrated in axial sections at the level of mid orbits. On the MR image it appeared there was a distinction between what seemed to be the midbrain or brain stem between the cerebral hemispheres. In addition, two folds suggestive of the surface of the cerebellum were also noted. None of those features were discernible on the MDCT image **[WS 4.119]**. The separation of the components of the brain seemed more evident on a near mid-sagittal section MR image. Again, the distinction was not as evident on the corresponding MDCT reformate **[WS 4.120]**. The smallpox lesions that were seem on the MDCT sections were not clearly visualized on the MR images suggestion very low water content **[WS 4.121]**.

At this point the examinations of the head and body data sets were not continued. However, during the fall of 2018 interest in reexamining the data sets was due to the airing of a Public Broadcasting Service documentary based on the recovery and subsequent study of the mummified remains (The Woman in the Iron Coffin, 2018). Both data sets were loaded onto a MacBook Pro with OsiriX™ MD. The study began with an examination of the head scan. The standard multiplanar reformates, axial, coronal and sagittal were displayed using the OsiriX™ MD default, maximum intensity projection, *MIP*, algorithm. The latter displays the volume elements, *Voxels*, with the highest HU values into the 2-D reformates. Once the images appear, the first operation was to adjust the orientations of the axial and coronal images to achieve a true mid-sagittal section. The process began with adjusting the axis representing the sagittal plane on the axial image **[WS 4.122A]**. The next step required the axial axis on the coronal image **[WS 4.122B]**. The result of the two axes manipulation was a true mid-sagittal section **[WS 4.122C]**.

OsiriX MD™ provided three other reconstruction algorithms, minimum intensity projection, mean and volume rendering, that could have been employed. Minimum intensity projection (minIP) displays low-density voxels while mean displays exactly that, the mean of the density values. Finally, volume rendering allows every density to contribute to the final reconstruction. A comparison of all four algorithms clearly demonstrated that the least suitable for mummified remains was the minIP **[WS 4.123]**. For thick sections the volume rendering permitted the visualization of the convoluted surface of the brain along with the demonstrated of the high-density smallpox lesions **[WS 4.124]**.

An examination of the pelvis was undertaken after using a coronal body section to acquire a more perfect axial projection of the pelvis **[WS 4.125]**. The newly generated reconstruction clearly demonstrated a dislocation of the left sacroiliac joint and a fracture to the posterior aspect of the sacrum. Once the true axial projection was established, it was possible to rotate the coronal axis to demonstrate the left hemipelvis and hip joint **[WS 4.126]**.

The new reformate revealed multiple fractures of the left ilium. With a true axial representation of the pelvis, it was also possible to reexamine the uterus that was first noted several years earlier with the Vitrea® viewer. A 21 mm coronal reformate revealed numerous smallpox lesions around what was thought to be the uterus, while a 19 mm near mid-sagittal reformate demonstrated what appeared to be the uterus and vagina **[WS 4.127]**.

Summary

This case study demonstrated several points. The accidental discovery of a smallpox victim that died over 150 years ago and sealed in an airtight iron coffin presented a very unique opportunity. At the time of the death of the last victim of the disease in 1977, none of the modalities—DR, MDCT, and MR—were yet developed. At the time, particularly in the victim's home country of Somalia, the only readily available image modality was radiography with images recorded on film that would not be capable of revealing lesions on organs. Therefore, probably most significant aspect of this case was the potential to employ multimodality imaging to correlate with the partial autopsy findings conducted by the CDC at the Queens OCME.

Locating a site to carry out the study was somewhat challenging, however, over a 20-year period, the Bioanthropology Research Institute had developed contacts that created a network of potential imaging centers across the country. The radiographers associated with the Institute not only had vast experience with non-traditional applications of advanced imaging modalities but had also been involved in developing and participating in documentaries that focused on mummified remains. This latter experience aided in accomplishing imaging studies in exchange for publicity or inclusion in a documentary instead of monetary compensation.

Finally, the ability to save data, particularly the MDCT data set, permitted the data to be reexamined years later. With digital plane radiographs and MR scan data, the images are static, only the contrast and density can be changed, the data cannot be manipulated to render a different prospective. However, the DICOM, MDCT data set can be uploaded to a laptop with DICOM reader software, such as OsiriX™, and sections can be generated in any plane or 3-D reconstructions created.

Groups of Mummies

Radiography studies of large groups of mummies present a completely different set of challenges. Because the sites where the remains are stored are frequently in remote locations, it is even more important to precisely define the objectives of the study. Generally, with a large group, the study will serve a triage function to not only attempt to acquire basic information, such as age at the time of death and the presents of pathology, but also determine with individuals would be the best candidates for possible future examination with advanced modalities, such as MDCT. The evolution of large group studies begins with the Chachapoya mummies in Peru.

Chachapoya-Inca Mummies: Leymebamba, Peru: 1998—Gerald Conlogue

In May 1997, Sonia Guillén, director of Centro Mallqui—Bioanthropology Foundation Peru, coordinated the recovery operation to rescue the mummified and skeletal remains, pottery and textiles of a recently discovered Chachapoya-Inka burial site in the remote mountainous cloud forest region of north-eastern Peru, Department of Amazonas. Because of looting and an accelerated deterioration of the remains, it was decided to move all the contents of the tombs, including artifacts, to a conservation laboratory established in the nearby village of Leymebamba (von Hagen and Guillén, 1998). This extensive undertaking took several months to accomplish before a total of 221 mummy bundles, many partially or nearly totally disturbed by looters, were safely deposited in the village.

Objective: It was determined that a radiographic survey would provide valuable information, such as the conditions of the remains, sex, age at the time of death, and evidence of pathologies.

In the spring of 1998, a field radiographic facility was established in the village with the primary objective to X-ray as many mummies as possible with minimal disruption to the remains. The ability to take radiographs in a remote area was, by itself a daunting task **[WS 4.128]** especially during that period due to flooding and washed out roads **[WS 4.129]**. With minimal funding and the impediments brought on by the field conditions, the challenges associated with this research project were intensified. The only radiographic film and cassettes available were donations from the clinical sites associated with the Diagnostic Imaging Program at Quinnipiac University in Hamden, Connecticut. During several expeditions over the next five-years, numerous brands of expired film, including Kodak T Max®, Konica CM®, Sterling Cronex®, and Agfa Crux® were donated and used to acquire the images. In addition to the radiographic film, several hundred sheets of single emulsion, Kodak Matrix Camera Film® were made available and also utilized. The latter was not intended to be the primary recording media for X-rays but rather to produce images acquired by a computed tomography unit and processed through a large format optical device, known as a matrix camera. Because of the constantly changing recording media, the radiographic exposures factors had to be continuously adjusted. In addition, due to the remote location, utilities such as electricity and water were not always reliable resulting in fluctuations in X-ray output and, at times, less than complete washing of films to remove excess fixer.

The X-ray source, for the first session, was a Kramex portable X-ray unit mounted on a custom made support system created in Egypt and transported to Peru by Dr. Gullén During other sessions when the Kramex unit was not available, a Picker Army Field unit X-ray source mounted on an EMT tubing frame was employed [**WS 4.130**]. The Kramex unit was equipped with a collimator to not only restrict the X-ray beam, but also indicate the area covered by the X-ray beam and beam center. Unfortunately, since the Picker unit lacked a collimator, it was necessary to determine the irradiated area with a cassette. The latter was opened and placed on the floor under the X-ray during. During the exposure, the area of intensifying screen fluorescence was noted and the floor marked to indicate the center of the beam and margins of the irradiated area [**WS 4.131**]. For lateral projections, regardless of which X-ray source was employed, and the remains could not be rotated into position, the X-ray tube was removed from the support system and placed on pile of objects to attain the required height for a horizontal beam [**WS 4.132**]. The average exposure with either unit was 50 kVp, 20 mA, and 0.8 sec with 40 inch (100 cm) SID.

A darkroom was constructed with a PVC pipe frame covered with black gardening plastic (see Figure 3.5 in Case Study 3: Skeletal Remains, this volume). Within the darkroom, a cassette was loaded with film, later exposed film removed from the film holder that was then reloaded. In addition, the darkroom served as the area to process the exposed films. Three wooden tanks lined with plastic contained the developer and fixer solutions along with an initial wash tank (see Figure 4.84 in Chapter 4 Plane Radiography, *Advances in Paleoimaging*). However, since it requires approximately 5 gallons (19 liters) of water to sufficiently wash a single 14×17 inch (36×43 cm) film, it was necessary to wash each film in a sink with running water [**WS 4.133**]. With perhaps 60 to 80 films per day requiring washing, using that volume of waster was a concern. To supplement the water provided from the sink, during the rainy season, rainwater was collected in large containers that was then used to wash films [**WS 4.134**]. Films were hung on cord lines to dry.

In order to ensure that no one was accidentally exposure to radiation, the X-ray equipment was set-up in a room away from everyone else in the building. The darkroom was established several rooms away. And prior to each exposure, "rayos x" was called out at least three times to make everyone in the house aware of what was about to happen.

For each of the mummies in bundles, the first radiograph determined the location of the individual within the bundle [**WS 4.135**]. All of the bodies were in a flexed position with the knees brought up to the chest, elbows placed close to or resting on the knees and the hands positioned over or at the sides of the face. Due to the flexed position, anterior-posterior (AP) radiographs resulted in superimposition of anatomical features with only a few structures being clearly demonstrated. Therefore, the lateral projection provided the most unobstructed view of the remains [**WS 4.136**]. When a suspicious area was noted on an image, such as a possible lesion, the remains were repositioned to more clearly visualize the region [**WS 4.137**]. Because the films were manually processed, with a development time of 4 minutes and an additional 8 minutes of fixing, it took a minimum of about 12 minutes before the radiographed could be initially examined before going into the wash. Therefore, any repeat due either to the setting inappropriate technical factors or a need to correct a position, significantly delayed the study. Because the film dimensions were 14×17 inches (36×43 cm), each image was of either the upper or lower half of the mummy. Even with the challenges encountered, a total of 1080 radiographs were taken between 1998 and 2001. All of the radiographs were transported back to Quinnipiac University for interpretation.

In 2003, an experienced retired radiologist, Anthony Bravo, MD, began reviewing the radiographs. Dr. Bravo limited his initial interpretations to an examination of the spine and calcifications within the chest. Seven categories were created to classify the radiographs: (1) normal; (2) congenital; (3) osteoarthritis; (4) osteomalacia; (5) trauma; (6) malignancies; and (7) infectious processes. Because certain individuals were found to have more than one condition, they were placed in more than one group (Bravo, Conlogue, and Gullén, 2001). Unfortunately, due to Dr. Bravo's death in 2003, the plan for an in-depth interpretation was not completed. In addition, as the 1080 radiographs weighted more than 50 lbs. (23 kg), it was not practical to send the images to other radiologists for interpretation. Another problem associated with the radiographs began to present itself. Over time, manually developed X-ray films that have been processed under less than optimal conditions begin to deteriorate. In addition, many of the types of film that were used in the study were not intended to be processed manually and therefore even more susceptible to deterioration.

Two factors enabled the project to resume. First, digitization of the radiographs made it possible to improve the image quality and reduce the sheer physical mass of radiographs. The process to scan all the radiographs began in 2003 and was completed in 2011. Second, two radiologists, one in the United States, Ramon Gonzalez, and the other in Hungary, Peter Zadori, accepted the challenge to interpret the images.

Prior to digitization, approximately 180 films that were considered overexposed were copied using a Lok-A-Bin Model 315® X-Ray Duplication Unit. The resulting copies appeared lighter or less exposed but with a loss of contrast, more shades of gray without distinct black and white.

The digitization process was accomplished with a Microtek ScanMaker® 9800XL equipped with a transparency adapter (see Figure 4.95 Chapter 4 Plane Radiography, *Advances in Paleoimaging*). Without the latter, it would not have been possible to scan a radiograph. The scanner employed SilverFast v6.5 lrla® software that was specifically developed for scanning radiographs. All scans were done at 16 Bit Grayscale, 300 dots-per-inch (dpi) and saved as TIFFs.

The process was time-consuming. The *prescan* took approximately one minute for a 14×17 inch (36×43 cm) radiograph, but it was necessary for several reasons. First, because the bed was only 12 inches (30.48 cm) wide, it allowed for adjustment of the radiograph to avoid exclusion of an important region that might have been along the edge of the image. Secondly, following acquisition of the *prescan*, the image contrast and density could be adjusted. This was the first opportunity to improve the appearance of the radiograph. Once the adjustments were completed, the actual digitization took approximately 5 minutes. Therefore, the minimum time required to digitize all 1080 radiographs was approximately 110 hours of scanning. Each image was about 35 MB; therefore, the entire series required approximately 38 GB.

Following digitization, each image was examined using Adobe Photoshop® CS3 software. This process provided a second opportunity to improve the appearance of an image. At this point images were placed into folders designated by the number assigned to each mummy by Centro Mallqui. The folders were saved on eight DVDs and an external hard drive.

Cave Mummies: Kabayan Region, Philippines (2001)—Gerald Conlogue and Ronald Beckett

Before considering another group of mummified remains in Peru, the discussion will move to an additional remote, isolated site with a group of mummies. The latter were located in Benguet Province in the rugged mountains of North Luzon about 208 miles (335 km) north of Manila in the Philippines. The project was developed as another episode of the Mummy Road Show (*Cave Mummies of the Philippines*, 2002). The National Geography Channel series made it possible to obtain the mobile CT study of the *Soap Lady*, in Philadelphia and enabled the first ever examination of *Sylvester*, in Seattle. However, as indicated earlier, there was a set of constraints imposed by the production company, Engel Brothers. The entire session, including flights to and from the Philippines extended for only 10 days, leaving approximately three days to investigate the mummies. Because of the tight schedule everyone needed to remain focused on the primary objective, to examine mummified remains in two caves.

A second set of limitations related to the isolated mountainous region where the caves were located. Film was not be an option as a recording media. Fortunately, the Polaroid Type 803®, 8×10 inch (20×25 cm) film, employed for the preliminary radiographs of *Sylvester*, served as a replacement. At approximately $11.00 per exposure, the cost would have been prohibitive had it not been for the large production budget. However, a problem had developed with the Polaroid processing unit: the roller system was periodically not providing an even distribution of the fluid used to transfer the image from the negative to create the positive print and there was no back-up system.

Without electricity, an electric generator needed to be physically carried to the caves to provide power to the 1950s vintage Picker Army Field Unit also employed for all the plane radiographs of *Sylvester*. Because the X-ray tube support constructed from EMT tubing was lightweight and easily configured, it provided the necessary flexibility to adapt to almost any situation. It was hoped the terrain would not prove too much of an obstacle to transport all the equipment to the site or sites.

The final set of challenges, for the most part, remained unknown until we met with the local community to discuss the project. Up to the arrival in the Philippines, the production company's contact person was Orlando V. Abinion, a conservation consultant at the National Museum of the Philippines in Manila. He had been attempting to document the heath, history and mummification practices of the ancient Ibaloy people. Of the nearly 100 ethnic groups in the Philippines, only the Ibaloy culture mummified their dead and placed the remains in caves. There were possibly dozens of caves containing hundreds of bodies with individual families utilizing specific caves. The tradition continued until attempts were made to the halt the practice in the sixteenth century by the invading Spaniards.

The long journey began with the 15-hour flight to Manila followed by a 6-hour drive to the province of Benguet, gateway to the Cordillera Mountain range. Because it was the rainy season, the ride gradually grew more difficult and treacherous due to mudslides and rock slides. In another three hours we finally reached the village of Kabayan **[WS 4.138]** and warmly greeted by the community including a group of singing women. In short order we were in a meeting with the community members including the mayor and an elder and local farmer, Baban Berong, who would also serve as our guide to the caves. The conditions were established: three black pigs, paid for by the New York based production company, were sacrificed and the livers read by the local shaman to determine if we would be permitted access; if the ancestors approved, Baban would lead the group to specific caves; finally, and most important from the point of view of the community, the remains could not, under any circumstances, be removed from the caves for examination. This latter constraint was completely unexpected and, because we had never seen the caves, all pre-conceived ideas regarding any specific imaging approach needed to be abandoned. However, one of the driving philosophies of the Bioanthropology Research Institute was not to challenge the limitations demanded by the community or an individual that controlled access to the remains.

According to the interpretations of the pig's livers, the ancestor did not object to our presence and the entire villages feasted on the roast pigs **[WS 4.139]**. Before beginning the trip to Mount Timbac and the caves, we visited the local museum that contained artifacts and a traditionally prepared female mummy. The latter, had been stolen from her burial site, eventually recovered and brought to the Museum, provided an excellent opportunity to test the imaging systems, both radiographic and endoscopic. According to Orlando, she was the about the best-preserved mummy he had seen. The Picker Field Army X-ray Source was set up on the assembled EMT tubing frame for horizontal beam AP and lateral projections of the mummy's chest. At a 30" SID, the distance was sufficient to cover the 8×10 inch (20×25 cm) Polaroid cassette and a 50 kVp, 13 mA at a 4-second exposure provided acceptable images **[WS 4.140]**. Not only was the first radiograph acceptable, but the AP clearly revealed tracheal rings somewhat superimposed over the spine. On the lateral image, the trachea was projected anterior to the spine and the bifurcation was plainly demonstrated indicating a high level of preservation. At a much later time, Ramon Gonzalez (September 26, 2017), a radiologist at Quinnipiac University, evaluated the images and, based on the lack of degenerative changes in the thoracic spine, estimated her age at the time of death to be less than 40 years old. Interestingly an incision was noted on the lower abdomen and, according to oral tradition, the Ibaloi did not eviscerate the dead. Endoscopy revealed some of the uterus was missing, but the intestines were present. Juliet Igloso (May 29, 2002 personal communication), who oversees the Kabayan Museum, recalled another tradition passed down orally regarding the fate of women dying in childbirth. Juliet was told that when the baby was due, her *stomach* would be cut using a sharp knife of sharpened bamboo to save the baby. The mother would be cared for in death while the surviving baby would have been tended to by the villagers. With the possibility of a primitive caesarean or c-section, this would have been the mummy to focus on; however, it was not the producer's focus for the episode and therefore abandoned.

The next morning, with police escort and a group of community representatives, the three-hour ride began to Timbac, 8192 feet (2497 m) above sea level, to set up a base camp on top of the mountain before the 15-minute descent to the two burial caves selected by Baban. On the ascent up the mountain, he told us how the dead were placed in the caves and rock shelters, beautiful places, to be protected and preserved, but unfortunately, over the years, many had been looted. Baban also recounted the mummification process: it entailed placing the dead in a *death chair*; plugging the ears, nose and mouths to prevent insect invasion, and a smoking process that took up to six months.

Unlike the village that had electricity, a generator had to be carried down the trail to the cave locations **[WS 4.141]**. Each cave had a wire grate in front of the entrance to inhibit access **[WS 4.142]**. Before opening the grate, Baban offered a prayer and spoke directly to his ancestors, "My ancestors, I'm telling them that please forgive us, if we are disturbing you. It should be known by the world what you have done. You are the cause of how Kabayan is known throughout the world. And as for you all, you did not come here if not for the mummies." He poured a little alcohol into the entrance, as we prepared to enter the cave, a tarp was set up to shield the equipment from the rain that began to fall. Once inside, he moved to a coffin that he said was built inside the cave in the 1700s and contained members of the same family **[WS 4.143]**. He pointed out that smaller coffins were dug out of tree trunks and date as far back as the 1300s.

The first mummy that Baban selected to be radiographed was a baby he said he often visited. As he placed the infant on foam wedges that was on top of an empty Polaroid Type 804 film box for the horizontally directed X-ray beam, he quietly spoke to the child's spirit explaining what we were going to do. The X-ray tube was balanced on rocks at the mouth of the cave to create a 33-inch (84 cm) SID **[WS 4.144]**. A series of four exposures were taken with one repeat at 50 kVp at 12 mA and a 4.5 second exposure. Because of the 8 × 10 inch (20 × 25 cm) size of the Polaroid film, it required four radiographs to cover the infant **[WS 4.145A–D]**. However, because neither the infant or the X-ray source were moved between exposures, it would be possible to stitch the four images together **[WS 4.146]**. The repeat was due to poor contact of the processing rollers resulting in the poor distribution of the chemicals from the processing pod, a concern considered before the leaving for the Philippines **[WS 4.147]**. Because there was no easy method to set-up the X-ray source for a horizontally directed beam and the lateral radiographs indicated an intact individual, the mummy was rotated 90° and a horizontally directed AP projection was acquired of the head and thorax **[WS 4.148A–B]**. Processing each Polaroid radiograph was a public event with community members, police, Orlando and Baban looking on adding to the stress of the moment **[WS 4.149]**. In some situations, such as the second cave, the X-ray source did not have to be brought into the cave. A disarticulated skull was brought to the mouth of the cave and the X-ray tube placed on a partially assembled EMT frame resting on rocks **[WS 4.150A–B]**.

Study Significance

The isolated location of the study, a tight, focused videotaping schedule imposed by the production company combined with not knowing the restrictions established by the local community created a great deal of uncertainty and made it difficult to develop a research study plan. Fortunately, the basic equipment shipped to the Philippines proved satisfactory to acquire the radiographs and endoscopic images required to achieve the goals of the production company and create an episode of the *Mummy Road Show*. The local community appeared satisfied that they were able to not only participant in a study of their relatives, but felt they contributed in its direction. Unfortunately, from an overall study prospective, it was somewhat lacking. With less than three days of actual research time, the study was certainly not sufficiently thorough to draw many conclusions or provide opportunities to reexamine remains, such as the female mummy in the Kabayan Museum.

Chiribaya: El Algarrobal, Peru, (1998)—Gerald Conlogue and Ron Beckett

Sonia Guillén, had another *Centro Mallqui* site in southern Peru near the coastal city of Ilo. In the Quechua language, Centro Mallqui translates as *mummy center*, and this facility was located in the Rio Osmore Valley about 10 miles (17 km) from the coast in the small village of El Algarrobal **[WS 4.151]**. Unlike the house that was used for the paleoimaging study in Leymebamba, this facility consisted of several buildings, including a, residence area, laboratory, and storage space for the human remains, ceramic and textiles. It therefore provided an opportunity to establish a permanent field facility to image all materials recovered from the excavated burials.

The valley floor is covered by olive groves planted in the sixteenth century by the Spaniards. Steep sandy slopes rise over 1300 feet (400 m) above the valley and the east slope contain a multitude of Chiribaya culture burial sites dating back perhaps 900 years **[WS 4.152]**. With its particular combination of temperature and moisture, the littoral desert on the coast of Peru provides an ideal matrix for natural mummification of human remains. Nestled among a few municipal buildings in the Valley, Dr. Guillén selected the site for the Center so as to reduce the distance the remains must be transported from recovery to safe storage.

Although an X-ray unit was already at the center, it was decided to transport as much equipment as possible to Peru. The first trip, in the summer of 1998, included six various sized used aluminum and plywood, Anvil® cases commonly used by musicians to transport sound equipment. One case contained two disassembled 1960s vintage X-ray units, a General Electric, GE (see Figure 4.34B, Chapter 4: Plane Radiography in *Advances in Paleoimaging*) and a Picker. While the rest were packed with outdated X-ray film, including Konica MC and C film, Adox blue medical X-ray film, and variety of used 14 × 17 inch (36 × 43 cm) cassettes such as Fuji EC-A and Dupont Cronex Hi-Plus both with 400 speed screens. Although 100-speed screens would have been provided higher resolution, none were available. Regarding the size of the cassettes, other sizes were available, but limiting the donations to a single size simplifies the process. The only exception was a single 14 × 36 inch (36 × 91 cm) cassette. It was donated because two of the five pressure clips that not only keep the cassette closed but also insures good film/screen contact **[WS 4.153A]**. While poor contact between the film and the screen would result in a less than sharp image, loaded with two 14 × 17 inch (36 × 43 cm) sheets of film **[WS 4.153B]**, it could provide a seamless 34 inches (86 cm) radiograph of mummified remains. In order to provide high-resolution radiographs, a cardboard non-screen film holder was also packed with the supplies **[WS 4.154A]**. However, a potential nonscreen film holder was located in each box of film. Within the box was a black, light-tight plastic envelop that contained the film. Once the box was empty, the envelope could be used as a nonscreen film holder **[WS 4.154B]**.

The cases also contained film hangers used to hold the film during development, lead numbers place on the cassettes prior to the exposure in order to identify the objects and even lead aprons to provide protection for the equipment operator. Three wooden boxes were constructed and included with the material shipped to serve as processing tanks in the darkroom **[WS 4.155]**. However, instead of the black plastic that was used as a tank liner in Leymebamba, leakproof liners were created by heat-sealing vinyl roofing material into the shape of an envelope by Charlie Maccalous, a clinical engineer from the University of Connecticut Medical Center in Farmington, Connecticut **[WS 4.156]**. Because there was a darkroom with running water already at the Center, the tanks were set into a deep tile covered sink. Unfortunately, the sink was not deep enough for the 14×17 inch (36×43 cm) film hangers, so the tanks were required for film processing.

After a 16-hour-by-bus journey from Lima to Ilo and an addition half-hour truck ride, we arrived at Centro Mallqui unloaded the cargo and got the first look at the X-ray unit in the Center. The tube head containing the X-ray tube and the transformer were welded to a frame and the latter secured to the concrete block wall **[WS 4.157]**. The Universal X-ray control unit was mounted on the wall close to the door into the room with the X-ray tube, but the mA and kV controls appeared very different. Instead of having numerical values for each of the settings, the mA choices were from A to L and the kV from M to X **[WS 4.158]**. The only information pertaining to the unit was a sticker on the control unit labeled Radiation Standards of the Commonwealth of Virginia with the number VDH #06990 and dated 1991. Unfortunately, the unit was not operational, however, because of Charlie's electrical expertise he worked to isolate the problems related to the control unit and the X-ray tube head **[WS 4.159]**. He had to rewire the circuit so that the hand switch activated the rotor supporting the anode in the X-ray tube and added another switch for the exposure **[WS 4.160]**.

The greater challenge was to get the X-ray tube operational. The unit was oil cooled and once the tube head was opened, Charlie noted that the oil bladder was damaged, requiring removal. With the acquisition of a replacement part not an option, he devised an ingenious solution to create an external bladder. First, he fashioned tubing by removing the copper core from a 16-gauge Teflon®-coated wire. The tubing fit into the receptacle for the oil around the X-ray tube. Next he ran the tube out the vent hole for the transformer housing and through the cap of a .5-l Pepsi® bottle **[WS 4.161]**. The system worked similar to the overflow on a car radiator: when the unit was cool, oil would remain in the bottle, as the X-ray tube heated, the oil flowed out of the bottle through the tubing into and around the outside of the X-ray tube.

With the unit functioning and a 34-inch (86 cm) SID, all radiographs were consistently taken at a kV setting of *M* and the mA at *C*. Depending on the object under examination, exposure times ranged from 1 to 3 seconds. However, because the X-ray tube head was welded into position, it was only used for vertical radiographs. If the human remains or ceramics could not be safely rotated for a second projection, one of the X-ray units transported to the Center was required **[WS 4.162]**. Because these units were manufactured for use in the United States, a step-down transformer, included with the shipped equipment, was required to convert the 220-volt Peruvian current to 110-volt. With the X-ray source directed horizontally, a greater SID was achieved and the 14×36 inch (36×91 cm) cassette, loaded with two, 14×17 inch (36×43 cm) films, was used to record the image. With a 120-inch (305 cm) SID required to cover the two sheets of film, the exposure was set at 50 kVp at 13 mA and 8 seconds.

During the first summer, 65 mummies, 21 adults, and 44 skeletally immature individuals many with evidence of intentional cranial modification, were radiographed **[WS 4.163A–D]**. Unlike Leymebamba—and because this was intended to be a permanent imaging facility—none of the radiographs were removed from the center. The newly formed Bioanthropology Research Institute at Quinnipiac University provided imaging assistance every summer until 2001 when a devastating earthquake partially destroyed the facility. However, due to Sonya Guillén's tremendous efforts, the center was rebuilt and continues to operate today. Unfortunately, due to poor health, Charlie never returned to Peru and died in 2007.

Museo de las Momias: Nineteenth- and Twentieth-Century- Mexican Mummies, Guanajuato, Mexico—Gerald Conlogue and Ronald Beckett

The Museo de las Momias de Guanajuato is a world-renowned museum located in the hilly, colonial city of Guanajuato, about a four-hour drive north of Mexico City. In 1947 Ray Bradbury published a short story, *The Next in Line*, inspired by the mummies that he observed in Guanajuato. Thirty-one years later, he republished the work retitled as *The Mummies of Guanajuato*, which included Archie Liberman's photographs of the mummies, the city, and local inhabitants of the city. By the early 1970s, the mummies' celebrity grew when, incorporated into a new film genre of unusual story lines and subjects, movies included masked wrestlers as super heroes fighting evil. The film, *El Robo de las Momias de Guanajuato*, staring three professional wrestlers, Blue Demon, Mil Máscaras, and Santo, was so popular that it resulted in a number of sequels and imitation.

In 2001, the mummies in the museum became the focus of another episode of the *Mummy Road Show* (*Muchas Mummias*). Frequently, exhibited mummified remains, such as *Sylvester* and the *Soap Lady*, have associated myths or stories. The 108 mummies in the museum were no exception. Examples of these stories include a mummy that was hanged, based on marks on her neck **[WS 4.164]** and another purportedly buried alive. Supposed proof of the latter was the positions of her arms and parallel furrows on her forehead, purportedly representing self-inflicted scratches **[WS 4.165]**. Thus, one of the objectives of the episode was to attempt to validate or refute these and other legends.

The museum staff was extremely helpful and accommodating in dealing with the short period of time available for the study. Originally, it was thought that 30 mummies could be examined and to minimize the time required to study each, it was decided to examine individual mummies either close to or where they were displayed. Most of the mummies were individually encased in horizontal wooden shelving **[WS 4.166]**, however, a few, including a six-month-old fetus, were placed in an upright position. Polaroid Type 803, the 800 ISO photographic film, enabled images to be available for viewing within several minutes of the exposure, however, because of the small size, 8×10 inches (20×25 cm), and the high cost, over $11.00 per sheet, it was not a cost-effective approach for the entire group of mummies. Therefore, it was necessary to create a light-tight area to load and unload X-ray cassettes before transporting the exposed film to a facility with an automatic processor. A temporary darkroom was fashioned by duct-taping sheets of black gardening plastic to the walls of a spiral staircase that led from the subterranean portion of the museum to the cemetery above. One of the stair steps served as a work surface while another held the transport case containing the exposed film. Unfortunately, due to the time limit, only a single trip was allotted to the hospital, Centro Medico La Presa, at least 30 minutes away, to process the films. Certainly, the Polaroid film assisted in establishing the exposure factors for the X-ray film, but the conditions associated with the processor certainly created an unknown.

Because the X-ray set-up would be different for each mummy, it was decided to use a folding ladder that could easily be moved as the X-ray tube support **[WS 4.167]**. For the woman who was supposedly buried alive, her remains were positioned upright resting against the wall and the EMT frame was assembled to support the X-ray tube. In this case the cassette was placed between the mummy and the wall and prevented from falling by sections of EMT cut to the required length **[WS 4.168]**. Because the remains of the woman, who purportedly died in childbirth, were stable and not fixed to the wall, she was removed and placed on a surface formed by several packing containers. In this position it was possible to easily acquire AP images **[WS 4.169]**.

Due to the nature of cable broadcast programs, it was necessary to produce some *immediate* results and address the most sensational stories, such as the woman who died from hanging. The Polaroid film provided results for the video camera within minutes of the exposure and did not require the 30-minute trip to the hospital to process radiographs that might be under- or overexposed. In fact, the Polaroid image did not reveal the characteristic fracture resulting from a hanging where the individual drops a certain distance and the sudden deceleration creates the fracture **[WS 4.170]**. Without a drop, many suicides by hanging lack the *hangman's fracture*, with death resulting from a crushed airway and asphyxiation. Endoscopy revealed an open airway with no indications of constriction **[WS 4.171]**. The Polaroid film also enabled a dramatic AP and lateral projection of the purported six-month fetus that was alleged to have been recovered from the woman who died in childbirth **[WS 4.172]**. The individual that was supposedly buried alive presented a problem; there would not be any radiographic or endoscopic indicators to substantiate or refute the claim. Therefore, that mummy was only radiographed on conventional radiographic film processed at the end of the study.

During the 29-hour period, extended over three days of the study, only 18 mummies were examined using endoscopy and radiography. A total of 42 radiographs were processed at the hospital and, unfortunately, due to poor quality **[WS 4.173]**, provided only the most basic findings, such as missing teeth and degenerative changes in the spine **[WS 4.174A–C]**. The narrow latitude of the film rendered minimal information regarding the age at the time of death of an infant but demonstrated the method of construction for one of the props associated with the mummy **[WS 4.175]**. Because of superimposition, the radiographs of the upper portion of the woman buried alive revealed very little except possible tooth loss postmortem and how she was maintained in the upright position against the wall **[WS 4.176]**. The results unequivocally demonstrated the problem associated with taking a large series of exposures and process the group just before leaving. However, the value of the study was in the relationship between the stories that were told about each mummy and what the actual data revealed.

In May 2007, Eduardo Romero Hick, MD, the mayor of Guanajuato, invited the Bioanthropology Research Institute to join Jerry Melbye, a forensic anthropologist from Texas State University to conduct a thorough comprehensive examination of the mummies in the recently renovated museum. Conlogue and Beckett were joined by Dr. Yvette Bailey, a radiologist who would provide image interpretation on scene. The presence of a radiologist eliminated the long delay encountered when the radiographs had to be transported back to Connecticut for interpretation. In addition, if after an initial examination of an X-ray by the radiologist on site, a slightly different position for clarification of suspected pathology or questionable feature was necessary, it was easily acquired.

In order to avoid all the problems associated with radiographic film as the recording media, such as the need for a darkroom and locating an automatic processor to develop the radiographs, it was decided to use Polaroid 8×10-inch (20×25 cm) photograph film for the entire study. Due to the small size and limited number of sheets of film, it was necessary to determine the minimum number of radiographs that would provide the maximum amount of data that could be acquired. Three factors, the age at the time of death, dental health and presence of pathology were considered the primary focus of the study. Therefore, for each of the mummies examined, the following projections were attempted: PA and lateral skull (calvarium); lateral mandible; PA apical portion of the chest; PA of the right and left upper chest; PA of the right and left lower chest; PA pelvis; PA of the right and left hips; right and left posterior oblique projections of the hips; and if the video-endoscope was introduced into the trachea, PA of the mid-chest. However, if anything suspicious was noted, additional films were acquired.

Another major difference compared to the 2001 study, mummified remains were located in two distinctly separate locations: either a storage or an exhibit area. In order to be less disruptive to the operation of the museum, the study began with the mummies that were not on exhibit. A room adjacent to the storage area was selected for three examination stations: anthropology; endoscopy and at the extreme end of the room, radiography. Placing the X-ray equipment at least 12 feet (4 meters) from the closest other station served as a component of the radiation protection plan for the site. In addition, before taking any exposure, it was announced several times prior to the exposure activation and everyone was verbally asked to leave the room.

The working area contained a frame structure that was designed to support a mummy on the equivalent of a shelf **[WS 4.177]**. For the vertically directed radiographs, the X-ray source was placed on the floor while the cassette was positioned over the anterior surface of the remains on a support made of empty cardboard boxes **[WS 4.178]**. With the remains resting on the middle shelf, a 41-inch (104 cm) SID was achieved. The same distance was employed for the horizontally directed lateral projects **[WS 4.179]**. For several stable infants, the horizontal X-ray beam was also employed to acquire AP projections **[WS 4.180]**.

The importance of having a radiologist present was demonstrated with a radiograph of the lower portion of the pelvis of mummy MH7. Dr. Bailey suspected a fracture of both the ischium and the pubis. In addition, she felt the soft tissue in the perineal area may have been displaced by a hematoma **[WS 4.181]**. Another radiograph was necessary; however, a lateral projection would be rendered useless due to superimposition of structures. The Quinnipiac radiography student, Jiazi Li, decided an oblique projection would suffice and rolled the mummy approximately 30° for an RPO, right posterior oblique **[WS 4.182A]**. The resulting radiograph confirmed the fractures of the ischium and the pubis. With no evidence of any periosteal reaction associated with the fracture sites, it suggested a lack of attempted healing and the trauma occurred shortly before death **[WS 4.182B]**.

The need for input from both the radiologist and anthropologist was illustrated in the interpretation of the extremities of an infant. A portion of Yvette Bailey's radiology training was in urban New York City, so when she reviewed the radiograph her first impression was lead lines **[WS 4.183]**. The findings were based on her experience with pediatric patients who had prolonged exposure to either the ingestion or inhalation to materials containing lead, such as peeling paint. However, Jerry Melbye, provided not only a historical context for the remains but also introduced her to the more likely possibility, Harris's Lines or growth arrest lines. The latter resulted from causes such as periodic episodes of malnutrition or parasitic infections.

At the end of three days, a total of 179 Polaroid images were acquired of 15 adult and four infant mummies. Over that period, approximately 60 X-rays were taken per day. Avoiding the use of conventional radiographic film provided an opportunity to view the images shortly after each was taken without having to travel to the hospital for film processing.

Significance

The study was a perfect example to demonstrate the concept of diagnosis by consensus. Dr. Bailey's extensive experience at recognition of abnormal patterns revealed in the radiographs offers a unique perspective in image interpretation. However, mummified remains present a several of obstacles. The shape and location of dehydrated soft tissue structures may be greatly altered. Interpretation may be compounded depending on the type of treatment of the body after death. With natural mummification, changes result from the combined effects of dehydration and decomposition. However, artificial mummification may include removal of organs.

Another complication in image analysis involves not only the position of the body, such as flexed or extended, but also the inability to eliminate superimpositions by moving extremities away from the body. Many radiologists who trained in the United States may not be either familiar with certain pathologies, such as leprosy, or with the appearance of untreated conditions, such as scoliosis. Anthropologists such as Jerry Melbye can provide clarification regarding factors such as cultural practices and taphonomy. In addition, they can provide a temporal context for elements such as the prevalence of specific diseases or periods of famine. Based on the findings of the study, it was interesting to note that the paleopathologies discovered among the mummies mirrored similar conditions expressed in the modern population of Guanajuato (Conlogue, Beckett, Bailey and Li, 232008).

Using the Polaroid film increase the throughput by eliminating the need to process the films at the hospital. However, the smaller size of the Polaroid product and the higher cost per sheet restricted the examination to the head and body, preventing the radiographic examination of the extremities. In order to completely assess the physical condition, including the documentation of old fractures or arthritic changes in the joints, the extremities must be included. After reviewing the results of the present study, it was decided to return and use conventional 14 × 17 inch radiographic film but also to process the films at the end of each day.

In January 2008, the team returned without Dr. Bailey, who had other commitments, but agreed to review the radiographs back in Connecticut. Although it eliminated the possibility of an immediate assessment, the image interpretation was be accomplished by the end of February.

With the exception of conventional radiographic film replacing Polaroid photographic film, the set-up from the earlier study was identical. Since the September 11, 2001, terrorist attack in New York, with the increase in airport security, it became more difficult to transport sealed boxes of film, including that used in radiography, from X-ray scanning prior to being loading onto a flight. In order to avoid that problem, Mediphot X-O/RP, 35 × 43 cm X-ray film was provided by the museum. The PVC pipe/black gardening plastic darkroom, first employed in 1998 in Peru, was brought to Mexico and assembled in the museum. At the end of each day exposed films were transported to the hospital, about a 30-minute trip each way, and developed with a Kodak M6B processor. To ensure a higher percentage of acceptable radiographs, a photographic technique, termed *bracketing*, inappropriate in the clinical setting, was employed. At the beginning of the study, at least two exposures, varying the mAs a minimum of 35%, for example from 4.2 to 5.7, were taken of each projection. Once the films were processed, usually only one of the two exposures proved satisfactory for review, but at times both images provided information. However, when the images were later digitized on a flatbed scanner, as done with the Chachapoya radiographs, and the contrast and density adjusted, the slight differences were eliminated. By the third day of the study, a routine had developed and, due to a certain degree of familiarity with the required exposure settings, little bracketing was necessary. However, the daily processing provided an opportunity to review the radiographs and acquire an addition film, such as an oblique projection, to clarify a feature noted in the previous image.

Over the five-day period of the study, 19 mummies and one skull were radiographed. A total of 200 exposures were taken or approximately 40 exposures per day. Once again, the time spent traveling round trip to the hospital reduced the throughput, however, bracketing the exposures insured that diagnostic quality images were acquired. Of the 200 radiographs processed, 160, or 80%, were considered acceptable for interpretation.

Upon return to Connecticut, Dr. Bailey reviewed all the radiographs and her impressions were compiled into a table of findings. However, as she was not present in Mexico, she requested additional radiographs to clarify her interpretations. An example was MM 27 [**WS 4.184A–B**], where lateral projections of the thoracic and lumbar spine would more clearly demonstrate the extensive degenerative changes. Because of superimposition, instead of a lateral, oblique projections of the hips would have provided the addition prospective of the pathology noted in that region. In addition, for cases like MM 27 she made a note this this would be a great mummy for a future computed tomography study. In all, she suggested 5 of the 19 mummies warranted further examinations employing CT. Regarding additional radiographs that she would have requested to confirm an interpretation had she been on site; Dr. Bailey indicated that for three mummies a single supplemental radiograph, for another mummy, two additional films and a single individual need three more images. In all, only eight additional radiographs or 5% of the total160 films were required for a complete interpretation. Once again, the results of the study were presented at the Annual North American Paleopathology Association Meeting (Li, Conlogue, and Beckett, 2009).

Interest in the Guanajuato mummies led to a company making an arrangement with the city and the museum to assemble a group of 36 mummies and transport them to the Detroit Science Center for an exhibit, *Accidental Mummies of Guanajuato*. The plan included plane radiography of the mummies and computed tomography of a select few. A cavernous large work area,

Eekstein Exhibit Shop, was selected for the plane radiographic phase of the project.

For the plane radiographs, a 14×36 inch (36×91 cm) Spectroline cassette equipped with Rarex Blue III intensifying screens was brought to Detroit. Since the matching film size was not available, outdated 11×14 (28×36 cm) Fuji Medical NHD green sensitive film was provided by one of Quinnipiac University's clinical sites. Although the intensifying screens emitted a light in the blue portion of the spectrum and the film was green light sensitive, the mismatch required an increase in the mAs to produce an acceptable exposure. With three sheets of the smaller size film loaded into the cassette, only 3 inches (8 cm) of the screens lacked film. Because the films would be processed in groups and to avoid misidentification, three lead markers were placed on the cassette to ensure that each sheet of film was marked **[WS 4.185]**.

In order for the X-ray beam to cover the entire mummy for the AP projects, a 144-inch (366 cm) SID was required. To achieve the needed distance, it was necessary to attach the X-ray source to the tines of a forklift truck **[WS 4.186]**. At this distance, four exposures at 55 kVp and 51 mAs were required to produce a satisfactory image. The radiation protection plan in such an immense space was a much easier task then in the confined areas of a museum. Prior to any exposure, a verbal announcement was made and once the few people in the area were at least 30 feet (10 m) away, the X-ray taken. For the radiographer, first the area irradiated was collimated to the size of the image receptor. Second, the cord for the exposure switch extended from the X-ray source to a height of approximately 6 feet (2 m) from the floor in front of a seat covered with lead aprons **[WS 4.187]**. An *X-ray table* was constructed using a .25-inch (6 mm) sheet of transparent Plexiglas with 1-inch (2.5 cm) rails to permit the cassette to be slid in under the mummy **[WS 4.188]**. Because neither the X-ray source nor the mummy were moved between the exposures **[WS 4.189]**, the total of six radiographs could be stitched together **[WS 4.190]**.

Because the superimposition of the lower extremities would not provide additional information, only a single 72-inch (183 cm) SID was required for the X-ray beam to cover the 14×36 inch (36×92 cm) cassette and acquire a lateral projection of the head to the pelvis **[WS 4.191A–B]**. With the reduced distance, the exposure was modified two exposures were made at 51 mAs and a third at 25 mAs, but the kVp was maintained at 55 for all the exposures.

The black gardening plastic, PVC pipe frame darkroom was set-up in a distant portion of the exhibit workshop. Following an exposure, the cassette was taken into the darkroom and the exposed film loaded into a light-tight transport box. The exposed films were transport to the VCA Animal Hospital in Royal Oak, Michigan, about 15 miles or a 25-minute drive from the workshop **[WS 4.192]**.

Prior to leaving Mexico, the production company selected four mummies for multidetector computed tomography studies when in Detroit. Following the plane radiography, the designated mummies were transported approximately 10 miles to Oakwood Hospital and Medical Center in Dearborn, Michigan. Dr. Emad Hamid from the Department of Radiology and Jim Forman from Siemens Healthcare were in charge of studies employing the Siemens 64-slice unit. The scans were acquired at 100 kVp, 100 mA, 1.25 mm thick slices and a pitch of 0.9, however the field of view was not recorded.

Following the scanning studies, Dr. Hamid prepared two presentations considering the findings (Hamid, 2010a, 4). Among the remains considered was MH 28 that had been radiographed earlier at the exhibit workshop. After reviewing the extent of degenerative changes, he estimated the age at the time of death to be between late 50s early 60s. Noted on the plane radiographs and confirmed on the MDCT images: cervical vertebrae 1 through 4 missing and a loose second cervical spine found in a dependent portion of the left chest **[WS 4.193]**. Also seen on the two-dimensional images, but much more dramatically demonstrated on 3D: dextrorotoscoliosis of the lumbosacral spine identified with truncal shift and pelvic tilt perhaps secondary to ankylosis of the left hip resulting in abnormally short, fixed malpositioned femur **[WS 4.194]**.

There was one final visit to Guanajuato in 2016, but before that episode of the story can be told it is necessary to leave Mexico and consider a group of mummies that were examined in Quito, Ecuador, in 2013. The significance of this particular study was that it marked the transition from film to a digital image receptor system.

Maranga Mummies: Museo Jacinto Jijon y Caamano, Quito, Ecuador—Gerald Conlogue, Ronald Beckett, and Andrew Nelson.

A graduate student from Cranfield University in England and an Ecuadorian, Maria Patricia Ordoñez, requested the Bioanthropology Research Institute at Quinnipiac University to organize a study of a group of mummies from the Maranga culture of Peru in Museo Jacinto Jijon y Caamano housed in the Universidad Catholica in Quito, Ecuador. In 1925 an Ecuadorian, Count Jacinto Jijon y Caamano (1890–1950), heir to one of the riches families in Quito, discovered a group of pre-Columbian mummy bundles (fardos funerarios) in Lima, Peru. The fardos were returned to Quito and joined the growing collections of archaeological pieces held by Jacinto's family. In 1963 the family collection, including the fardos, was donated to the Cultural Center of the Universidad Catholica de Quito and housed in the Museo Jacinto Jijon y Caamano.

Ron Beckett was able to secure a National Geographic grant to fund the study, including $7,562.00 for the round-trip cost to ship two containers of radiographic equipment from Quinnipiac University in North Haven Connecticut to Quito, Ecuador [**WS 4.195**]. The larger case contained the computer radiography, CR, reader, while the smaller container held all the other items, such as the CR plates, laptop computer, the X-ray tube, required for the project.

Because the mummies were flexed within the fardos, it was thought that a majority of each bundle would be included on two of the imaging plates. If neither the mummy nor the X-ray source was moved between exposures, the two images could be stitched together. Therefore, it was determined a 72-inch (183 cm) SID would provide a sufficient distance to cover the required area. The basis for the Kubtec Xtend™ 100HF X-ray tube was supported was the base of a bathtub seat (see Plane Radiography Chapter 4, Figure 4.42 in *Advances in Paleoimaging*). In order to achieve the necessary height, four 72-inch (183 cm) broom handles were purchased at a local hardware store (ferretería) and the end of each broom handle fit was inserted into the legs of the bathtub seat [**WS 4.196**]. Below the point where the wooden handles fit into the bathtub legs. duct tape was used to stabilize the four legs of the support system. Duct tape was also employed to secure the legs to the floor.

The radiation safety plan included a verbal warning of an impending X-ray exposure and waiting until everyone was out of the room prior to the exposure. To provide a sufficient distance for the radiographer, the cord for the exposure switch was extended 12 feet (4 m) and suspended from the top step of a stepladder [**WS 4.197**].

The CR station was set up approximately 10 feet (3 m) from the X-ray tube support system. The large CR reader was placed on top of the large transport case it has been used for shipping the unit to Ecuador. A small desk was placed next to the reader for the monitor and keyboard [**WS 4.198**].

The CR plates were put directly on the floor and two 1-inch (2.5 cm) wooden slats were duct-taped to the floor to serve as a track for the image receptors. For the first exposure, the plate was pushed to the farthest end of the track. While the second exposure required the end of the plate to stop at the nearest portion of the track [**WS 4.199**]. Over the top of the wooden slats taped to the floor, a sheet of wood was placed to form the tabletop. With this configuration, two radiographs were acquired, for example of the lower half of the fardo. Once acquired, the images could be stitched together to form a single image [**WS 4.200A–C**].

For lateral projects when the fardo could not be rolled 90° or for an infant mummy, a horizontal beam was employed. It required the X-ray tube be removed from the vertical support system and placed on the smaller transport case [**WS 4.201**]. A series of boxes were stacked to attain the necessary height and a foam rectangle was positioned on the boxes to allow the mummy to be slightly elevated. Finally, the image receptor was propped up in the vertical positions and supported by another group of boxes. The arrangement worked well for infant mummies [**WS 4.202**]. Because the 72-inch (183 cm) SID would cover more than one plate and several of the infant mummies would not fit on a single plate, two images could be stitched together [**WS 4.203A–C**].

Several small specimens were encountered during the study, such as the mandible of an infant mummy. The vertical support system provided an excellent opportunity to capture magnification radiographs. If the specimen was suspended halfway between the source and image receptor, or in this case 36 inches (91 cm), the object was magnified by a factor of two [**WS 4.204**]. If the same procedure was carried out using film as an image receptor, the image would appear fuzzy due to penumbra. However, with digital radiography the margins of the image, processed by an algorithm, will appear more well defined. In addition, post-processing manipulation can be applied to enhance the edges.

At the end of the five days allotted for the study, a total of 38 fardos, 33 containing human remains, and several nonwrapped cranial were examined. Aside for transitioning from film to a digital image receptor system, the total number of hours spent acquiring the radiographs were monitored [**WS Table 4.1**]. The digital images were reviewed at Quinnipiac University by Dr. Ramon Gonzalez and the findings included in a publication (Ordoñez et al., 2015).

Significance

The study represented a major departure from past group mummy studies. By eliminating film as the image recording media, without the need to consider constructing a darkroom, the on-site preparation was simplified. The time between exposures was reduced from approximately 12 minutes necessary for manual processing to about two minutes, the time required to process the digital plate. In order to track to time between exposures, a log was maintained for later analysis. The number of exposures per hour increased each day as the team became more efficient at moving the remains from the radiographic area to the endoscopy and anthropological measurements station. However, it was noted that there was a tendency to study the radiographs after each mummy, creating a delay before the next mummy was radiographed. Calculating the amount of time spent to acquire images seemed more significant because the study was funded by a grant. For this project, the only cost, $7,562, was for transporting the equipment. Since 193 images were acquired, the cost per image was $39.18.

Priest Mummies: Gangi, Sicily—Gerald Conlogue, Ronald Beckett, and Mark Viner

In January 2015 another opportunity to radiograph a group of mummified remains in a field situation presented itself. Dario Piombino-Mascali, an Italian anthropologist requested a radiographic study of group of mummified priests in burial crypts in the Chiesa Madre de San Nicolo in Gangi, Sicily. The 60 mummies dated from the early 18th and 19th centuries and have been referred to as the *waxed mummies*, as the faces have wax-like masks [**WS 4.205**]. Each mummy was positioned in a niche within the crypt [**WS 4.206**] and various methods were employed to maintain each in a vertical position [**WS 4.207A–B**]. Some have been actively embalmed while others were dried on racks of ceramic pipes. Once again, Ron Beckett sought funding from the National Geographic Society/Waitt Foundation.

Objectives: The overall objectives were to conduct a paleoimaging, including digital radiography, video-endoscopy, and XRF scanning, along with bioarchaeological analysis of the entire group of 60 mummies.

There were two major radiographic differences between this study and the one conducted in Quito, Ecuador. First, instead of computed radiography that required a reader to process the images, a direct DR system was going to be the image recoding media for this study. Second, two DR stations were going to be established: one for AP projections and the other for horizontal beam radiographs.

The lateral station was established by Mark Viner using a Sedecal SP-HF X-ray source and a Canon Lanmix™ CXDI DR plate set to a 40-inch (100 cm) SID. The X-ray tube rested on a thin transport case, while the DR plate was put directly on the floor resting against the wall [**WS 4.208A**]. The mummies were placed on a melamine tabletop raised slightly above the surface of the floor. The laptop control unit was placed on top of a transport case approximately 10 feet (3 m) from the X-ray source [**WS 4.208B**]. Because several of the mummies were flexed slightly at the waist, the lateral station was used to acquire AP projections [**WS 4.209**]. Using what was available, a support was created to maintain the position of the image receptor [**WS 4.210A**] and another support system for the X-ray tube [**WS 4.210B**]. This case also demonstrated a tremendous advantage of the DR system. Because of the complex nature of the setup, it was not necessary to remove the imaging plate for processing. It was possible, within a few seconds, to check the positioning and technical factors [**WS 4.210C**]. If any adjustment were required, it would have easily been accomplished.

The AP radiographic station involved more preparation to setup. Unlike the Sedecal X-ray source and the Canon DR system that have dual voltage and be used with either 110–120 or 220–240 volts, the equipment shipped for the United States required a transformer to operate on the 220- to 240-volt Italian current. A transformer was found in Palermo, Sicily, prior to the drive to Gangi and installed in the crypt of the church [**WS 4.211**]. A mummy support system was created using sections of PVC and clear vinyl [**WS 4.212**]. A canvas drop cloth was placed on the floor under the assembled mummy table. The function of the drop cloth was to minimize dust and dirt from coming in contact with the DR plate.

Contrasting the Cannon DR system that required a cable to connect to the laptop computer, the Kubtec DIGIVIEW™ 395 DR unit was wirelessly connected to its laptop [**WS 4.213**]. In addition, because the system was battery operated, a charging unit was necessary to insure a fully charged battery was always ready. Replacing the wooden broom poles used in Quito, Ecuador, four aluminum extension tubes were brought for the t X-ray tube support system [**WS 4.214–4.215**]. Because the plan for the AP station was to have the X-ray beam high enough to cover an area of 38 inches (97 cm), a 95-inch (241 cm) SID was necessary. With that area of coverage, the entire mummy was radiographed with a minimum of two moves [**WS 4.215**]. In order to get the radiographer as far as possible during an exposure, the cord for the exposure switch was extended 15 feet (4.5 m) [**WS 4.216**].

Because of the curved nature of some of the mummies, it was necessary to utilized available objects as positioning aids [**WS 4.217A–B**]. However, because the positioning aids did not always prevent slight movement of the remains, malalignment of the images resulted [**WS 4.218**]. Because the position of the X-ray source and image receptor moved for each lateral projection, it was not possible to stitch the radiographs together [**WS 4.219**].

Another advantage of a digital image receptor system was demonstrated by the AP station radiographs. As with most mummies, the remains were clothed, however, the vestments draped over the shoulders of each priest had a unique design using metallic threads. The ability to switch between positive and negative images enhanced the viewing. In addition, the wide latitude, inherent in digital radiography made it possible to visual bone, soft tissue and a wood pole in the same image **[WS 4.220]**.

By the end of the arranged 2.5-day period, 36 of the 60 mummies had been radiographed. Once again, all the radiographs were reviewed at Quinnipiac University by Dr. Ramon Gonzalez and aside from pathologic findings (Catapano et al., 2016) and a technical presentation (DiCesare et al., 2016), several basic observations of the condition of the mummies were made and nicely demonstrated by the radiographic study. The outward appearance of the waxlike mask and vertical position of the mummy provide no indication of the underlying condition of the skeleton **[WS 4.221]**. Radiographs of other mummies revealed an extensive use of wire to maintain the upright position within the niche **[WS 4.222]**.

A review of the throughput indicated that the AP station completed 245 images or 98 images per day while the lateral station completed 326 images in the same period or 130 images per day. Those numbers represent significant increases over the throughput during the Quito study (Table 4.2). It is a fact that the CR system requires approximately two-minutes to process the data from the exposed plate while the DR image appears in only several seconds following an exposure. However, there were several other reasons for the increased throughput. Three Quinnipiac University radiologic science students were among the team in Gangi. They assisted at both workstations with transport of the remains, positioning and documenting the process with both recordkeeping and photography. The latter was particularly important in recording the setup for each mummy at both workstations for later review of the entire process with the intension of improving efficiency and use in future presentations and publications.

Having two workstations certainly improved the throughput. This arrangement eliminated the need to continually remove the X-ray tube from the support system in order to acquire orthogonal projections as was the case in Quito. Certainly, replacing the CR with a DR image recording system reduced the wait time between exposures. However, there were two other factors that increased the efficiency of this study. The first was having the radiologic science students assisting with the project enabling the senior investigators more time to concentrate on image and data acquisition. The other reason for the increased productivity was to have the mummies queued up and ready to be examined eliminating idle waiting time. Aside from the sheer increased in the number of radiographs acquired, the true reflection of productivity was demonstrated in the cost per image. For the AP station, as Kubtec waived the rental fee, the only cost was the round-trip shipping between the United States and Italy, $6,875. Therefore, the average cost for each of the 245 radiographs was approximately $28. Even with the cost of the lateral station including, not only shipping charges by also equipment rental and insurance fees, the total was only $3,586. The primary reason for the lower price was the reduced shipping distance between England to Italy. As 326 radiographs were acquired at the lateral station, the average cost per image was $11. The combined average cost for image for both stations was $18.32 or less than half the $38.18 per radiograph for the Quito study.

Significance

The primary significance of this study was the use of two radiographic workstations and employing DR image recording system at each. By incorporating radiologic science students in the team and queuing up the remains, the increased efficiency was clearly demonstrated.

Museo de las Momias: Guanajuato, Mexico (2016)—Gerald Conlogue and Ronald Beckett

Finally, back to Guanajuato for the apparent final chapter of that story. The lessons learned in both Quito, Ecuador, and Gangi, Sicily, were about to be applied to a familiar group of mummified remains and present the opportunity to compare a study that extended over a period of nearly 15 years. Funding for the study was provided by the city with the intention of incorporating the imaging findings into the Museum exhibits. However, the funding was only sufficient to setup a single radiographic workstation.

Objectives

Basically, the principle objective was to radiograph all the mummies that had not been previously examined. In addition, a secondary goal was to reduce the weight of the material that would be shipped and, prior to the arrival of the team, have a mummy table constructed in Guanajuato.

The X-ray tube support system was created out of section of electro-mechanical tubing, EMT, so that no section was longer than 22 inches (56 cm) and would fit into a duffle bag as carry-on luggage **[WS 4.223–4.224]**. The Kubtec XTEND™ 100 HF was secured to the top of the support system by an aluminum plate and two bolts **[WS 4.225]**. Several months prior to fly to Mexico, the design for a mummy table was sent to Michael Wright, the contact person and coordinator in Guanajuato **[WS 4.226]**.

Once the team arrived at the museum in Guanajuato the final preparations were made to establish the field radiographic facility. The DR system was the Kubtec DIGIVIEW® 395 plate that was used in Gangi, Sicily. Once again, the company waived the rental fee but sent along Chest Lowe, PhD, their chief technology officer, to join the team and to assist in the image acquisitions. Instead of using it in the wireless mode, a 21-foot (6.4-m) cable connected the plate to the laptop computer. The plate was wrapped in a plastic garbage bag secured with duct tape. In addition, two *pull-tabs* were created using duct tape to enable the plate to be moved beneath the *mummy table* [**WS 4.227–4.228**].

For AP radiographs, the mummy was placed on the table under the X-ray support system. Unlike other situations, the acquired images were not intended to be stitched together, but rather be viewed as single images. Therefore the X-ray tube was set at an 80-inch (100 cm) SID. Because the X-ray support system had wheels at the base, following an exposure, it was rolled to the next position as the DR plate was pulled into place to line up with the X-ray tube [**WS 4.229**]. After acquiring the AP projects from the head to the feet, the X-ray tube was removed from the support system and positioned for horizontal beam lateral projections [**WS 4.230**]. Generally, laterals were only acquired for the head, chest, abdomen and pelvis. Due to superimposition of structures, laterals were not obtained of the lower extremities.

The resulting radiographs dramatically demonstrated the difference in latitude between the radiographs acquired on film from a previous trip to Guanajuato and those captured using the DR format [**WS 4.231**]. Because the DIGIVIEW® system was not intended for clinical applications, it provided higher resolution that was seen on the resulting images [**WS 4.232A–B**]. Back in Connecticut when the radiographs were reviewed, the wide latitude and increased resolution resulted in Dr. Ramon Gonzalez determining a gall bladder was visualized on one of the mummies [**WS 4.233A–B**].

The wide latitude inherent with the system brought about an unexpected consequence for the study. Because of the wide range of densities that were revealed on each image, it was possible to demonstrate clothing covering the bodies and the leather forming shoes. Guanajuato has been known as a shoe manufacturing center and the X-rays provided documentation of shoe construction over time [**WS 4.234A–B**].

Significance

This last digital radiography study in Guanajuato provided an excellent example to view the evolution of field radiography from an image recording prospective (Table 4.3). In 2001, with film as the image receptor, an average of only 20 images were acquired. As the years progressed and the procedures improved, film still kept the average to no more than 49 X-rays per day. However, with the transition to a DR system, the average exposures per day shot up to 101.

References

Beckett, RG, J Conlogue, G Posh, D Double, MC Henderson, MC Sonntag, A Guzik. 2006. The Legend of Sylvester: One Tough Cowboy. 33rd Annual North American Paleopathology Association Meeting, Anchorage, AK.

Conlogue, G. 1999. Low Kilovoltage, Nonscreen Mummy Radiography. *Radio. Technol.* 71(2):125–132.

Conlogue, G. 2010. Another Cheney Bird Hunting Accident? Bring Your Own Slides (BYOS). Proceedings of the 62 Annual Scientific Meeting American Academy of Forensic Sciences, Seattle, Washington, DC.

Conlogue, GJ, W Hennessy, RG Beckett, J Posh. 1999. Nondestructive Analysis of Mummified and Skeletal Remains: Approaches to Maximizing Imaging Outcomes. 26th Annual Meeting of the Paleopathology Association. Columbus, OH.

Conlogue, GJ, W Hennessy. 1997. Back to Basics: A New Look at an Old Approach to Imaging Mummified Remains. 25th Annual Meeting of the Paleopathology Association, St. Louis, MI.

McFarland, J. 1942. Dr. Joseph Leidy's Petrified Lady. *Ann. Med. Hist.* 4:268–275.

Monster Museums Mystery Hunters III. 2007. Apartment 11 Productions, Montreal, Canada. Discovery Channel. Premier: January 2007.

Nelson, A, G Conlogue. 1997. Field Radiology in Archaeology: Penetrating Problems and Illuminating Research in Osteology. 25th Annual Meeting of the Canadian Association for Physical Anthropology. London, Ontario.

One Tough Cowboy. The Mummy Road Show. Engle Brothers Media Inc., New York. The National Geographic Channel. Premier: October 2001.

Posh, JC, G Conlogue, R Beckett, J Cooney, G Double, D Echelard, M Olson. 2006. The Role of MRI in the Evaluation of Mummified Human Remains Preserved with Arsenic. 15th Annual Scientific Meeting Section of Magnetic Resonance Technologists (SMRT), Seattle, Washington, DC.

Posh, JC, G Conlogue, R Beckett. 2007. The Use of MRI in the Evaluation of Three Mummies with Varying Methods of Preservation. 34th Annual North American Paleopathology Association Meeting, Philadelphia, PA.

Soap Lady. The Mummy Road Show. Engle Brothers Media Inc., New York. The National Geographic Channel. Premier: October 2001.

The Gunslinger Mummy. Mummies Alive. Saloon Media (Toronto, Canada) and Impossible Factual (London, UK). History Channel Canada, Episode 1, Premier: April 19, 2015. Smithsonian Channel (USA), Episode 1, Premier: June 7, 2015.

Mystery of the Masks

Anonymous Mrs. P.T. Barnum Weds: Widow of the Great Showman Marries a Greek. Friday, August 9, 1895 Williamsport, Pennsylvania Daily Gazette and Bulletin.

Saxon, AH. 1989. *P.T. Barnum: The Legend and the Man.* Columbia University Press, New York.
Scheuer, L, S Black. 2000. *Developmental Juvenile Osteology.* Academic Press, London, UK.

Cave Mummies of the Philippines

Bradbury, R. 1947. *The Next in Line in Dark Carnival.* Arkham House, Sauk City, WI.
Bravo, AJ, GJ Conlogue, S Gullén. November, 2001. Dead Men Walking: A Radiographic Survey of Spinal Pathology in Peruvian Chachapoya Mummies. Presented at the 87th Scientific Assembly and Annual Meeting of the Radiological Society of North America. Chicago, IL.
Cave Mummies of the Philippines. The Mummy Road Show. Engle Brothers Media Inc., New York, New York. The National Geographic Channel. Premier: October 2002.
El Robo de las Momias de Guanajuato. 1972. Producciones Filmicas Agrasánchez S.A., Tikal Internacional.
von Hagen A, S Guillén. 1998. Tombs with a View. *Archaeology* 51(2):48–54.

Muchas Mummias

Catapano, A, J Curry, R Gonzalez, G Conlogue, M Viner, D Piombino-Mascali, R Beckett. 2016. A Differential Diagnosis of Spinal Pathology Among the Gangi Mummies. 43rd Annual Meeting of the Paleopathology Association. Atlanta, Georgia.
Conlogue, G, R Beckett, Y Bailey, J Li. 2008. A Preliminary Radiographic and Endoscopic Examination of 21 Mummies at the "Museo de Las Momias" in Guanajuato, Mexico and the Importance of a Team Approach to Imaging Interpretation. 35th Annual North American Paleopathology Association Meeting. Columbus, OH.
Dicesare, A, D Piombino-Mascali, R Beckett, M Viner, G Conlogue, A Catapano, J Curry, KJ Harper-Beckett. 2016. The use of Dual Imaging Stations for Increased Productivity for Large Scale Radiographic Examination of Mummified Remains. 43rd Annual Meeting of the Paleopathology Association. Atlanta, Georgia.
Hamid, E, G Conlogue, V Henoch, H Pierson, J Finger, R. Beckett. 2010a. The Current Postmortem Condition of a Century Old Mummy: A Pictorial Assay Based on MDCT and Radiographic Findings. 37th Annual North American Paleopathology Association Meeting. Albuquerque, NM.
Hamid, E, G Conlogue, V Henoch, J Finger, R. Beckett. 2010b. Learning from the Past. 37th Annual North American Paleopathology Association Meeting. Albuquerque, New Mexico.
Li, J, G Conlogue, R Beckett. 2009. Radiographic Interpretation by Consensus: Diagnosing Pelvic Pathology in Mummies from Guanajuato, Mexico. 36th Annual North American Paleopathology Association Meeting. Chicago, IL.
Ordoñez, MP, R Beckett, A Nelson, G Conlogue. 2015. Paleoimagen y análisis bioantropológico de la colección Maranga del Museo Jacinto Jijón y Caamaño. *Antropología Cuadernos de Investigación* 15:63–79.
"The Woman in the Iron Coffin". Secrets of the Dead, Episode 1. Public Broadcasting Service. Premier: October 3, 2018.

Manufactured or Created Objects

5

GERALD J. CONLOGUE AND ROBERT LOMBARDO

Contents

This group contains a wide range of objects that were either created or manufactured. Particular items were crafted with the specific intent to deceive a potential collector while others constructed to produce a sense of wonder or for purely artistic reasons. There are basically four categories of questions addressed in this section:

Is it real or a fake?
How was it made?
What is inside the object?
What is the condition of the object?

There is also a fifth category that is not a question, but rather a statement: The pure esthetic nature of the radiograph of the object.

The intent is to discuss imaging approaches and not a complete explanation for every example.

Fakes

In order to convincingly deceive the potential buyer, the individual that manufactures the item must have some convincing components. This was the case with a baboon mummy at the Rosicrucian Egyptian Museum in San Jose, California. The object was coincidentally radiographed in 2002 during an episode of the *Mummy Road Show* (*Egypt California Style*). The Museum houses over 4,000 artifacts, the largest display of Egyptian relics west of the Mississippi River. The actual focus of the episode was the contents of what was thought to be an empty Egyptian coffin purchased by the museum in 1971 from the upscale department store Neiman Marcus in Texas. When the coffin arrived in California and was opened, an unwrapped mummy was found inside. The mummy was probably a victim of a Victorian era unwrapping party in the hope of finding amulets or other artifact within the warping. While the mummy was being examined with video-endoscopy, a baboon mummy on a pedestal was noticed (Figure 5.1). With about a 30-minute wait before the next radiography segment to be videotaped, it was determined to spend the time imaging the animal mummy. Several sheets of Polaroid film were taped to the wall behind the fragile baboon and the radiographs were taken. Because the film was

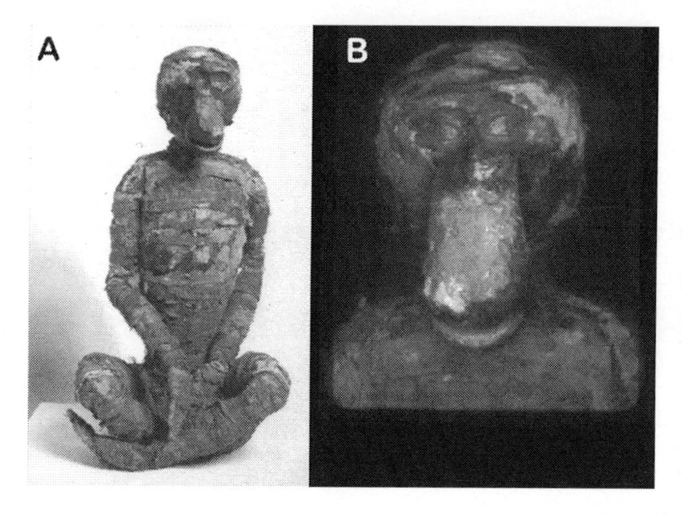

Figure 5.1. (A) The entire wrapped baboon mummy at the Rosicrucian Egyptian Museum in San Jose, California. (B) A close-up of the baboon face.

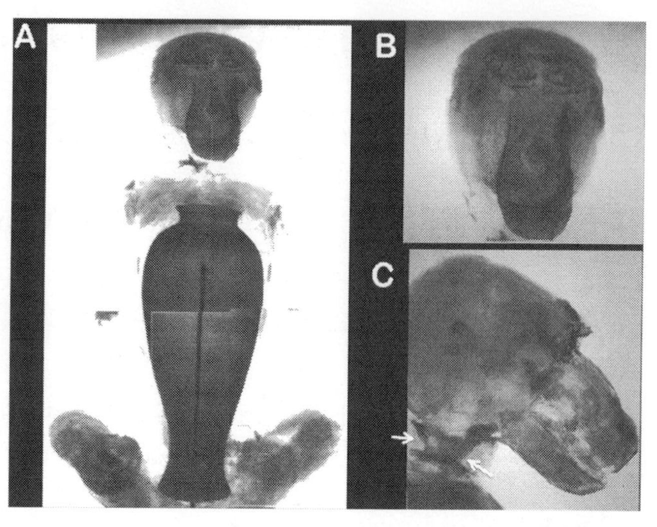

Figure 5.2. (A) The composite Polaroid radiographs of the entire baboon mummy revealing a vase for a body and a carved head. (B) A close-up AP projection of the baboon head. (C) A close-up lateral projection of the baboon head: Note the tapered neck.

not loaded into an intensifying screen, an exposure lasting 100-seconds at 55 kVp was required. The resulting images revealed a vase where the body should have been and a carved wooden head. A closer look at the neck revealed a tapered neck, similar to a cork to fit it into the top of the bottle (Figure 5.2). How could this have been perpetrated? Recall the previously mentioned mummy unwrapping party. Many thousands of mummies were unwrapped and destroyed. It would not have been a difficult task to acquire authentic wrappings and use them to cover anything. Apparently, the wrapping on the baboon mummy were test and once discovered to be authentic, the mummy was purchased.

In the late 19th and early 20th centuries, wealthy European and American tourists visiting Egypt wanted to bring souvenirs home, particularly mummified remains, either animal or human. If they couldn't take an entire mummy, they were happy to bring home parts, such as a mummified hand. What were the origins of this fascination with Egyptian mummies? In part it may be traced back to Napoleon and the extensive scientific study he initiated after his campaign in Egypt between 1798 and 1801. By the mid-nineteenth century, the mummy unwrapping parties mentioned earlier became social events in England. In American, another unique institution was found, the Dime Museum. Although there were other showman before P.T. Barnum, he can be attributed with the great age of the American dime museum (Dennett, 1997), opening the American Museum in New York in 1841. By providing amusements, emphasizing their educational benefits, it appealed to a diverse audience including both the elite wealthy and working masses, regardless of ethnicity or gender, crowded into the museum. Barnum offered everything from stuffed animal and dioramas to menageries and human oddities. Of course, Barnum had to include mummified remains among the numerous other natural history specimens in his museum (Wolf, 2009).

Because the Dime Museum was a fixed entity, visitors had to travel to the city to view the extraordinary collect of oddities, thus the traveling museum was created. Barnum organized one in 1851 that included a 110-foot (33.5 m) tent and toured for four years (Dennett, 1997). Entrepreneurs realizing the possibilities met the demand by creating objects, such as a mummified hand **[WS 5.3]**. During the early twentieth century, according to John Robinson (Sideshow World), the Nelson Supply House located at 514 East 4th Street South, Boston, Massachusetts manufactured, among other things, mummified curiosities. It has been suggested that the craftsmen, employed by Nelson, created the objects by a combination of taxidermy of actual parts of humans and animal bones, skin, fingernails, and hair. Not only did the company produce the objects but also the banners to attract the customers and a complete story that elaborated the most amazing and outrageous facts to solidify the gaff.

In 1999, the American Dine Museum was founded in Baltimore, Maryland, as the world's only exhibit space recreating a nineteenth century collection of the novelty and varied exhibition business, featuring actual and "gaffed" manufactured objects. Among the items in the collection was the *1000-year-old 9-feet tall* (3 m) *Peruvian Amazonian Giantess* attributed to the Nelson Supply House **[WS 5.4]**. The actual techniques employed to create the object were never documented and Dick Horne, a cofounder of the museum and an artist who manufactures gaffed artifacts, wanted a view inside the *Giantess*. Therefore in 2001, a *Mummy Road Show* crew (*Faking It*) traveled to Baltimore to examine this unique aspect of Americana and focus on the *Giantess*, among other items in the museum.

On visual inspection of the *Giantess*, a large opening was noted in the chest and what clearly appeared to be actual large ribs were seen. Because the only two options to record images were conventional X-ray film and Polaroid photographic film, the latter was selected as method to establish the technical factors required for the conventional radiographic film. Unfortunately, the 8 × 10 inch (20 × 25 cm) Polaroid film size was too small to examine the entire 9-foot (3 m) object. The X-ray source employed for all the episodes of the *National Geographic Channel* series was a Korean War vintage Picker Army Field Unit than unfortunately weighed approximately 40 pounds (18 kg). Due to the heavy weight and the cramped quarters of the museum, a 40-inch (100 cm) SID was used of all of the images. At that distance, 50 kVp, 10 mA, and a six second exposure was set for all the Polaroid radiographs. Several lateral and an AP projection of the head confirmed that the structure lacked a real skull and suggested to Dick Horne that the materials that were possibly used in the construction: *papier maché* and clay **[WS 5.5]**. AP radiographs acquired of the mandible and neck implied that the head and neck were attached to the upper torso by nailing it to a block of wood **[WS 5.6]**. Also identified on the lateral projection was a corrugated or wiggle nail that has been generally employed to fasten miter joints in furniture or picture frame construction **[WS 5.7]**.

Once the technical factors had been established, the 14 × 17 inch (36 × 43 cm) cassettes were employed to image larger areas of the *Giantess*. A film changing area was established in a Museum closet and the exposed films were placed in a light-tight transport case (see Chapter 4, Figure 4.74, *Advances in Paleoimaging*). At the completion of the study, the exposed films were transported to a local veterinary clinic and put through an automatic processor. AP projects were acquired of the chest, abdominal and pelvic regions revealing boards as framing material, numerous nails as fasteners, and wire as framing for fingers and simulate tendons in the back of the hand **[WS 5.8]**. The opening between the ribs on the left side of the chest was created to expose three large ribs, probably beef, as proof that the mummy was authentic. However, the opening provided access for video-endoscopy. The endoscope revealed the presence of excelsior packing material. Used as a substance to stuff mattresses, furniture cushions, toy animals and taxidermy, excelsior or wood shavings were also used in packing around fragile objects was eliminated after the second world war in favor of foam rubber.

Surprised by the findings, Dick had expected a frame of chicken wire, also known as poultry netting or hardware cloth. The wire mesh, dating back to the mid-1800s, could easily have been covered with something like burlap saturated in glue. Instead it appeared to be a wood frame with excelsior employed as a filler or packing material, similar to upholstering, and then covered.

There was more to be learned at the museum, but first the tale of the *Giantess* did not end in 2001. Unfortunately, the museum closed in 2003 and the holdings were auctioned off, with the *Giantess* being purchased by the magician David Copperfield for his private museum in Las Vegas, Nevada. In 2007, Copperfield wanted to learn more regarding the construction of the object and requested a more complete imaging study. The intent was to locate a facility with a computed tomography unit in the Las Vegas area that would permit the *Giantess* to be scanned. The thought of a CT scan back in 2001 was never a consideration, and the stability of the object was never assessed. Unfortunately, upon arriving at the museum, it was determined that the case containing the mummy was too wide to fit into the CT gantry **[WS 5.9]**. In addition, the object was too fragile to be removed from the case.

With the CT scanning no longer an option, the examination consisted of a more extensive plane radiography and endoscopy. Since the 2001 study, the old Picker portable X-ray source was replaced by a MinXray™ source equipped with a high-frequency generator. The new unit was much lighter, as it weighed only 24 pounds (11 kg) and was more efficient at converting electrical energy to X-ray. In addition, unlike the separate, 20-pound (9 kg) control unit that accompanied the Picker unit, the controls for the new system were built into the X-ray source.

Because the museum was actually a warehouse with high ceilings, instead of the cramped confines of the Dime Museum in Baltimore, it was possible to attain a greater SID to stitch the resulting radiographs together. As with most warehouses, in order to place objects and crates on the upper tier of the shelving units, a forklift was available. A board was inserted through the handle of the MinXray™ source and rested on the tines of the forklift. Once the X-ray source was in place, it was secured with duct tape **[WS 5.10]**. Test exposures were taken at a 27-inch (69 cm) SID of a number of everyday objects **[WS 5.11]**. Once the satisfactory exposure was acquired, the direct square law, discussed in Chapter 4 Plane Radiography (*Advances in Paleoimaging*), was applied for the final SID. With the X-ray source secure, the tines of the forklift were elevated to reach a 110-inch (279 cm) SID to enable the X-ray beam to cover an area from the top of the head to the base of the pelvis [**WS 5.12**].

Test radiographs were taken with a 27-inch (69 cm) SID at 60 Kvp at 0.3 mAs and then the mAs was recalculated to 4.8 mAs for the 110-inch (279 cm) SID. A total of 20 Polaroid images were taken [**WS 5.13A**], however, after bumping into the case containing the Giantess between images number 14 and 15, the remaining five images could not be stitched with the earlier radiographs [**WS 5.13B, C**]. Because the increased SID made it possible to cover a larger area than in the initial study in Baltimore, a board constituting a component of an internal frame was revealed extending from the top of the left shoulder region to below the left *hip* [**WS 5.13D**].

The most exciting aspect of the study was inclusion of the Fuji computed radiograph, CR, system. Four imaging plates, IP, each in a cardboard holder, were sent via FedEx™ from the Fuji Non-Destructive Testing, NDT, facility in Stamford, Connecticut. In Las Vegas, each plate was exposed to the fluorescent lights in the Museum for one hour then replaced in their respective cardboard holders. All four plates were exposed using the same technical factors employed with the Polaroid film. The exposed plates were repackaged and shipped back to Connecticut by FedEx™. It took approximately four days between the time the plates were send and processed at the Connecticut facility by Bob Lombardo [**WS 5.14**]. The ability to reprocess the data collected from the plates was dramatically demonstrated with radiographs of the right *chest* [**WS 5.15**]. Since both Polaroid and Fuji CR images were taken of the same region, it was possible to compare the two imaging approaches. The larger CR plates required fewer exposures to image the same region and the wider latitude revealed even low-density structures, such as the left arms not visualized on the Polaroid film [**WS 5.16**].

Because of the small size restriction of the computed tomography gantry, the imaging of the Giantess that traveled from Baltimore to Las Vegas was over. However, approximately three years later another possible Nelson Supply House *mummy*, in the hand of a private collector, Hilary Lester, in Wilsonville, Oregon, made the use of an advanced imaging modality possible. Arrangements were made to meet Ms. Lester and her mummy, known as *Gretchen*, at the Department of Clinical Services in the College of Veterinary Medicine at the Oregon State University in Corvallis, Oregon for a multi-detector computed tomography, MDCT, scan. Unlike the Giantess, Gretchen was only 53-inches (135 cm) long, 11-inches (30 cm) wide and 10-inches (25 cm) thick, certainly small enough to go though the CT unit gantry. Because the mummy was on a plank, 57×17×1-inch (145×43×2.5 cm), stability of the mummy was also not a concern.

According to Hilary, the mummy had been on display at the Cliff House and Sutro Baths Museum in San Francisco for 70 years until closing in the 1960s. At that time, it was purchased by Hathaway and Bowers, collectors and dealers of automatic musical instruments. In the 1970s Hilary's father bought the mummy with the intention of exhibiting it at his Antique Music and Wheels Museum in North Carolina. It never reached North Carolina and after her father's death in 2010 she had considered selling it on eBay.

At the Veterinary School, prior to the MDCT study, Dr. Susan Steiger-Vanegas, a veterinary radiologist, suggested acquiring CR images for a preliminary evaluation. Due to the short length of the mummy, only four 14×17-inch (36×43 cm) radiographs covered the entire object and reveal a more simple structure than that noted in the Giantess [**WS 5.17**]. However, there were a number of similarities. Multiple types of fasteners were employed in the construction along with openings or *windows* cut into the chest to reveal ribs in an attempt to prove it to be real and not a fake.Jason Wiest, a radiographer and Computed Tomography Coordinator directed the study with the Toshiba™ Aquilion 64-slice using the following factors: 64-slices per rotation; 0.5 mm thick slices; 120 kVp; 75 mAs; a helical pitch of 21.0; and FC 81, an algorithm that maximizes edge enhancement. The reconstructed images provided detailed information regarding the construction that was later interpreted by individuals at the Smithsonian Institution in Washington, DC. Not only did the reconstructions confirm the frame was wood, but provided evidence that much of it had been previously used. One axial image revealed a board within the mummy with a tongue to be used with tongue and groove construction. The same section also included a board that had a routed edge and another, below the object, that had a drill hole made with a hand drill [**WS 5.18**]. Empty drill holes, including one with the impression of a screw head were seen in another axial section [**WS 5.19**]. Eliminating superimposition viewed the CR images provided clarification of a square shape that possibly extending into the skull. The axial section revealed not only that the square-shaped block was under the skull, but also enclosed in wrapping that continues over the head. In addition, under the square-shaped block was a board with surface that appeared milled and served only to raise the block [**WS 5.20**]. The same section afforded information regarding the construction of the mummy, such as the skull filled with excelsior, also known as wood wool. In the region of the abdomen, a magnified portion of another axial reconstruction afforded a more characteristic image of the fine wood shavings [**WS 5.21**]. That material, produced by a device termed a slivering machine dating back to the early 1800s, was used to stuff mattresses, in taxidermy and the filling for toy animals, such as teddy bears.

A clay or plastic-like material covered most of the skull and extended over the board behind the skull. In order to demonstrate the possible applications of MDCT software, a Region-Of-Interest, ROI, value was acquired to quantify the density of the material covering the right posterior region of the skull **[WS 5.22]**. The mean value, 815 HU, Hounsfield Units, had a density similar to bone, however, to draw any conclusions from the density value, many more ROIs would be needed from this object and also from samples of clay and plaster dating to the same period. Moving inferiorly into lower portion of the head with the shoulders beginning to appear, the square-shaped block was no longer present, however, a rounded pole-like wooden support next to a smaller rectangular shaped piece of wood was seen surrounded by excelsior. The head was supported to two boards screwed together and partially covered by the clay/plaster-like material **[WS 5.23]**.

Continuing into the upper chest region, the two supports from the head were still visible along with a dowel in each arm as framing material. What appeared to be some type of fabric enclosed the chest filled that was stuffed with excelsior and continued around the back of the mummy formed by a board with a tongue edge. Over the anterior surface of the mummy, form was provided with the clay/plaster-like substance covered with a layer of material **[WS 5.24]**. An axial image, near the base of the object demonstrated a warp and weft pattern of the material. By utilizing the measurement tool it was possible to calculate a thread count of 12 per in (30 per cm), suggesting the covering was a course material, such as burlap. The identical pattern was also observed in a coronal reconstruction in the abdominal region **[WS 5.25]**.

Utilizing multiple planes provided an explanation for the particular appearance of structures or objects. An example was two screws noted in the lower pelvic region. On the AP CR image the screws appeared parallel to the imaging plane at the end of a board **[WS 5.26A]**. The axial section only provided an image of the screws in cross section **[WS 5.26B]**. However, a coronal image through the level of the board containing the screws demonstrated, not only the position of the fasteners, but also the grain of the wood, including a knot, and the relative location of the other fasteners seen on the AP radiograph **[WS 5.26C–D]**. Because of the location of the two screws, it appeared that neither were used as fasteners in the construction of Gretchen and were probably already in the wood when the mummy was put together. From the coronal section, botanists at the Smithsonian, who later reviewed the images, suggested the wood was pine.

With the data collection protocol set to create isotropic voxels (see CT Chapter 7 in *Advances in Paleoimaging*), the MDCT system will permit high-resolution images in virtually any plane. For example, a structure or object only partially visualized in the commonly employed planes, axial, coronal and sagittal, an oblique section can provide valuable information. In assessing the construction techniques used to produce Gretchen, an oblique section positioned along the long axis of a fastener provided helpful insights. An axial section was employed to determine the position and angle of the oblique reconstruction through the long axis of the fastener. The resulting image demonstrated the screws were used to connect supports to the based running along the side of the mummy **[WS 5.27]**.

A common feature seen in the Giantess and Gretchen was a window cut into the chest region with ribs exposed. Because only plane radiographs were acquired of the Giantess, it was not possible to confirm it actual ribs were incorporated into the construction. An axial section of Gretchen revealed the unequivocal presence of ribs imbedded into the clay/plaster-like material **[WS 5.28]**.

Once the study was completed and the scan data reviewed, a series of images were sent to the Smithsonian Institution for assistance in analysis of the materials used in construction. As indicated above, a botanist identified the wood as pine and might include a piece or two of oak. An individual, familiar with hardware, thought the screws indicated a time period after 1900 and more like post 1920s, depending on the pitch and type of head manufacturing method, such as filed or machine made slot in the head. From the reconstructions, several types of screws were identified, such as tapered and un-tapered shank wood screws **[WS 5.29]**, but a more detailed identification was not possible from the images alone.

Significance

The opportunity to examine the Giantess on two separate occasions using two types of film, conventional radiographic and Polaroid, in additional to Fuji CR plates, provided a rare comparison of the recording media. The least acceptable radiographs resulted from the conventional radiographic film that lacked the latitude to demonstrate low-density structures, such as the covering material. With wider latitude, the Polaroid film provided more information, however, the small format required 20 exposures to cover the same area that would have been visualized with four 14×17-inch (36×43 cm) cassettes. In addition, the more frequent exchange of exposed and unexposed plate resulted in slightly moving the object and eliminating the ability to stitch the last five images with the previous 15 radiographs. By far the best results were obtained using the Fuji CR plates with the ability to apply a wide range of industrial algorithms in order to acquire the optimal results. However, only the video-endoscopy was capable of visualizing the excelsior stuffing material.

Due to superimposition, none of the plane radiographic recording medias could reveal details regarding the board framing, such as routed edges or empty screw holes, visualized on the MDCT scans. The multiplanar images clearly demonstrated the excelsior stuffing along with the warp and weft of the covering material. Applications, such as the measurement tool and the ability to acquire quantitative density values in Hounsfield Units also provided valuable insights without the need to open up the object.

Finally because of the co-operation of the team at the Oregon State University College of Veterinary Medicine, it was possible to compare two different algorithms in order to determine which provided the highest resolution. The only method to determine the optimal protocol is to change only one of the factors at a time and compare the resulting images. The algorithm selected processes the acquired raw data with varying degrees of either edge enhancement or smoothing depending on the region of the body under examination. This equipment was developed for clinical use on live patients with hydrated organs. Therefore, a logical choice for an algorithm to scan the body of a mummy would be a body algorithm or filter convolution, FC, for example FC12. However, a body scan on a patient would automatically apply smoothing to the edges of structures, such as the liver. With the Toshiba™ *Aquilion* Unit, the algorithm with the highest degree of edge enhancement is FC81 intended for scans of the temporal bone, location of the auditory ossicles. Without knowing the effects of each algorithm on edge enhancement, there would be little chance of selecting FC81 to scan an object other than the temporal bone of a patient. However, a comparison of images processed with FC12 and F81 leave little doubt regarding which should be selected for a non-patient scan **[WS 5.30]**.

With the discussion regarding the Giantess and Gretchen completed, it is time to return to the Dime Museum in Baltimore for more of Dick Horne's insights into the creation of gaffs. Radiographic interpretation is based on the recognition and identification of shapes and an understanding of object densities relative to X-ray attenuation. With the two sideshow mummies previously considered, it was fairly easy to recognize fasteners, such as screws and nails. However, for more sophisticated objects, observing Dick actually create a gaff and X-raying other items in the Dime Museum collection, provided a greater understanding of what was viewed on a radiograph.

For the Nation Geographic Channel episode, Dick went to his workshop on the second floor of the Museum. He began with the head of a mannequin he found in a garbage dumpster and estimated it probably dated to the 1930s. Inside the head he found old newspapers, which he did not remove because he felt it would confuse someone trying to determine when the completed object was made. His plan was to transform the mannequin into the head of a mummy and place it into a little box that was on the shelf above his workbench. He explained the box was originally a doll's truck and would add a degree of "creepiness" to the final creation. His first step was to smash out the mannequin's eyes and make it more into a "skull-like shape". As Dick worked, he pointed out, that to be successful, each object must have a fantastic or elaborate story with a touch of credibility associated with it. He mentioned that, in the nineteenth century, tourists actually purchased parts of mummies, such as hands and heads, as souvenirs. While providing a bit of historical background, Dick was building up the facial features with a putty he identified as *rock hard*. He indicated it was commonly used in to early part of the twentieth century and may have been what formed the face of the Giantess. He also confessed that his motivation was to make something good enough that people will look at it and say it's real and good enough to fool someone 100 years from now. The completed mummy head was radiographed on Polaroid photographic film before it was placed in the box and the finishing touches achieved. On superficial examination, the head appeared convincingly good, however the lateral image was obviously not a real skull **[WS 5.31]**.

Several years prior to meeting Dick, a private collector contacted the Bioanthropology Research Institute requesting radiographs of two objects he had purchased to confirm the authenticity. Both were supposed to be mummified skull: one Egyptian; and the other a *trophy*. The 1950s vintage Picker™ Army Field unit X-ray source, a Polaroid processing system recovered from Thomas Jefferson University Hospital in the 1980s and two par-speed 14×17-inch (36×43 cm) radiographic cassettes loaded with film were transported to the collector's private residence. Neither object could be removed from the case they were sealed within. The first was described as an Egyptian mummified skull with a heavy glass pyramid case.

Because there was little space in the house to carry out the examination, it was decided to conduct the study on the stairs **[WS 5.32]**. The latter offered several advantages. Employing a horizontal beam, the stairs provided a means to readily attaint the correct height and support for the image receptor. In addition, behind the stairway was a closet filled with material to absorb any scatter radiation. Two milk crates were placed on the floor and a 1 × 12-inch (2.5 × 30 cm) shelf on top of the containers. The heavy glass pyramid was positioned on the shelf and the Polaroid cassette on the step behind the pyramid. To insure the cassette was perpendicular, an empty cardboard box was placed behind the cassette.

The AP and lateral projections revealed large frontal sinuses, proving without a doubt, the skull was genuine, but could not verify if it was ancient Egyptian [**WS 5.33**]. The other object was accompanied by an elaborate story describing the origins of this trophy skull. With the technical factors established with the Polaroid film, the two conventional radiographic cassettes were used to acquire the AP and lateral images. Once the films were exposed, the cassettes were taken to a local chiropractors office and processed. The X-rays revealed an object similar to what was seen in the Dime Museum years later [**WS 5.34**]. Back at Quinnipiac, a plastic skull model was obtained from a local hobby shop and a lateral radiograph was taken on Polaroid film. The resulting image revealed the plastic skull was less dense than the material used in the construction of the mannequin head seen in Baltimore [**WS 5.35**]. Having paid a great deal of money for what turned out to be a fake, the collector was certainly unhappy with the results.

Before finally leaving the Dime Museum, one last technique employed by Dick must be considered and will lead the discussion to the next topic. He mentioned the artisans creating the objects also employed techniques utilized in taxidermy. A favorite subject for gaffs, mermaids were even advertised as an item in the Nelson Supply House catalogue [**WS 5.36**]. In 1843, P.T. Barnum entered into an agreement with the owner of the Fejee Mermaid and manipulated the publicity surrounding the object before finally exhibiting it (Dennett, 1997). It created such excitement that crowds came to view the object that, according to Dennett, was so cleverly manufactured it was difficult to believe it was not real. Today, in the Barnum Museum in Bridgeport, Connecticut, a Fiji Mermaid, created for a 1986 made-for-TV movie titled *Barnum!* staring Burt Lancaster can be seen and was radiographed [**WS 5.37**]. Dick crafted a very realistic looking mermaid and sealed it within a glass bell jar. The sealed container, made it more difficult to closely examine the object, a principle requirement for successful gaffs like the mummified skull owned by the private collector. Radiographs of the object revealed it was fashioned from two preserved specimens: what appears to be the head and chest of a primate and the lower portion of a fish [**WS 5.38**]. Dick's use of preserved material also brought to mind his previous comment that the artisans at the Nelson Supply House were familiar with taxidermy techniques.

A Penis—Real or Fake

In the summer of 2011, Brooke Sabonis, from Left Field Picture, a New York based production company, called and asked if it was possible to use X-ray to determine if a mummified penis was real. She explained that the study would be included in an episode of the third season of the series, *Oddities*, on the Science Channel. The documentary/reality style program followed the day-to day operation of the unique shop, *Obscura Antiques and Oddities*, in the East Village of New York City. The backstory for this segment, a customer came into the shop, with, what he claimed was a mummified penis mounted on a wooden display stand. The owners of the shop, Mike Zohn and Evan Michelson, wanted to know if the object was genuine before paying the thousands of dollars requested to purchase the object.

Although the objective was quite simple, a single axial section acquired with multi-detector computed tomography, MDCT, would answer the question but not meet the requirements of the program. Not all imaging studies may be intended for a scientific publication, but rather to serve both an educational and entertaining presentations. Although virtually all the episodes of the *Mummy Road Show* were transformed into scientific publications or presentations at academic meetings, the findings of the *Oddities* study were more for dramatic effect. Therefore, a 3D reconstruction that could be rotated and virtually sectioned would provide the best imaging approach.

Fortunately, the Bioanthropology Research Institute had previously scanned a male mummy that had been exhibited in the sideshow circuit during the early twentieth century. The penis, in cross-section, even mummified, has a very characteristic appearance: two rounded side-by-side structures, the corpora cavernosa, and a single, less rounded opening below, the corpus spongiosum [**WS 5.39**].

The object brought from New York had a very unusual appearance. Approximately 8-inches (20 cm) long, the head rested on the wooden base and the distal end supported by a supposed pair of testicles. The location where the organ had been supposedly cut from the body was covered over in what appeared an unrealistic manner. There was little confidence from an external examination that this had been removed from a mummified individual. The object was scanned with the Toshiba™ Aquilion 64-slice unit and went directly to the 3D reconstruction using a color pallet that had been developed for mummified remains (see Case Study 4: Mummified Remains). The resulting data set was saved as an apparent movie or *cine* with 72 images that rotated 360° [**WS 5.40**]. After the rotational presentation, the rotation was stopped and an axial section acquire posterior to the supposed testicles, revealing a hollow tube [**WS 5.41**]. The procedure was repeated with a virtual sagittal sectioning of the object again demonstrating a hollow tubular structure and similarly designed testicles [**WS 5.42**]. In additional, the purported location where the organ had been cut from the body appeared to have been formed as part of the entire cylindrical object. Therefore, without a doubt the object was a fake. However, it constituted several minutes of the final version of the episode meeting both the radiographic and entertainment requirements.

Almost to the day, one year latter Brooke called back with another penis. The situation was basically identical except this was now season four of the program. The team, including the shop owners Mike and Evan, returned to the Quinnipiac campus. However, the object looked quite different with an apparent cut surface and not mounted on a wooden stand.

Once again the images acquired from the actual mummy were recalled, including the 3D reconstructions. The 3D sagittal image of the pelvic region demonstrated a small flaccid penis above the testicles [**WS 5.43**]. On the 0.5 mm thick sagittal reformate through the penis and testicles, not only were those structures revealed but also the position of the genitalia relative to the pubis and the remaining prepuce on the penis [**WS 5.44**]. With a similar rational to the study one year earlier, the acquired data from the object in question was immediately processed as a 3D reconstruction. The resulting images were strikingly similar to those acquired from the intact mummified male [**WS 5.45**]. However, there was one major difference, on the intact mummy the prepuce was present, but on the object brought for evaluation, the glans penis was visualized suggesting circumcision. Of course the confirmation that this was a real excised specimen was made from the axial reformate. The image demonstrated the very characteristic pair of corpora cavernosa and a small, barely discernable, but still present, corpus spongiosum [**WS 5.46**]. Also noted on the section was a clearly defined testicle.

Significance

Similar to the program that aired the previous year, the imaging study, particularly the 3D reconstruction, was allowed several minutes of the final running time of the episode. From the academic prospective, both studies have been used in discussions of applying MDCT to determine if object were real or fake, but little else was done with the data. The production company was viewed as a client rather than a patient. Instead of making the diagnosis, the radiographer, taking into account the imaging objectives of the client, determined the optimal imaging approach. Although there was no charge for either study, a cost could have been determined and requested for the service.

Taxidermy—What Is Inside? Determine the Internal Construction

As part of an imaging project with the Barnum Museum in Bridgeport, Connecticut, in 2014 two taxidermy mounts provided an opportunity to examine the preparation methods. The first animal was a two-headed calf enclosed in a clear acrylic case [**WS 5.47**]. The mount was originally part of a traveling museum owned by a father and daughter team dating back to the 1940s. According to Adrienne Saint Pierre, Curator at the Barnum Museum, the calf was in their possession in 1951 because there was a telegram offering to purchase it that year.

The imaging approach is considered in more detail in Case Study 1: Large Objects, however a brief description will be given here. After a visual inspection of the calf, it was determined the most information with the least disturbance to the object would be provided by a lateral project. Instead of acquiring a series of radiographs, moving the central portion of the X-ray beam to the center of each image receptor, a sufficiently long SID would enable the beam to cover the entire animal. Consequently, if neither the X-ray source nor the object is moved between exposures, the resulting radiographs could be stitched together. The latter would be facilitated by using a CR system, providing digital images, in place of film that would require the additional step of digitization. As noted from the CR images of the Giantess and Gretchen, the digital image receptor also rendered wider latitude images.

A frame, constructed from PVC pipe and aluminum channeling to hold the imaging plates, IP, was developed and built by Bob Lombardo [**WS 5.48**]. The mount was elevated by creating first a platform using a wooden pallet on top of which two 3 × 3-inch (8 × 8 cm) PVC columns were placed. Finally, the mount was placed on the PVC columns [**WS 5.49**]. With a 144-inch (366 cm) SID, the X-ray beam produced by the Kubtec™ 100HF was sufficiently large enough to cover the entire mount. By placing the central portion of the beam at a level below the feet of the animal, the mount was projected up onto the imaging plates [**WS 5.50**]. With two CR plates available, it was possible to expose both plates with a single exposure [**WS 5.51**]. In all, a total of 12-plates were necessary to image the calf **[WS 5.52]**. On gross inspection of the assembled radiographs, the extensive use of wire-framing material was noted. On close observation, it was revealed that the animal was skinned down to tarsal joints on the hind legs and to the carpal joints on the fore legs **[WS 5.53]**. Above those joints, no bones appeared to be present with the exception of the skull seen in one of the heads **[WS 5.54]**. The muzzles of both heads were covered with a dense material similar to that seen with the Giantess, Gretchen and the mummified head created by Dick Horne.

Artistic Creations: How Were They Made?

Severed Chinese Heads

Many of the objects in the Dime Museum were intended as gaffs to fool visitors; however, other objects have been created not necessarily meant to deceive, but to look extremely realistic. Some of these creations were so well conceived that they defy an explanation for the method of construction. Two of these objects, *severed Chinese heads*, provided an excellent example. The first was in the collection of the Mütter Museum at the College of Physicians in Philadelphia. Museum records indicated the object was donated by Dr. Charles Hart in 1896. He claimed the extremely realistic head was produced by a Japanese artisan as a trophy head, probably for the First Sino-Japanese War (1894–1895). In 1995 Gretchen Warden, Director of the Museum, requested a radiographic examination in the hope that the images would reveal the techniques employed to create the head.

A visual examination of the head, resting on a wooden disk, appeared to substantiate the description provided by Dr. Hart. If it did represent a Chinese prisoner, the seized individual might have been wounded during capture or tortured prior to execution, accounting for the *gash* on the left check. The attempt to promote the level of realism was noted by individual hairs forming the eyebrows and several hairs emerging from the mole adjacent to the right lip **[WS 5.55]**. The process of beheading often required more than one blow to complete the act. A deep cut on the posterior aspect of the neck suggested an initial attempt. However, the severed surface of the neck had a more stylized appearance and several inaccuracies **[WS 5.56]**. The exposed muscles in the neck were completely misrepresented, displaying more of a swirling, instead of a cut surface. Although the head looked to have been severed at the level of the mid-cervical spine, the vertebrae noted in cross-section lacks transverse foramen, suggesting a thoracic spine. However, more significantly, the opening in the vertebrae to accommodate the spinal cord, the vertebral foramen, was not even present. Similarly, the cross section of the trachea demonstrated the level where the airway bifurcates or splits into right and left main-stem bronchi, an anatomic feature seen at the level of the 6th or 7th thoracic vertebrae certainly not in the neck.

Two vessels were present on either side of the trachea but inaccurately represented. First, the vessels were colored red and blue representing the carotid artery and the jugular vein; in reality tissues do not appear differentially colored as such. Although anatomical models use red to indicate oxygenated blood carried in arteries and blue for deoxygenated blood carried in veins. Second, the position of the vessels were anatomically reversed, the artery should have been medially located with the vein laterally positioned. Finally, both vessels appeared to have thickened, muscular walls, whereas only the arteries are thick walled; veins are thin walled. In fact, the severed veins should have been made as collapsed and not easily discernible and the cut carotid arteries should have been retracted from view.

In order to establish the technical factors, the initial lateral projection was taken using the medical Polaroid imaging system and the Picker™ Army Field Unit set at a 40-inch (100 cm) SID; 50 kVp, 10 mA, and 0.5 seconds **[WS 5.57]**. Once it was determined the exposure factors were satisfactory, lateral and frontal or AP projections were acquired and processed back at Thomas Jefferson University Radiologic Technology program laboratory. The lateral radiograph revealed a seam dividing the head into front and back sections. The eye and mouthpiece containing the teeth appeared to have been inserted into the back of the front piece. Similarly, rectangular blocks contain each ear were inserted into each side of the posterior section. A third section, the base of the neck, appeared to fit into the joined front and back sections **[WS 5.58]**.

Fortunately Gretchen located another severed Chinese head in the holdings of a private collector, the same individual who had the previously discussed mummified Egyptian skull in the glass pyramid. The second severed head was very similar to the one at the Mütter with incredible detail **[WS 5.59]**. However, there were differences: the moles were on opposite sides of the lips; there was a larger wound near the right temple region compared to a gash in the left cheek; and the eyelids were almost closed **[WS 5.60]**. The other major difference between the two objects, consisted of the one in the private collection having some superficial damage **[WS 5.61]**. The most identical feature was the base of the neck **[WS 5.62]**.

As with the mummified head within the glass pyramid, the Picker™ Army Field Unit was employed as the X-ray source. Instead of utilizing the stairs, as was the case in the previous study, an X-ray table was constructed by resting a 1 × 12 inch (2.5 × 30 cm) board across two milk crates. Images were recorded on 14×17-inch (36×43 cm) par speed cassettes brought for the study [**WS 5.63**]. Four projections, a lateral, AP, oblique and, as termed in the clinical radiography, a reverse Water's or occipitomental view were acquired. In the clinical setting, the latter provided better visualization of facial bones and sinuses, but in this situation, it provided a better perspective of the mouth insert. As with the external appearance, there were internal similarities and differences. The lateral radiograph revealed a seam between the front and back halves with an inserted base. In addition, the margins of the wig and ear inserts were seen [**WS 5.64A**]. However, the eye inserted had a different appearance on the lateral radiograph and on the AP projection, were less dense [**WS 5.64B**]. There was also a very dense rectangular shaped structure noted on both projects that seemed to be more associated with the front half on the lateral and in a midline position on the AP projection. The two additional radiographic projections not taken at the Mütter Museum were the oblique and reverse occipitomental views. These were added to the series in order to provide additional information not available from the first two views and a common procedure in the clinical setting for complex structures such as the skull. Today, plane skull radiography has been replaced by computed tomography, and few radiographs trained in the past decade are familiar with the addition projections. Both projections demonstrated much smaller less radiopaque eye inserts and provided the best unobstructed view of the mouth insert. In the base of the neck, the two depressions that formed the bifurcated trachea appeared to be shorter and possibly not separated at the apex as noted in the Mütter object. Finally, unfortunately due to the lack of latitude of the image receptor system, no definitive attachments were seen to be associated with the dense rectangular shaped object [**WS 5.65**].

Significance

Having more than one severed Chinese head to examine provided a unique opportunity to compare the construction techniques employed for both objects. With a narrow latitude, the film recording media offered visualization of larger components, such as the three pieces that formed the object and the inserts for the eyes, ears, nares and mouth. However, the more subtle features, such as the function of the dense rectangular structure seen within the head owned by the private collector, were more elusive. The two additional, non-orthogonal projections included in the second study, provided additional information regarding the eyes and mouth inserts but failed to elucidate the role of the dense rectangular shape.

Digital radiography, not available at the time of either study, with the wide latitude previously discussed, would have provided more information regarding the internal construction. Certainly, computed tomography would furnish the most precise representation and specific orientation of all the components.

Seated Buddha: How Was It Made and What Is Inside?

Carol Snow, Deputy Chief Conservator at the Yale Art Gallery had two primary questions she hoped could be addressed using MDCT to *look inside* a 9 $^{7}/_{8}$ -inch (25.1 cm) high, gilt wood seated Buddha: first, could the advanced imaging modality detect and identify the possible contents hidden inside the object; and second, could computed tomography provide "addition information on the carving and other fabrication techniques" (Snow, 18 April 2017).

The object came into the University's collection in 1957 and visual inspection dated it to the Japanese, Edo period (1615–1868). Radiocarbon analysis of a wood sample by the University of Arizona provided two time frames 1447AD to 1522AD or 1590AD to 1623AD, but Carol felt it probably dated closer to 1615. She stated, "these Buddhas were typically carved from pieces of wood jointed together with hollow interiors and then carved". Offerings, such as scraps of paper with inscriptions, fabric scraps, false organs, or a whole range of other materials, were occasionally found inside. In requesting the CT examination, she accurately pointed out that the CT study would "show the bundle more clearly than x-radiographs". Referring back to the studies of the severed Chinese heads, the plane radiographs were incapable of elucidating the steps or methods employed in construction.

The following protocol was set for Toshiba™ Aquilion 64-slice unit: 0.5 mm thick sections; 64 slices per rotation; one complete rotation in 0.5 seconds; 100 kV; 150 mA; helical pitch (HP) of 41 or pitch factor (PF) of 0.641; 240 mm Scanning Field of View (SFOV); and processed by an algorithm or filter convolution (FC) that provided the highest level of edge enhancement, FC81. In order to enhance the 3D reformates from the volume reconstructions, the 0.5 mm sections were stacked at 0.3 mm intervals, creating an overlapping of slices. The second, easier question to address was the delineation of the components that comprise the Buddha simply by using multi-planar reformates. Coronal and sagittal reconstructions demonstrated the two-piece head and neck were fit into the upper portion of the body and the presence of an unexplained more radiopaque wedge-shaped object **[WS 5.66]**. Because both the lower and higher density structures did not entirely exist in the standard planes, axial, coronal and sagittal, oblique sectioning was employed for better visualization. An oblique reformat was directed along the long axis of the block-shaped structure that appeared to be posterior to the eye inserts **[WS 5.67A]**. The resulting reconstruction revealed a curve anterior surface of the structure pressing against the eye inserts **[WS 5.67B]**. The higher density structures seemed to be fixing the position of the lower density object, however, none of the former were in the imaging plane. In addition, the 0.5 mm thick slice was too thin to clearly demonstrate the relationship of all the structures posterior to the eye inserts.

By expanding the sagittal and coronal section thicknesses from 0.5 to 20 mm, a more thorough understanding of the inter-relationship of all the components within the head was clarified **[WS 5.68]**. It appeared the function of the wooden block, posterior to the eye insert, was to maintain the position of the latter. The five long wedge-shaped objects appeared to hold the wood block in place. However, an oblique section along the long axis of each wedge-shaped fastener was necessary to completely document their contribution to the complex of objects within the head. Five oblique reformats following the path of each wedge confirmed the wedges were fasteners driven into the wooden front piece to hold the block behind the eye inserts in place **[WS 5.69]**. Four of the five wedges were confirmed to function as fasteners, but the oblique reconstruction of the fifth wedges demonstrated it's tip was not embedded in any wood **[WS 5.70]**. This finding also suggested that the first wedge-shaped, noted in the coronal section **[see WS 5.66A]**, was loose in the head-neck space.

The relationship between the structures within the head were clearly demonstrated by the multi-planar reformats including oblique sections, but more perfectly suited to this situation was the ability of MDCT to create 3D reconstruction and the associated applications used to enhance the final images. A more complete discussion of the process to be described is presented in the Chapter 7: Computed Tomography (see Figure 7.119). Once the color 3D algorithms, monochromatic lung and multi-colored organ, were selected and combined, the next step was to eliminate the overlying structures. A process, termed *clipping*, was applied first to a coronal reformat **[WS 5.71A]** and then to the sagittal reconstruction **[WS 5.71B]**. Clipping permits areas parallel to coronal, sagittal or axial planes to be removed from the 3D reconstruction data set. The resulting 3D reconstruction clearly demonstrated the relationship of the structures within the head **[WS 5.72]**.

The body and base appeared to have been constructed of multiple pieces of wood and required numerous sagittal and axial sections to document all the components and reveal the spaces within the statue. The complete series of images will not be presented here, however a few representative views will be used to convey the process. A sagittal section through the right side of the statue showed a front and back pieces and a small chamber. In addition, the gilt covering created a linear artifact that could have been confused as a seam **[WS 5.73 and 5.74]**. An unusual honeycomb pattern was noted in the front section of the base of the statue **[WS 5.74 and 5.75]**.

Since the thick base was parallel to the surface of the MDCT table, axial reconstructions were most helpful in understanding the construction. The same honeycomb pattern previously noted was also seen in several axial sections **[WS 5.76]**. A final axial reconstruction through the recess in the base revealed it was composed of numerous pieces of wood covered by a dense, radiopaque gilt layer **[WS 5.77]**.

Following a review of the MDCT images, Carol indicated a borescope examination of the interior of the statue was completed. The direct visualization of the honeycomb pattern revealed it was most likely due to insect activity **[WS 5.78]**. However, this last procedure confirmed that other than the remnants of insect activity, no other objects were hidden within the statue.

Significance

There were no plane radiographs of the seated Buddha statue; none were required. The question of how it was constructed and was there anything hidden inside eliminated the intermediate step and moved directly to an MDCT study. Although the conventional multiplanar reconstructions provided a majority to the information regarding construction techniques, the oblique reformats addressed the specific details regarding the relationship between elements found within the head. The borescope provided direct visualization into the hollow spaces within the statue and confirmed the presence of structures revealed by the MDCT.

Time Capsule: What Is Inside?

Hurricane or *Superstorm* Sandy cut a path of destruction through Connecticut on 29 October 2012. Among the many trees toppled or uprooted by the storm was a 60–70 foot oak located on the New Haven Green. During the initial stages of the cleanup, the following day, two

Figure 5.3. The stone monument found on the ground next to the toppled tree.

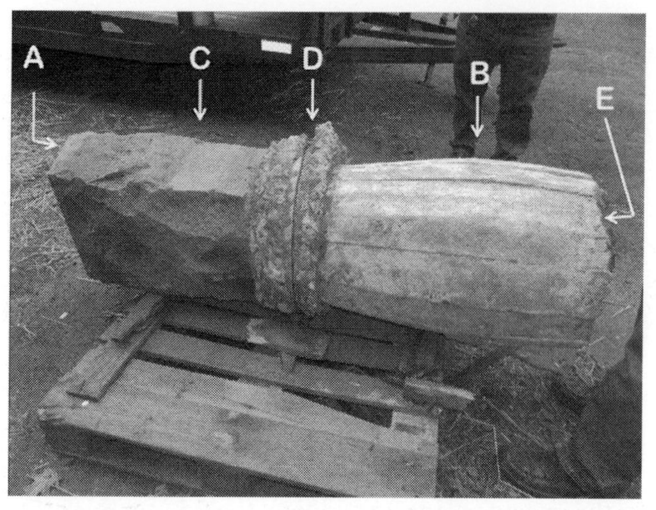

Figure 5.4. The stone monument/concrete complex: (A) the face of the marker with the inscription; (B) concrete filled barrel with the impressions of the staves still visible; (C) the stone monument was inserted into the top of the barrel; (D) the concrete displaced by the stone formed the mushroom-like collar; (E) the base of the concrete.

unusual findings related to that particular tree became the focus of attention. The first, on the ground next to the tree was a stone monument inscribed (Figure 5.3):

Although the inscribed monument had been visible on the surface of the ground on the Green, the barrel shaped base that secured it in place below the surface, had vanished from memory. The other, more startling discovery was a human skull nestled within the root ball of the tree. The New Haven Green, like many other village commons, had served, for a time, as a burial ground and between 1638 until the later 1790s as many as 10,000 individuals had been interred there.

A team from the Office of the Chief Medical Examiner for the State of Connecticut, OCME, was sent from Farmington, Connecticut to recover the skeletal remains and transport them back to office. Due to the fragmented nature of the bones, they were not radiographed at the OCME facility, but transported to the Yale University Biological Anthropology Laboratory back in New Haven. Gary Aronsen, a bioarchaeologist and supervisor of the Yale laboratory along with Nick Bellantoni, the Connecticut State Archaeologist, had continued to excavate at the base of the uprooted tree and recovered the bone of five other individuals. Eventually, all the bone fragments were brought to the Diagnostic Imaging Program Laboratory at Quinnipiac University for plane radiography and MDCT studies (Pelletier et al, 2013). During this period, little attention had been paid to the Lincoln monument.

In April, 2013, Nick contacted the Bioanthropology Research Institute to explore the idea of searching for a time capsule that might have been associated with the monument. After researching the origins of the monument in the New Haven library, Rob Greenburg, a local artist and historian, suspected a time capsule was entombed in the concrete attached to the base of the monument and Nick was hopefully optimistic. The tree was planted by veterans of the Grand Army of the Republic, GAR, on 9 April 1909 to commemorate the 44th anniversary of the surrender at Appomattox. Rob succeeded in convincing the New Haven Bomb Squad to acquire a digital image using a Golden™ X-Ray Unit. However, due to poor resolution resulting from the large focal, the image only suggested a *hollow core* inside the concrete block that now resided on a wooden pallet at the New Haven Park and Recreation's Office and Garage complex.

A visual inspection of the monument with attached concrete block suggested how it was constructed (Figure 5.4). It appeared a barrel had been placed into the hole and filled with concrete. The base of the stone monument was then lowered into the wet concrete, displacing a volume and creating mushroom-like collar that was below the surface of the ground. Over time, the wooden staves of the barrel deteriorated, leaving the distinct barrel stave pattern on the surface of the concrete. Bone fragments of a child were still imbedded in the base of the concrete suggested the hole for the monument extended directly into the child's grave (Figure 5.5).

If a time capsule was present, it would have been located within the barrel prior to pouring concrete. Based on that assumption, Ron Beckett drilled into the concrete in search of the hollow space suggested by the Bomb Squad radiograph. At a point that was estimated to be approximately the center of the barrel, Ron removed the drill and replaced it with a video

Figure 5.5. (A) Nick Bellantoni (on the left) and Ron Beckett (on the right) inspecting the base of the concrete. (B) A fragment of the bones (arrow) from a child imbedded in the cement.

Figure 5.6. (A) Ron drilling into the concrete base with the intention of hitting the *hollow core* suggested by the New Haven Bomb Squad image. (B) After drilling approximately half way into the structure, Ron took a look with the endoscope.

Figure 5.7. A captured frame of the video-endoscopy through the hole drilled into the concrete block.

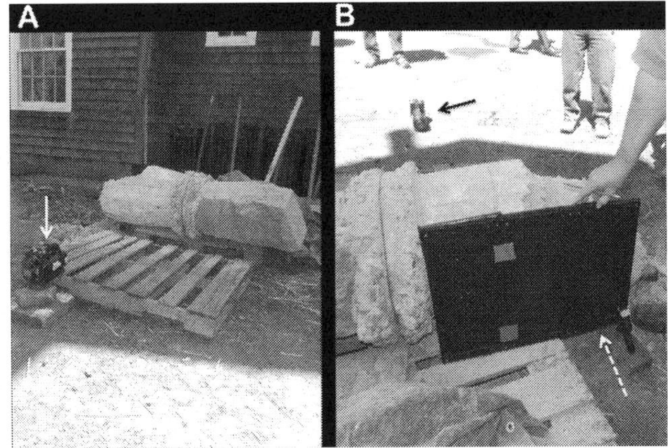

Figure 5.8. (A) The battery operated Golden XRS4 pulsed X-ray Unit (solid arrow) was positioned approximately ten feet (3 m) from the image receptor. (B) The top of the digital imaging plate (hashed arrow) was placed just below the portion of concrete that had mushroomed out of the barrel.

endoscope (Figure 5.6). While running the endoscope through the drilled hole (Figure 5.7), Ron saw something like the glint of metal, but was unsuccessful in discovering the space.

The next approach was to bring in first a concrete saw and then a power chisel in an attempt to locate the hollow core [**WS 5.84**]. After approximately three hours with little progress, it was decided more powerful equipment and possibly another image by the Bomb Squad was necessary. Two weeks lapsed before it was possible to reconvene all the interested parties and the Bomb Squad acquired another image with a battery operated Golden XRS4 pulsed X-ray source (Figure 5.8). One again, the radiograph suggested *something* was below the mushroom shaped extrusion of concrete above the top of the barrel-shaped mass. The new approach was to employ a large water-cooled saw to slice slabs from the bottom of the barrel and hopefully not cut into the something that was suggested on the Bomb Squad image [**WS 5.86**]. After several layers had been sliced off, concern grew that this less than delicate approach might slice through the capsule, if it occupied the suspected space. The final device brought to bear on the concrete block was a jackhammer. In the hands of a very skilled operator, within approximately 30 minutes, the corner of a copper cylinder emerged and a short time latter, the entire capsule was exposed (Figure 5.9). Once the time capsule was removed, to the surprise of everyone, part of another copper cylinder was revealed. Before the second object could be removed, the first cylinder was taken to the Quinnipiac Diagnostic Imaging Laboratory for radiography. At the University, a Kubtec™ XTEND 100HF portable X-ray unit and a Kubscan™ 3600 CR system

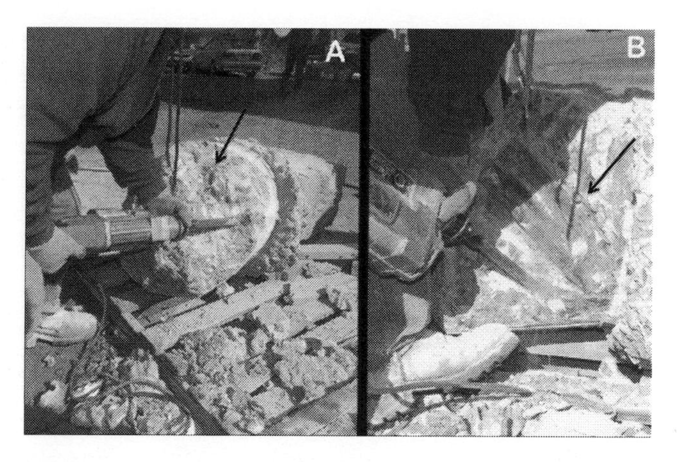

Figure 5.9. (A) Within approximately 30 minutes, in the skill hands very skilled individual, the jackhammer revealed the corner of a copper cylinder (arrow) became. (B) A short time later, the entire capsule (arrow) was exposed.

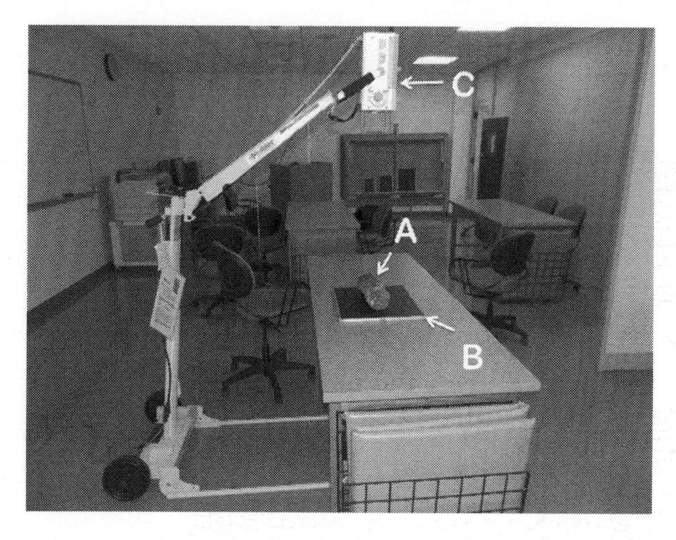

Figure 5.10. The time capsule (A) positioned for the first exposure on the Kubscan CR plate (B). The XTEND HF 100 portable X-ray source (C) was mounted on tube stand developed by Kubtec.

were employed to acquire three projections of the object (Figure 5.10): the first, with the cylinder placed on the side; the second, the objected rotated 90°; and the third, with the capsule resting on end. The first radiograph revealed a hole suggesting Ron had drilled through the time capsule. In addition, it provided information regarding the construction of the object: a seam indicating a sheet of copper rolled into a cylindrical shape; a crimped bottom; and a cap. Inside the cap was a dense circular shaped object (Figure 5.11A). On the second X-ray, the circular object maintained that shape, indicating it was probably rounded. Adjacent to it was an equally dense, irregularly shaped item (Figure 5.11B). The third projection proved most helpful, confirming the presence of the dense, round object while suggesting a more rectangular shape to the other radiopaque item. In addition, what appeared to be layers of rolled up material created a central empty space. With the exception of the two dense objects, within the cap, there did not appear to be any other radiopaque items in the capsule (Figure 5.11C).

By the time the images were completed on the first time capsule, the second cylinder had been removed and arrived at the University. The identical projects were acquired, but demonstrated a different pattern and location of radiopaque objects. The first radiograph revealed a container of similar construction with a cap, well defined seam and a crimped bottom that appeared somewhat dented. However, not only were the dense radiopaque items located at the bottom instead of the top of the container, but what appeared to be pins, staples and odd shape paper clips were scatter throughout the cylinder (Figure 5.12). On the second image, the dense objects had a flattened appearance and the other items, including the pins, staples and paper clips were all located below the cap (Figure 5.13). The final X-ray revealed what seemed to be points of a star on one of the flattened objects (Figure 5.14). In addition, the same layers of a rolled up pattern visualized in the first capsule were noted.

In an attempt to obtain higher resolution images, both time capsules were transported less then 20 miles to Kubtec Medical Imaging, then located in Milford, Connecticut. Three systems were available for the study beginning with the XPERT™ 80L cabinet equipped with a 17×17inch (43×43 cm) DR plate providing 48 μm resolution. The resulting radiographs had much higher resolution with sharper edges noticeable on the thinner items such as the paper clips, pins and staples then were visualized on the medical CR system (Figure 5.15). In addition, the position of one of the coin-like objects was now seen in the cap portion of the time capsule, demonstrating the possible consequence of transporting items.

For the next series of images the identical X-ray source employed at the Quinnipiac lab was used, but with a DR plate, a DIGIVIEW™ 395, composed of 100 μm pixels. Due to the inherent algorithm of the system processing the data, that radiographs had a wider latitude, demonstrating more shapes of gray than the two previous imaging systems described. This feature was most evident with the end-on projection of the second time capsule (Figure 5.16). Not only was the complete outline of the star pattern visualized, but also an object shaped like a stylized eagle was seen. By toggling between negative and positive images, the patterns became more discernable.

Finally, due to the metallic nature of the time capsules, a large custom-built industrial radiography cabinet was used. The unit was equipped with a 225 kVP

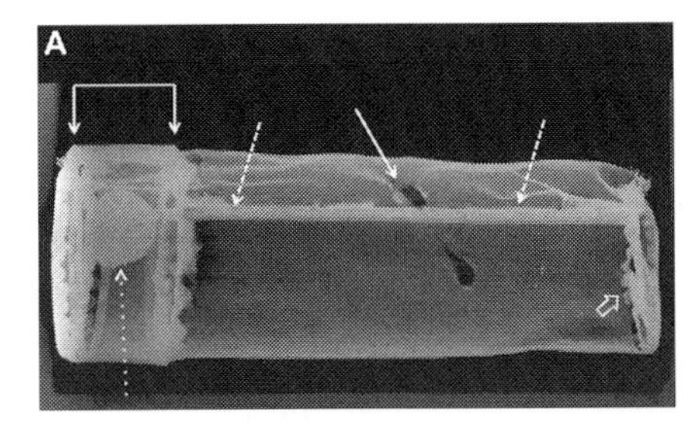

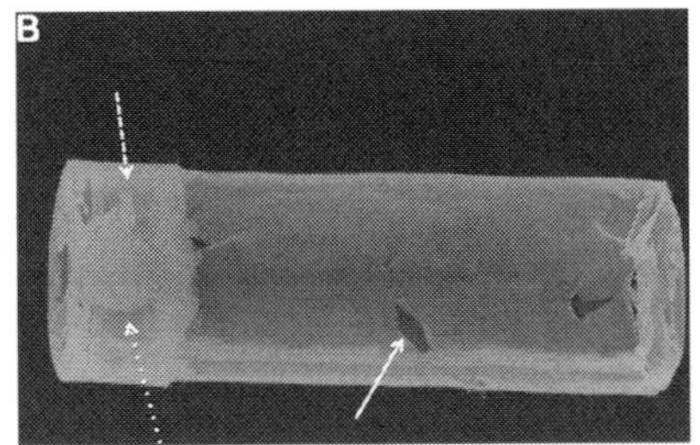

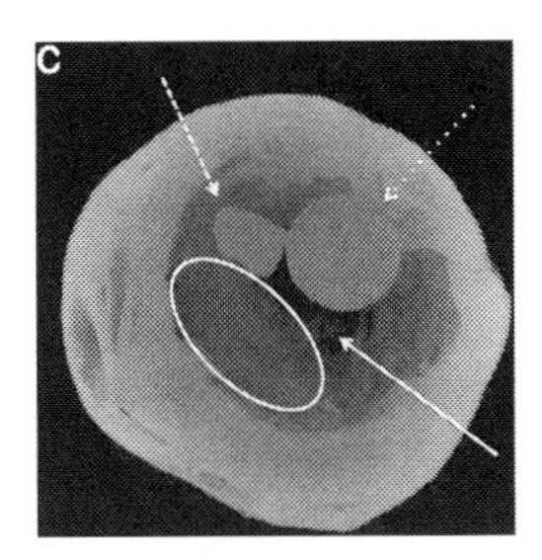

Figure 5.11. (A) The first image reveal a hole through the contained created by Ron's drilling on the first day (solid arrow). A number of other features regarding construction of the container were also demonstrated including the "cap" (two headed arrow), "crimping" to seal the bottom (open arrows), and a seam along the side (dashed arrow). Within the capsule there appeared to be a circular object (dotted arrow). (B) The second radiograph with the capsule rotated approximately 90°. The circular object (dotted arrow) visible on the first radiograph still appears rounded and another irregularly shaped object (dashed arrow) appeared to be located within the "cap" area of the capsule: Note the hole created by Ron (solid arrow). (C) The third radiograph was taken with the capsule on end. The rounded (dotted arrow) and irregularly shaped (dashed arrow) objects were still seen in this projection. There appeared to be material that was in layers (within the oval) and a radiolucent central area that suggest a space (solid arrow).

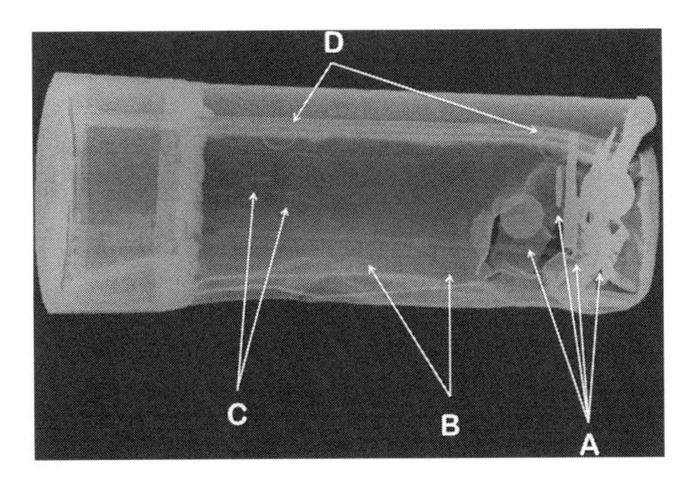

Figure 5.12. The first projection of the second capsule had radiopaque objected located in the bottom of the container (A). In addition, the appeared to be pins (B), staples (C) and odd shaped paper clips (D) throughout the length of the cylinder.

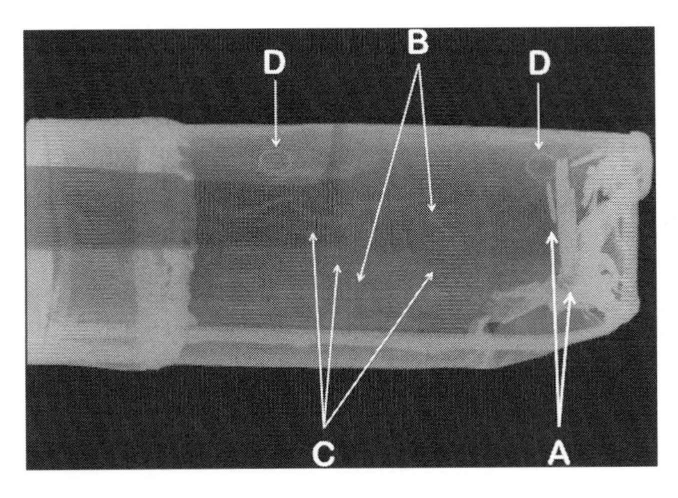

Figure 5.13. On the second projection, the objects at the bottom (A) of the container appeared flattened. All the other items including the pins (B), staples (C) and the paper clips (D) were all located below the cap.

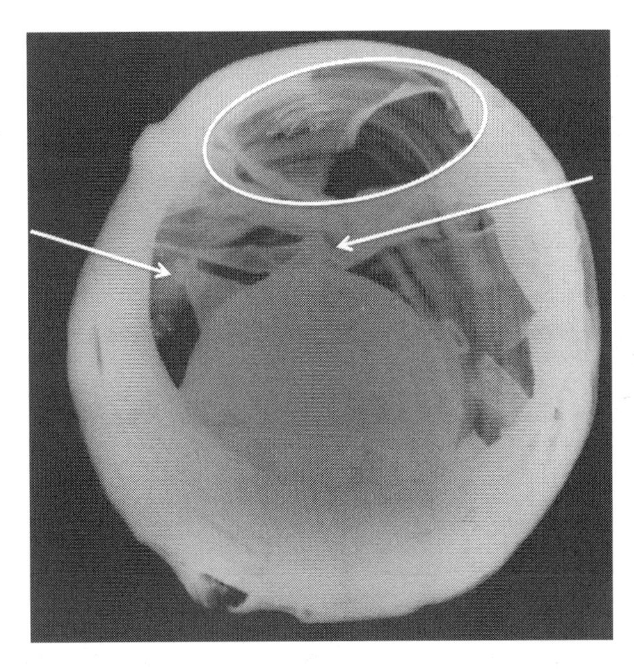

Figure 5.14. The end-on radiograph revealed a star-shaped object (arrows) among the coins and two points of a star.

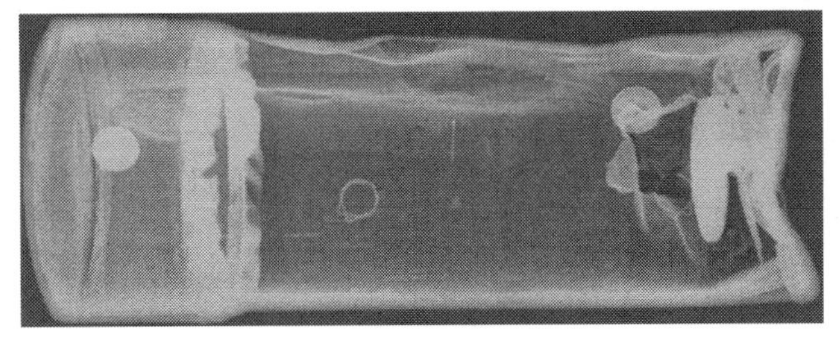

Figure 5.15. The cabinet system produced higher resolution images than were obtained with the CR images obtained at Quinnipiac. Note that transporting the container from the North Haven campus to Milford changed the position of the coins.

micro-focus X-ray source and a 17 × 17-inch (43 × 43 cm) DIGIVIEW™ 4020 detector with 200 μm pixels (Figure 5.17). All the images were acquired with 90 kVp, sufficient to penetrate the coins, and 20 μA. One of the radiographs clearly demonstrated the words "one dime" and a pattern that Nick Bellantoni recognized as a Barber dime (Figure 5.18). Charles E. Barber was the United States Bureau of the Mint Chief Engraver who designed a dime and quarter minted between 1892–1916 and half-dollars between 1892–1915.

Once all the images were analyzed, Nick began the slow process of opening each time capsule. The first cylinder revealed a collection of rolled up local newspapers (Figure 5.19). After a careful process of unrolling the over 109 year old contents, it was noted all the newspapers were dated 12 February to commemorate Lincoln's birthday **[WS 5.98]**. In all there were a total of nine newspapers enclosed in the two time capsules. Why so many newspapers? Nick reminded us that before radio, television and the internet, newspapers were the chroniclers of events. In the space created at the center of the roll of papers was an envelope that indicated the contents were grape shot and a deformed minié ball recovered from Gettysburg (Figure 5.20). The latter was termed *minié* or *minni* after Claude-Étienne Minié who developed the 0.58 caliber, conical, hollow based, muzzle-loading, spin-stabilized rifle bullet that caused devastating wound during the Civil War. Once out of the envelope, it was easy to match the two objects to what was visualized on the first end-on radiograph **[WS 5.99B]**.

Similarly, when Nick removed the contents of the second time capsule the items confirmed general

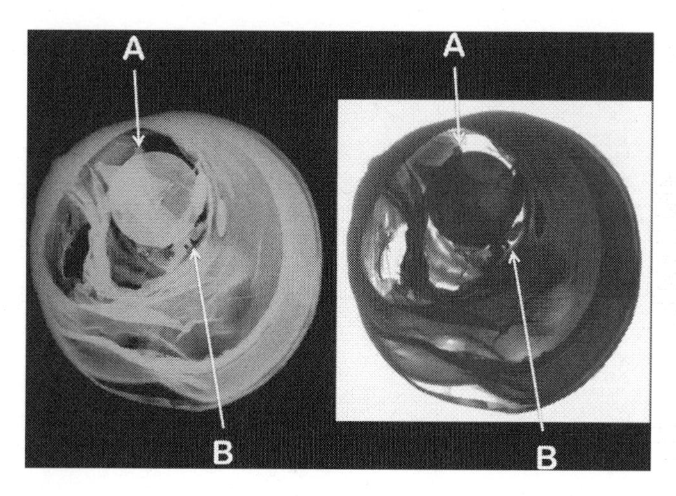

Figure 5.16. Negative and positive end-on projection of the second time capsule recorded with the DR plate. Not only is the "star" more clearly defined, bit the shape of what appears to be an eagle (B) is visible.

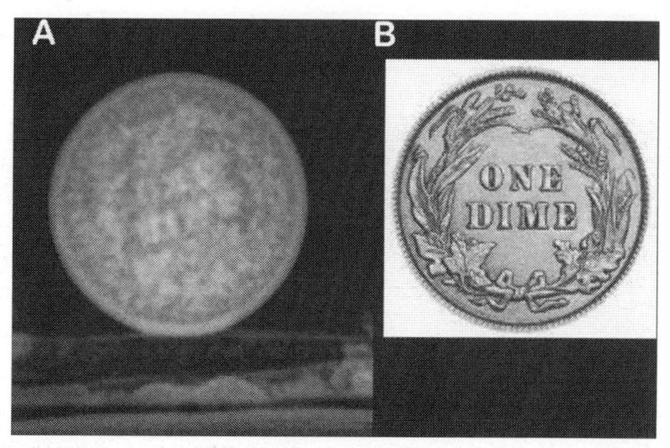

Figure 5.18. (A) The image acquired with the large industrial cabinet provided the penetration necessary to demonstrate the pattern on one of the coins in the second capsule. (B) The patter matches that of a Barber dime minted from 1892–1916.

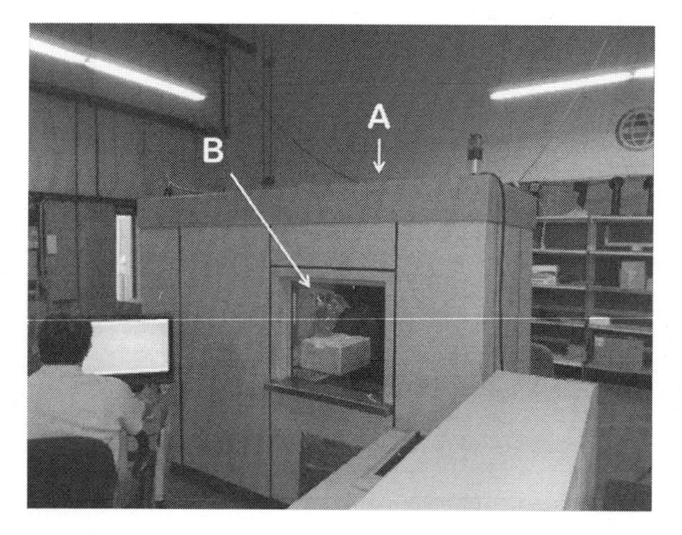

Figure 5.17. Chester Lowe seated at the computer next to the large industrial cabinet (A) with the first capsule (B) visible through the cabinet window.

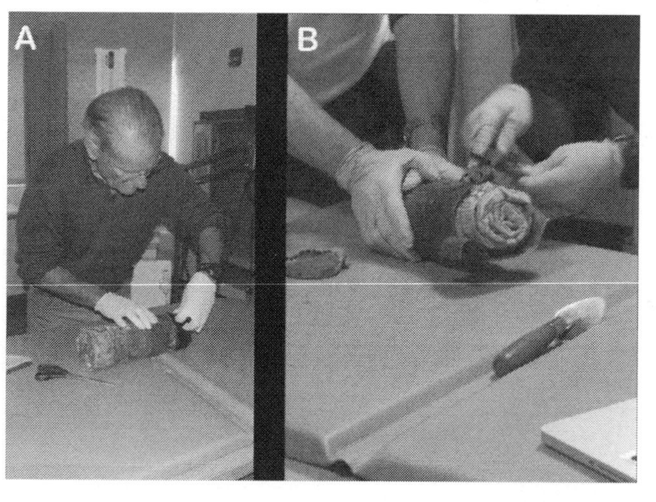

Figure 5.19. (A) Nick Bellantoni opening the first time capsule. (B) Pealing back the sides of the container revealing newspapers.

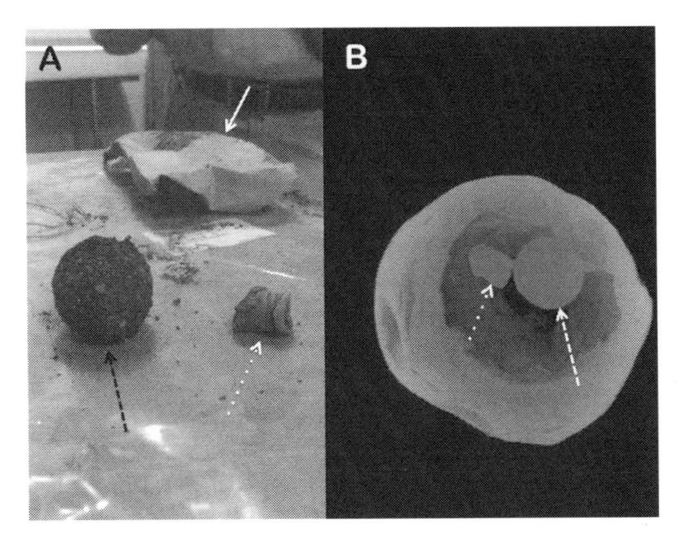

Figure 5.20. (A) The envelope (solid arrow) with text describing the contents as grape shot (dashed arrow) and a deformed musket minié ball (dotted arrow) recovered from Gettysburg. (B) Radiograph of same objects.

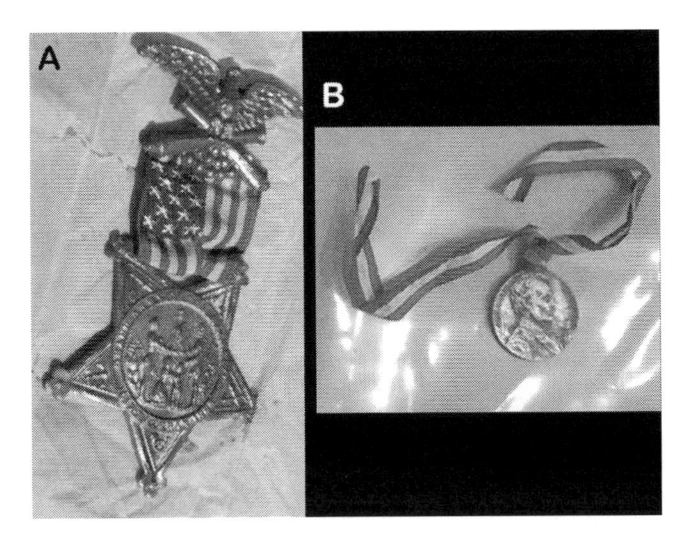

Figure 5.21. (A) The star and eagle of the Grand Army of the Republic metal. (B) Abraham Lincoln commemorative metal.

appearance noted on the radiographs. The rolled paper material included a program for the Lincoln Oak Tree Planting along with a series of lecture notes that were held together by staples, paper clips and pins [**WS 5.100**]. Loose in the center of the cylinder surround by the rolled up papers were several coins, including a 1907 Barber dime, a 1902 Barber quarter and a 1906 Indian head penny. The Lincoln head penny was not issued until August 1909, four months after the tree planting ceremony. In addition to the coins were two commemorative medals: a Grand Army of the Republic medal with a star connected to an eagle by a cloth replica of the American flag; and one commemorating Abraham Lincoln (Figure 5.21).

Significance

In order to demonstrate the contents of both time capsule a combination of radiographic sources and image receptor systems were employed. It was important to identify the contents and determine the relative locations of the items in order to plan the best approach to opening each container.

All images, regardless of the radiographic system employed, provided information regarding the contents of each time capsule. However, the larger focal spot of 1.2 × 1.2 mm on the X-ray source combine with the medical CR system used at the University provided much lower resolution than the X-ray cabinet system with a 50 × 5 μm focal spot and DR image recording. Due to the software processing the image data, image quality and wider latitude were improved over the previous images using the DIGIVIEW 395 system even with the larger focal spot X-ray source. Finally, the large custom-built industrial X-ray cabinet provided the penetrating power and resolution to enable the "one dime" to read off the image coin. Therefore, the non-medical DR systems provide consistently better images in this situation.

One other important point demonstrated by this study, moving the object can cause items within the object to change position. By acquiring the first set of images at the University and repeating them after a less than 20-mile transport clearly showed the coin in the second time capsule had moved. This was not an important factor in this study, but in certain situations it may be a consideration and emphasizes the possible need for radiography closest to the recovery site.

P.T. Barnum Bust: Is There Unseen Damage?

On 24 June 2010 an EF1 tornado briefly touched down in Bridgeport, Connecticut resulting in damage to the structural integrity of the Barnum Museum. Several months later, Kathleen Maher, executive director, stated a reassessment of the damage raised the cost of repairs from an estimated $2.4 million to probably exceed $6 million (Torres, 2010). Following the disaster, the contents of the Museum were moved to the People's United Bank Gallery located behind the damaged building. In 2013 a project to employ plane radiography to evaluate items for possible storm damage was jointly undertaken by the Barnum Museum, the Bioanthropology Research Institute and Diagnostic Imaging Program both from Quinnipiac University less that 25 miles from Bridgeport. The project expanded to include radiography of other objects in the collection and provide an opportunity for the University's radiography students to experience non-clinical, field radiography.

The first object examined was a plaster bust of P.T. Barnum created by Thomas Ball dating to 1883 [**WS 5.102**]. It was made from life in preparation for a full, seated statue finished in 1887. The work won a medal at the International Exhibition in Munich in 1888. Upon returning from Europe, it was stored in a warehouse in Hoboken, New Jersey where Barnum and his family and friends saw it in 1889. Barnum later wrote his assessment to Bell, "the best executed statue and the most perfect likeness we ever before saw" (Saxon). After his death in 1891, the statue was transported to the circus's winter quarters until it was placed in Seaside Park near the location of two of Barnum's houses.

The bust was on a pedestal in a rather crowded area in the temporary Museum space and could not be easily moved. The safest approach was to place the MinXray™ unit on a stack of milk crates to attain the height of the bust [**WS 5.103**]. With the 108-inch (274 cm) SID, a sufficient distant was obtained for the collimated X-ray beam to cover the entire bust. As an image receptor system, the Kubtec™ KUBSCAN 3000 CR unit was also transported to the Museum. The PVC pipe imaging receptor support system, previously describe was employed to place the CR plate in the necessary position to evaluate the head portion of the bust. Due to the thickness of the object, the image receptor was placed about 10-inches (25 cm) from the head enabling the air-gap technique (see Chapter 4: Plane Radiography) to be employed to reduce the scatter radiation and enhance the resulting X-ray [**WS 5.104**]. In addition, with the plate in that position, it was also possible to lower the height of the support device without the need to increase the distance to avoid contact with the lower portion of the bust. A total of six exposures at 80 kVp and 10 mAs were made for the radiograph of the head [**WS 5.105**]. Not only did there appear to be a large radiolucent area suggesting a hollow space within the head, but more importantly a crack was visualized in the nose that was not visible externally. Interestingly, on the radiograph, Barnum's curly appeared as cerebral convolutions, but because he was balding did not extend into the frontal region [**WS 5.106**].

Because the lower portion of the statue was thicker below the head, the number of exposures was increased from six to ten. In the lower portion of the bust there appeared to be a small space in the center of the piece under the neck and into the shoulder regions. A much large open area extended into the base of the bust [**WS 5.107**]. Because neither the bust nor the X-ray source was moved between exposures, the two radiographs could be stitched together [**WS 5.108**].

Reproof: Can an Old Repair Be Demonstrated?

In the 1960s or 1970s a statue entitled *Reproof* was donated to the Barnum Museum from the Bridgeport Library. One of several created Edward R. Thaxter sometime between 1878–1880, the Carrara marble neo-classical statue is of a disapprovingly looking young girl scolding a cat awkwardly clutched to her chest. A dead bird lies at her feet and feathers are around the cat's mouth. According to the Smithsonian American Art Museum Website (https://americanart.si.edu/artwork/reproof-23921), the "scene is a prelude to the responsibilities of motherhood: the young girl who is now reprimanding her cat will have to ensure that her own children are well behaved in the future".

The statue, donated to the Bridgeport Library in the 1940s, was displayed in the children's room when four fingers somehow were broken off (Saint-Pierre, 2018). Unfortunately, the original fingers were lost so a local artisan sculpted the replacements and completed the repair. Following the repair, the statue went back to the children's room, but unfortunately the forth and fifth fingers were again broken and instead of another repair, the donation was made to the Barnum Museum. Radiographs were requested to visualize the method employed in the first repair. Since there are various methods used to repair a sculpture, a radiograph can provide a conservator with insights into a previous approach and needs to be addressed in a future treatment plan.

Similar to the radiographic approach taken with B.T. Barnum's bust, the PVC pipe image receptor support system was employed to hold the CR plate in place [**WS 5.109**]. In addition, the X-ray sourced was positioned with a 108-inch (274 cm) SID and six exposures were taken at 80 kVp and 10 mAs, but without the air-gap between the object and the image receptor [**WS 5.110**]. Unlike the plaster bust of Barnum, the *Reproof* was solid marble and it would not have been possible to penetrate the thicker sections of the statue [**WS 5.111**].

Significance

Equipment designed for mobile or portable medical radiography generally can only provide about 100 kVp, insufficient penetrating force to produce satisfactory radiographs of thick dense objects such as marble statues. However, for larger less dense objects like a plaster bust, an air-gap technique can be employed to reduce scatter radiation and produce sufficient resolution to demonstrate a crack. For thinner dense material, such as the small marble hand of the statue of the little girl, the central X-ray beam directed close to the suspected repair site minimized distortion, but did not require the air-gap.

The Schwein: The Pure Esthetics of the Radiograph

Laura Lindgren, an editor, book designer, publisher, colleague of Gretchen Worden at the Mütter Museum and familiar with the radiography of the Severed Chinese Head and the Soap Lady (see Case Study 4: Mummified Remains) inquired if there would be interest in a radiographic study of a mechanical pig. Laura knew the artist, Paul Etienne Lincoln, who created the piece and thought it would produce an interesting and esthetically pleasing image.

Laura provided the following description, "*The Bad Bentheim Schwein*, a life-size mechanical pig designed by Paul was modeled on the Bunte Bentheimer Schwein, a pig bred in the lower Saxony area of Germany, that had gone nearly extinct by the 1950s. The pig's hollow interior housed an elaborate system, similar to the pig's digestive tract, that gilds acorns introduced into the pig's maw, moved by a mechanical jaw. The greater part of the pig is filled by an organ, in front of which is a speech synthesizer loosely based on a device made by Joseph Faber (c. 1800–1850). The tail serves as a hand crank that turns a punched Mylar roll encoded with a variation of an 1856 *Vereinslied* and that pumps air through twenty specially prepared pipes to produce the pig's vocalization. The pig has nine teats, which are pulled to allow air to pass, enabling the pig to grunt in a musical fashion; a randomizing device ensures that the pig never sings the same song twice."

When asked to describe the material used to construct the Schwein, Paul stated, "it was made of pig metal (pewter), actually ground up tankard tops to German ceramic beer flagons, mixed with polyester resin binder. The inner workings were a combination of non-corrosive metals, DuPont™ Delrin® acetal resin, wood, and Mylar". Knowing the type of metal and thickness used in the construction is an important consideration in the selection of an X-ray source. Equipment intended for medical use will generally provide a maximum of 110 to 120 kVp. At that level it is possible to easily penetrate 0.5-inch (1.3 mm) of aluminum, but thicker or more dense metals would require an industrial unit **[WS 5.112]**.

As to why it was created, Laura explained, "The mechanical pig is an integral part of Lincoln's *Bad Bentheim Schwein* project, conceived as an elaborate system to replant, over two decades, a lost eighteenth-century garden in the Bentheim Forest in lower Saxony, Germany. Lincoln was selected by Kunstwegen in Germany to install his unique project in Bad Bentheim, and through its inspired artistry to draw attention to the plight of an endangered species and engage the populace in the restoration of a once-magnificence garden."

In May 2015, Laura and Paul transported the Schwein to the Quinnipiac Diagnostic Imaging Laboratory in North Haven, Connecticut from New York City **[WS 5.113]**. The Bioanthropology Research Institute had recently completed radiographic studies on two large objects, a mounted centaur skeleton and the taxidermy mount of the two year old elephant (see Case Studies 1: Large Objects), in addition to the two headed calf described earlier all at the Barnum Museum in Bridgeport, Connecticut. For all the studies, a PVC pipe frame, designed by Bob Lombardo, to hold the CR plates was utilized and enabled the resulting radiographs to be stitched together.

Since the objective was to produce the best set of images to demonstrate the inner workings of the object, it was decided to begin with lateral projections, evaluate the results and determine if addition projections were necessary. The *Schwein* was placed standing on the X-ray table and the PVC pipe frame assembled behind it. With three 14×17-inch (36×43 cm) KUBSCAN 3000 CR plates available, three radiographs were acquired with a single exposure **[WS 5.114]**. In order to cover the entire object with the X-ray beam it was necessary to obtain a 180-inch (457 cm) SID. That distance was determined by opening the collimator as wide as possible until the light covered the entire object. So as to minimize the shadow of the X-ray table, the center of the X-ray beam cross hairs was then lowered to about the level of the edge of the abdomen **[WS 5.115]**.

At that distance, the battery operated Shimadzu™ *Evolution* mobile X-ray unit was set at 110 kVp and 250 mAs. Because the room had lead-lined walls, the radiation protection plan was quite simple. With the mobile unit positioned in the doorway and the beam directed into the room, it was possible to extend the exposure cord down the hall about 120 inches (305 cm) **[WS 5.116]**.

Since each plate had to be placed into the reader, there was an approximate delay of about 90 seconds before each image could be viewed **[WS 5.117]**. Therefore, when three plates were employed for an exposure, it was generally about five minutes before the next set of radiographs were acquired. However, latitude and resolution of each X-ray was so satisfactory that the wait was not an issue. There were also delays do to resetting the PVC frame for the next row of images **[WS 5.118]**. Because the frame was not specifically built for the dimensions of this object, on site modifications, such as using duct tape to secure a plate that extending beyond the frame rails, were necessary **[WS 5.119]**. Paul was satisfied with the lateral radiographs and felt it accurately reflected the internal mechanics [**WS 5.120**]. In all, over a period of about three hours, 20 radiographs were required to cover the entire *Schwein* and later stitched together as both negative and positive images by Laura Lindgren [**WS 5.121**].

Once the lateral projects were completed and reviewed, a possible second projection was considered. A view from above or dorsal-ventral projection would be interesting, unfortunately, due to the restriction of the ceiling height, there wasn't enough distance to achieve the minimum SID of 144-inches (366 cm). The other possible projection was to direct the X-ray beam from the head to the tail of the *Schwein*. The major problem with that approach would have been magnification. With the tail end of the object closest to the CR plates, there would be little magnification, however, because the head would be farthest away, it would be extremely magnified.

Significance

Since Paul Lincoln created the *Schwein*, there was not a question regarding the contents. This study was done purely to create an esthetic *life size* image of a manufactured object and demonstrate a non-diagnostic application of plane radiography.

The Chest: What Does It Contain?

The Mütter Museum at the College of Physicians in Philadelphia has been mentioned in other case studies dealing with mummified remains and contrast media injections. However, the Museum has a vast number of objects in the collect that are not categorized as human remains. In May 2016, several objects were brought to the Diagnostic Imaging Laboratory at Quinnipiac University for examination including an inlay chest. It was thought the chest contained medical instruments, however, opening it would have required the lock to be broken. Since the objective was simply to identify the contents, plane digital radiographs provided a simple solution.

Similar to the time capsule, an arbitrary first projection was taken. The X-ray beam was directed through the front to the back of the chest where the hinges were located [**WS 5.122A**]. The resulting radiograph provided the preliminary indication of the contents including what appears to be decanters, wine glasses and documents the location of hinges [**WS 5.122B**]. There appeared to be a smooth descanter superimposed over one of the carved liquor containers.

For the second projection, 90° to the first, it was decided to direct the X-ray beam through the sides of the chest [**WS 5.123A**]. The radiograph revealed two smooth surface decanters closest to the back of the chest with the hinges [**WS 5.123B**]. It was decided a third projection would provided additional documentation of the position of the objects within the chest. Since an X-ray beam directed from the top to the bottom of the chest would only provide images with superimposition from top to bottom. It was decided an oblique projection with the X-ray beam through the corner of the chest would more clearly identify the position of all four decanters [**WS 5.124A**]. The image confirmed the smooth decanters were located in the back of the chest beneath the hinges [**WS 5.124B**].

Since there was an MDCT unit available in the Quinnipiac Laboratory and the chest was small enough, it was decided to acquire a scan and compare the images. The chest was scanned and did provide some useful information. On one of the axial images through both decanters, it was easy to differentiate the two: the carved vessel created extensive artifacts indicating incorporated into the glass was a dense material such as lead; while there was no artifacts generated by the small glass container. In addition, streak artifacts were created by metal at other locations of the chest [**WS 5.125**]. Therefore, due to the extensive artifacts, the image quality was poor, but the sectional view provided a clear view of the stopper in the smooth glass decanter without superimposition.

The Toshiba *Aquilion*™ scanner did have a 3D algorithm that was intended to demonstrate metallic objects. When applied to the acquire data set and the threshold Hounsfield values adjusted, it was possible to visualize the glasses along with the dense carved glass decanter and metallic objects attached to the chest. Although the 3D rendering could be rotated and tilted in any direction, it did not provide any additional information than the set of plane radiographs [**WS 5.126**].

Significance

The study demonstrated that plane radiography can be employed to address specific questions. Since that imaging modality will be more readily available the MDCT, there is not need to locate an imaging facility with the latter.

Moulages: How Was It Made and What Is Inside?

Wax anatomic models known as *moulages* constitute another category of objects at the Mütter Museum. Ballestriero (2010) attributes the first anatomic teaching wax models to a seventeenth century Sicilian wax modeler, Gaetano Giulio Zumbo, and French surgeon, Guillaume Desnoues. Moulages represented a strikingly realistic method of presenting anatomic preparations before there were dependable methods of preserving human tissues. Pastor, *et al*, (2016) using multi-detector computed tomography, MDCT, demonstrated that a mid-nineteenth-century model created by the Vasseur-Tramond studio in France used human bones as a frame under the wax. The Mütter has a total of 27 moulages that were arbitrarily divided into three groups for radiographic purposes: large (7); small (6); and those enclosed within glass containers (14). There was a single primary objective for the radiographic examination: to determine if there were any human bones used as a frame for the models. Since a single radiograph would either confirm or refute the presence of bones, only one radiograph of each model would be required to achieve the objective. Proceeding through the sequence of questions presented in Chapter 9, Section 2: Determining the Imaging Needs; knowing the dimensions of the largest wax model provided information for the best configuration of the X-ray support system. With the largest model not being longer than 20 in (51 cm), a single 14 × 17 in (36 × 43 cm) image receptor at a 43 in (109 cm) SID was sufficient to image the object and address the single objective. A wooden frame X-ray tube support system was constructed that could be disassembled, transported to Philadelphia and re-assembled in the basement of the Museum where the study was to be conducted **[WS 5.127]**. For those wax models that could be positioned horizontally under a vertically oriented X-ray beam, a table that would fit into the support structure was also built. A sheet of Bakelite™, acquired from equipment discarded from a chiropractor's office, served as the tabletop. Under the Bakelite™, a shelf was constructed with a plywood base and rails to serve as guides for the image receptor. Strips of tape on the table-top indicated the precise location of the image receptor in the tray below **[WS 5.128]**. For objects that required a horizontally directed X-ray beam, the X-ray source support system permitted three easily achievable heights **[WS 5.129]**.

In addition to inquiring about the largest moulage to be radiographed, a request was made for the Museum staff to pull all the wax models prior to beginning the study in order to create a queue ready to be X-rayed. With this approach to improve throughput, it was possible to examine 13 moulages, using 18 plates in a total of 96 minutes or approximately 7.4 minutes per wax model. The radiograph of the first large moulage (# 8004), a prosection of the right axilla lacked evidence of any skeletal structures. However, a radiologist examining the image felt the branching nature of the artery and associated soft tissue suggest the tissue was derived from an injected cadaver (Gonzalez, 2018) **[WS 5.130]**. XRF analysis confirmed the presence of mercury (Hg) and lead (Pb), both radiopaque materials **[WS 5.131]**. Cinnabar, the ore for mercury is intensely red and was used as a pigment in vermillion paint.

The next wax model (# 8003), the largest moulage, represented the upper chest, neck, and lower half of the skull, exceeding the size of the image receptor. The principle area of dissection of the highly detailed model was the neck, demonstrating the relationship of muscle, vasculature and lymphatic system **[WS 5.132]**. Due to the size of the object, the first radiograph captured the chest and neck but not the entire skull component of the model **[WS 5.132B]**. Surprisingly, it appeared all the skeletal components of the region presented were included. However, since the vertebral foramen of the thoracic vertebrae were well visualized, a wired section of the model curved the spine anteriorly and was not attached to the cervical vertebrae **[WS 5.133]**. A second radiograph was acquired to include the skull component of the model. Aside from confirming the presence of human remains, the X-ray demonstrated the cut ends of the carotid arteries seen on the model **[WS 5.134]**. Unfortunately, due to the extensive superimposition of structures including hardware such as wires, pins and nails, the relationship of all the internal elements were not clearly visualized. Therefore a lateral radiograph was required to better demonstrate the relative positions of components. The next day, after the X-ray tube was moved for a horizontal beam radiographs, the lateral X-ray was acquired **[WS 5.135]**. The image revealed the cervical spine was wired into an extended position. Anterior to vertebrae, a more radiopaque carotid artery and less radiopaque jugular vein were visualized. In addition, there appeared to be dental attrition in the maxilla.

Through an existing opening in the mouth an endoscopic examination of the teeth was completed **[WS 5.136]**. The endoscopic images and radiographs were reviewed by the Chair of Oral and Maxillofacial Radiology at the University of Connecticut Health Center (Lurie, 2018). Although the extensive superimposition on the radiographs obscured clear visualization of the dentition, the supplemental endoscopic images assisted in the assessment. Dr. Lurie noted more marginal bone loss in the maxilla and a lack of premolars and molars. A possible abscess was noted on the right central incisor (tooth #8). The mandible also exhibited marginal bone loss due to periodontal disease. The right side 2nd premolar and 1st and 2nd molars were missing with totally new-appearing sockets consistent with recent extractions or traumatic avulsion.

XRF analysis of the artery and vein confirmed a difference in composition. The more radiopaque artery had a higher concentration of mercury (Hg)

[WS 5.137A] while the mercury level was lower in the less radiopaque vein **[WS 5.137B]**.

Two similar moulages, demonstrating the lymphatic system in a prosected chest, abdomens and pelvis were radiographed next **[WS 5.138]**. Since both were slightly larger than the image receptor, multiple images were required to cover the entire object. No skeletal elements were visualized **[WS 5.139]**. However, the superior and inferior vena cavae were radiopaque. XRF analysis of the inferior vena cava revealed low levels of mercury (Hg), but high levels of lead (Pb) **[WS 5.140]**.

It required less than five minutes to reposition the X-ray tube for a horizontally directed beam and to complete the remaining 14 wax models and to take an additional lateral projection of one of the large moulages **[WS 5.141]**. For the horizontal beam projections, a PVC pipe frame was constructed. Since only a single X-ray was required to determine if bone was present in any of these models, it was possible to acquire 15 images in 59 minutes. No bones were found in any of the other wax models.

Significance

This case study demonstrates the utility of using a multi-modal approach to data collection to maximize the interpretability of the findings. Integrating XRF and endoscopy with radiography provided valuable information regarding the study at hand. The portable nature of the instrumentation as well as determining the imaging needs prior to the study, and having the objects available and ready for analysis greatly impacted not only the efficiency of the project but also the efficacy in acquisition of interpretable data.

Having a team of colleagues who would assist with data interpretation exemplifies the diagnosis by consensus approach. The images were reviewed by both a clinical radiologist and a dental radiologist greatly enhancing the value of the data collected.

These findings add value to the Museum as they now have a greater understanding of their collection. Many of the wax models from this study are on display among the museum's exhibit space. The imaging data can now add value by helping visitors of the exhibit gain greater knowledge than they would have prior to these findings. The images too may enhance the exhibit presentation by providing visual content in the form of images (X-rays, endoscopic, XRF plots) supporting new and richer explanations of these objects. Important as well are the findings themselves. The fact that there are actually human remains within some of the wax models allows us to understand how these models were created in such a life-like manner. Instead of art imitating life, at least in some of these models, art employed life.

References

Ballestriero, R. Anatomic models and wax Venuses: art masterpieces or scientific craft works. *J Anat* (2010) 216:223–234.

Blyth, N.T., R. Lombardo, G. Conlogue, G. Aronsen. The Advantages and Disadvantages of Multi-Detector Computed Tomography (MDCT) and Computed Radiography (CR) for the Radiographic Examination of Human Skeletal Remains from a Mid-19th Century Cemetery in Connecticut. In a Symposium: Multidisciplinary Analysis of Human Skeletal Remains from a Mid-19th Century Cemetery in Connecticut. *78th Annual Meeting of the Society for American Archaeology*, Honolulu, Hawaii, April 2013.

Dennett, A.S. 1997. *Weird and Wonderful: The Dime Museum in American*. New York University Press, New York.

Egypt California Style. Mummy Road Show. 2002, National Geographic Channel.

Faking It. Mummy Road Show. 2002, National Geographic Channel.

Gonzalez, R. Personal Communication. 23 July 2018.

Lincoln, Paul Etienne. Personal Communication. 22 January 2018.

Lurie, A. Personal Communication. 9 August 2018.

Mummy's Private Collection. Oddities. Science Channel (Season 3), Episode 9, February 4, 2012.

Pastor, J.F., B. Gutiérrez, J.M. Montes, R. Ballestriero. Uncovered secret of a Vasseur-Tramond wax model. *J Anat* (2016) 228(1):184–189.

Robinson, J. Sideshow World. www.sideshowworld.com/40-ATS/2013/Nelson/Supply.html. 2013.

Saint-Pierre, Adrienne. Personal Communication. 26 January 2018.

Saxon, A.H. P.T. Barnum Statue Needs Restoration, Care. *New York Time*. 31 October 1993.

Snow, Carol. Personal Communication. 18 April 2017.

The Mummy Phallus Returns. Oddities. Science Channel (Season 4), Episode 11, June 8, 2013.

Torres, Keila. Barnum Museum's tornado damage could exceed $6 million. *Connecticut Post*. 21 September 2010.

Wolf, S.J. 2009. *Mummies in Nineteenth Century America*. McFarland & Company, Jefferson, NC.

Teeth: Plane Radiography (Film); Clinical CT; MicroCT

6

ANDREW J. NELSON AND STAN KOGON

Contents

Introduction

We have chosen an Egyptian mummy as the subject of this case study on dental paleoimaging for two main reasons. The first is that the Ancient Egyptians are well known to have been in generally very poor dental health, particularly in terms of dental wear and the sequelae of advanced wear including destruction of the pulp, apical abscesses, and chronic suppurative periodontal disease (Ruffer 1920; Schwarz 1979; Weeks 1980; Harris et al. 1998; Forshaw 2009; Cramer et al. 2018). Caries is a condition that appears to have been present in all periods, but with a very low prevalence early in the dynastic period that gradually increased through time (Ruffer 1920; Triambelas 2014). It would appear that the Ancient Egyptians did not have tooth brushes, although there is some evidence of cleaning instruments at select sites (e.g. Merowe and Faras, Ruffer 1920). Thus, dental "issues" would have been part of the life of almost every Ancient Egyptian, pharaohs and commoners alike (Harris et al. 1998). Over the past century, there has been a lively debate about whether or not a dental profession existed in Ancient Egypt. Evidence includes possible bridges, papyri and direct evidence of surgical intervention. Authors who do not see the evidence as being convincing include Ruffer (1920), Leek (1967, 1972), Schwarz (1979) and Becker (1999). Those who see that there is evidence of a dental profession (evidence of dental surgery, implants, other interventions, documentary evidence etc.) include Hooton (1917), Weinberger (1946, 1947), Ghaliuongui (1971), Harris et al. (1975), Harris et al. (1998), Irish (2004), and Wade et al. (2012).

The subject of this case study is "Lady Hudson" (Figure 6.1). Lady Hudson is an Egyptian Mummy who resides in the Department of Anthropology at the University of Western Ontario. "Lady Hudson," short for "Our Lady of Hudson's Bay" is the name she bore when she came into our care, which reflected the belief that the blanket that she lies on in her wooden coffin was a Hudson's Bay Blanket (which it is not… but we have kept the name). Her origins in Egypt are, unfortunately not known. This mummy came into our care in 2003 after a complicated journey that took her from Egypt to Brussels to Ottawa, around North America, back to Ottawa, on to Toronto and ultimately to her current home in London, Ontario. A full accounting of what is known of her afterlife can be found in Nelson (2019). For our purposes here, it is sufficient to say that the afterlife has not treated her well, as she resides in a coffin made for a male that is about 1000 years older than she is and her remains are in

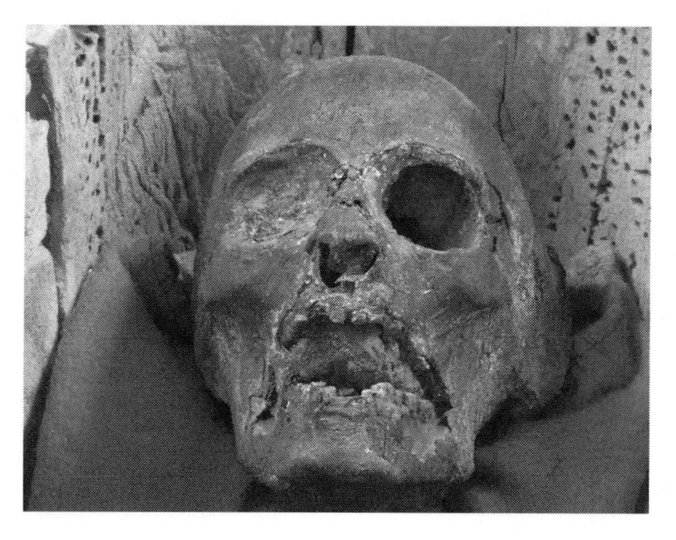

Figure 6.1. Lady Hudson's face. Note the oral packing and the poor state of her dentition. Photo credit—Jennifer Maxwell.

a poor state of preservation. Her head is separate from her thorax, both of her arms are fairly well persevered with the herringbone wrapping characteristic of the Roman Period, but her thorax and abdomen are only represented by bone fragments. Her pelvis and thighs are unwrapped and bare to the bone, but her lower legs are intact and still preserve the original wrappings. Finally, she has no feet. However, the fact that her head is separate from the rest of her body means that we can take it for endoscopic inspections (Holler et al. 2006), as well as visits to the dentist's office, CT suite, MR scanner and micro-CT scanner. The use of multiple imaging modalities, combined with a very poor state of dental health make her the ideal subject for a case study on dental paleoimaging.

Osteobiography

An osteobiography is the story of an individual's life as told in their bones (Saul & Saul 1989), or in the case of a mummy, from their skeleton and preserved soft tissues. In the case of a skeleton the reconstruction of the osteobiography involves direct examination of the bones for evidence of age, sex, pathological conditions, trauma, activity patterns and so on—all elements of one's identity that are etched onto the skeleton (Knudson & Stojanowski 2009). In the case of a mummy, the ideal course of analysis is not to disturb the wrappings to expose the bones underneath, but to use nondestructive imaging techniques to gather information about not only the skeleton, but the soft tissue, wrappings, and funerary preparation.

Lady Hudson was determined to be female on the basis of the morphology of her pelvis and the gracile form of her cranium. Measurement of her long bones, entered into predictive equations, suggest that she was 155 ± 4.25 cm (5 ft 1 inch ± 1.7 inches) tall in life. Her state of osteonal remodeling, reduced cortical thickness and degree of cranial suture closure suggest that she was in her 30 s when she died. This age is consistent with a lack of osteophyte formation or evidence for degenerative joint disease. Carbon and nitrogen isotopic analysis suggests that her diet was based on C3 plants, including fruit, vegetables and wheat and that she either had a high protein component to her diet or she lived in one of Egypt's desert oases (Beauchesne et al. 2008). See Nelson (2019) for a more complete profile.

Lady Hudson dates to the Roman period (30 BCE to CE 395 (Shaw 2000)) on the basis of the herringbone pattern of her wrappings and the individual wrapping treatment of her fingers (Nelson 2019). She was clearly eviscerated, as there is a resin soaked wad of textile where her abdominal organs would have been. However, the poor preservation of her thorax and abdomen mean that we do not know the details of how she was eviscerated. Her brain was removed through her nose, resin was poured into the empty vault and a resin soaked tampon was used to plug the hole through the cribriform plate. Her mouth was filled with resin-soaked linen. See Nelson (2019) for more details.

Paleodentistry

For effective interdisciplinary collaboration between bioarchaeologists and dental experts, we must ensure that we are using common nomenclature (or at least that we understand each other's language). In addition, to facilitate communication between dental experts and bioarchaeologist it is helpful to produce images which are commonly used in dental practice (see the Plane Imaging Chapter 4 in *Advances in Paleoimaging* for a similar discussion of clinical views of skeletal elements).

Nomenclature/Notation

There are numerous clinical dental charting/coding systems in use around the world. Three of the most common are the Zsigmondy-Palmer system, the Universal system, and the FDI World Dental Federation system. Of those, the Universal system and FDI system are most commonly used; the Universal system is almost exclusively used in the United States and the FDI system in the rest of the world (Harris 2005). As the FDI system is the one used in Canada and internationally we will use it in this case study. In the FDI system each permanent tooth is identified by two digits. The first digit indicates

	right															left
upper	18	17	16	15	14	13	12	11	21	22	23	24	25	26	27	28
	M^3	M^2	M^1	PM^2	PM^1	C	I^1	I^1	I^1	I^1	C	PM^1	PM^2	M^1	M^2	M^3
	M_3	M_2	M_1	PM_2	PM_1	C	I_2	I_1	I_1	I_2	C	PM_1	PM_2	M_1	M_2	M_3
lower	48	47	46	45	44	43	42	41	31	32	33	34	35	36	37	38

Figure 6.2. A comparison of the FDI 2 digit system of dental notation for permanent teeth used by most clinical dentists outside of the USA with that used by many anthropologists.

the quadrant in the mouth: 1 denotes the upper right quadrant, 2 denotes the upper left, quadrant, 3 denotes the lower left quadrant, and 4 denotes the lower right quadrant (Harris 2005). The second digit is the position in the quadrant starting with the central incisor (1) and ending with the third molar (8). In the anthropological/bioarchaeological field, Buikstra and Ubelaker (1994) (aka *Standards*) use the US-based Universal system, while many anthropologists, particularly those with an evolutionary interest use a system based on the identification of the tooth's quadrant (upper right, upper left etc.), the tooth's type (incisor, canine [cuspid], premolar [bicuspid], molar), and the tooth's position counting from the medial (central incisor) to the posterior of the tooth row (c.f. Hillson 1990; İşcan & Steyn 2013). So an upper right first molar would be a #16 in the FDI system and a URM1, or often a RM^1, in the system favored by many anthropologists. We will use both systems here. Note: Strictly and evolutionarily speaking, the PM1 and PM2 should be PM3 and PM4, as the actual PM1 and PM2 were lost early on in the primate lineage (Hillson 1990; Jheon et al. 2013). However, most bioarchaeologists opt for the PM1, PM2 nomenclature and we will stick with that here. See Figure 6.2 for a concordance of the FDI and anthropological nomenclature systems.

There is little uniformity in the charting/coding of the deciduous dentition. The FDI system uses the same 4 quadrants as the first digit: 5 denotes the upper right quadrant, 6 denotes the upper left, quadrant, 7 denotes the lower left quadrant, and 8 denotes the lower right quadrant (Harris 2005). The anthropological/paleontological system denotes deciduous teeth with a lower case letter, i for incisor, c for canine, m for molar, and a superscript position for upper and lower. So a lower left deciduous first molar would be #74 in the FDI system and lm_1 in the anthropological/paleontological system (Hillson 1990).

Dental Paleoimaging

Dental imaging can be very challenging due to the key issue outlined in the Plane Imaging Chapter 4 in the *Advances in Paleoimaging* volume—the superimposition of three-dimensional structures (in this case the two sides of the jaws and teeth) onto a two-dimensional image. Dental clinicians have developed a standard set of radiographic projections to best visualize particular teeth and dental lesions. A thorough dental imaging study would include:

- bitewing and periapical views to visualize the crowns and roots of the molars
- lateral oblique projections to document dental eruption and dental decay by positioning the film and X-ray source oblique to the patient's face, thereby minimizing superimposition of the molars and premolars
- a panoramic radiograph to visualize the mandible, maxilla and midface, seeking bone abnormalities, impactions, state of eruption and so on
- and dentist's offices are increasingly equipped with cone beam CT scanners to capture the patient's head as a volume, which can be manipulated in many different ways to visualize the jaws, teeth and facial soft tissue and bone structure.

Bitewing Radiographs

Bitewing radiographs (also known as interproximal radiographs) are used in dental practice to depict the crowns and the alveolar bone of the molars and bicuspids (premolars). The standard size of the bitewing film/sensor is 31 * 41 mm (1.2″ * 1.6″) and the film/sensor is placed directly against the lingual surface of the teeth and the X-ray beam is projected slightly upward and through the contact points to minimize overlap. The value of this projection technique is that there is no superimposition and the images show very fine details. In the clinical setting bitewings are taken with the mandible and maxillary teeth in occlusion (see White & Pharoah 2014: 114 ff).

When the teeth cannot be put into occlusion, this projection can be approximated by using the same alignment. The mandibular molar, or distal, projection and the mandibular bicuspid (PM), or anterior projection, produces similar images as the bitewing without the opposing dentition (see Wood 2014: Figure 34–6). Similar distal and anterior molar and bicuspid (premolar) views can be made in the maxilla. However, because of the shape of the palate the sensor must be placed somewhat medial to the teeth. For all of these dental views the sensor can be held parallel to the axial inclination of the tooth or teeth and the beam projected about 90° to the sensor and through the contact point to minimize overlap.

Lateral Oblique Projections

Lateral oblique projections are taken with the head rotated and angled to reduce the superimposition of the tooth rows that takes place in a lateral projection (lateral cephalometric projection). It is used to document the position or presence/absence of teeth and to look for fractures or lesions (Viner & Robson 2017).

Panoramic Radiograph

In panoramic imaging (or tomography) the source moves 180° around the patient's face, while the film/detector moves in synchrony on the opposite side of the face. The effect is to produce a single radiograph that includes all teeth along with the bony structure of the midface, maxilla and mandible (Mallya & Lurie 2014). These images are useful to detect cysts, unerupted or impacted teeth, advanced periodontal disease, abscesses and so on (Viner & Robson 2017).

Cone Beam CT

Dental cone beam CT resolution (approximated on the basis of voxel size) ranges between 90 µm and 400 µm (Scarfe & Farman 2008). As CT volumes, cone beam studies offer great flexibility in terms of the views that can be reconstructed, eliminating the superimposition of structures that characterizes plane radiographs. With the appropriate software, oblique projections can be created and curved reformats done to create "synthetic" bitewing and panoramic views (Pauwels et al. 2015).

Lady Hudson's Dental Check Up

Images Acquired

Lady Hudson's head (see Figure 6.1) has been imaged using a variety of imaging modalities. Intra-oral projections (bite wing, periapical, and occlusal) could not be performed because of the linen stuffing in her mouth. From the list given earlier, lateral oblique X-rays and panoramic X-rays were obtained. In addition, a lateral plane radiograph (lateral cephalometric projections in dental parlance) and clinical CT scans were obtained of Lady Hudson's head. These studies were obtained using equipment in the Department of Radiology and Nuclear Medicine in the University Hospital at the University of Western Ontario. The CT scans were taken using a GE Medical Systems Lightspeed Plus scanner. Slice thickness was 0.625 mm (pixel size in the X-Y plane was 0.4883 mm, so the voxels were not isotropic—see the Computed Tomography Chapter 7 in the *Advances in Paleoimaging* volume for a discussion about setting the field of view to get isotropic voxels), peak voltage was 120 kVp and the tube current was 170 mAs. Finally, a micro-CT scan was undertaken using the Nikon XT H 225 ST micro-CT scanner housed at Sustainable Archaeology, the University of Western Ontario. Voxel size for the scan was 122 µm, peak voltage was 195 kVp, the X-ray current was 48 µA, a 0.5 mm copper filter was used, and the volume was reconstructed from 3141 projections.

The CT and micro-CT data was visualized using ORS Visual^{si} or Dragonfly (Object Research Systems Inc. (https://theobjects.com/).

3-D Views of the Occlusal Surface of the Dental Arcades

Three-dimensional renderings of the occlusal views of the mandibular and maxillary arcades (Figure 6.3A & B) were created from the micro-CT scan data to approximate what a dentist or bioarchaeologist would see when first assessing a patient or skull, respectively. In the maxilla, the upper left M^1 (#26 in FDI 2-digit notation) and PM^2 (#25) are missing leaving a wide gap in the tooth row. These teeth have been missing for quite some time as their sockets have completely remodeled. In addition, the upper right I^2 (#12) is missing and its socket is well closed and remodeled. A recent clinical study of 250 patients (Berti et al. 2018) suggests that complete remodeling occurs after a mean of 13.6 months after extraction (range 4 to 36 months), suggesting that these teeth were lost some years before Lady Hudson's death. This view also reveals the crown of the impacted upper left canine (#23) behind the lateral incisor (#22). Allowing for the loss of the PM^2 (#25), there are 5 tooth roots to account for the incisors, canine and first premolar, so the deciduous canine (#63) must have been retained, possibly accounting for the impaction of the canine (cuspid). Note that this reconstruction is not entirely certain, due to the wear of the crowns and overlap of the roots.

In the occlusal view of the mandible, both central incisors (#31 and #41) are missing and their sockets are remodeled and the alveolar bone is well resorbed, also indicating that the teeth had been lost for some time.

Bitewings—Because of the linen packing in Lady Hudson's mouth, it was not possible to take regular bitewing radiographs. However, by reformatting

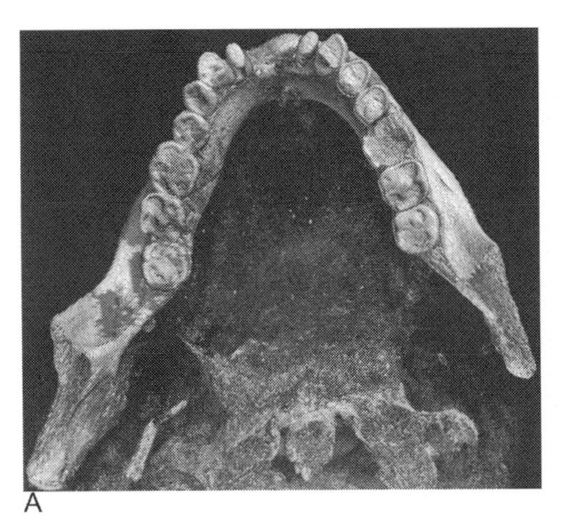

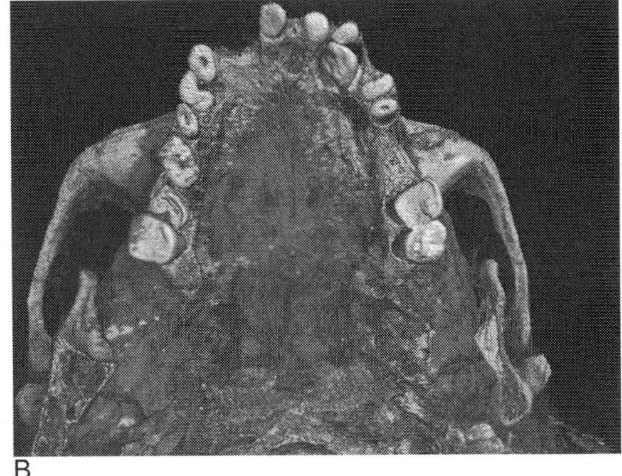

Figure 6.3. Occlusal views of the 3-D renderings of Lady Hudson's mandible (A) (left) and maxilla (B) (right).

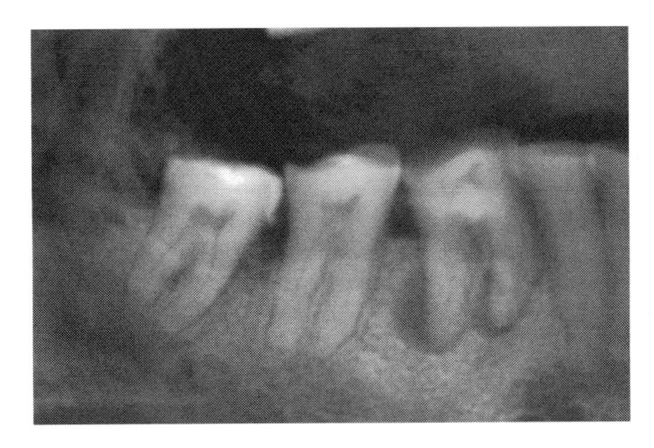

Figure 6.4. Synthetic bitewing of right mandibular molars (#46, #47 & #48). Average intensity projection based on the micro-CT scan.

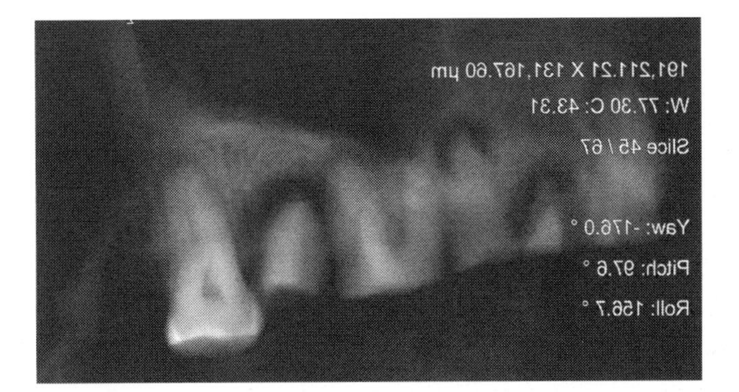

Figure 6.5. Synthetic bitewing of right maxillary premolars and molars (#14 to #18). Average intensity projection based on the micro-CT scan.

the micro-CT slices and making an average intensity projection with a slab the width of the tooth row, a "synthetic bitewing" can be generated. The synthetic bitewing for the 3 right mandibular molars (#46, #47 & #48) (see Figure 6.4) shows two apical abscesses for the first molar (#46).

The synthetic bitewing of the right maxillary molars (#16, #17 & #18) (see Figure 6.5) shows a large abscess around the root of the second molar (#17), an abscess at the apex of the distal root of the first molar (#16) and large apical abscesses for the first and second premolars (# 14 & #15). Alveolar resorption has eliminated most of the boney socket for the second molar (#17) and first premolar (#14), which are clearly only being held in the mouth by soft tissue.

A synthetic bitewing of the right maxilla slightly offset to the anterior relative to Figure 6.5 (Figure 6.6) allows the viewing of the tooth row from the third molar (#18) to the canine (#13). This view shows that there are abscesses at the apex of each tooth from the second molar (#17) to the canine (#13).

The synthetic bitewing of the posterior portion of the left maxilla (Figure 6.7) shows the impacted canine (#23), the roots of the deciduous canine (#63), first premolar (#24), the gap where the second premolar and first molar used to be (#25 & #26), and the second and third molars (#27 & #28). Note the radiolucency at the root of the first premolar (#24) indicating an apical abscess.

The synthetic bitewing of the posterior portion of the left mandible (Figure 6.8) shows the left mandibular premolars (#34 & #35) and molars (#36, #37 & #38). Note the slight radiolucency at the tip of the posterior root of the third molar (#38) indicating an apical abscess. Hypercementosis (excessive deposition of cementum) can be seen on the roots of the first molar (#36).

Panoramic radiograph—The panoramic radiograph provides an overall survey of the maxilla, mandible and midface (see Figure 6.9). The overall impression is one of heavy wear removing much of the cuspal enamel. Details of the upper anterior dentition (including the impacted canine) are difficult to discern because of superimposition with the boney anatomy of the cranial base. The postcanine dentition on the right side is

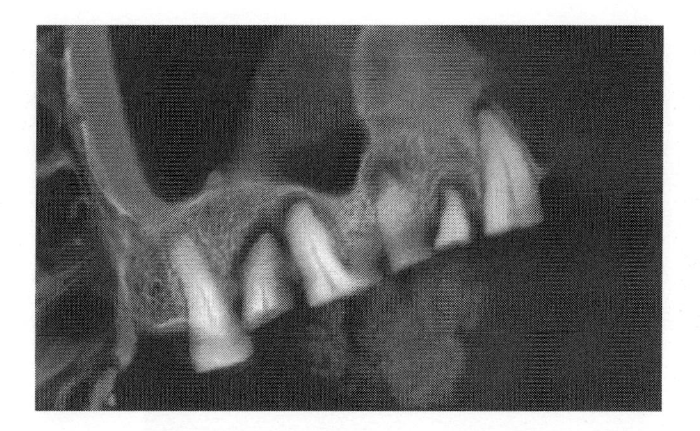

Figure 6.6. Synthetic bitewing of right maxilla slightly offset from Figure 6 showing the from the third molar (#18) canine to the (#13). Average intensity projection based on the micro-CT scan.

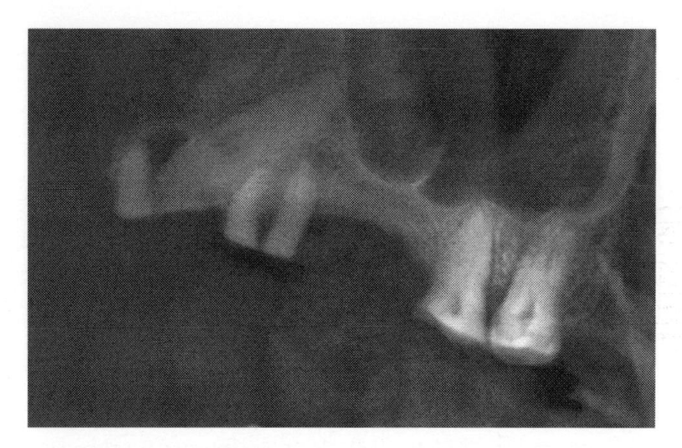

Figure 6.7. Synthetic bitewing of left maxilla showing the impacted canine (#23) to the second and third molars (#27 & #28). Average intensity projection based on the micro-CT scan.

severely worn with advanced alveolar bone loss, likely due to periodontal disease. There are abscesses associated with the root apices of several of the teeth.

The panoramic radiograph (Figure 6.9) confirms the loss of the lower left and right central incisors (#31 & #41, respectively). The lateral lower incisors (#32 and #42) have no remaining enamel and they appear to be tilted laterally. The abscess is apparent at the apex of lower right first molar (#46).

Lateral oblique radiographs—The positioning of the lateral oblique radiographs was not ideal, as superimposition renders them very difficult to interpret. The right lateral oblique radiograph (Figure 6.10) confirms that the space left by the missing left first molar (#26) is quite large, likely larger than the single tooth, suggesting that the left second premolar (# 25) is also missing as discussed above. The loss of bone around the sockets of the right premolars (#14 & #15) can be seen through that gap. The right anterior oblique radiograph (see Figure 6.11) shows the presence of the impacted left

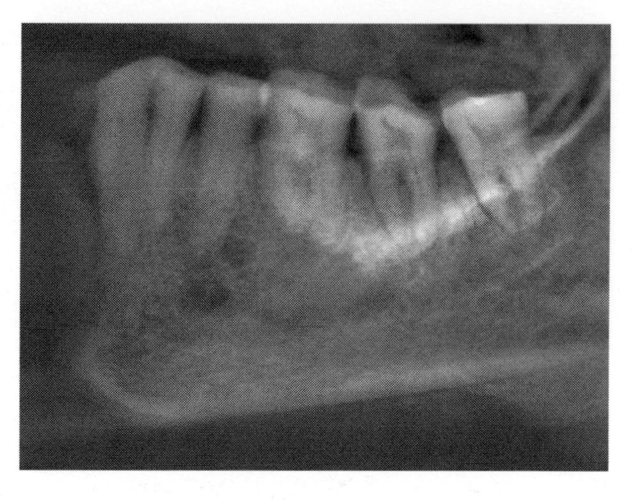

Figure 6.8. Synthetic bitewing of left mandibular premolars (#34 & #35) and molars (#36, #37 & #38). Average intensity projection based on the micro-CT scan.

upper canine (#23) and the loss of bone around the root of the upper right first premolar (#14).

CT scans—Lady Hudson has not been scanned using a dental cone beam scanner. However, she has been scanned by both clinical CT and industrial and micro-CT. Figure 6.12 shows the medial-lateral plane radiograph (Figure 6.12A), the midsagittal reformat slice from the clinical CT scan (0.625 mm or 625 μm slice thickness) (Figure 6.12B), a down sampled micro-CT slice to mimic the resolution of a cone beam scanner (244 μm voxels) (Figure 6.12C) and the micro-CT slice (122 μm voxels) (Figure 6.12D).

The difference in resolution of the clinical and micro-CT scans is very clearly illustrated in Figure 6.13. Figures 6.13A and B show the 3-D rendering of the maxillary dental arcade using clinical CT (13A) and micro-CT (13B).

The micro-CT 3-D volume reconstruction allows detailed interrogation of the condition of each tooth in any plane. This detailed inspection revealed apical abscesses of the mandibular lateral incisors (#32 & #42) that were not seen in other views (Figure 6.14).

Figure 6.15 shows the volume rendering of Lady Hudson's face (windowed & leveled to show bone) showing the right and left sides of the face based on the micro-CT scan data. Note the considerable loss of alveolar bone

Summary

General Dental Assessment

The radiographic imaging array depicts a dental apparatus that is severely diseased. There is significant wear throughout. Although there are remnants of enamel, for the most part all crowns of the molars and premolars

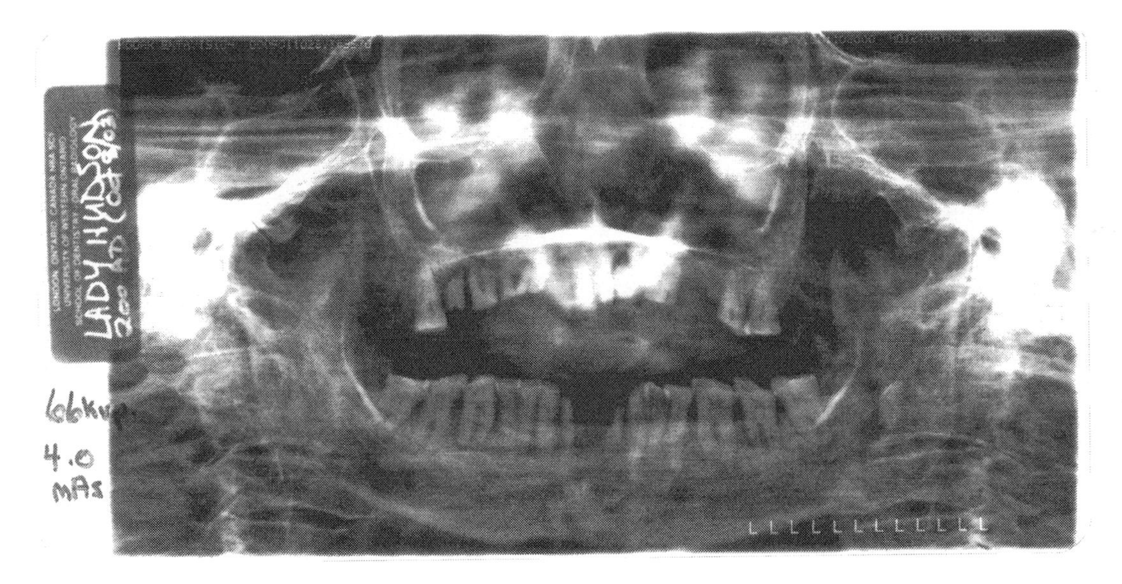

Figure 6.9. Panoramic X-ray of Lady Hudson. X-ray courtesy of the Schulich School of Medicine and Dentistry, The University of Western Ontario.

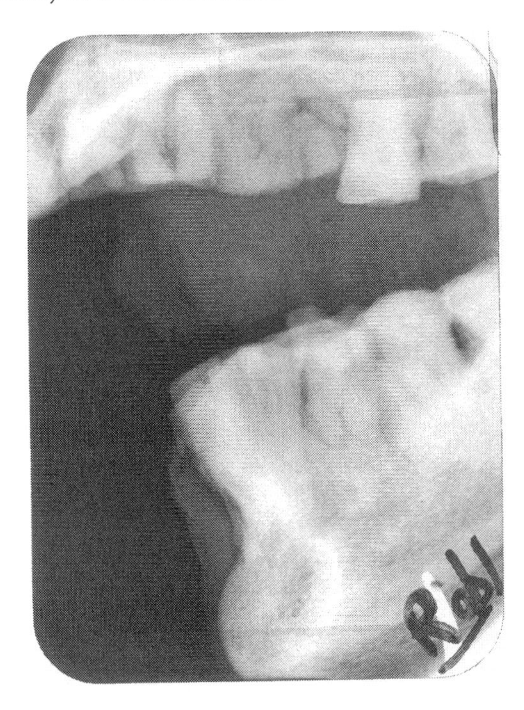

Figure 6.10. Right lateral oblique X-ray. X-ray courtesy of the Schulich School of Medicine and Dentistry, The University of Western Ontario.

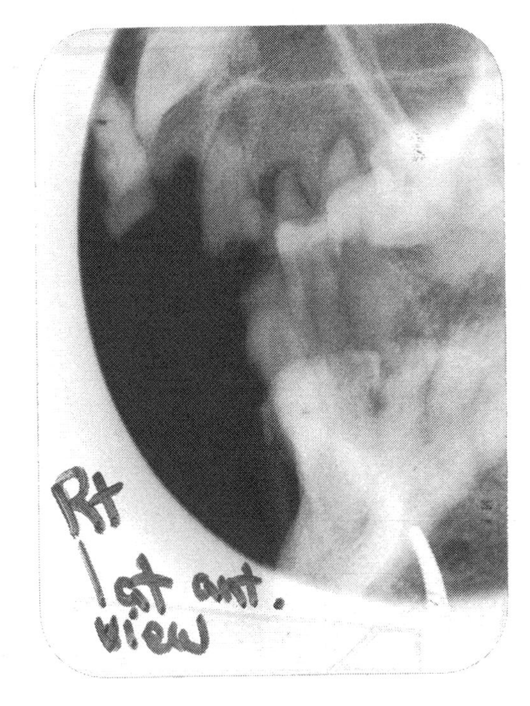

Figure 6.11. Right lateral anterior oblique X-ray. X-ray courtesy of the Schulich School of Medicine and Dentistry, The University of Western Ontario.

(bicuspids) have been worn flat leaving the dentine exposed.

Lady Hudson is missing 5 teeth: upper right M^1 and PM^2 (#26 and #25), lower I^1's (#31 and #41), and the upper right I^2 (#12). These were lost at least a year premortem as the sockets are all well remodeled.

The upper left maxillary canine (#23) is impacted with the tip of the cusp emerging through the palate. It is difficult to say whether this tooth would have erupted through the soft tissue into the mouth, but even if it had not, there would have been an elevation of the palatal tissues over the cusp. This tooth is severely tipped so that the root extends distally and palatal to the root of the remaining premolar (bicuspid). The deciduous upper left canine (#63) has been retained. This is not an unusual circumstance when the root of the deciduous tooth is not resorbed by its permanent successor. The root of this tooth would have blocked the normal eruption trajectory of the permanent canine (#23)

There is moderate to advanced periodontal bone loss in all quadrants. Some calculus deposits can be detected.

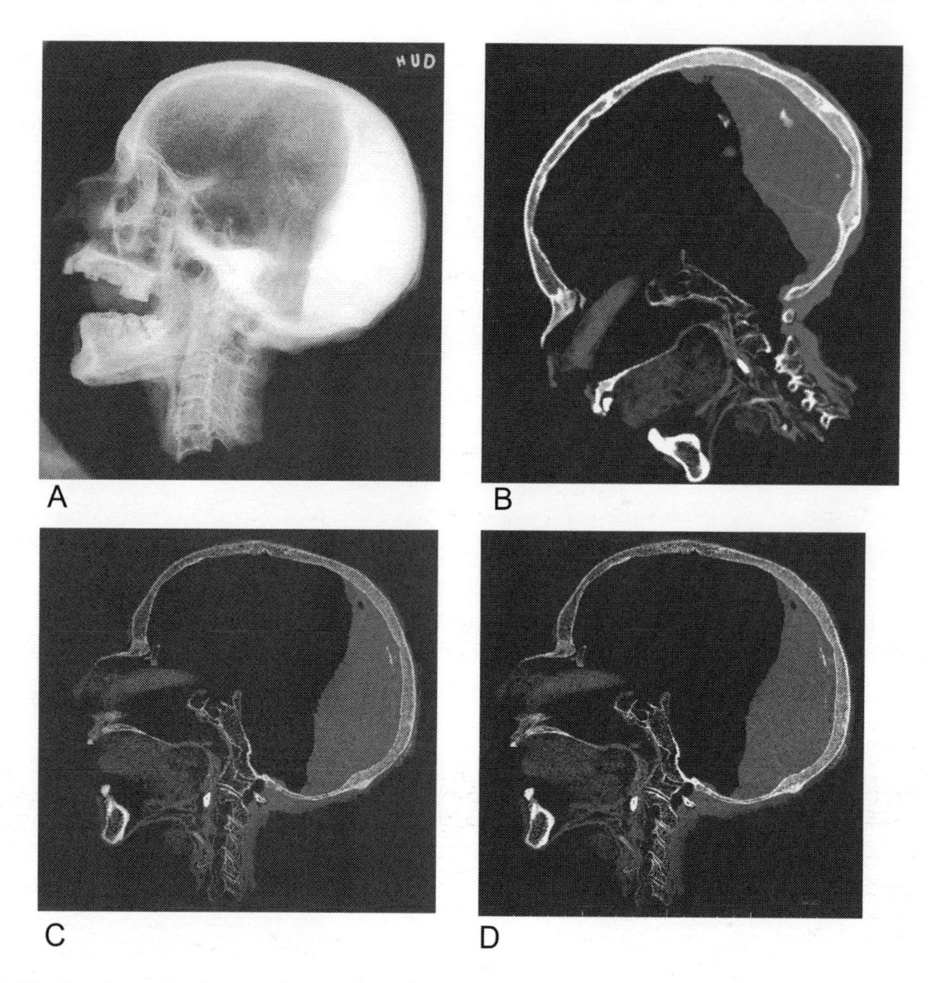

Figure 6.12. (A) Medial lateral plane radiograph. (B) Midsagittal CT slice—0.625 mm slice thickness, X * Y plane pixels—0.4883 mm. (C) Down sampled midsagittal micro-CT slice—244 μm voxels. (D) Midsagittal micro-CT slice—122 μm voxels.

For most teeth, the crown/root ratio is unfavourable. This is usually accompanied with some degree of tooth mobility and results from bone loss associated with periodontitis (Penny & Kraal 1979). Furcation defects (advanced bone loss which exposes the bifurcation or trifurcation of the roots) are detected in most molars. The 3-D rendered images of Lady Hudson's face (Figure 6.15) show advanced recession of facial periodontal bone support.

In the maxilla, periapical radiolucencies due to chronic inflammation from necrotic dental pulps and root canals are seen in a remarkable 8 teeth. They are seen in the maxilla at the apices of the upper right first and second molars (#16 & #17), premolars (#15 & #14, and canine (#13), and left first premolar (#24). In the mandible these radiolucencies can be seen at the root apex of the left third molar (#38) and right first molar (#46). The etiology of the periapical infections was likely due to the exposure of pulp horns as the dental wear advanced at a higher rate than secondary dentine could be deposited. When pulp necrosis is associated with avenues for exudate drainage there may be minor degrees or no odontalgia. Where periapical abscesses cannot drain sufficiently through the crown there will be pain accompanied with facial inflammatory disease until another drainage route is established. This drainage can occur by penetrating the buccal cortical bone, the floor of the sinus, or occasionally the floor of the nose.

Minor amounts of hypercementosis were found on #36. In most cases the cause of hypercementosis cannot be determined but it is often associated with inflammation (Lam 2014).

There is no radiographic evidence of caries.

Conclusions

Lady Hudson presents a severely diseased dentition with inefficient mastication, tooth mobility, and intermittent or persistent sepsis. The loss of dental enamel and tooth mobility would have made it difficult for her to process anything but the softest forms of foods. The abscesses that did not drain would have caused her a considerable amount of dental pain and facial swelling, and those

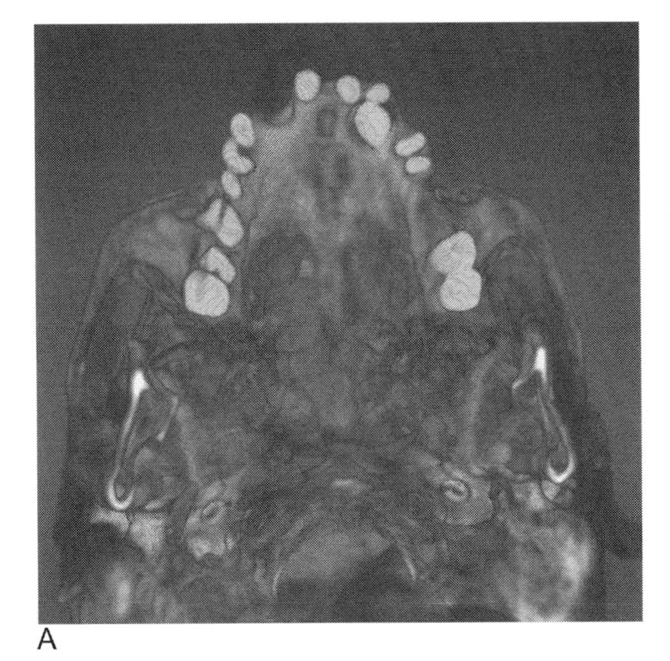

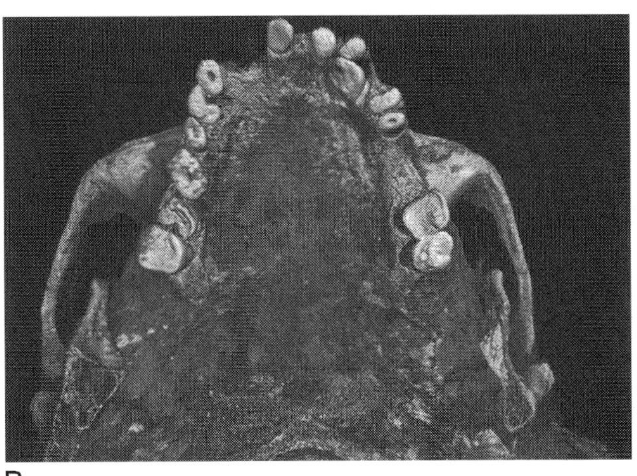

Figure 6.13. (A) Volumetric reconstruction of the occlusal surface of the maxillary arcade—clinical scan (625 µm slice thickness, X * Y pixels = 488.3 µm). (B) Volumetric reconstruction of the occlusal surface of the maxillary arcade—micro-CT scan (122 µm voxel size).

abscesses that did drain would have left her with fetid breath and a foul taste in her mouth.

It is likely that dental infections and their sequelae led to the deaths of many people in antiquity (Langsjoen 1998; Forshaw 2009). As recently as the turn of the nineteenth to twentieth century, dental infections had a mortality rate of 40% (Turner Thomas 1908) and dental sepsis continues to have significant associated morbidity and mortality amongst individuals who have not had effective dental care (Walsh 1997; Robertson & Smith 2009). We cannot know for sure if a dental infection caused Lady Hudson's death, but it is a very real possibility. Even if it did not cause her death directly, her dental condition would have left her susceptible to other diseases.

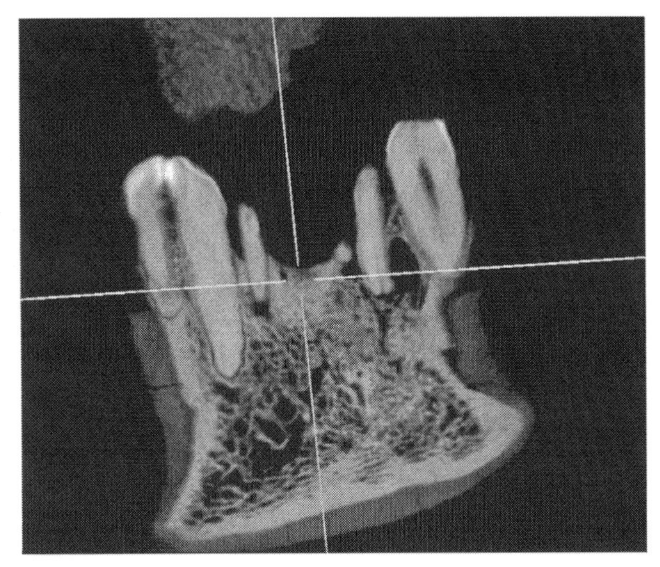

Figure 6.14. Micro-CT slice through lower anterior dentition. Lower lateral incisors with apical abscesses.

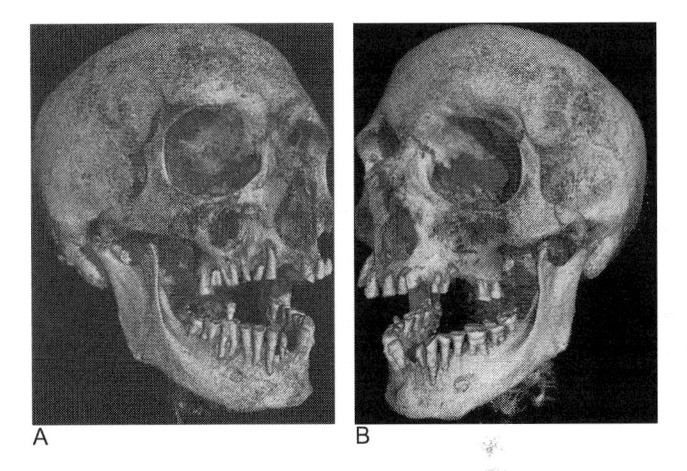

Figure 6.15. 3-D renderings of Lady Hudson's face (micro-CT scan data). (A) Oblique view from right. (B) Oblique view from left.

The issue of lack of effective dental care brings us back to the lively debate discussed at the opening of this case study: was there a dental profession in ancient Egypt? Lady Hudson's poor state of dental health would seem to speak against that proposition, or at least if there were professional dentists, that she did not have access to them. But a consideration of the symptoms that she must have experienced—and many other people experienced as well—would suggest that there certainly was a need for the development of methods of relieving symptoms (cf. Wade et al. 2012). Perhaps the relief of symptoms could have been accomplished by having a specialist extract the diseased tooth. Unfortunately, a single case cannot resolve the debate, but it does contribute to our understanding of dental health in ancient Egypt, and to our understanding of the lived experience of many ancient Egyptians.

Case Study

Within the context of the *Advances in Paleoimaging* volume, the goal of this case study was to explore the application of multiple imaging modalities to the analysis of the dentition of a woman who lived in ancient Egypt. The importance of the close collaboration between the bioarchaeologist and dental expert is central to this analysis. This collaboration is facilitated by the use of clear terminology and the selection of appropriate image projections. This example also highlights how different modalities, from the very basic to the latest technology, all have a role to play in paleoimaging.

Literature Cited

Beauchesne, P., Colquhoun, I., Cross, A., Longstaffe, F., Marciano, L., Metcalfe, J., Nelson, A.J., Pawlowski, A., Wheeler, S., White, C.D. & Williams, L. 2008. The lady hudson project. In P. Atoche, C. Rodriguez & M.A. Ramirez (eds) *Mummies and Science. World Mummies Research.* Proceedings of the VI World Congress on Mummy Studies, pp. 637–640. Academia Canaria de la Historia, Santa Cruz de Tenerife.

Becker, M.J. 1999. Ancient "dental implants": A recently proposed example from France evaluated with other spurious examples. *The International Journal of Oral and Maxillofacial Implants* 14(1): 19–29.

Berti, K., Kukla, E.B., Albugami, R., Beck, F., Gahleitner, A. & Stavropoulos, A. 2018. Timeframe of socket cortication after tooth extraction: A retrospective radiographic study. *Clinical Oral Implants Research* 29(1): 130–138.

Buikstra, J.E. & Ubelaker, D.H. (eds) 1994. Standards for data collection from human skeletal remains. Arkansas Archaeological Survey Research Series No. 44.

Cramer, L., Brix, A., Matin, E., Rühli, F. & Hussein, K. 2018. Computed tomography detected paleopathologies in ancient Egyptian mummies. *Current Problems in Diagnostic Radiology* 47: 225–232.

Forshaw, R.J. 2009. Dental health and disease in ancient Egypt. *British Dental Journal* 206: 421–424.

Ghaliuongui, P. 1971. Did a dental profession exist in Ancient Egypt? *Medical History* 15(1): 92–94.

Harris, E.F. 2005. Tooth-coding systems in the clinical dental setting. *Dental Anthropology* 18(2): 43–49.

Harris, J.E., Iskander, Z. & Farid, S. 1975. Restorative dentistry in ancient Egypt: An archaeological fact! *Journal of the Michigan Dental Association* 57: 401–404.

Harris, J.E., Ponitz, P.V. & Ingalls, B.K. 1998. Dental health in ancient Egypt. In A. Cockburn, E. Cockburn & T.A. Reyman (eds) *Mummies, Disease and Ancient Cultures,* 2nd edition, pp. 59–68. Cambridge: Cambridge University Press.

Hillson, S. 1990. *Teeth.* Cambridge: Cambridge University Press.

Holler, T., Wright, E.D., Chhem, R. & Nelson AJ. 2006, May. Lady Hudson: A case of transnasal craniotomy in Ancient Egypt. *Canadian Society of Otolaryngology-Head and Neck Surgery* (poster).

Hooton, E.A. 1917. Oral surgery in Egypt during the Old Empire. *Harvard African Studies* 1: 29–32.

Irish, J.D. 2004. A 5,500 year old artificial human tooth from Ancient Egypt: A historical note. *International Journal of Oral and Maxillofacial Implants* 19: 645–647.

İşcan, M.Y. & Steyn, M. 2013. *The Human Skeleton in Forensic Medicine*, 3rd edition. Springfield, IL: Charles C Thomas Publisher, Ltd.

Jheon, A.H., Seidel, K., Biehs, B. & Klein, O.D. 2013, From molecules to mastication: The development and evolution of teeth. *Wiley Interdisciplinary Reviews of Developmental Biology* 2(2): 165–183.

Knudson, K.J. & Stojanowski, C.M. 2009. The bioarchaeology of identity. In K.J. Knudson & C.M. Stojanowski (eds) *Archaeology and Identity in the Americas*, pp. 1–23. Gainsville, FL: University of Florida Press.

Lam, E.W.N. 2014. Dental anomalies. In S.C. White & M.J. Pharoah (eds) *Oral Radiology. Principles and Interpretation*, 7th edition, pp. 582–611. St. Louis, MI: Elsevier Mosby.

Langsjoen, O. 1998 Diseases of the dentition. In A.C. Aufderheide & C. Rodriguez-Martin (eds) *The Cambridge Encyclopedia of Human Paleopathology*, pp 393–412. Cambridge: Cambridge University Press.

Leek, F.F. 1967. The practice of dentistry in ancient Egypt. *Egyptian Archaeological Journal*, 53: 51–58.

Leek, F.F. 1972. Did a dental profession exist in Ancient Egypt during the 3rd millennium BC? *Medical History Medical* 16(4): 404–406.

Mallya, S.M. & Lurie, A.G. 2014. Panoramic imaging. In S.C. White & M.J. Pharoah (eds) *Oral Radiology. Principles and Interpretation*, 7th edition, pp. 166–184. St. Louis, MI: Elsevier Mosby.

Nelson, A.J. 2019. Mummies, memories and marginalization: the changing social roles of mummies from antiquity to today. In M.L. Mant & Holland, A.J. (eds) *Bioarchaeology of Marginalized People*, pp. 11–32. London: Academic Press.

Pauwels, R., Araki, K., Siewerdsen, J.H. & Thongvigitmanee, S.S. 2015. Technical aspects of dental CBCT: State of the art. *Dentomaxillofac Radiol* 44: 20140224.

Penny, R.E. & Kraal, J.H. 1979. Crown-to-root ratio: Its significance in restorative dentistry. *The Journal of Prosthetic Dentistry* 42(1): 34–38.

Robertson, D. & Smith, A.J., 2009. The microbiology of the acute dental abscess. *Journal of Medical Microbiology* 58(2), 155–162.

Ruffer, Sir M. A. 1920. Study of abnormalities and pathology of ancient Egyptian teeth. *American Journal of Physical Anthropology* 3: 335–382.

Saul, F. & Saul, J. 1989. Osteobiography: A Maya example. In M. Iscan & K.A.R. Kenned (eds) *Reconstruction of Life from the Skeleton*, pp. 287–301. New York: Alan R. Liss.

Scarfe, W.C. & Farman, A.G. 2008. What is cone-beam CT and how does it work? *The Dental Clinics of North America* 52: 707–730.

Schwarz, J-C. 1979. La medicine dentaire dans l'Egypt pharaonique. *Bulletin de la Société d'Égyptologie, Genève* 2: 37–43.

Shaw, I. 2000. *Oxford History of Ancient Egypt*. Oxford: Oxford University Press.

Triambelas, K. 2014. Caries prevalence in ancient Egyptians and Nubians. Unpublished MA Thesis, Department of Anthropology, University of Fairbanks, Alaska.

Turner Thomas, T. 1908. Ludwig's Angina: An anatomical, clinical and statistical study. Part I & Part II. *Annals of Surgery* 46: 161–183, 335–372.

Viner, M.D. & Robson, J. 2017. Post-mortem forensic dental radiography—A review of current techniques and future developments. *Journal of Forensic Radiology and Imaging* 8: 22–37.

Wade, A.D., Hurnanen, J., Lawson, B., Tampieri, D. & Nelson, A.J. 2012. Dentition of the Redpath 'Theban Male': Early dental intervention and habitual tooth wear. *International Journal of Paleopathology* 2(4): 217–222.

Walsh, L.J. 1997. Serious complications of endodontic infections: some cautionary tales. *Australian Dental Journal* 42: 156–159.

Weeks, K.R. 1980. Ancient Egyptian dentistry. In J.E. Harris & E.F. Wente (eds) *An X-ray Atlas of the Royal Mummies*, pp. 99–119. Chicago, IL: The University of Chicago Press.

Weinberger, B.W. 1946. Further evidence that dentistry was practiced in Ancient Egypt, Phoenicia and Greece. *Bulletin of the History of Medicine* 20: 188–195.

Weinberger, B.W. 1947. The dental art in ancient Egypt. *The Journal of the American Dental Association* 34(1): 170–184.

White, S.C. & Pharoah, M.J. 2014. *Oral Radiology. Principles and Interpretation*, 7th edition. St. Louis, MI: Elsevier Mosby.

Wood, R.E. 2014. Forensics. In S.C. White & M.J. Pharoah (eds) *Oral Radiology. Principles and Interpretation*, 7th edition, pp. 646–652. St. Louis, MI: Elsevier Mosby.

Contrast Media Injections

7

GERALD J. CONLOGUE, RONALD G. BECKETT,
JOHN POSH, AND BRUCE YOUNG

Contents

Modalities: Plane radiography (Polaroid photographic film, conventional radiographic film and CR); Microradiography; Tomosynthesis; MDCT and MR; XRF

Imaging Objective: Demonstrate the circulatory, respiratory and cerebral ventricular systems in animal and human specimens.

In Chapter 5, Contrast Media (*Advances in Paleoimaging*), two prosected neonates in the collection of the Mütter Museum in Philadelphia were introduced and several images presented. In this context the multimodality imaging approach and analysis will be considered. Although the specimen preparation occurred centuries before, the imaging objectives include an attempt to determine how the prosections were prepared and the age of the individuals at the time of death. The first individual to be considered is a prosection that was in private possession until 2015 when it was donated to the Mütter. According to family lore, around 1850, the cadaver had been found by a shopkeeper in the bottom of a molasses barrel. A few doors away from the shop a physician, Dr. John Gernon, was notified and given permission to dissect the body. He attributed the lack of decomposition to the sugar acting as an excellent preservative.

The remains were shipped to the Bioanthropology Research Institute at Quinnipiac University in Hamden, Connecticut, and imaging studies were carried out in the Diagnostic Imaging Programs' Imaging Laboratories on the North Haven campus. Preliminary images were acquired with CR followed by MDCT and MR. Even before the images were obtained, a visual inspection of the mummy revealed that there were obvious inconsistencies between the story passed down for generations and the actual procedure performed on the cadaver. It was apparent from the initial CR images that a dense radiopaque material had been injected into the circulatory system (Chapter 5 Advances in Paleoimaging, Figure 5.10). Filling of the popliteal arteries behind the knees revealed not only good vascular filling (Chapter 5 Advances in Paleoimaging, Figure 5.12), but provided evidence of an injection done shortly after death rather than months postmortem, as the original story suggested.

All of the MDCT data was acquired with a Toshiba *Aquilion*™ 64 slice unit using the following factors: detector width of 0.5 mm; 64 detectors per rotation; 0.5 second rotation time; 100 kVp; 200 mA; 240 mm Display Field of View (DFOV); 41.0 Helical Pitch (0.641 Pitch Factor). The raw data was processed with a high-resolution bone algorithm (FC 81) that provided maximum edge enhancement. The three-dimensional volumes were reconstructed at 0.5 mm intervals with 0.3 mm of overlap.

Thick section coronal **[WS 7.1]** and sagittal **[WS 7.2]** images correlate well with the CR images. The axial images revealed good filling to the base of the brain **[WS 7.3]** and indicated the injection was completed, the material permitted to solidify, followed by careful, precise removal of the cerebral hemispheres. Axial sections of the heart provided a means to view individual chambers within the structure hidden by superimposition on the CR images **[WS 7.4]**.

Age at the time of death determinations were done by examining epiphyseal development and diaphyseal lengths. An assessment of the epiphyses at various joints was carried out using curve-linear reconstruction of, for example the left **[WS 7.5]** and right wrists **[WS 7.6]**. According to standards established by Scheuer and Black (2000), the lack of visible ossification centers in both carpals suggested the individual was perinatal. No epiphyses were noted on either distal radius confirming that the individual was under one year old.

In addition to the curve-linear reconstruction application, oblique section reconstructions were also employed to assess bone development in both left **[WS 7.7]** and right **[WS 7.8]** feet. The ossification noted in the tarsal region of both feet confirmed the findings of the assessment of the carpals suggesting a perinatal individual. Unfortunately, since it appears several epiphyses have been lost over time [**WS 7.9**], the bone development assessment at other locations was not possible.

Oblique sections were also employed for age estimation by examining diaphyseal length of the femurs [**WS 7.10**], tibias [**WS 7.11**] and both humeri [**WS 7.12 and 7.13**]. Once again, with Scheuer and Black as the reference, the femoral and tibia diaphyseal length measurements indicated between 39 to 40 weeks' gestation. The measurements of the humeral diaphysis suggested an age greater than 40 weeks' gestation.

A third method to estimate the age of the individual at the time of death was to examine the development of the teeth using curve-linear reformate. The resulting image resembles a film based imaging procedure known as a dental panoramic radiograph [**WS 7.14**]. Unfortunately, with the small size of the skull, the reconstruction with the software available with Aquilion™ unit did not render a high-resolution image [**WS 7.15**]. The DICOM data was downloaded onto a DVD and brought to the University of Connecticut Dental School where it was uploaded onto a laptop computer with OsiriX™ software [**WS 7.16**]. With a skilled dental radiologist manipulating the data, higher-resolution images of the maxilla and mandible [**WS 7.17**] were acquired and an age estimate determined. After evaluating the developing deciduous tooth mineralization patterns throughout the gnathic bones, Lurie (2008), estimated the age to be approximately 18 weeks postnatal (Table 7.1).

In an attempt to determine the density of the injected material and utilize the quantitative nature of computed tomography, Hounsfield Units (HU) or CT#s were acquired from several injected regions of the mummy. Because the heart was large with considerable material within its chambers, it was the site for data collection. First measurements were collected from the wall of the right ventricle on an axial section [**WS 7.18**]. The high standard deviations of the density measurements indicated a nonhomogeneous nature of the tissue examined suggesting the material injected was in the muscle via the coronary arteries. Measurements were then acquired from within the chambers and vessels of the heart on the same axial section [**WS 7.19**]. Densities of the injected material within the heart were also collected on a coronal projection of the organ [**WS 7.20**]. Because the coronal image was larger than the axial projection, the sizes of the region-of-interest (ROI) were smaller on the former plane. In order to compare the density values related with the material injected to the tissue not associated with the injection, the density in four other areas; the costal cartilage, vertebral body, anterior and posterior ribs were sampled at the same level in the axial plane as the heart [**WS 7.21**]. However, the high standard deviation value and difference between means for multiple collections, suggestion the ROI was too large. Another approach was to gather multiple pixel values instead of the ROI method. To test the idea, an axial section at the base of the skull was selected where both carotids and basilar arteries were visualized. Pixel values were obtained from all three arteries and then a 7.0 mm ROI, the smallest size that could be selected, were acquired for the three vessels [**WS 7.22**]. The pixel values were similar but much greater than the mean values acquired from the same vessels. With the exception of the right carotid artery, both of the other values fell within the standard deviation.

The three-dimensional reconstruction of the chest and abdominal areas also provided valuable information suggesting how the specimen was prepared.

Table 7.1. The age estimation of the developing deciduous tooth mineralization based on the cone beam computed tomography images

Developing Deciduous Tooth Mineralization		
Region	Characteristics	Likely Age (weeks)
Anterior teeth maxilla	i1 ⅓ coronal i2 ¼ coronal c cusp tips	About 17–18
Posterior teeth maxilla	m1 occlusal surfaces (relatively complete cusps) m2 very start of cusp tips	18–23
Anterior teeth mandible	i1 ½ coronal i2 ⅓ coronal c full cusps, just starting crown	About 18
Posterior teeth mandible	m1 occlusal surfaces (cusps complete) m2 barely beginning cusp tips	18

Source: Dental Anatomy, Physiology and Occlusion—Development and Eruption of the Teeth (http://what-when-how.com/dental-anatomy-physiology-and-occlus…)

Data derived from Smith, which derived from Moorrees et al., Sunderland et al., Anderson et al., Kronfeld, Lysell et al., and Hume

A ligature was noted on the superior vena cava, indicating it was tied off after the injection and before the distal end was severed [**WS 7.23**]. Evidence of dissection following injection was also noted in the abdomen where the cut across the inferior vena cava just superior to the bifurcation had a sharp edge [**WS 7.24**]. In addition, the displaced superior portion of the inferior vena cava, absence of the kidneys and other organs with the abdomen, but an intact abdominal aorta was observed. The umbilical vein was present filled with the injection material implying it may have been the route of injection and accounts for the filling of the superior vena cava and brachiocephalic veins. The elevated and superiorly rotated position of the right atrium indicated that the heart was positioned before the specimen was dried in order to demonstrate the vessels on the posterior aspect of the heart. The coloring of the myocardium confirmed the findings noted during the collection of ROI values that the injection material was present in the coronary arteries [**WS 7.25**].

After the MDCT was completed the mummy was transported to the Kubtec Medical Imaging manufacturing facility in Stratford, Connecticut, for an examination of the head with a Kubtec Parameter™ tomosynthesis unit. The objective was to clearly demonstrate the injected vessels at the base of the brain. Anterior-posterior (Chapter 5 *Advances in Paleoimaging*, Figure 5.15) and lateral [**WS 7.26**] projections provided sharp images, eliminating the superimposition of calvarium, were obtained in a few minutes.

The final imaging modality for this series was magnetic resonance with a Toshiba Vantage™ 1.5T unit. In order to enable the unit to function with a completely dehydrated specimen, a water bottle had to be incorporated into the magnetic field and, in order to receive sufficient signal, thick sections were acquired. During the study, axial, coronal, and sagittal images were acquired with the specific parameter for each. In order to correlate the anatomy visualized with the thick MR sections, those images were correlated with CT images from the same regions [**WS 7.27, 7.28, and 7.29**]. Because high signals were received from the area of the heart, it suggests the injected material was paramagnetic.

Reviewing the findings of the mummified remains, now frequently referred to as the *Molasses Baby*, there appears to be little evidence to support the original story passed down through several generations. All indications suggest the injection was done shortly after death. If a long time had elapsed, the filling would not have been complete. As indicated by skeletal development, the age at the time of death was full term. Although the tooth development did not match that finding, an injection through the umbilical vein supports the perinatal age. The preparator was very skilled not only in the method and materials used in the injection, but also in the extensive dissection with the intent to demonstrate specific anatomic features. The latter is most notable in the removal of the brain while leaving the falx cerebri and tentorium cerebelli in place. The second suggestion of intent to demonstrate anatomical structure was the rotation of the heart to provide visualization of both the aorta and point where the inferior vena cava enters the organ. In addition, the position of the arms suggest the prosection was prepared to enable facilitate transportation of the remains minimizing the potential of damage to the upper extremities.

The success of the *Molasses Baby* study led to a decision by the Mütter Museum to have a similar study carried out on another perinatal mummy, identified as 1090.55, referred to as a *Sugar Mummy* (Chapter 5 *Advances in Paleoimaging*, Figure 5.16). The CR images were very similar to both the Burns specimen and the *Molasses Baby* (Chapter 5 *Advances in Paleoimaging*, Figure 5.17). With the 72-inch (183 cm) SID, three 14×17 in (36×43 cm) inch plates were required to cover the entire mummy [**WS 7.30A**]. Because neither the X-ray source or mummified remains were moved between exposures, it was possible to stitch the images to produce a single image [**WS 7.30B**]. However, because the upper extremities were partially extended, only the AP plane radiographs were acquired. The images demonstrated more extensive arterial and venous filling of the circulatory system that extended clearly into the feet. The varying sized *bright white* spots, radiopacities, noted within the body did not conform to the shape of the associated vessels, but may represent crystals formed by material used in the preservation process. The largest radiopacity was found in the pelvis [**WS 7.31**]. Unlike the previous mummy, sagittal and axial reconstructions of the skull revealed extensive arterial and venous filling without removal of the brain. The latter appeared to be dehydrated and in a gravity dependent position, suggesting the remains were in a supine position during the process of preparation (Chapter 5 *Advances in Paleoimaging*, Figure 5.18).

The identical MDCT protocol that was employed for the previous individual was used with this neonate. Confirming what was seen on the CR images, the circulatory system of this individual was more completely filled than the prior prosection. Because there was no evidence of an umbilical vein, the individual was definitely older. Age determination was accomplished by measuring diaphyseal lengths. Employing the oblique sectioning application, the lengths of the femurs [**WS 7.32**], tibias [**WS 7.33**], and humeri [**WS 7.34**] were calculated. Corresponding to the Scheuer and Black (2000) determination, the individual was probably less than two months old at the time of death (Table 7.2).

Table 7.2. The age at the time of death estimation based on the diaphyseal lengths of three of the long bones obtained from the MDCT oblique sections (Scheuer and Black, 2000)

	Measurement taken from ROI		
Bone	Right (mm)	Left (mm)	Age (months)
Femur	90.2	93.1	1.5–3
Tibia	74.8	74.9	≈ 1
Humerus	71.0	70.6	< 2

Scheuer, L. and S. Black. Developmental Juvenile Osteology. Academic Press 2000.

Measurements of the density of the injection material were achieved with ROIs of axial images of the heart **[WS 7.35]** and sagittal sections of the heart and associated vessels **[WS 7.36]**. The Hounsfield unit values were at least twice as high as noted in the previous prosection, clearly demonstrating that a different, more dense material was injected into the circulatory system.

In an attempt to determine what was injected into the circulatory system, three colored injection masses were produced (Table 7.3) and placed into three sizes of polyethylene tubing (Table 7.4). Each tube was plugged with cotton at either end and sealed with a bead of hot glue. The tubes were packaged and sent from the Mütter Museum to Quinnipiac University for imaging. Prior to the MDCT scanning, the three tubes filled with the same color, but varying in diameter, were laid on a foam sponge. The latter had slits cut to accommodate each tube **[WS 7.37]** to ensure that the tubing would be surrounded by a uniform material during the scan. The foam block containing the tubing was placed on top of another foam block to raise the sample to be scanned farther from the couch surface **[WS 7.38]**. The same protocol that was used to scan the prosected neonate was employed to scan the tubing. Both ROIs and pixel values were acquired from axial sections **[WS 7.39]**. As expected, because the smallest diameter ROI available was 0.9 mm^2, the smaller the diameter of the tubing resulted in a greater standard deviation of HU values. Pixels provided only single HU values and to arrive at what may be considered an accurate representation, many samples would need to be collected, a procedure to be included in future studies. However, a generalized preliminary assessment indicated that the least dense material was the pale blue and most dense the white material **[WS 7.40]**.

Table 7.4. Outer and inner diameter of polyethylene Tubing

Outer Diameter (in)	Inner Diameter (in)
1/4 (0.25)	5/32 (0.156)
1/8 (0.125)	3/32 (0.094)
3/32 (0.094)	3/64(0.047)

The results from the two perinatal mummies examined at Quinnipiac University provided the motivation to include other preserved prosections in the Mütter Museum collect to be examined. The opportunity was realized when the museum requested a study of wax anatomic models known as moulages in July 2018 (see Case Study 5: Manufactured or Created Objects). Because the scheduled study also included endoscopy and XRF analysis, it provided additional perspectives that were unavailable during the spring 2016 study session.

Neither of the two very different prosections were currently on exhibit at the museum. The first, identified as 1090.56, was a definite fetus with accompanying umbilical cord and was housed in a cut foam container. The position of the body resembled the *Sugar Mummy* and somewhat reminiscent of Leonardo de Vinci's *L'Uomo Vitruviano* or *Vitruvian Man* (Figure 7.1). The arteries appeared red and the veins blue in this small specimen with the diaphragm in place but with the lungs and most of the abdominal organs removed (Figure 7.2).

Prior to the radiographic examination, XRF analysis was accomplished. Analysis of the arterial branch demonstrated the high mercury (Hg) content associated with red color characteristic of the ore of the element cinnabar, used to produce vermilion pigment (Figure 7.3). However, the assessment of the umbilicus, with little red color, showed much lower levels of mercury (Hg), but

Table 7.3. Composition of colored materials

Red		White		Pale Blue	
Material	Scaled Quantity	Material	Scaled Quantity	Material	Scaled Quantity
Yellow Bees Wax	45.28 gm	Yellow Bees Wax	45.28 gm	Yellow Bees Wax	45.28 gm
White Resin	22.64 gm	White Resin	22.64 gm	White Resin	22.64 gm
Turpentine Varnish	17.76 ml	Turpentine Varnish	17.76 ml	Turpentine Varnish	17.76 ml
Vermillion	8.88 gm	Flake White		Flake White	10.2 gm
				Blue Smalt	10.2 gm

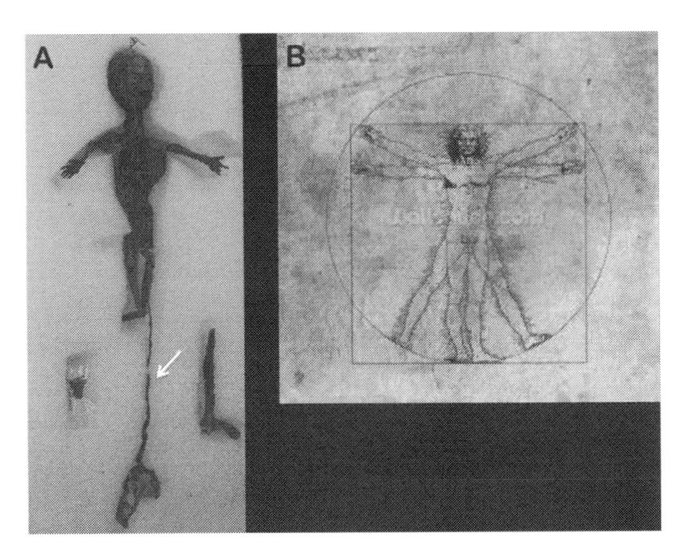

Figure 7.1. (A) The prosection identified as 1090.56 was stored in a foam container cut to accommodate the specimen: note the attached umbilical cord (arrow). (B) Leonardo da Vinci's *L'Uomo Vitruviano* or *Vitruvian Man*.

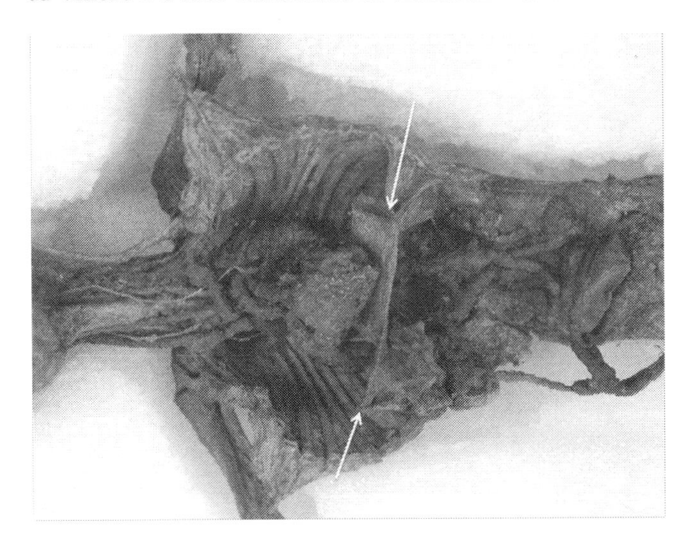

Figure 7.2. The chest and abdominal cavities were exposed with the dried diaphragm (arrows) forming a distinct separation between the two. Clearly the arteries were injected red and the veins blue.

high levels of arsenic (As) and lead (Pb) that might have been employed as a preservative (Figure 7.4). The single AP radiograph of the specimen did reveal the presence of radiopaque material in both the arterial and venous system and the bight white speckles noted on the prosection, 1090.55, radiographed at Quinnipiac University (Figure 7.5). A comparison of the photograph and the radiograph of the chest with the heart and associated vasculature show little or no difference in the densities between the red arteries and blue veins (Figure 7.6).

The other prosection, an adult in a similar position, was hanging in a storage area with other skeletal remains (Figure 7.7). The situation, with a nearby available desktop, was perfectly suited for both XRF analysis and endoscopic examination (Figure 7.8). Four locations were assessed with the XRF: the aortic arch (Figure 7.9); right femoral artery (Figure 7.10); left surface of the leg (Figure 7.11); and external wad in the mouth (Figure 7.12). The XRF analysis of the aortic arch and femoral artery presented nearly identical elemental profiles with high levels of mercury (Hg). Similarly, XRF analysis of the surface of the leg and external wad over the mouth provided virtually the same profiles of high arsenic concentrations suggesting the element was employed in the preservation of the remains. The opening beneath the left mandible provided an access route for the endoscope (Figure 7.13).

Because the primary objective of the trip to Philadelphia was to radiograph the wax models, the setup was not designed to radiograph an entire adult with outstretched arms. A return visit to the museum was planned for three or four months in the future. The prosection was transferred to a rolling frame and brought into the area where the wax models were radiographed. The X-ray tube was mounted in the top position on the wooden frame and the tube rotated 90° in order to project the beam horizontally to the level of the skull. The CR plate was placed in a holder created from PVC pipe [**WS 7.54**]. The AP CR image of the head and neck revealed a radiopaque structure that corresponds to the vessel seen on the photograph of the area (Figure 7.14).

Naturally Occurring Contrast Media

In 1986, a course for radiography students at Thomas Jefferson University (TJU) in Philadelphia, Pennsylvania, required students to select a historic study and attempt to replicate it while adapting the protocol to modern equipment. As a representative example, Goby's earthworm study, referred to in Chapter 5 of *Advances in Paleoimaging*, was presented where the objective was to determine the quantity of calcium within the worm's gut (Conlogue and Marcinowski 1986). According to Goby, high calcium levels reflected calcium rich healthy soil. An earthworm was acquired from a section of Philadelphia's Fairmont Park where the lawn was quite lush. The live annelid was transport to the imaging laboratory of the TJU Radiography Program. The parameters for Goby's original study included a dead worm placed on a photosensitive glass plate and exposed to X-ray for nearly an hour. The plate was then processed and the resulting image magnified. Because the resulting image was viewed under magnification, Goby termed the procedure *microradiography.* Due to the long exposure, it was necessary to have a dead worm. However, the modification presented to the students spared the life of the worm that

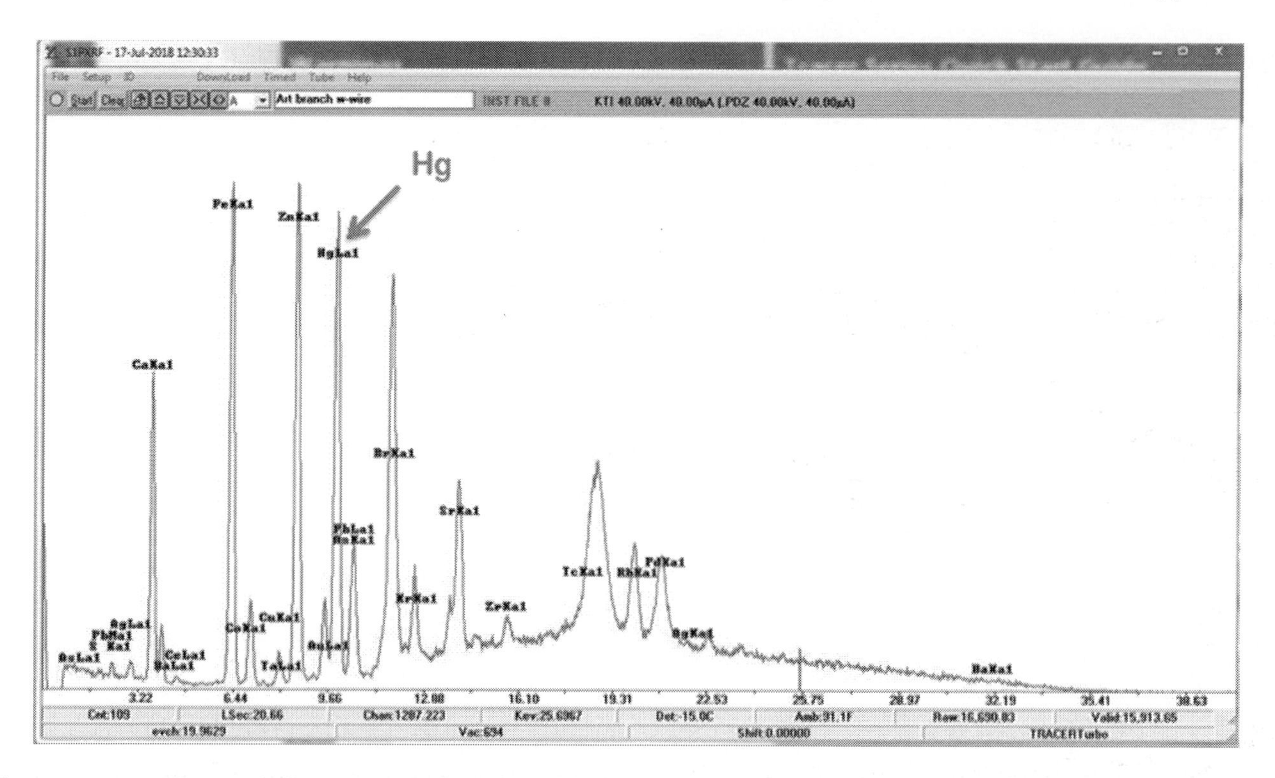

Figure 7.3. The XRF analysis of the arterial branch demonstrating a high content of mercury (Hg) content associated with red, vermilion, pigment.

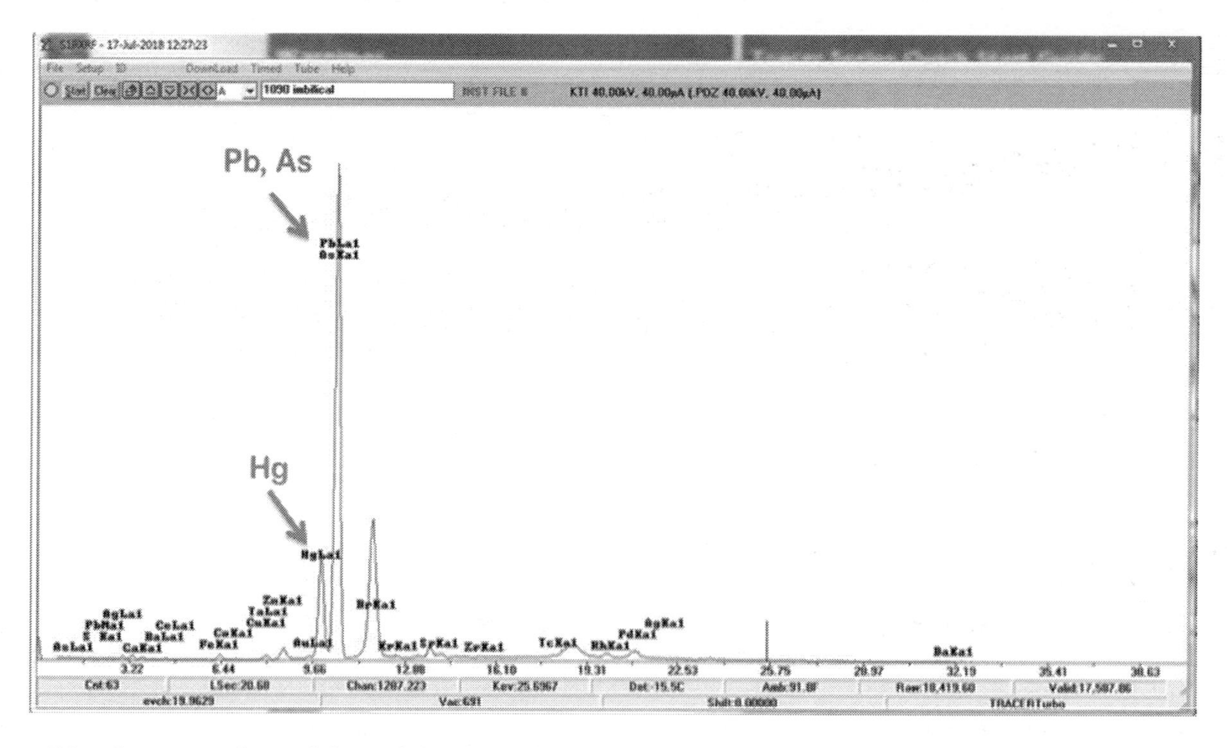

Figure 7.4. The XRF analysis of the umbilical cord showed low concentrations of mercury (Hg) but high levels of arsenic (As) and lead (Pb) the might have been used in the preservation process.

was eventually returned to the park. Therefore, not only did the worm need to be rendered motionless for the duration of the radiographic exposure, but sufficient resolution was acquired to demonstrate calcium within the digestive system. Placing the worm in refrigeration was considered, but the minimum required length of chilling was not known nor if the process might harm the worm. It was decided to place the worm in a drinking straw and seal the end. With the head-end of worm held vertically, the entire body stretched out. After several attempts, it

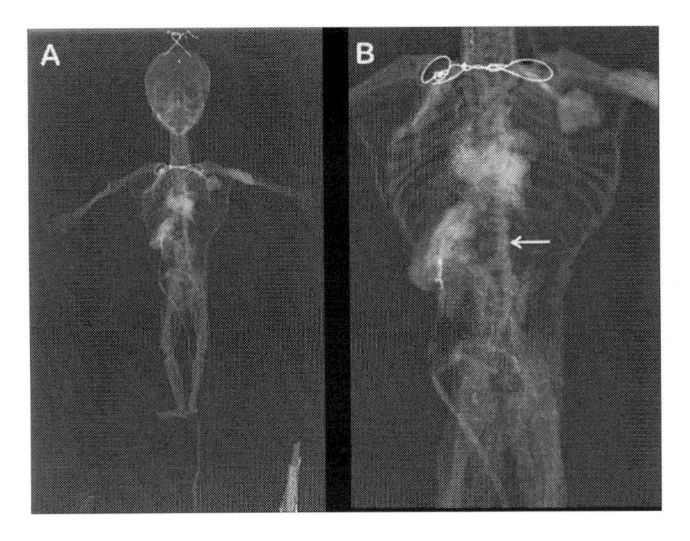

Figure 7.5. (A) The anterior-posterior, AP, radiograph of the prosected specimen, 1090.56. (B) An enlarged image more clearly demonstrating the abdominal aorta (arrow) and the bright white radiopacities in the abdomen and covering the thighs.

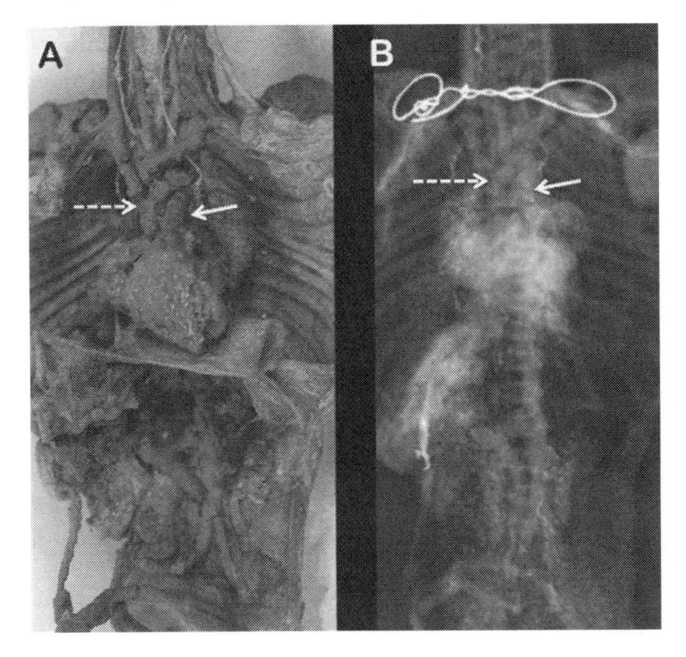

Figure 7.6. A comparison of the photograph (A) and radiograph (B) of the chest with the heart and associated vasculature: Note the blue pulmonary artery (solid arrow) leaving the right ventricle and the red aorta (dashed arrow) leaving the left ventricle have virtually the same radiographic density.

was possible to get the outstretched worm into the drinking straw. Both ends of the straw were folded over and taped. The now *restrained* annelid was placed on a cassette equipped with a 100 speed screen and the exposure taken at 50 kVp @ 100 mA (small focal spot) @ 0.02 seconds @ 40 inch (101 cm) SID. The resulting image, although not presenting the highest resolution, enabled clear visualization of the radiopaque material within the gut and the worm returned to the Park **[WS 7.56]**.

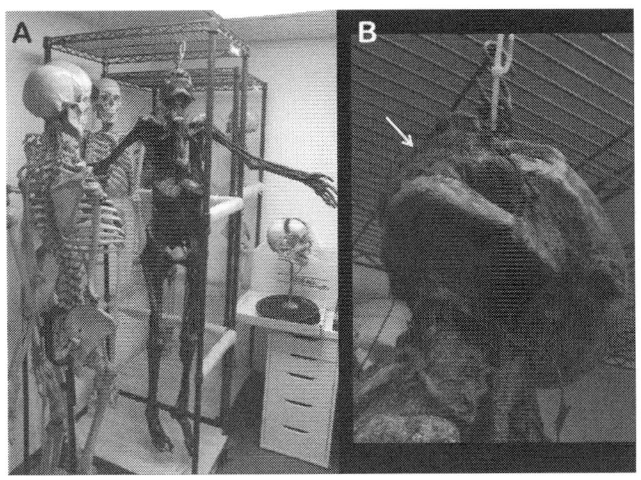

Figure 7.7. (A) The adult prosection was hanging in a storage area with other skeletal remains. (B) The mouth appeared to be sealed (arrow) preventing direct visualization of the dentition.

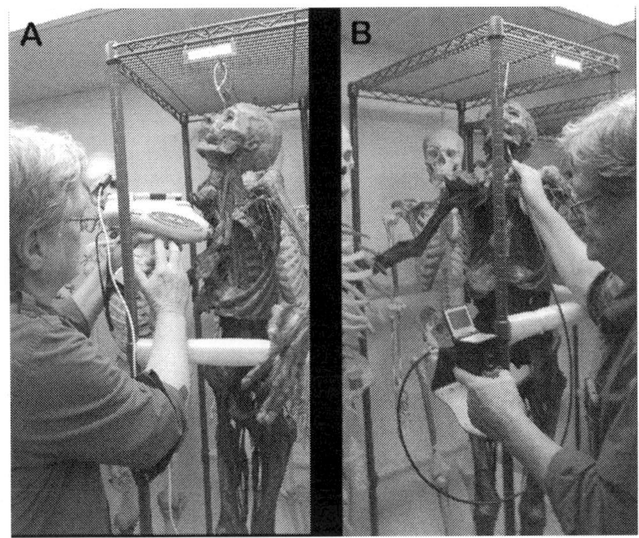

Figure 7.8. (A) Ron Beckett conducting an XRF analysis of the aortic arch. (B) An endoscopic examination of the dentition behind the sealed mouth.

An Artificially Produced Contrast Media

In 1970 the objective of a project was to demonstrate the lateral line canal system around the head of *Microgadus tomcod,* Atlantic tomcod or winter cod. The canal, lying just beneath the skin, is a sensory system in aquatic vertebrates used to detect movement, vibrations and pressure gradients in the surrounding water. Specimens were stored in 70% alcohol for several weeks prior to the study. Before the procedure specimens were removed from the preservative and place into a 95°F (35°C) water bath for an hour. The heated barium-gelatin contrast medium described in Chapter 5 of *Advances in Paleoimaging* was introduced through a 25-gauge needle into the lateral

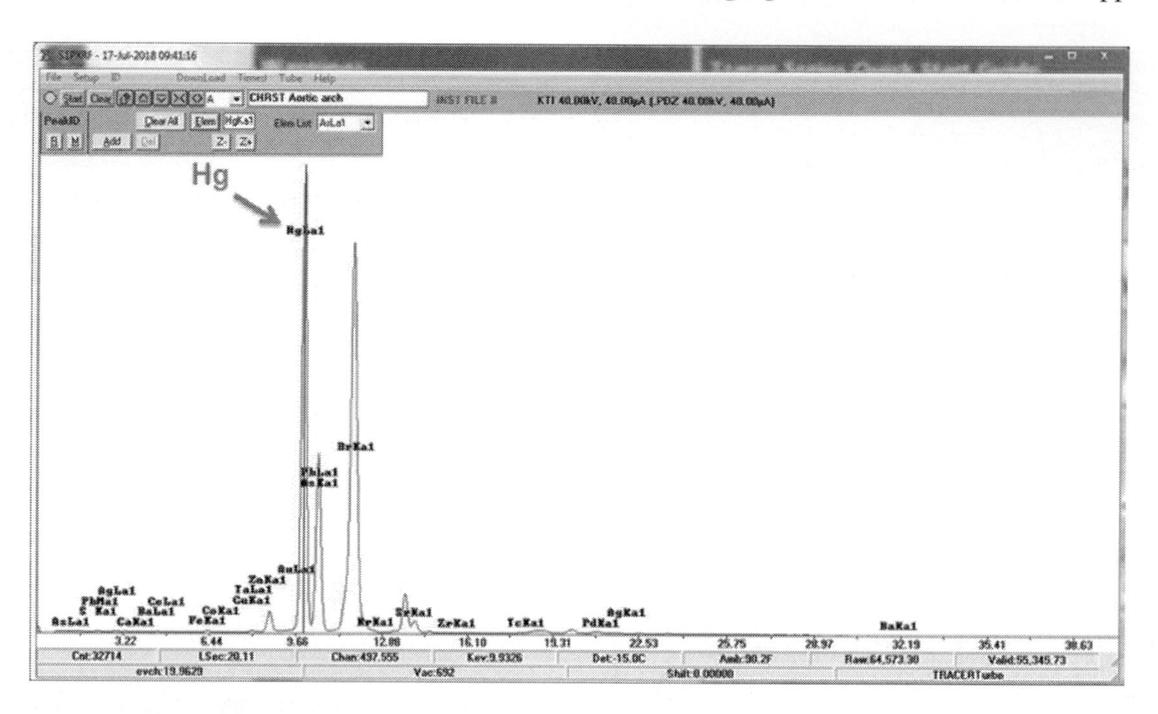

Figure 7.9. The XRF analysis of the aortic arch revealing high levels of mercury (Hg).

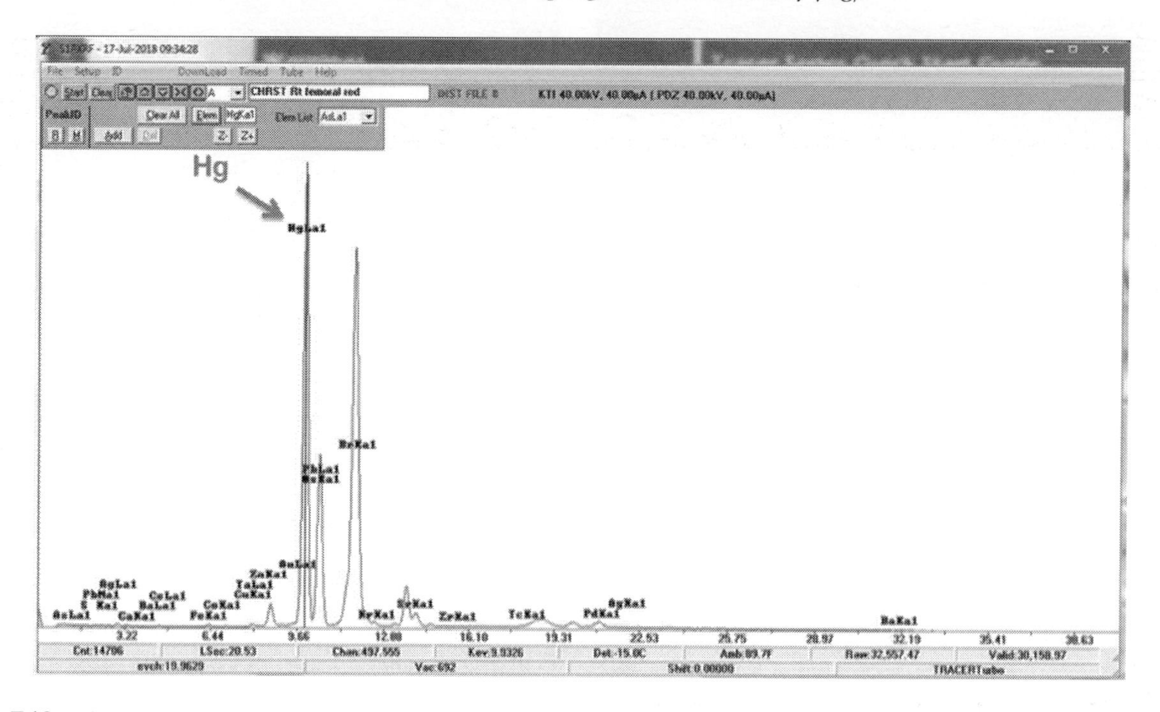

Figure 7.10. The XRF analysis of the right femoral red demonstrating an almost identical elemental profile as the aortic arch.

line canal just posterior of the gill **[WS 7.57]**. The hand injection was terminated when it appeared the canal system was well filled. After one hour in an ice bath the specimen was returned to alcohol. Because high resolution was required, non-screen Agfa-Gevaert STRUCTIX™ bipac radiographic film was selected for the study. Bipac indicated two sheet of film were loaded into the disposable paper envelope. Because the X-ray sensitivity of each sheet of film in the packet differed, one radiograph was slightly more dense or darker than the other. The slight difference provided a bit of flexibility in the selection of exposure factors, similar to bracketing in photographic exposures. In order to reduce scatter radiation and improve image quality, a metallic mask, with an opening large enough to accommodate each head, was first placed over the film packet **[WS 7.58]**. Three projections were obtained with the dorsal-ventral, DV, radiograph taken first followed by a lateral. If the exposure was satisfactory, the head was removed posterior to the gills, split mid-sagittally, in order to eliminate superimposition of

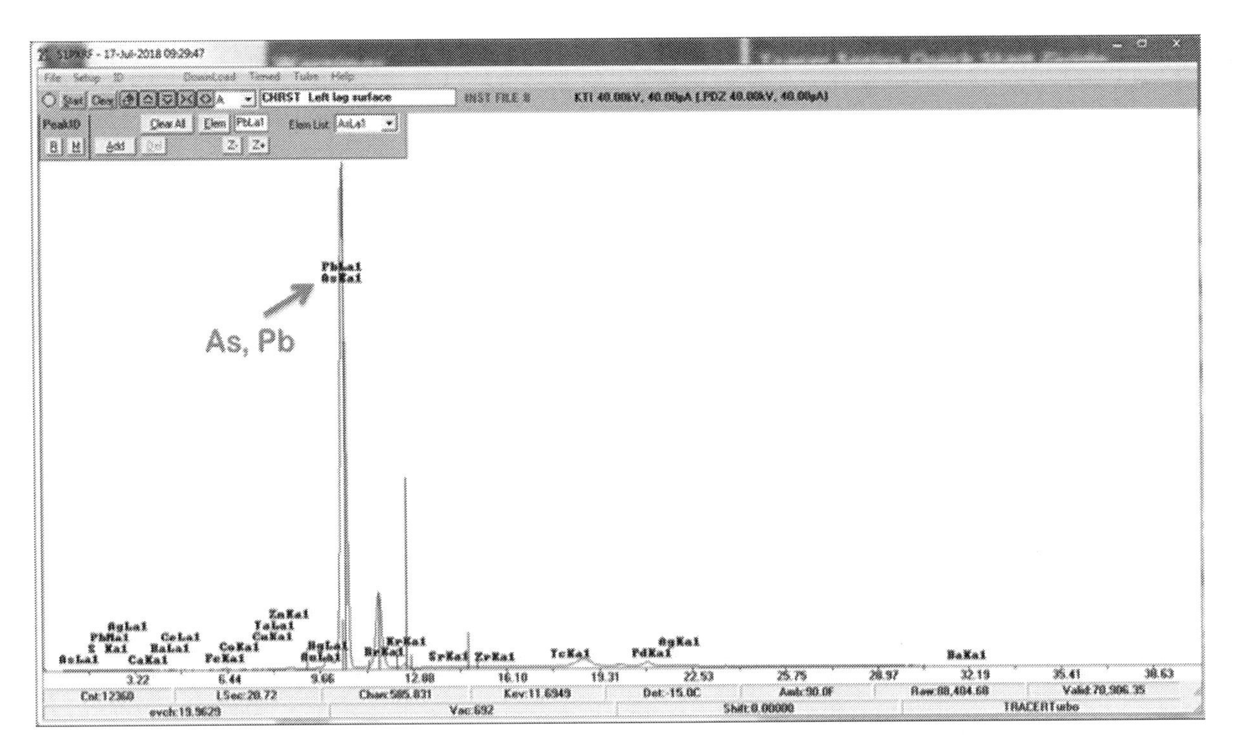

Figure 7.11. The XRF analysis of the surface of the left leg showing high concentrations of arsenic (As) and lead (Pb).

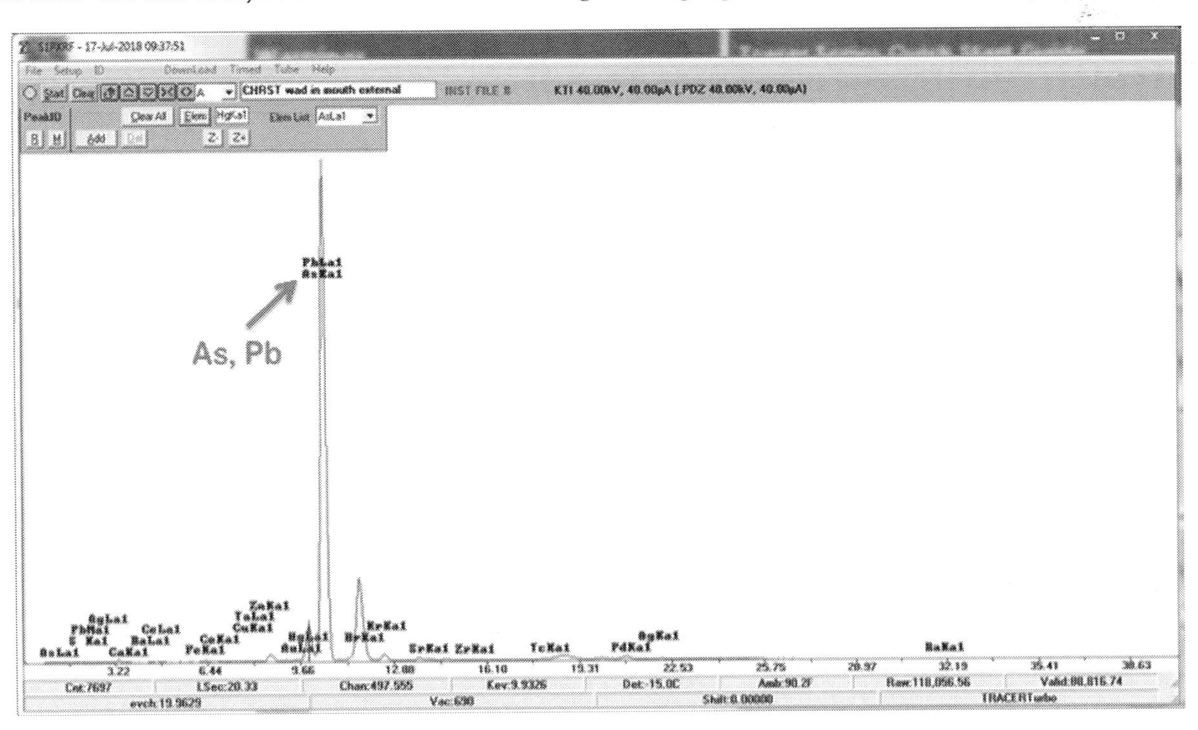

Figure 7.12. The XRF analysis of the external wad over the mouth provided a nearly identical profile with high concentrations of arsenic (As) suggesting the element was employed in the preservation of the remains.

structures, before the third radiograph was acquired [**WS 7.59**]. All exposures were taken with a General Electric portable radiographic unit with a 72-inch (182 cm) SID set at 40 kVp, 15 mA and a 10-second exposure time [**WS 7.59**]. Films were processed with Dupont Standard manual processing chemistry: developed for 5 minutes at 68°F (20°C); fixer for 10 minutes; and washed for 20 minutes. Once the films were dry, each was cut to fit into a 35 mm slide mount for viewing in a slide projector [**WS 7.60**].

For a number of reasons, the animal frequently selected for ophthalmological studies is the New Zealand white rabbit. Compared to other small mammals, with the exception of pigs and primates, rabbit eyes are most

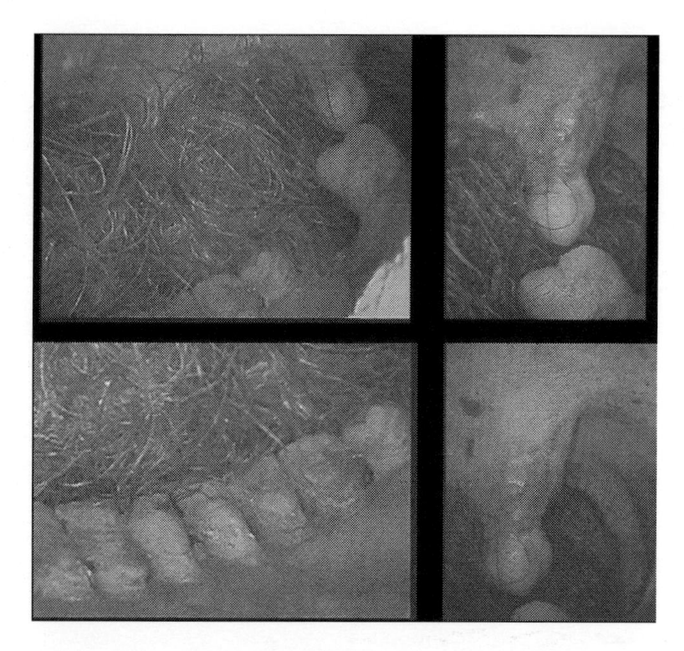

Figure 7.13. The endoscopic images of the mouth.

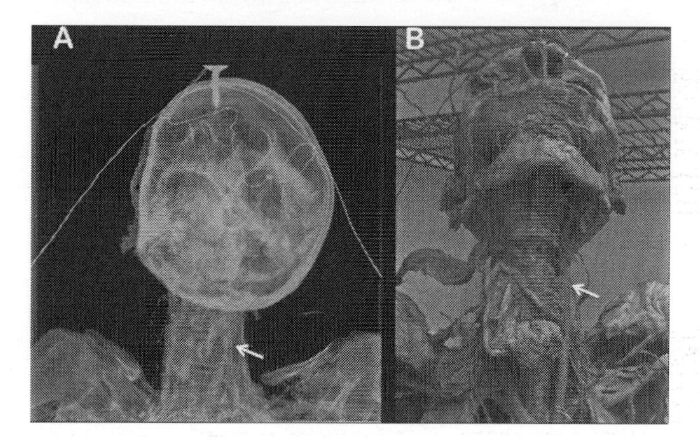

Figure 7.14. (A) The anterior-posterior, AP, radiograph of the head and neck demonstrating a radiopaque structure on the left side of the neck (yellow arrow). (B). The same structure (yellow arrow) seen on the photograph of the same area.

similar to humans. Rabbits also cost less to maintain and governed by less stringent regulations than pigs or primates. Most significant, from a radiographic perspective, their eyes can be proptosed or displaced out of the orbit without severing muscles, vessels and nerves. If done properly, the rabbit should hardly care (Mead 2016).

In 1972, the Ophthalmology Department at Yale University wanted to develop not only *in vivo* radiographic studies of the ocular circulation but also document the microcirculation of the rabbit eyes (Dueker et al., 1974). For the in vivo procedure, once the 4.4 to 6.6 lbs (2- to 3-kg) rabbit was anesthetized with intravenous sodium pentabarbitol and a periorbital injection of 2% Lidocaine, the eye was proptosed. Iodinated contrast medium, *Renografin® 60* (Diatrizoate Meglumine and Diatrizoate Sodium Injection UPS), was injected via a #4 French catheter that has been placed into the carotid artery. The circulation around the iris, the major arterial circle, was documented on dental film held by a clamp attached to a ring stand. In order to minimize scatter radiation and improve image quality, an extension tube was affixed to the front of the X-ray tube [**WS 7.62**]. Because the rabbit was alive and the dental films could only capture a portion of the arterial/venous cycle, several exposure were required to document the complete arterial phase of circulation around the iris [**WS 7.62 and 7.63**]. Although the objective to radiographically demonstrate the ocular circulation was achieved, the lack of sharpness was an inherent with dental film, not intended for macroradiography.

In order to demonstrate the ocular microcirculation, the contrast medium needed to remains in the vessels following dissection so the barium-gelatin mixture, previously described, was employed. Prior to being killed with sodium pentobarbital, rabbits were injected with 1000 units of heparin as an anticoagulant. Once the rabbit was dead, a #4 French polyethylene catheter was inserted into one of the common carotid arteries and the jugular vein on the opposite side was also catheterized to serve as a drain. Next, approximately 7 ml of warm normal saline was injected into the carotid catheter to flush the circulatory system. When a blush was noted in the vessels around the eye, tongue and gums it served as an indicator that the arterial system was flushed. Finally, 7.0 ml of heated barium-gelatin was introduced through the arterial catheter and continued until filling was noted in the conjunctival and iris vessels. The head was removed at the level of C6–C7 and placed in refrigeration at 40°F (4°C) for 24 hours to allow the gelatin to harden. The next day the injected eye was enucleated and place into 10% buffered formalin. After approximately fourteen days of fixation, the globe was dissected into several components: the optic nerve, retina, choroid and anterior segments. The specimens were sealed into thin (0.004 μ) plastic envelopes using a Futura Portable Heat Sealer. Sealing served several purposes. Because of the long exposure times necessary for microradiography and, if exposed to air, formalin fixed specimens would have quickly dry out and shrivel. During the initial phases of the study, specimens were not sealed in the plastic envelope and the long exposure caused the specimen to dry resulting in apparent motion on the processed radiograph [**WS 7.64**]. Sealing the specimen also created a stable microenvironment within the envelope. Specimens in envelopes were also easier to immobilize, handle and store for future examination.

All the microradiographs were taken with a unit constructed specifically for the Radiology Research Laboratory (Conlogue et al., 1984). The unit was a water-cooled with a chromium copper target, 0.2 × 1.0 mm focal spot and a beryllium window **[WS 7.65]**. Specimens were exposed at 20 kVp and 20 mA with the times varying from 5 to 8 minutes, depending on the thickness of the tissue. All images were recorded on single emulsion, Kodak Type R film that were hand processed in Kodak D19 developer at 68°F (20°C) for 8 minutes, fixed for 16 minutes, washed for 30 minutes, and hung to air dry.

With the success of the rabbit project, the study group expanded to include cats (Rothman, Kier, Dueker, 1975) and a number of more exotic species. Particularly for the latter group, because of the rarity of a number of animals available, the injections included the entire artery circulation. In all cases, 5000 units of heparin was administered prior to killing the animal with sodium pentobarbital. Once the animal was dead, two injection approaches were utilized. In the first, the sternum was split, pericardium opened and the aorta ligated at its root. An incision was made above the ligation and a #4 French catheter introduced approximately 5.0 mm into the aortic arch and tied in place. The abdomen was then opened with a midline incision extending from the level of L1 to slightly below the aortic bifurcation. The inferior vena cava was ligated at the same level and a K50 connector tube inserted above the ligation and tied into place to allow the blood to drain from the animal (Figures 7.15 and 7.16). The second injection route required the femoral artery to be isolated and catheterized while the femoral vein on the opposite side was exposed and catheterized to serve as a drain (Figure 7.17). Regardless of the approach, 100 ml of warm saline was injected into the catheter followed immediately by the same volume of the barium-gelatin. As previously indicated, the conjunctival vessels were monitored to observe the presence of the white contrast medium. Following termination of the injection the animal was placed in 40°F (4°C) refrigerated for 24 hours prior to enucleating the eye and fixation in 10% buffered formalin. Following fixation and dissection, as with the rabbits, the contrast medium remained in the vessels **[WS 7.69]**.

In a number of cases, the eyes were not removed but, regardless, in all instances the animals were skinned and the abdominal and chest cavities were opened before immersing the carcass into a tank of 10% buffered formalin. Skinning and opening the cavities allowed the fixative to penetrate tissues and reach organs. In all, 383 animals were injected and remained in tanks of preservative until 1994 when they were transferred from formalin, considered hazardous, to a somewhat harmless solution of Ward's® WARDSafe™ (Ward's Science). In 2010 a new phase of the project began. Many of the animals had been injected, but lacked even plane radiographs before they were stored for preservation. A survey of the specimens, now known as the Kier/Conlogue Collection began with plane digital radiography to determine the extent of filling. The next planned step was to examine the specimens with imaging modalities that were not available four decades ago, such as computed tomography and magnetic resonance. However, before expanding the discussion into the more recently revealed properties of the contrast medium, the evolving versatility that was demonstrated more than 40 years must be considered.

Also in 1972, Dr. William Allen III, a neuroradiology fellow at Yale, began an investigation of spinal trauma using cats as the anatomic model (Allen et al., 1974, Dohrmann and Allen 1975). Anesthetized cats were placed on a ventilator and maintained at 98°F

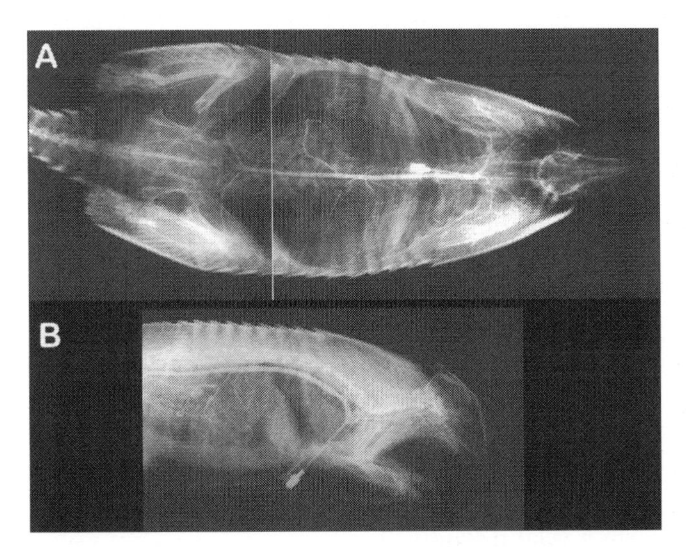

Figure 7.15. An AP (A) and lateral (B) radiographs of an aortic approach on an armadillo (*Dasypus novemcinctus*).

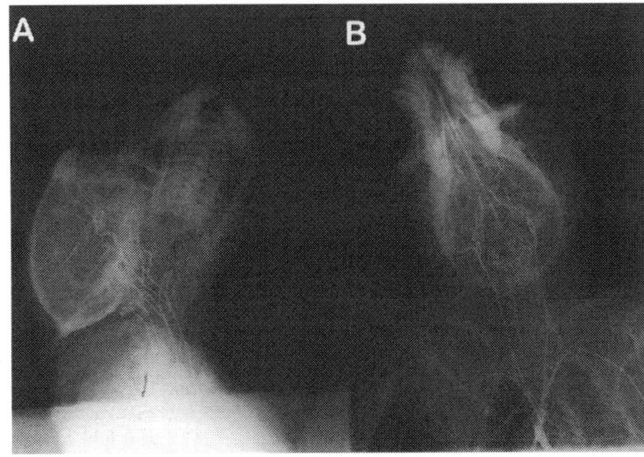

Figure 7.16. A lateral (A) and dorsal-ventral, DV, (B) projections of a stump-tailed macaque (*Macaca arctoides*) with an aortic route injection.

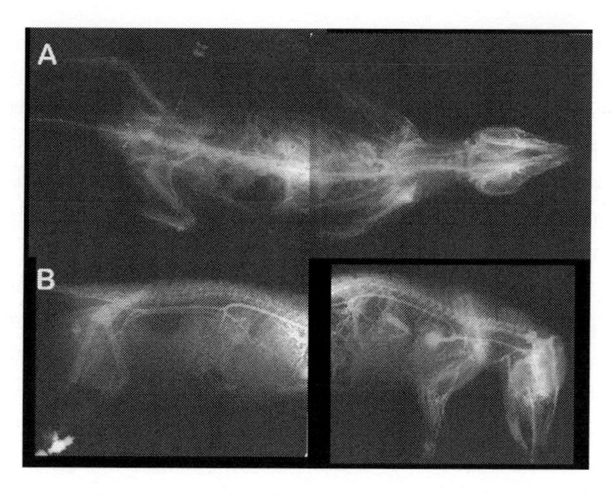

Figure 7.17. An AP (A) and lateral (B) radiographs of the femoral artery injection route of an opossum (*Didelphis virginianus*).

(37°C) with the aid of a heating pad. A laminectomy then exposed the dura mater covering the spinal cord from C7 to T1. Other than the control animals that received no trauma, two levels of trauma, either 300 or 500 gram-centimeter (gm-cm) contusions were delivered to the cord. The former was sufficient to produce transitory, while the latter enough to create permanent paraplegia. A vertically oriented tube was placed over the exposed cord to deliver the trauma. Either a 15 gm (0.033 lb) or 25 gm (0.055 lb) weight was dropped from a height of 20 cm to produce the desired effects.

A polyethylene catheter was introduced into the left axillary artery to approximately the level of aortic arch as a route to introduce the heated barium-gelatin contrast media. Prior to the termination of the procedure, 5000 units of heparin were administered as an anticoagulant. Finally, an intravenous injection of potassium chloride was administered to stop the heart at one of three time intervals postcontusion: immediately (0–5 min); 15 to 30 minutes; 1 or 2 hours. Following an injection of 50 ml of contrast medium, the spinal cord was frozen *in situ* with liquid nitrogen then removed en bloc from C-1 to T-2 and placed in a −4°F (−20°C) freezer for one hour. Once removed from the freezer, the specimen was placed in 10% buffered formalin for a period of two-weeks. The preserved spinal cord was dissected from the vertebral column and dura remove, before packaging as described earlier. AP and lateral projections of the entire cord were acquired using the previous described radiographic unit at 20 kVp, 20 mA, and a six-minute exposure time on Kodak Type R film. The exposed film was manually processed with Kodak D19 developer for eight minutes at 68°F (20°C). Fixing time was twice the development period and finally washed in water for 30 to 35 minutes [**WS 7.70**]. In all, for each projection, about one hour was required from the time the specimen was placed into the X-ray unit until the *wet* radiograph could be viewed. Following examination of the two projections, cross-sections, approximately 3 mm (0.118 inch) in thickness, were cut, packaged and radiographed at the settings indicated earlier, but the exposure time reduced to three minutes [**WS 7.71**].

The barium-gelatin preformed well under the thin sectioning by cutting cleanly, remaining within the vessels and maintaining its shape after fixation. In addition, it was sufficiently radiopaque to provide high X-ray photon attenuation for the microradiographic studies of the rabbit, cat and exotic species eyes as well as the spinal cord trauma studies on the cat. Dr. E. Leon Kier, Chief of Neuroradiology in the Yale Radiology Department, wanted to expand the use of the contrast medium to demonstrate the cerebral ventricles. It was due to his interests in comparative anatomy and embryology that enabled the previously described study to proceed beyond merely ocular circulation.

The ventricular system of the 90 to 100 cm (35.4 to 39.3 inches) long sharks (*Squalua acanthias*), 15–18 cm (5.9 to 7.08 inches) frogs (*Rana catesbeiana*) and, on average, 160 cm (62.99 inches) iguanas (*Iguana iguana*) were injected through the fourth ventricle. Using a rongeur, a scoop-shaped tip surgical instrument, the inferior-medial portion of the occipital bone was removed to expose the roof of the fourth ventricle. The *tela choroidea*, the triangularly shaped fold of pia mater, was carefully elevated posterior-inferiorly. The tip of a 20-gauge Teflon catheter attached to a syringe filled with the barium-gelatin mixture warmed to 95°F (35°C) was gently introduced into the ventricle directly anteriorly towards the cerebral aqueduct. The volume injected ranged from 0.4 ml (frog) to 1.0 ml (shark).

Since manual processing of the single emulsion radiographic film required at least one hour per projection, it was decided to accept the lower resolution and use screen film that could be processed with an automatic processing unit loaded into a non-screen film holder. All animals were radiographed at 55 kVp, 1000 mAs at a 40-inch (100 cm) SID. Because the body of the frog was anteriorly-posterior compressed, only a dorsal-ventral, DV, projection was acquired [**WS 7.72**]. For sharks, with a cartilaginous skeleton, both DV and lateral images were obtained [**WS 7.73**]. Due to the dense bone surround the brain of the iguana, the lateral projection provided the most information regarding the level of filling (Figure 7.18). Following the described preliminary radiographs, each animal was placed in 40°F (4°C) refrigeration for 24 hours to ensure that the barium-gelatin solidified.

After the cooling period, small animals, such as the frogs, were placed directly into containers with 10%

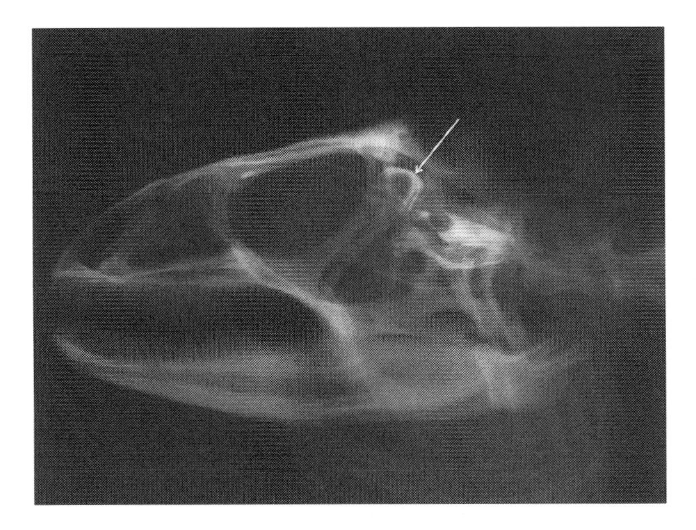

Figure 7.18. Lateral projection of the iguana *(Iguana iguana)* skull showing the contrast media filled cerebral ventricles (arrow).

Figure 7.20. Lateral radiograph of an iguana brain demonstrating the contrast media filled cerebral ventricles on Kodak Type R single emulsion film: Note the olfactory bulbs (arrows).

buffered formalin. Larger specimens, such as the sharks and iguanas were decapitated at approximately the level of C-3 and deposited into containers with the preservative. All specimens remained in the fixative for at least two weeks prior to any additional studies. In order to get a more accurate representation of the ventricular filling and eliminate superimposed bony structures, such as in the iguana, another modality was necessary. As computed tomography was not readily available in the mid 1970s, conventional tomography was employed (Figure 7.19A and B). For specimens with exceptional filling, like this iguana, the brain was removed and radiographed on single emulsion Kodak Type R film (Figure 7.20).

In order to introduce the contrast medium into the ventricular system of mammals a different method was developed. All mammals including rabbits (*Lepus cuniculus*), sheep (*Ovis aries*), cats (*Felis catus*), dogs (*Canis familiaris*) African green monkeys (*Cercapithecus aethiops*) and Stump-tailed macaques (*Macaca arctoides*), the injections made directly into a lateral ventricle was an easier approach than the craniotomy performed on the non-mammals. Initially, a high cervical laminectomy was performed to provide direct visualization of the cervical subarachnoid space. A burr hole was then drilled lateral to the mid-line to reveal the dura mater before it was nicked to expose the brain. The exact position of the hole varied with species, for example on 2–4 kg (4.4 to 8.8 lbs) cats it was 4.5 mm (0.177 inch) from the midline at a level of the most lateral aspect of the zygomatic process. In order to accurately introduce the barium-gelatin into the ventricle, a simple device was constructed by a machinist, Mr. Vincent Gillette of Wilcott, Connecticut. It consisted of a vertical microscope stage that served both for rigid fixation and precise control the injection needle. The latter, a 20-gauge Jelco® needle, consisted of a Teflon catheter in which a beveled metallic needle

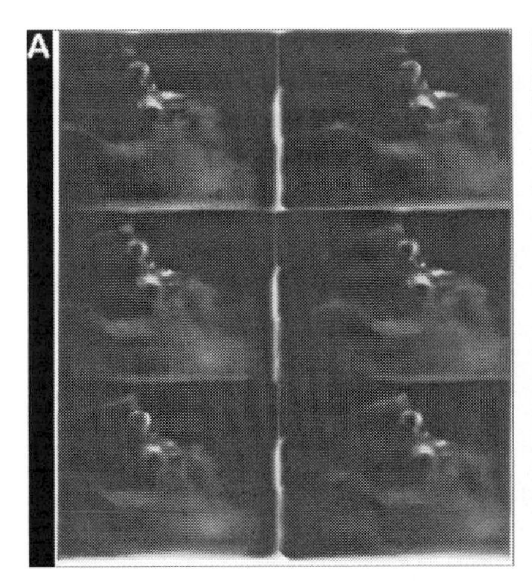

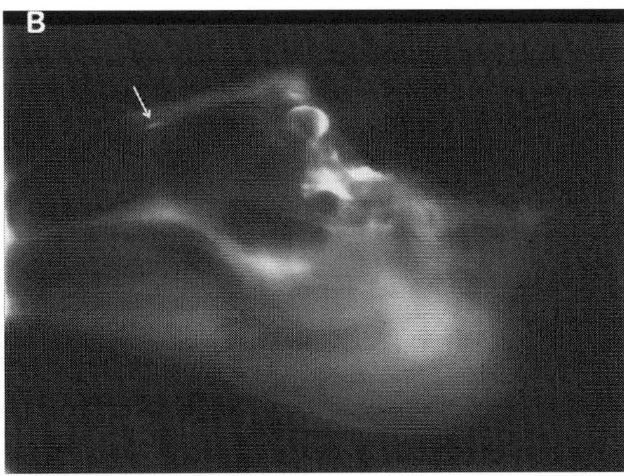

Figure 7.19. (A) A series of six lateral tomography exposures a different levels to better visual the contrast filled cerebral ventricles of the iguana. (B) A single tomographic slice demonstrating contrast media into the olfactory bulb (arrow).

protrudes from the catheter [**WS 7.77**]. The controls on the microscope stage permitted the needle to be advanced to a specific depth. Once within the lateral ventricle, the metallic needle was removed. A connecting tube was attached to a syringe filled with the 95°F (35°C) barium-gelatin mixture. After advancing the contrast medium through the tubing, in order to eliminate the introduction of air, it was attached to the Jelco catheter and the injection was terminated when the white mixture was observed in the cervical subarachnoid space. Following the completion of the injection, either plane radiography or fluoroscopy was employed with the tubing attached to observe the level of filling before the animal was placed into the 40°F (4°C) refrigeration for 24 hours [**WS 7.78**].

The next day at least AP and lateral radiographs [**WS 7.79**] were taken after the connecting tube was disconnected and removal of the Jelco catheter from the brain. As this was during the period of the introduction of computed tomography into the clinical setting, the modality was not available for specimen imaging. Therefore, conventional tomography was employed to eliminate superimposition of the bony elements of the skull and provide better visualization of the components of the cerebral ventricles. For example, due to the small size of the cat skull, the most complex tomography motion, hypocycloidal, was required to demonstrate the ventricles of the cat [**WS 7.80**].

With the assistance of Dr. Edmund S. Crelin, professor of anatomy and director of the Human Growth and Development Study Unit at the Yale University Medical School, the research expanded to include human fetuses acquired by the Anatomy Department. For the study of cerebral circulation, human fetus that had been fixed in 10% buffered formalin and stored in the Anatomy Department were used. Three injection approaches were employed. In the first, a thoracotomy-type incision was made and the left lung reflected medially to expose the thoracic aorta. In between the intercostal branches of the aorta, a Teflon #5 French catheter was introduced, advanced to the level of the aortic arch and tied into place with a triple-0 cardiovascular suture. For smaller fetuses, a second approach was developed, the heart was exposed by opening the pericardium and the aortic arch was catheterized at its origin with the largest possible diameter polyethylene tube. The third method introduced the contrast media into the circulation by utilizing the umbilical vein. Regardless of the approach, the fetus and bottle containing the barium-gelatin mixture were placed into a water bath warmed to 98°F (37°C). Once the contrast medium was thoroughly liquefied, the solution was drawn up into a syringe. The fetus was removed from the water bath and, with the aid of fluoroscopic visualization, the contrast medium was hand injected through the catheter. The injection was continued until either a rupture was noted or sufficient filling had been achieved. Following the injection, the fetus with attached tubing was placed in 40°F (4°C) refrigeration for 24 hours, before the injection tubing was removed and AP and lateral radiographs were taken [**WS 7.81**].

During this period, Dr. Crelin suggested injecting an adult cadaver donated to the Yale Medical School for dissection, but the individual did not meet the criteria for the program. Following the embalming procedure, the same catheter in the femoral artery used to introduce the preservative fluids was also employed to introduce the barium-gelatin contrast media. Due to the size of the cadaver, it was not possible to put the remains in a refrigeration unit for 24 hours to cool the gelatin. However, as the contrast media followed the injection of the formalin based embalming fluid, it was decided to wait 24 hours at room temperature before cutting into the body. The upper and lower extremities were removed by the Department of Orthopaedics without any noticeable lose of the contrast media. In order to ensure that the preservative fluids would also surround the brain, a coronal incision extending anterior to each external auditory canal and across the top of the head was made to expose the skull. After pealing back the scalp, a circular cut was made around the calvarium to expose the brain. Once submerged, the bone skull-cap was put back in place and the scalp returned to the original position.

After the extremities were removed and brain exposed, the remaining head and torso was placed in a tank of 10% buffered formalin. Because there was not a radiographic facility where the partially dissected remains could be easily radiographed, the cadaver remained in a tank for nearly 20 years before it could be imaged.

Dr. Kier dissected a number of the animals and human fetuses, isolating the brains for photographs [**WS 7.82**] and additional radiographs free of the overlying bony structures [**WS 7.83**] (Kier 1974, 1975, and 1977). However, nearly 20 years later, in the mid-1990s, the project was resumed to employ imaging modalities, such as digital radiography, multi-detector computed tomography, MDCT, magnetic resonance, MR, imaging. Plane radiographs of the adult cadaver revealed that the barium-gelatin had remained intact with *cracking* noted in the large vessels of the injected adult cadaver [**WS 7.84**]. For the MDCT studies the specimens, including the adult cadaver, were wrapped in plastic wrap to contain the remains and protect the scanner couch [**WS 7.85**]. As noted in Chapter 5 (*Advances in Paleoimaging*), clinical protocols must be modified for specimen imaging [**WS 7.86**]. The initial scout or scano images acquired before the actual scan, because of the wider latitude of the digital data, more clearly demonstrated the cracks in the contrast media [**WS 7.87**] than the images recorded on film [**WS 7.84**]. On MDCT sections what appeared to be clots were visualized in the coronal [**WS 7.88**] and sagittal [**WS 7.89**] sections of the chest. Streak artifact, created by the density of the contrast media, was most evident in regions with large volumes of the barium gelatin, such as the aortic arch [**WS 7.90**]. With the high concentrations of contrast media in the ascending and thoracic aorta, using the ROI application, density values indicated high HU values [**WS 7.91**]. Because of the high density, the cerebral arterial circulation was well demonstrated with both mean and MIP settings on multiplanar reconstructions [**WS 7.92**]. The plane computed radiography, CR, images revealed a well-preserved brain indicating that the opening of the skull to permit the preservative to reach the surface of the organ was successful [**WS 7.93**]. In addition, both superficial and cerebral arterial vasculature were well filled. However, the extensive filling and accompanying superimposition made it difficult to evaluate specific components of the circulation. However, 0.5 mm MPR images revealed an apparent clot in the right internal carotid artery using the software on the Toshiba Aquilion™ used to acquire the data [**WS 7.94**] and downloaded to be examined with OsiriX™ software on a MAC Pro laptop computer [**WS 7.95**]. Because the head of the preserved specimen could not be positioned prior to the scanning procedure, the right and left cerebral circulation could not be easily compared. Applying the oblique sectioning function on the Aquilion™ [**WS 7.96**] presented the resulting off-axis coronal slices demonstrating the lack of contrast filled right middle cerebral artery [**WS 7.97**]. The same filling defect was noted on the thick oblique sections with the OsiriX™ software [**WS 7.98**].

Three-dimensional reconstructions utilizing the Aquilion™ *basket* 3D algorithm provided an excellent demonstration of the barium-gelatin contrast media [**WS 7.99**]. A combination of applying the 3D algorithm, rendering the bone semi-transparent and providing a somewhat pink background produced a striking demonstration of the contrast filled vessels [**WS 7.100**]. However, in order to isolate the cerebral circulation, an application known as *clipping*, described in Chapter 5 (*Advances in Paleoimaging*), was utilized to eliminated a number of structures around the brain [**WS 7.101**]. The result was an unobstructed view of the arterial circulation in the head and neck revealing the apparent clot seen on the MPR images [**WS 7.102**].

The barium-gelatin injected cadaver illustrated several points. The contrast media filled even small vessels distant from the injection site, remained intact for over twenty years and provided adequate radiopacity to be well demonstrated without significant streak artifact, on a clinical MDCT unit. However, a nonclinically applicable scanning protocol was required to maximize the resolution to enable visualization of the smaller contrast filled vessels. This detail was best exemplified by the visualization of the artery of Adamkiewicz, the vessel supplying blood to the lumbar and sacral spine, seen on MPR [**WS 7.103**] and 3D reconstruction [**WS 7.104**].

Because the contrast media lacked paramagnetic properties, it was not visualized using magnetic resonance imaging. However, although the brain was shrunken due to dehydration, internal structures, such as gray and white matter were easily differentiated [**WS 7.105**].

The clinical MDCT unit did not provide acceptable resolution for specimens smaller than 6 inches (15 cm) specimens [**WS 7.106**]. Other imaging modalities, such as CR [**WS 7.107**], provided a quick easy method to triage the nearly 400 specimens prepared in the early 1970s to determine the best candidates for another imaging modality, microCT. The latter, discussed in Chapter 7 (*Advances in Paleoimaging*), provides sections between 50 and 100 µm (0.05–0.1 mm). Depending on specimen size, two different units were used. The first, a General Electric eXplore™ 120 Preclinical MicroCT unit, had a maximum 75-mm diameter scan area, therefore specimens larger than the head of a cat would not fit into the unit. Specimens were scanned, on average, at 90 kVP, 40 mA and a 10-minutes acquisition time and produced isotropic reconstruction voxels between 50–100 µm (0.05–0.1 mm). This unit provided superb resolution of the smallest brains dissected from the skull [**WS 7.108**].

The other unit, the Nikon Metrology™ XTH225L MicroCT system can accommodate larger specimens due to the 16 × 16 inch (41 × 41 cm) scan area. Specimens were scanned using 135 kVp, 95 µA, and a 6-minute acquisition time and rendered 89 µm (0.089 mm) isotropic reconstruction voxels. A good example of the capabilities of the system is illustrated with an intact cat skull radiographed in 1972 following the injection of the contrast media (Figure 7.21) a 3D MIP MicroCT image (Figure 7.22), and OsiriX™ software MPR reconstructions (Figure 7.23). A cat brain removed from the skull and scanned with a GE CT-120™ MicroCT unit provided concrete documentation a fine vessel filling (Figure 7.24).

Everything to this point has considered injections shortly after death in preserved specimens or intact remains. However, contrast media injections can be accomplished a day or two after death if certain conditions are observed. An example was a horse head removed shortly after death and transported several hours to the Quinnipiac Diagnostic imaging laboratory. The objective of the study was to demonstrate correlative anatomy of the skull and brain employing MDCT

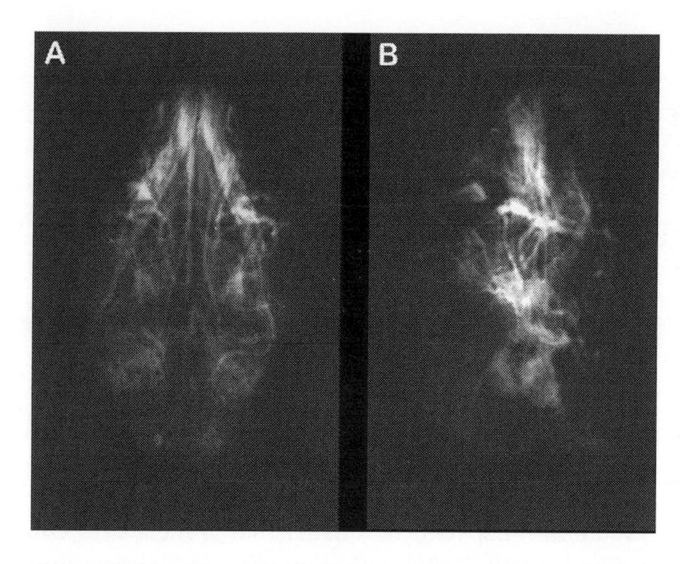

Figure 7.21. (A) A dorsal-ventral, DV, and (B) lateral projections following a cerebral vascular injection of a cat skull taken in 1972.

and MR. In order to remove as many air-bubbles as possible, a fresh batch of the barium-gelatin contrast media was prepared, as described in Chapter 5 (*Advances in Paleoimaging*), two days prior to the arrival of the specimen. Following the preliminary CR images, to establish

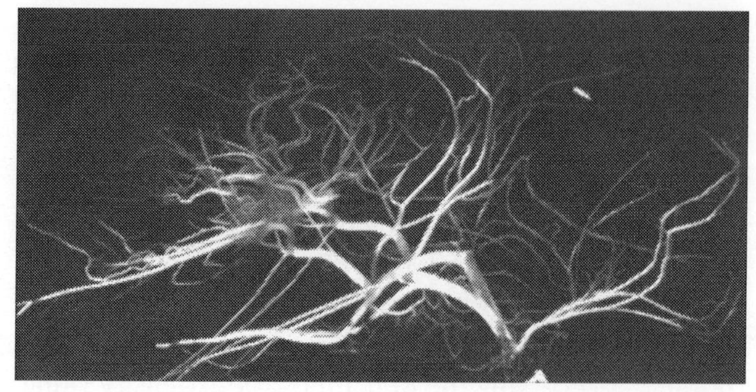

Figure 7.22. A sagittal 3D MIP image acquired using the Nikon Metrology™ XTH225L MicroCT of the cat skull injected in 1972.

the optimal technical factors, the right common carotid artery was isolated, catheterized with a polyethylene tube attached to a *Christmas tree* adapter and a three-way stopcock and flushed with normal saline **[WS 7.113]**. The bottled contrast media was warmed in a 95°F (35°C) water bath until completely liquefied. Approximately 120 ml was then injected through the catheter before leakage of the contrast media was noted from severed arterial branches. The DV and lateral radiographs acquired after the injection revealed good filling via the right carotid

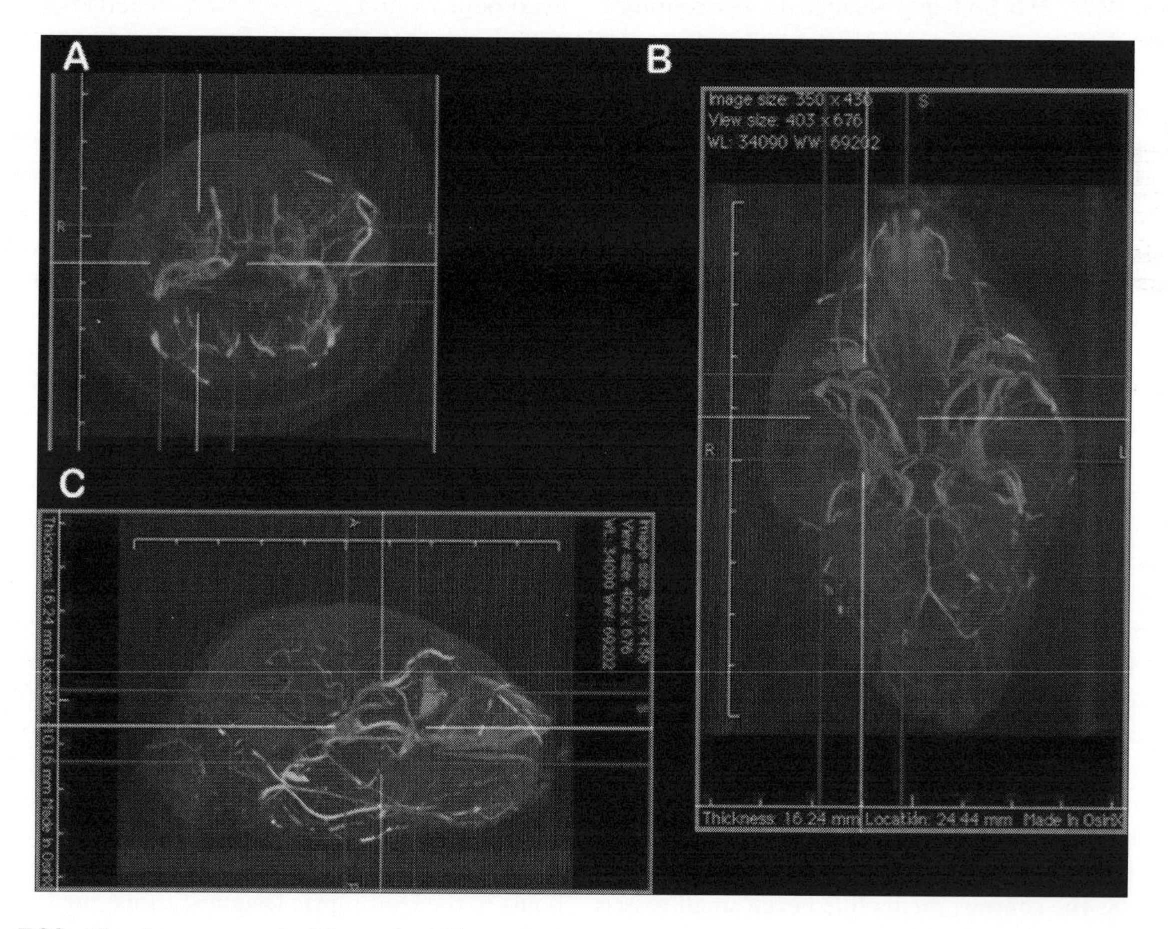

Figure 7.23. The data set acquired from the Nikron MicroCT unit processed using Osirix™ into 3D coronal (A), axial (B) and sagittal MPR images.

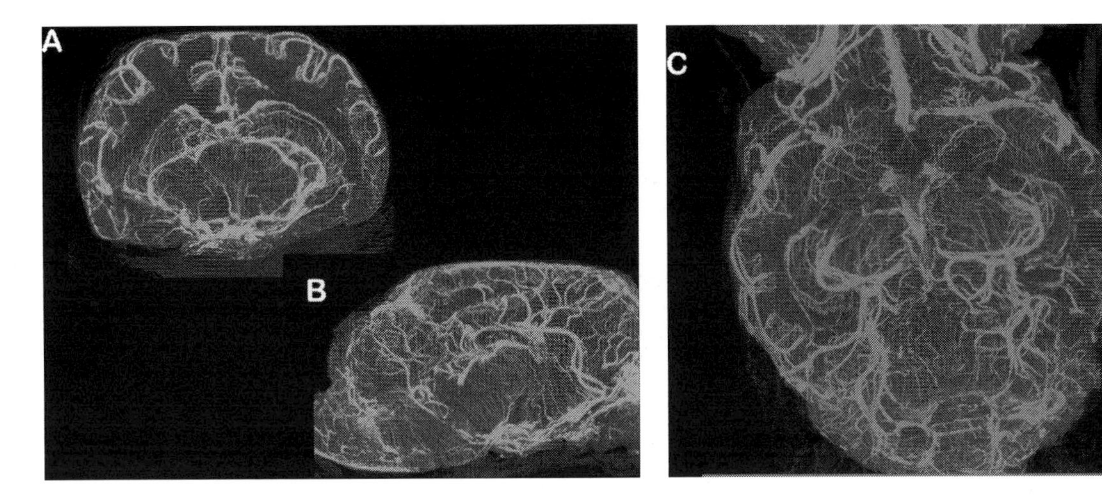

Figure 7.24. A cat brain microCT 20 mm thick MIP coronal (A) and sagittal (B) sections. (C) A 10 mm thick axial section of the cat brain.

artery [**WS 7.114**]. Because none of the severed branches on the right side were ligated, continued injected would have resulted in greater leakage, but insufficient contrast media had been injected to completely fill the opposite side via the circle of Willis. Without delay, the head was scanned with the Toshiba Aquilion™ with the following protocol: 120 kVp; 200 mA; 64 slices; 0.5 mm thick; 240 mm FOV; FC81 (maximum edge enhancement). Because the intent was to demonstrate correlative anatomy and only limited arterial filling was achieved, it was decided to move straight to 3D reconstruction. Based on the success with the injected adult cadaver, the basket algorithm was selected for presentation of the circulatory component [**WS 7.115**]. The semi-transparent algorithm was added in order to reveal the relative position of the brain and cord relative to the arteries [**WS 7.116**].

References

Allen WE III, CM D'Angelo, and EL Kier. 1974. Correlation of Microangiographic and Electrophysiologic Changes in Experimental Spinal Cord Trauma. *Radiology.* 111(1):107–115.

Conlogue, GJ and F Marcinowski. 1986. Microradiography: A Theoretical Basis and Practical Applications. *Radiologic Technology.* 58:301–309.

Conlogue, GJ, EV Warmoth, and J Wetmore. 1984. Microradiography Using a Non-Commercially Constructed Grenz Ray Unit. *Radiologic Technology.* 55:813–816.

Dohrmann, GJ and WE Allen III. 1975. Microcirculation of Traumatized Spinal Cord: A Correlation of Microangiography and Blood Flow Patterns in Transitory and Permant Paraplegia. *Journal of Trauma-Injury Infection & Critical Care.* 15(11):1003–1013.

Dueker, DK, EL Kier, and SL Rothman. 1974. Microangiography of the Rabbit Eye: A Radiographic Study. *Investigative Ophthalmology.* 13(7):543–547.

Kier EL. The Cerebral Ventricles: A Phylogenetic and Onotogenetic Study. In: *Radiology of the Skull and Brain*, Vol. III. T.H. Newton and D.G. Potts (eds), C.V. Mosby Company, St. Louis, MO, 1977, pp. 2787–2914.

Kier EL. The Evolutionary Basis of Cerebral Arterial Patterns. In: *Advances in Cerebral Angiography.* G. Salamon (ed.), Springer, Berlin, Germany, 1975.

Kier EL. The Fetal Cerebral Arteries: A Phylogenetic and Ontogenetic Study. Contributing author. In: *Radiology of the Skull and Brain*, Vol. II. T.H. Newton and D.G. Potts (eds), C.V. Mosby Company, St. Louis, MO, 1974, pp. 1089–1130.

Lurie, A. Personal communication. May, 2008.

Mead, Alden. Personal communication. 17 July 2016.

Rothman, SL, EL Kier, and DK Dueker. 1975. Microangiographic Anatomy of the Cat's Eye. *Investigative Radiology.* 10(1):53–61.

Scheuer and Black (2000) *Developmental Juvenile Osteology.* Academic Press, London, UK.

Endoscopy and XRF Cases

8

RONALD G. BECKETT AND GERALD J. CONLOGUE

Contents

Introduction

It is apparent to the reader that paleoimaging is enhanced when multiple modalities are employed in concert with one another. In this case study we present several mini-cases where data collected through the application of video-endoscopy. Depending on the research context, often the only radiographic modality possible is plane radiography. As described in Chapter 2 of *Advances in Paleoimaging* (CRC Press, 2020), endoscopy is a versatile and very portable modality that serves to complement a plan radiographic image. Additionally, endoscopy when applied following the anthropological approach can describe targets that may suggest additional radiographic approaches. The complementary nature of modalities was also mentioned in Case Study 4 mummified remains regarding the excerebration route in Pa-Ib where endoscopy was used in concert with fluoroscopy to determine the

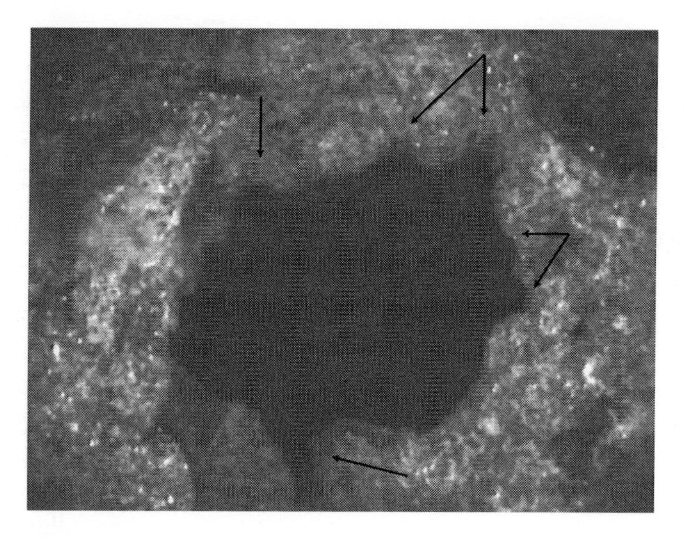

Figure 8.1. Excerebration route in the area of the cribiform plate in the Egytian Mummy know as Pa-Ib (Barnum Museum). Note the in and out "grooves" associated with the brain matter removal procedure (arrows).

nature and extend of the cribriform plate destruction. In that case, the actual in and out action of the excerebration tool used to liquify the brain matter could be directly visualized (Figure 8.1). Endoscopy has been able to contribute studies and in a variety of ways including the presence of paleopathologies, the nature of artifact inclusions in mummified remains, analysis of ceramics, determination of the presence of internal organs not seen on a plane radiograph as well as the internal stability of mummified remains, as a guide to conservation efforts, preexcavation tomb assessment, direct biopsy efforts, and the discovery of unexpected findings.

We also present a few mini cases demonstrating the contributions made by XRF methodologies. XRF provides an analysis of the elements associated with the target material.

Case 8.1: Paleopathologies

Our first case demonstrates the utility of approaching paleoimaging research using multiple modalities. To represent the complementary aspects of multimodal imaging we present the case of 'Sabia'. Sabia is a mummy from Pachacamac, in what is now Peru. She was excavated and transported to the University of Pennsylvania (UPenn) in the late 1800s or early 1900s by Max Uhle.

Friedrich Max Uhle (1856–1944) was from Germany and is considered the "father" of South American Archaeology. Uhle conducted archaeological work in Peru, Bolivia, Chile and Ecuador. While he worked for several universities, he sent hundreds of mummified remains to UPenn in the late 1800s, many of which originated from Pachacamac.

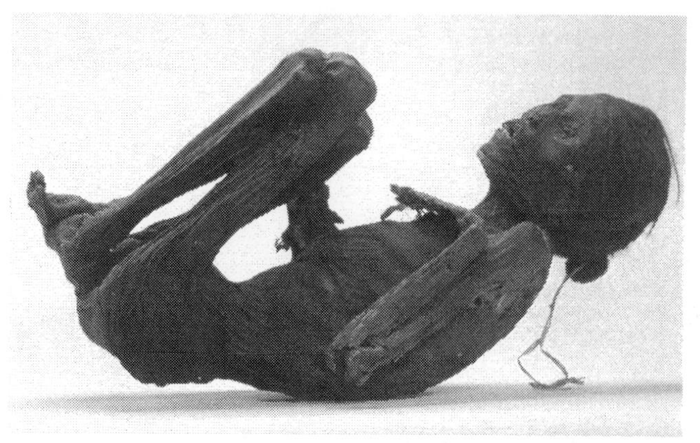

Figure 8.2. Sabia: a mummified woman from Pachacamac. An individual from the Max Uhle collection at the Museum of Anthropology and Archaeology, University of Pennsylvania.

Pachacamac is a well-known archaeological site about 20–30 miles (40kms) southeast of what is now Lima, Peru. It is estimated that the site was developed in about 200 AD and was an important religious and pilgrimage site where many burials have been discovered. Pachacamac is considered one of the longest continually inhabited cultural centers among Andean cultures being active until the Spanish Conquest in the 1530s, some 1300 years. The name originates from the Quechua language the creator god Pacha Kamaq, meaning "Earth Maker." When the Inca empire expanded, Pacha Kamaq was enveloped into their own 'world view'

The UPenn Collection

A large number of mummies arrived at UPenn Museum of Archaeology and Anthropology in the late 1800s and early 1900s, so many that they were challenged to process them all due to minimal resources at the time. As resources, methods, and knowledge progressed, the mummies began to receive the attention that the museum hoped for. While the BRIQ conducted on-site paleoimaging data collection on the vast majority of the mummies, one mummy later called Sabia (Figure 8.2), was sent to the BRIQ paleoimaging research laboratory in 1997 for additional analysis. William Hennessy conducted a thorough radiologic exam using plane radiography and presented his findings to the Deputy Chief Medical Examiner for the state of Connecticut. Plane radiography revealed several interesting findings; a parry fracture to the right radius, fractured rib, broken phalanges of the left foot, vertebral compression fracture (Figure 8.3), and a fractured maxillary incisor (Figure 8.4). In the case of Sabia, based on the specific pattern of perimortem fractures in various parts of the

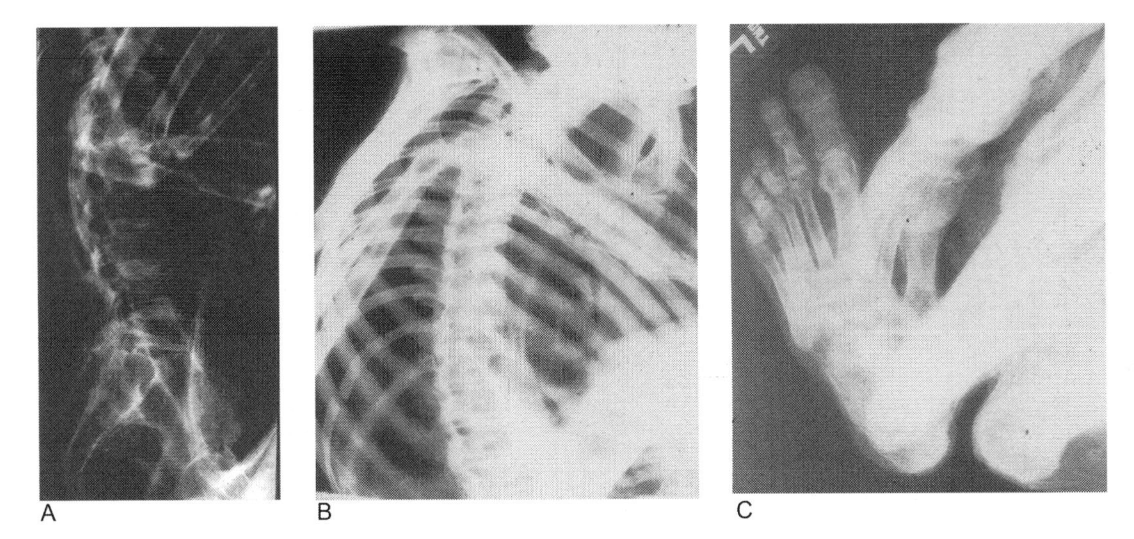

Figure 8.3. Sabia: Radiographs showing parry fracture (A), fractured rib (B), and fractured phalanges of left foot (C).

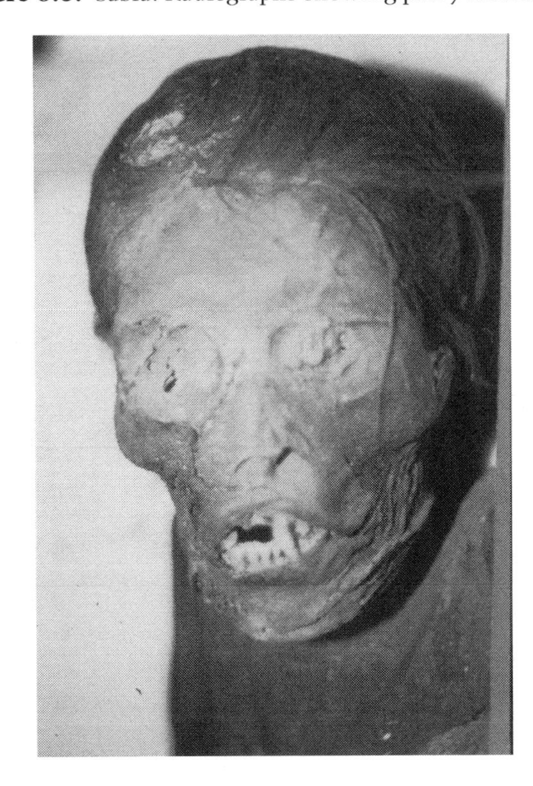

Figure 8.4. Sabia. Fractured maxillary incisors.

skeletal system, the manner of death was likely an accidental fall, a nonaccidental fall, or a violent attack.

The missing incisor provided a route of entry for endoscopy. A 6 mm (0.24 inch) Olympus industrial endoscope with a cold halogen light source was used for the study. The scope was introduced much in the way a medical bronchoscopy would be conducted. The first interesting endoscopic image was that of a sublaryngeal narrowing of the trachea (Figure 8.5). This narrowing was not picked up on the plane radiographs due to the narrowing originating in the soft tissues rather than the bony structures. Additionally, superimposition of shadows on the X-rays may have obscured and evidence. The narrowing would have certainly constricted the passage of air into the lungs. Garroting was ruled out as the hyoid bone was intact and there were no residual markings or impressions on the neck that would suggest a strangulation. The images were shared with Dr. Michael MacNamee, MD, a pulmonologist who was the then director of intensive care at Wallingford Hospital in Connecticut. Dr. MacNamee examined the radiographs, the external characteristics of the neck region and the endoscopic image and concluded that the narrowing represented a paratracheal lymphadenopathy that would have been present at the time of death. A paratracheal lymphadenopathy could be the result of a variety of system wide infectious processes resulting in reactive hyperplasia. However, given Sabia's original context, the most likely culprit would be tuberculosis. This brings another potential into the discussion when attempting to determine how Sabia may have died. Was in an accidental or violent end or was it the result of an advancing infectious process? Biopsy of the lymph tissue was not conducted in this study.

As the endoscope was maneuvered past the narrowing it was introduced past the carina and into the right mainstem bronchus. Here, what looked like a tooth fragment was visualized How the tooth fragment came to be lodged in the right main stem bronchus generated some debate. Given the theory of a possible violent death (multiple fractures seen on X-ray), one possibility was that this was a portion of the incisor and was fractured during the possible violence or accident and was then aspirated into the lung airway structure. Another possibility was the fracture could have been simply a result of taphonomic change which became dislodged while in transport to the museum from South America.

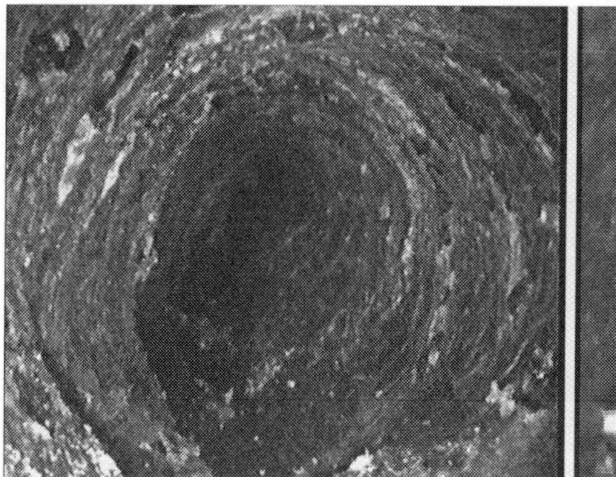
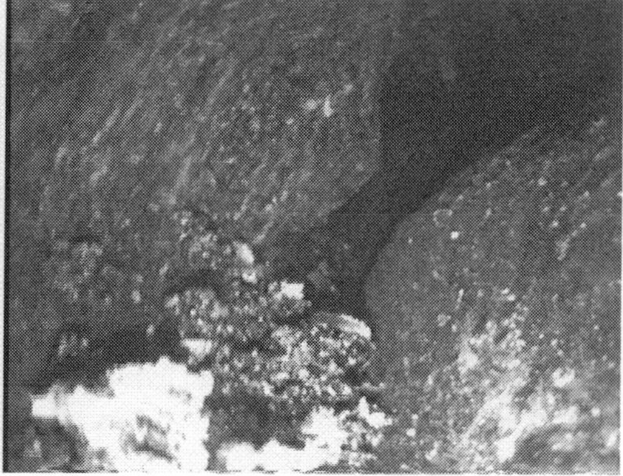

Figure 8.5. Sabia: Videoendoscopic images of the trachea of a mummy from Pachacamac. The image on the left shows proximal tracheal rings with distal tracheal narrowing. The narrowing is likely due to a paratracheal lymphadenopathy encroaching on the tracheal lumen. The image on the right is a closer view of the narrowing.

Given that this mummy helped us develop methodological applications in so many ways, we referred to her as Sabia, or, a wise woman.

Significance of This Case

We may not know if it was TB or if there was violence at death, but this case does illustrate the importance of using multiple modalities when examining any mummy. There is great potential in discovery of significant information when methods are combines. In this case, the paratracheal lymphadenopathy would not have been discovered nor would be the tooth fragment lodged in the right mains stem bronchus had endoscopy not been employed in concert with extensive plane radiography.

Figure 8.6. Osmore river valley in the Atacama Desert near El Algarrobal.

Case 8.2: El Viejo (the old)

Another useful example of the complementary nature of standard field radiography and endoscopy as related to target artifact analysis is found in a case we have come to call "El Viejo" (Beckett and Guillen 2000).

El Viejo was discovered in a tomb among the vast cemetery of the pre-Columbian culture known as the Chiribaya (AD 900–1350). The Chiribaya inhabited the Osmore river valley near the contemporary village of El Algarrobal (Figure 8.6) and about 10.6 miles (17 kilometers) from the fishing town of Ilo, in southern Peru. El Viejo was recovered from a typical Chiribaya style tomb in this remote region of the Atacama Desert. The rock-lined tomb was discovered about one meter below the surface. Figure 8.7 shows typical grave goods associated with Chiribaya burials. El Viejo and his associated grave goods were documented and excavated, then transported to the nearby research facility of Centro Mallqui under the direction of Dra. Sonia Guillen. A preliminary radiographic survey was conducted at the research facility.

Among the anthropological and paleopathological data collected via radiography it was determined that El Viejo was around 60 years of age (> 50) when he died, older than the majority of the approximately 800 mummies examined at the research facility. Pelvic bone morphology, along with the prominent brow ridge and large mastoid processes, indicated that this was a male. The initial lateral radiographic also revealed a unique ceramic artifact that appeared to be inside the mummy's thorax. Additionally, the radiographs revealed that this mummy, unlike all the others at this site, had been eviscerated with the pelvic, abdominal and lower thoracic cavities being packed with cotton-like substance or llama wool. Because of the superimposition of shadows associated with X-ray, it wasn't clear from this initial radiographic view if the ceramic artifact was within the thoracic cavity or outside of the body.

Figure 8.7. Typical associated grave goods of the Chiribaya culture.

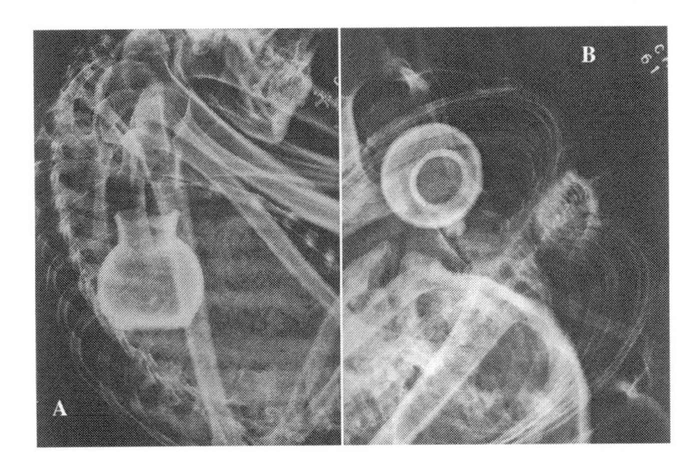

Figure 8.8. Conventional lateral radiograph (A) showing ceramic artifact associated with "El Viejo." Another view (B) was used to determine that the ceramic was in fact within the thoracic cage of the mummy. Note: It is not possible to tell if the ceramic had anything inside from these radiographs.

Since the mummy was in a flexed position, the knees drawn up to the chest, the arms wrapped around the legs and the head tilted to one side, a lateral projection would not eliminate much of the superimposition. It was decided that a more unique radiographic position was required to determine the relative location of the ceramic artifact. The X-ray beam was directed from the superior to inferior aspects of the body. This image revealed that the ceramic artifact was indeed within the right thorax of the mummy and not on the outside (Figure 8.8).

Initial associations were made between the radiographic findings and the anthropological and paleopathological data collected thus far. He appeared older at the time of his death than the general population whose age at death was generally in the mid-life age range. He

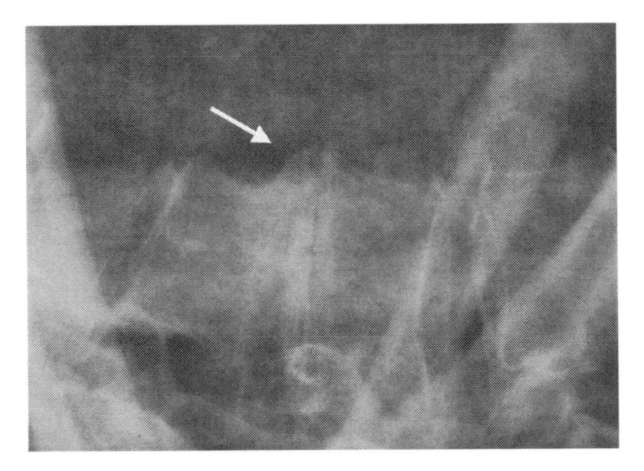

Figure 8.9. Lateral radiograph of the lumbar spine showing moderate arthritic changes on the anterior aspect of the vertebrae (arrow).

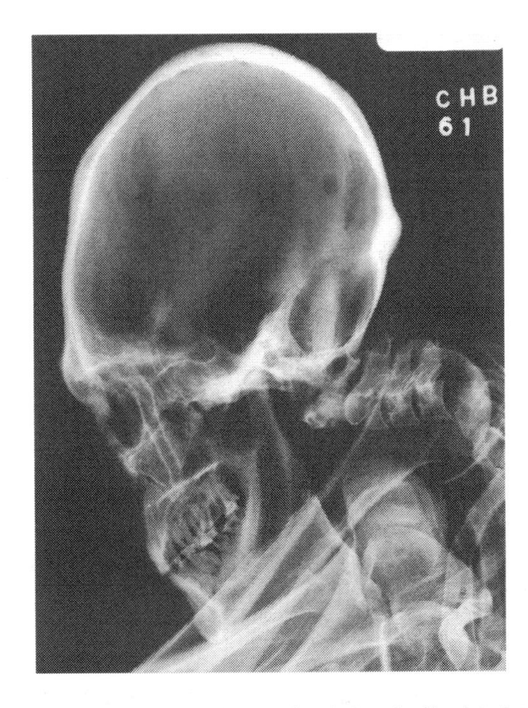

Figure 8.10. Lateral radiograph of the skull of "El Viejo" demonstrates the extensive dental surface wear due to sand in the food.

showed some degenerative or arthritic changes of the spinal column (Figure 8.9) and had extensive wear of his teeth from sand being in the food yet minimal attrition (Figure 8.10). The burning question was: Why was this mummy processed so differently when compared to the hundreds of other mummies from this site? Was his longevity enough to be treated in this unique manner at his death? Was his diet somehow different than others in this group leading to less dental pathology? Had he traveled from another culture and died among the Chiribaya? On the visual inspection component of the physical exam, he had earrings made from cui (guinea pig) pelts that were passing through a large opening

Figure 8.11. Cui (guinea pig) pelt earrings (arrow) on "El Viejo."

formed in each enlarged earlobe (Figure 8.11). Grave goods found in the tomb with the mummy included a ceramic plate with remnants of corn and llama hooves. The textiles that made up his wrappings were modest and in need of conservation.

As the wrapping textiles were removed for conservation, an opening into the left thoracic cavity was discovered at the superior aspect of the left clavicle offering a route for endoscopic examination. Additional routes were also discovered in the lower pelvic region and at the base of the skull posteriorly.

Preliminary endoscopic examination was conducted as described Chapter 6 of *Paleoimaging: Field Applications for Cultural Remains and Artifacts* (CRC Press, 2010), as procedural step one, a survey of accessible body cavities. The pelvic entry route was selected first to determine if there were any other low-density artifacts not seen on the initial X-rays. Endoscopic images revealed the llama-like wool packing seen as irregular low-density shadows on the initial X-ray and ruled out cotton as the packing material (Figure 8.12). The endoscopic images further confirmed that the individual had been eviscerated. The survey of the abdominopelvic region complemented the X-ray by revealing artificial sutures on the interior surface of the abdominal wall (Figure 8.13) not visualized radiographically. The skin surrounding the suture sites showed no healing or adherence suggesting that the suture procedure was

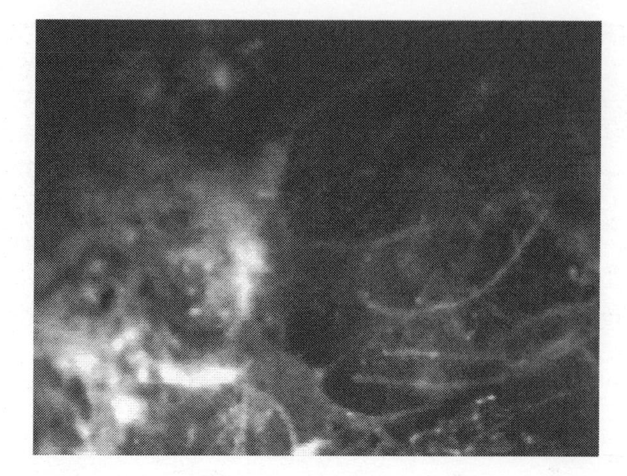

Figure 8.12. Endoscopic image of the internal abdominopelvic cavity showing a wool like packing rather than cotton.

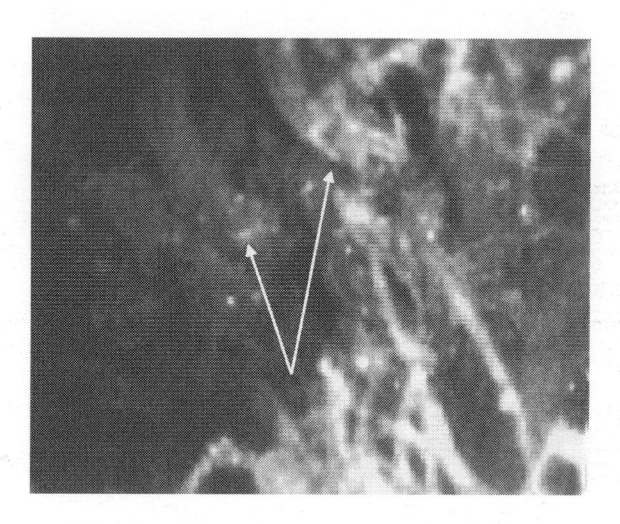

Figure 8.13. Endoscopic image of artificial sutures (arrows) seen on the internal surface of the abdominal wall.

conducted soon after the individual had died. The discovery of the sutures supported the theory that this individual was not only eviscerated, but suggests a route for the evisceration procedure. The suture artifact further supported the premise that this individual was treated in death very differently than others at this cemetery.

Continued endoscopic survey of the oral and thoracic cavities revealed additional artifacts not seen on the radiographs. Endoscopic images revealed coca leaves adhering to the anterior aspect of the thoracic vertebra and coca leaves within the oral cavity (Figure 8.14). It also appeared that the interior cavities were "treated" with a substance that enhanced the coca leaves attachment to the organic structures. The endoscope revealed that there were coca leaves throughout the accessible body cavities. In addition, endoscopy further documented the arthritic changes seen on the X-rays (Figure 8.15) and the dental status showing extensive wear with little dental attrition (Figure 8.16).

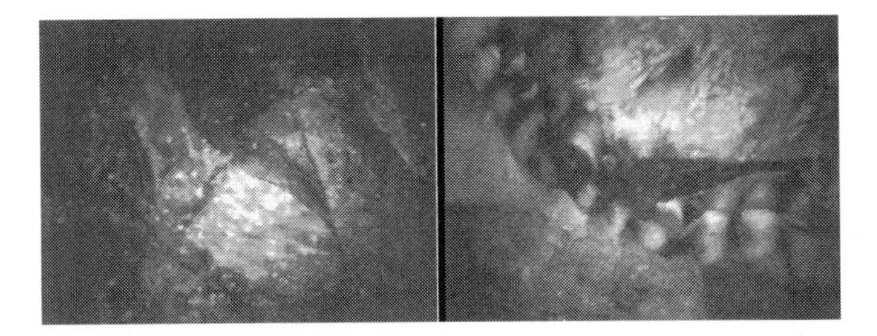

Figure 8.14. Endoscopic images of the wide distribution of coca leaves within various body cavities. Note how the coca leaf is adhered to the anterior aspect of the vertebrae in image on the left.

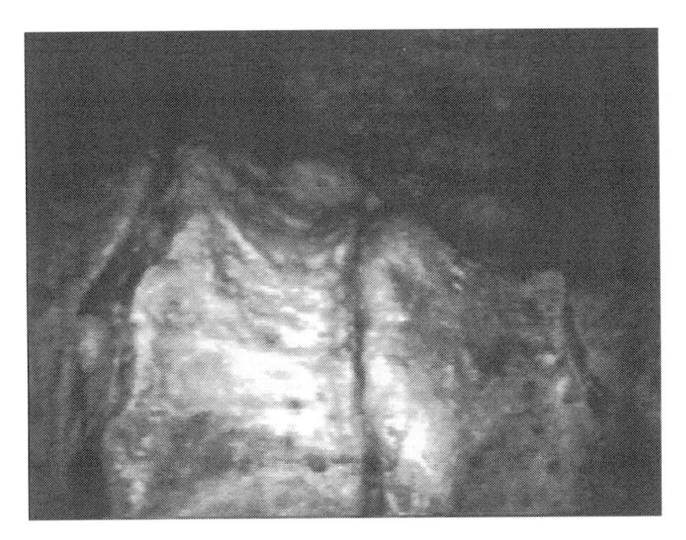

Figure 8.15. Endoscopic image of arthritic changes complementing radiographic image of the same region.

Following the endoscopic survey, target analysis was conducted using the supra-clavicular entry route for introduction of the endoscope. Traversing the thoracic cavity from the left to the right, the ceramic artifact was visualized within the right side of the cavity. The shape, color, and contour of the small pot were all documented from the endoscopic image. Additionally, the outer surface of the ceramic also had coca leaves adhering to it in a similar manner as the coca leaves seen on the surface of the internal thoracic vertebra. There were also coca leaves extruding from the mouth of the pot (Figure 8.17).

It was determined that as we had documented the ceramic, its contents, and features, extraction of this artifact at this time would not be necessary leaving the internal context intact for future research. Furthermore, it was also determined that transporting the mummy for advanced imaging would not be warranted in this case due to the fact that the site was quite remote and travel to a facility would likely harm the mummy and possibly alter the internal context of the ceramic artifact. Additionally, it was felt that advanced imaging would not add to the field paleoimaging data collected.

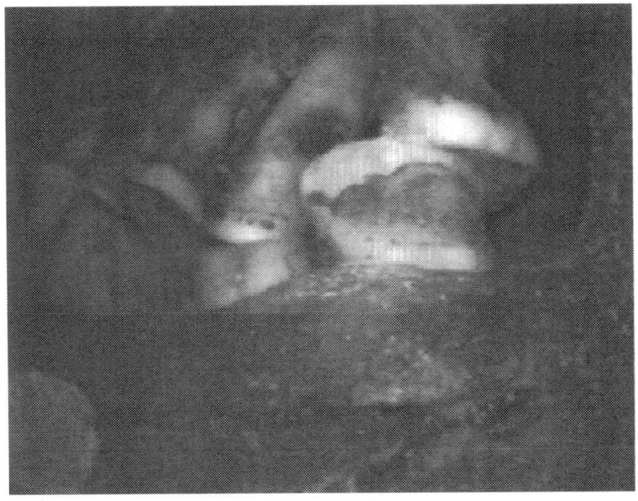

Figure 8.16. Endoscopic image of extensive dental wear pattern complementing the radiographic image. Also note the presence of carries formation.

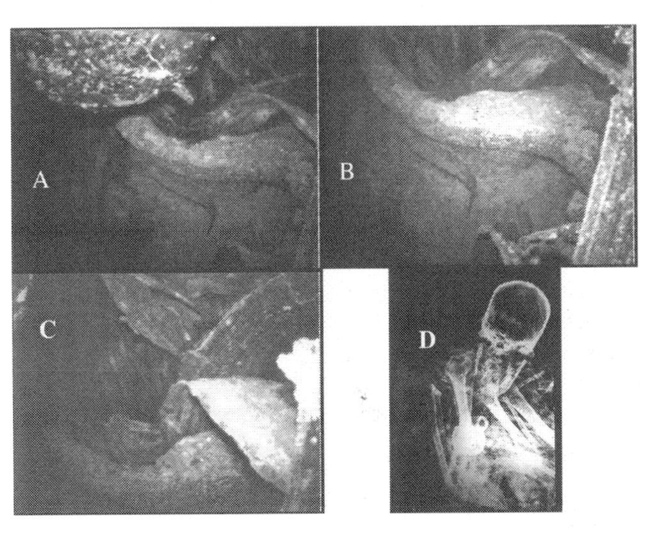

Figure 8.17. Several endoscopic images of the ceramic artifact within the thorax of "El Viejo." The images complement the radiograph (D) in that they allow for the assessment of what was held within the ceramic (C), some of its construction features (B), and the presence of coca leaves adhering to the exterior surface (A).

Significance

In the case of El Viejo, the complementary nature of the two paleoimaging procedures, field radiography and endoscopy, when properly employed, can amass more information than observational methods alone. It is imperative, however, that procedural standards be followed in order to maximize the data collected. For example, in the case presented, if only target artifact endoscopic analysis were conducted, the internal sutures and broad distribution of coca leaves found during the initial survey would have been missed reducing the analyzable data.

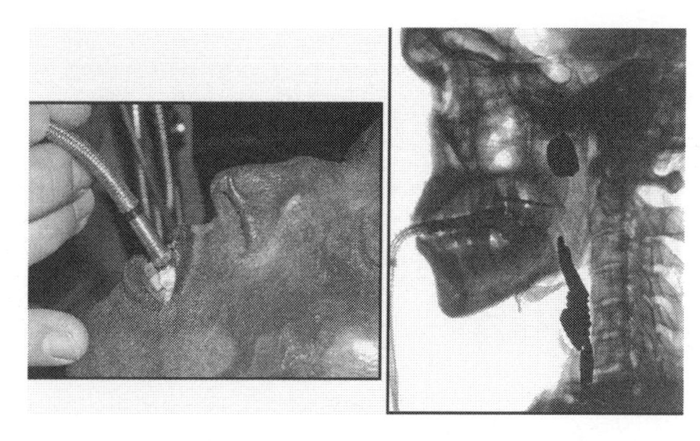

Figure 8.18. Oral endoscopic route of entry on "James Penn." Lateral conventional radiograph of "James Penn" showing "coin-like" structures in the oral and laryngo pharynx as well as the upper esophagus. Note that the radiograph also shows the endoscope location.

Case 8.3: James Penn

In this case, we again see the importance of using several mobile imaging methods to gain as much information as possible while not in an imaging facility. The case also illustrates a sequential process of decision making regarding how and when to use another modality. The case begins with field radiography, video endoscopy, portable fluoroscopy, and mobile CT scanning.

The mummified remains of a male individual have been in the care of the Theodore C. Auman Funeral Home in Reading, Pennsylvania for over 100 years. The remains said to be that of a James Penn, an imprisoned burglar who died in 1895, was embalmed by Theodore Auman in an attempt to allow any family members time to claim their relative. The embalming solution used, an early formulation of formaldehyde, preserved the body so well that the remains are still in excellent condition (Conlogue et al. 2008). No previous examination of the remains has been recorded. Several newspaper accounts of James Penn's life, death, and mummification were reported. However, the very same source reported that someone named James Penn was buried. If that were true, who was this mummy and when was he mummified? Anecdotal accounts of public viewings in the funeral home have been reported. Internal context artifact analysis became a factor in this case regarding the temporal context associated with these remains.

Artifact Analysis: Paleoimaging Findings

There were two unexpected findings from the imaging studies. On the conventional X-rays using Polaroid film as the image receptor, multiple flat circular, coin-like objects appeared to be located between the oro and laryngopharynx, or upper esophagus (Figure 8.18).

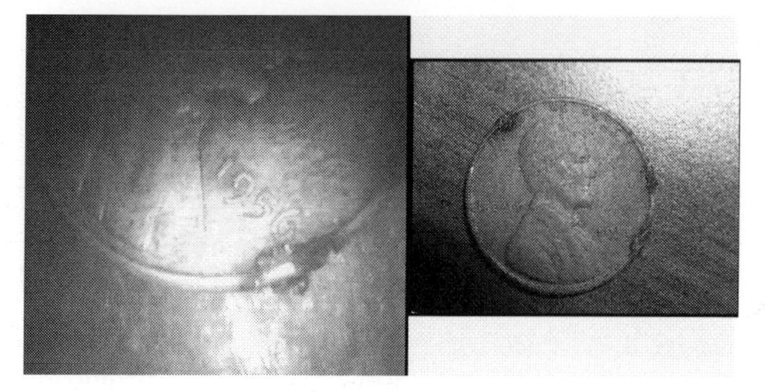

Figure 8.19. Endoscopic image of a 1956 US penny in the oropharynx of "James Penn" and a photograph once it was removed.

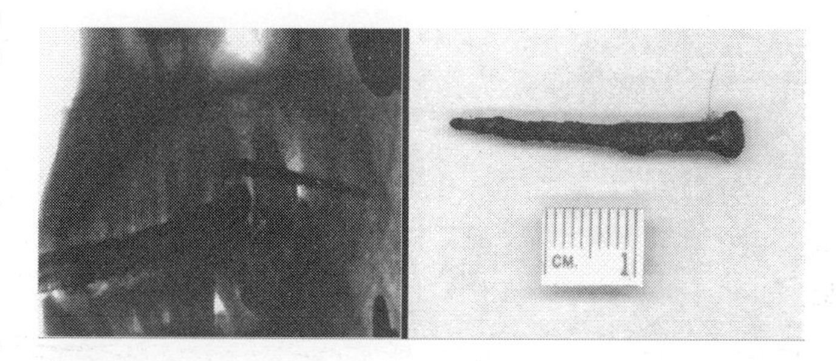

Figure 8.20. Lateral radiograph demonstrating thin metallic object within "James Penn," which turned out to be a nail.

Fiber-optic video-endoscopy was used and verified the presence of stacked United States coins, specifically pennies (Figure 8.19). Endoscopic image could make out the date on one of the pennies. After considerable manipulation using clinical postural drainage positions and the use of a bronchoscope cytology brush under fluoroscopic guidance to dislodge the coins, a total of 21 United States pennies dating from 1896 to 1961 were eventually retrieved.

The second unexpected finding was a thin metallic object seen on the X-rays in the area along the superior portion of the mouth on left side (Figure 8.20). Endoscopy revealed that the object was lodged under the tongue and with a little manipulation, what appeared to be an oxidized nail was removed. The Connecticut state archaeologist, Nick Bellantoni examined the artifact and determined that it was a factory cut nail dating to the late 19th and early 20th centuries (Bellantoni 2005). Bellantoni felt that it could be a finishing nail or a shingle/lathe nail. The shape of this type of nail prevented the cracking of wood often experienced when using a wire nail. Bellantoni was certain it was not a fastener that was used in coffin or casket manufacturing.

The coins discovered in the upper esophagus were an interesting find. Given the date range of the coins, it suggests that they had been placed there over a long period. It suggests that the mummy had been viewed at the funeral home, perhaps as a dramatic example of the embalming prowess at the Auman Funeral Home. The coins may have been placed according to the custom of giving the dead hidden money to pay the boatman who will transport the recently dead across the river Styx, or, perhaps, the mummy was simply an unusual wishing well.

The artifacts associated with this case, the coins and the nail, seem to verify the temporal period reported in the late nineteenth-century newspaper accounts of James Penn. An additional piece of information from direct observation points to the same time period. That is, the style of stitching used at the embalming sites, a baseball stitch that was in vogue around the turn of that century.

Significance

This case demonstrates the suggested procedure for artifact analysis using paleoimaging methodologies. First, a survey was conducted using both standard radiography and on site CT scans. Target analysis was accomplished using standard radiography and endoscopy. And finally, artifact extraction was conducted under both fluoroscopic and endoscopic guidance. Based upon the on-site evaluation, a decision was made to move the mummy. This decision was based on the stability of the mummy and the additional paleopathological data that could be derived from a state of the art MDCT scanner. It was agreed by the research team that this would be a low risk, high benefit endeavor. Several paleopathological data associated with "James Penn," including pulmonary adhesions, lesions, and liver pathology, were accomplished using MDCT.

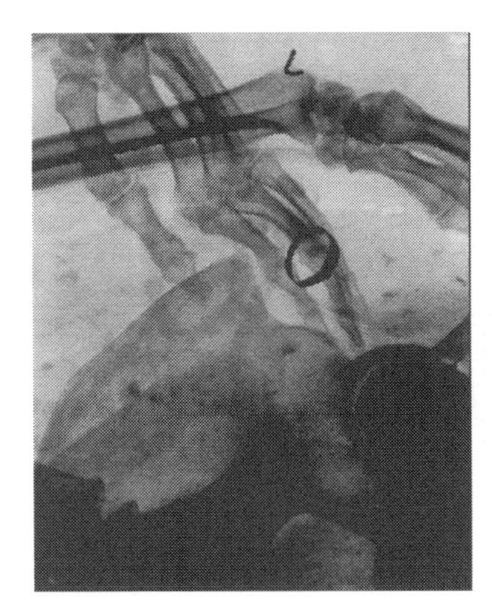
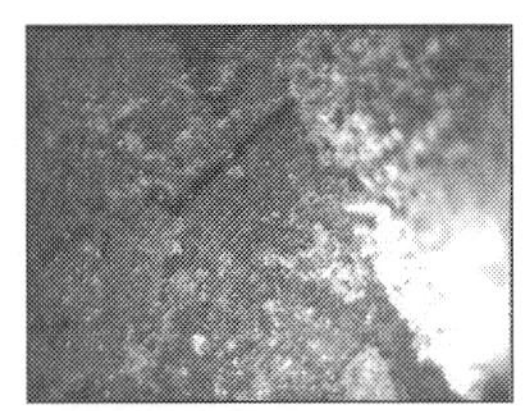
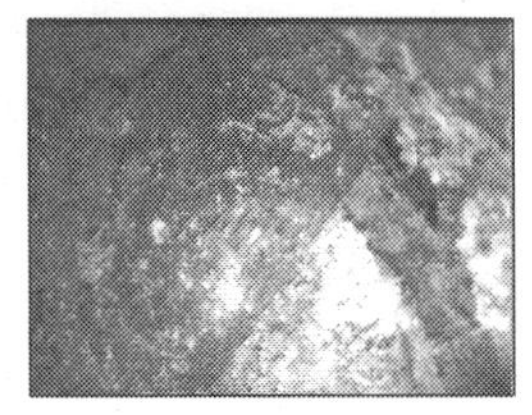

Figure 8.21. Radiograph showing a ring on the finger of a crypt mummy from Popoli, Italy. The accompanying endoscopic image of the ring adds the characteristics of color and contour to the analysis.

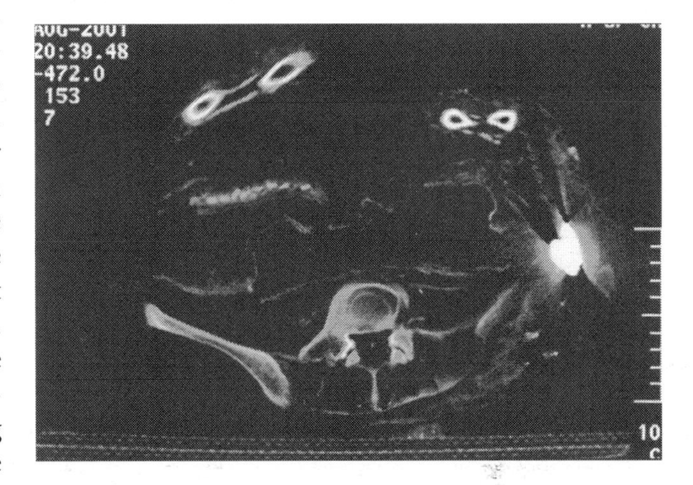

Figure 8.22. Axial CT image of a coin sized metallic object within the folds of clothing of the "nobleman" of Popoli (see text).

Case 8.4: The Nobleman of Popoli: Biopsy, Renal Stone, and Saint Philomena

BRIQ was invited by Dr. Gino Fornaciari, MD, a paleopathologist, to participate in a study of mummified remains in South central Italy. The mummified remains of a male individual were discovered in a crypt below the floorboards of the Church of the Holy Trinity in Popoli, Italy (Ventura et al. 2004). It was first believed that the remains were that of a priest based on the burial location in the sacristy within the church. However, on visual inspection the remains were dressed in fine patterned clothes suggesting that rather than a priest, these may be the remains of a benefactor, or nobleman, associated with the church. One of the initial radiographs and subsequent endoscopic images shows a ring on the finger of the "nobleman" (Figure 8.21). The remains were well preserved and after a radiographic examination conducted in the crypt, a coin-sized metallic object was seen at the side of the mummy. The stability of the mummy was found to be exceptional so it was decided to remove the mummy from the crypt and transport the mummy to the local hospital where a CT scan was conducted. The CT scan confirmed the metallic object at the side of the mummy (Figure 8.22). The mummy was returned to the church where endoscopic image was conducted. Using endoscopy, a pouch underneath the overcoat of the mummy, which contained the object was visualized and ultimately extracted under endoscopic guidance (Figure 8.23). The pouch was opened and what was thought to be a coin was in fact a medallion of Saint Philomena (Figure 8.24). Saint Philomena was canonized in 1837, therefore the individual could not have been interred prior to that date as this artifact was intimately associated with the remains.

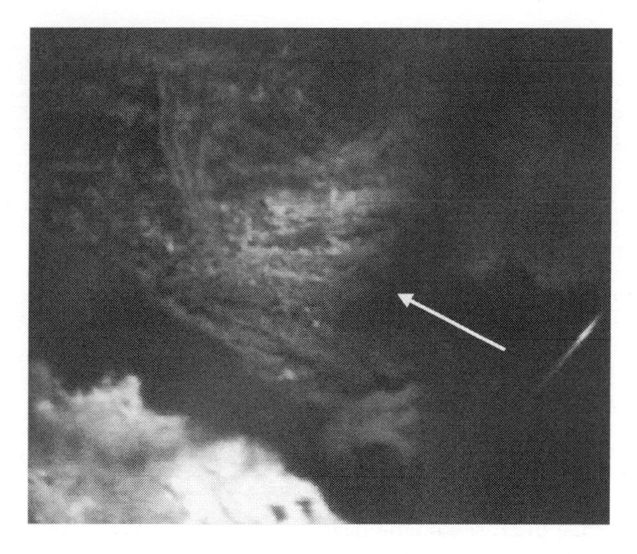

Figure 8.23. Endoscopic image of a small pouch which contained the medallion of Saint Philomena in direct association with the "nobleman:of Popoli.

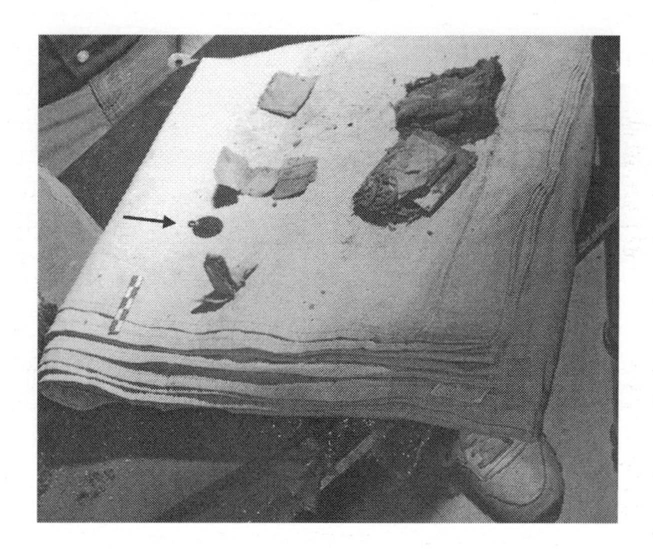

Figure 8.24. Artifacts discovered within the pouch of the "nobleman" from Popoli. The medallion of Saint Philomena (arrow) was among the items.

One of the primary uses of the medical endoscope is to obtain samples for pathological analysis. These analyses can help determine tissue type and the presence of disease. It follows that endoscopy used for anthropological research can accomplish those same goals. In mummified human remains, tissue elements of organs and organ systems are not necessarily in their appropriate anatomical position. Nor is their morphology the same as while living. In the "nobleman" in Popoli, an exploratory biopsy was taken though existing openings along the right costal margin using a laparoscopic technique. The target was to be lung tissue. After rehydration of that tissue, it was found to be diaphragm and not lung tissue. Even so once the tissue was stained and examined microscopically, the sample demonstrated calcifications

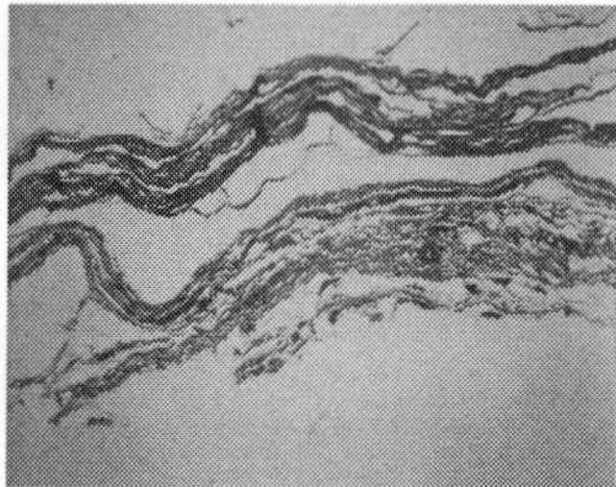

Figure 8.25. Rehydrated and stained diaphragm tissue showing calcifications. Tissue samples were collected under videoendoscopic visualization.

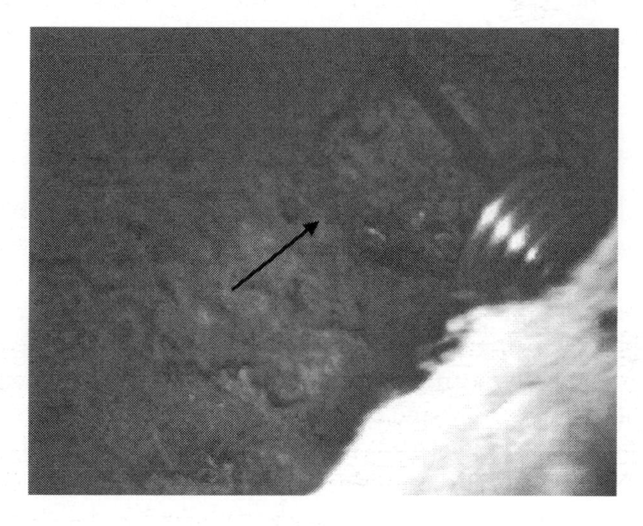

Figure 8.26. Videoendoscope image of a renal stone (arrow) removal procedure using the laparoscopic method.

(Figure 8.25) indicating a long standing disease process (Ventura et al. 2004).

The CT scan also revealed a spherical density in the region of the right kidney. The renal stone was removed under endoscopic guidance (Figure 8.26) using the laparoscopic technique described in Chapter 2 of *Advances in Paleoimaging*. The stone was further analyzed and found to contain the same features and chemical makeup as modern-day renal stones.

Significance

The case study demonstrates the high degree of information that can be derived when combining paleoimaging modalities. Radiographs and CT scan revealed both artifacts and potential pathology. The endoscopic application contributed in locating and extracting artifacts that were critical to determining the temporal context in this case. Additionally, the endoscope was used to guide the biopsy of thoracic tissue, as well as the removal of a renal stone. Both of these findings informed researchers regarding the state of health of the individual while alive.

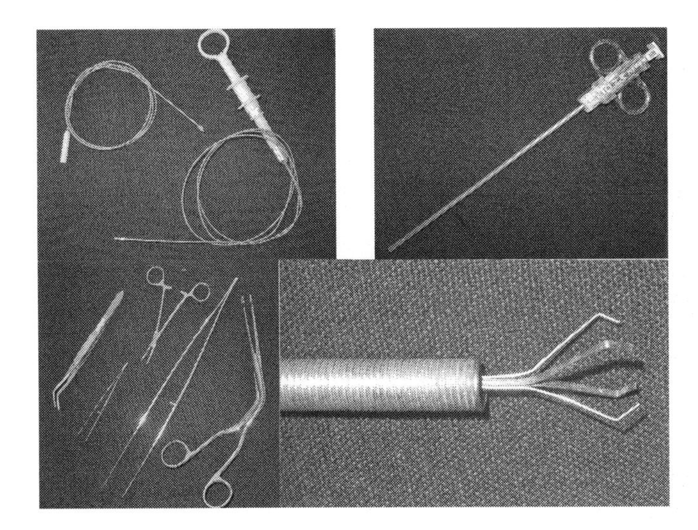

Figure 8.27. Various instruments used for tissue biopsy. Top left—Medical biopsy forceps and cytology brush. Top right—Percutaneous needle. Bottom left—Miscellaneous medical instruments. Bottom right—Mechanics gripping device for larger samples.

Biopsy and tissue sampling add a great deal to our understanding of several variables associated with mummified remains. Tissue sampling can be used to determine if the tissue remnants are in fact organs, thereby suggesting a mummification method that did or did not remove internal organs. Furthermore, lymph tissue, calcifications seen on X-ray, and bony lesions can be biopsied and further analyzed for traces of disease. Following rehydration, the ancient tissue can be pathologically examined and probability data may be statistically determined if the population size is large enough.

Biopsy can be conducted in a variety of ways. Biopsy using CT guidance and the laparoscopic biopsy technique using endoscopic guidance demonstrate proven methods for target specific biopsy. Standard medical biopsy forceps work well but the yield is often too small for diagnosis. Larger collection tools and needle biopsy instruments can be used to enhance the yield and the diagnostic capability (Figure 8.27). Samples should be handled with the same care as if from a living individual. Contamination should be avoided and sterile containers should be used.

Case 8.5: The conservation of Jeremy Bentham

Paleoimaging is often utilized to gather information which will assists in the evaluation of an object of antiquity or, as is seen in this case, noted human remains. The evaluation informs the researchers as to the state of preservation of the object and the discovery of any conservation need. The information gathered through imaging modalities as such details are typically hidden from direct observation. In this case, we were asked to assist in determining the condition of the skeletal remains and mummified head of Jeremy Bentham. The imaging data collected would be used to guide in the conservation efforts. Portable field radiography and endoscopy were used on site to gather the data.

Jeremy Bentham (1748–1832) was a forward thinker in London, England. Bentham is frequently associated with the founding of the University of London, specifically University College London (UCL), although in fact he was 78 years old when UCL opened in 1826, and played no active part in its establishment (*Mummy Road Show,* A Head for Science, 2003). However, it is likely that without his inspiration, UCL would not have been created. Bentham strongly believed that education should be more widely available, particularly to those who were not wealthy or who did not belong to the established church, both of which were required of students by Oxford and Cambridge. As UCL was the first English university to admit all, regardless of race, creed, or political belief, it was largely consistent with Bentham's vision. Bentham is credited with advocating the philosophical social construct of Utilitarianism, which, simply stated, suggests that the needs on the many outweigh the needs of the few, or the one.

With this construct as a backdrop, Bentham supported the donation of deceased bodies for medical study and science, a concept that was not popular at the time. Before he died, Bentham made arrangements to preserve his body to demonstrate that more people could benefit from his passing than merely burying him in the ground. If fact, Bentham himself selected the glass eyes that were to be used in his preserved head. He was said to have carried the eyes in his pocket for quite some time before his death and frequently could be heard jingling them in his pocket as he strolled around London. When he did die, an autopsy was performed on his remains in the medical amphitheater, which was illegal at the time, and his head was mummified by a colleague, according to Bentham's instructions, using a Maori technique of placing the head in a plume of smoke in order to preserve it. With some minor modifications in technique, particularly using sulfur fumes instead of only wood smoke, the head of Jeremy Bentham is extremely well preserved. Before the smoking process additional scientific tests consistent with the times were conducted on the remains (more on that a bit later in this section). Bentham's postcranial skeleton was dried and then reassembled using standard hardware of the era. The skeleton was then covered with several layers of packing, building it up to Bentham's approximate body volume in life, clothed with Bentham's own clothes, and put on display at the University.

As requested in his will, his body, called his "Auto-Icon" was maintained and stored in a wooden cabinet. Originally kept by his disciple Dr. Southwood Smith, it was acquired by University College London in 1850. The Auto-Icon is kept on public display at the end of the South Cloisters in the main building of the college. For the 100th and 150th anniversaries of the college, the Auto-Icon was brought to the meeting of the College Council, where he was listed as "present but not voting." Tradition holds that if the council's vote on any motion is tied, the Auto-Icon always breaks the tie by voting in favor of the motion.

The Auto-Icon has always had a wax head, as Bentham's head was less life-like after the mummification process. The real head was displayed in the same case for many years, but became the target of repeated student pranks including being "borrowed" on more than one occasion. At the time of this study his actual remains were being conserved in the University College London Anthropology department. Bentham's mummified head is now kept safely locked in a vault.

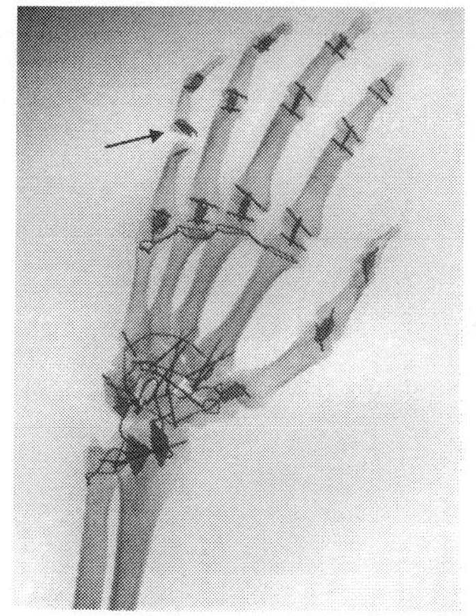

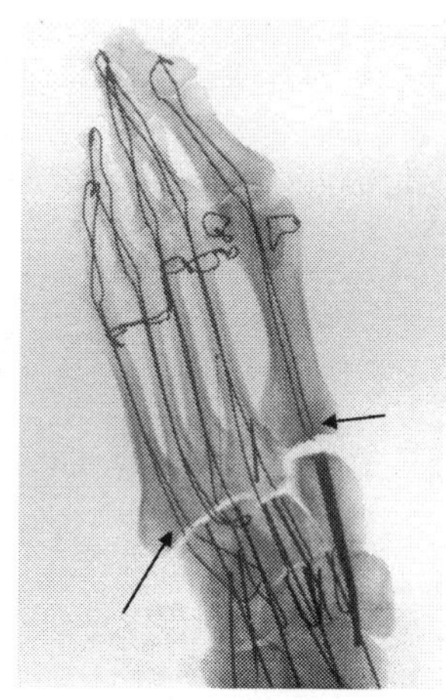

Figure 8.28. (A) A Polaroid image of Jeremy Bentham's left hand demonstrating the pins, plates, and wire used to articulate the skeleton. Note the broken plate (arrow) that formed the joint between the proximal and middle phalange of the fifth digit. (B) An AP projection of the left foot showing that most of the wires (arrows) across the metatarsal phalangeal joints were broken.

Case Objectives

The major objective of this study was to determine the condition of the post cranial skeleton and the mummified head of Jeremy Bentham, in an attempt to better understand the construction features and the help direct future conservation efforts. Standard radiographs were taken of the wrapped skeletal remains at the University College of London in an attempt to discover the condition of the skeleton and the status of the original articulation hardware. Instant film was selected to eliminate the need for 'wet' developing and to provide on the spot data for assessment. Radiographs were taken of each articulation. Review of the data revealed that the wires and small metal plates used to articulate the phalanges of the hand were well oxidized and several were in need of conservation (Figure 8.28A). An X-ray revealed that the left foot was also in need of conservation (Figure 8.28B). Without the radiographic data, movement of these joints could have caused disarticulation and possible damage to the skeletal material. The radiographs of the remainder of the post-cranial skeleton demonstrated the techniques used to articulate the remains (Figure 8.29). Endoscopy was employed to directly visualize the articulation hardware at accessible joints (Figure 8.30). While much of the hardware was in good condition, an understanding of the construction features articulating Jeremy Bentham's skeleton was valuable information to the conservators, allowing them to anticipate future repair needs and to establish reasonable handling procedures that would not cause damage.

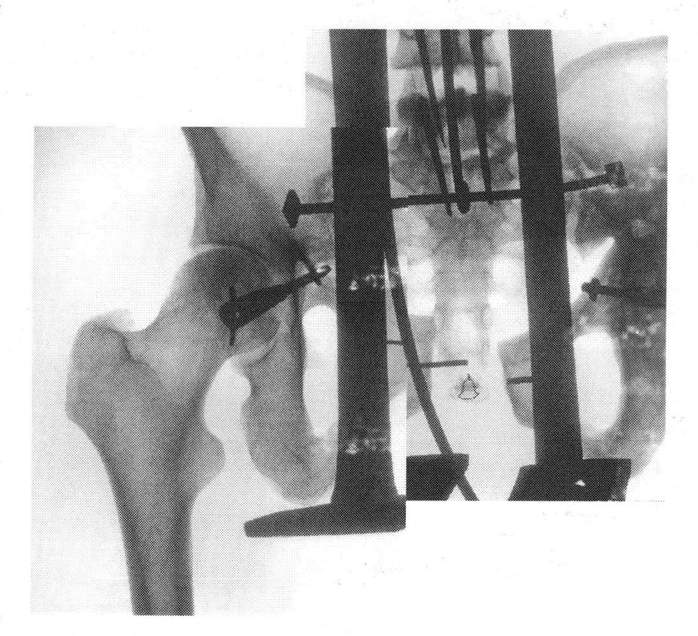

Figure 8.29. Composite Polaroid images showing the hardware used to articulate the pelvis, spine and right hip.

Radiographs were then taken of Jeremy Bentham's mummified head. While otherwise unremarkable, the radiographs clearly demonstrated a pair of interesting artifacts, the glass eyes that Bentham used to carry around in his pocket prior to his death (Figure 8.31A). Because of the superimposition of the eyes on the initial lateral radiograph, an oblique projection was taken making it easier to assess the glass eyes (Figure 8.31B). Endoscopic images demonstrated the packing material

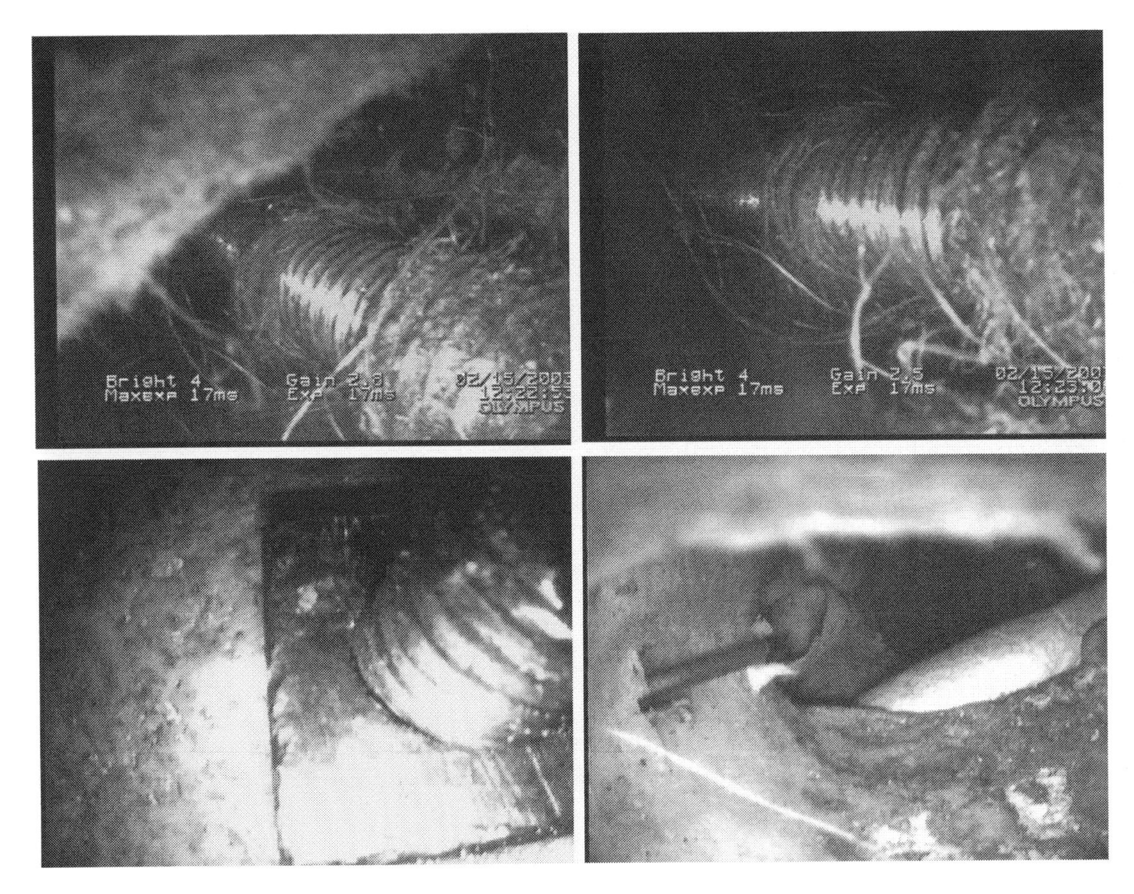

Figure 8.30. Endoscopic images showing various hardware used to rearticulate the skeleton of Jeremy Bentham. The bolts and nuts appear to be in reasonable condition with no critical oxidation. The image in the lower right shows a wire used to hold the individual vertebrae together as seen from the vertebral canal.

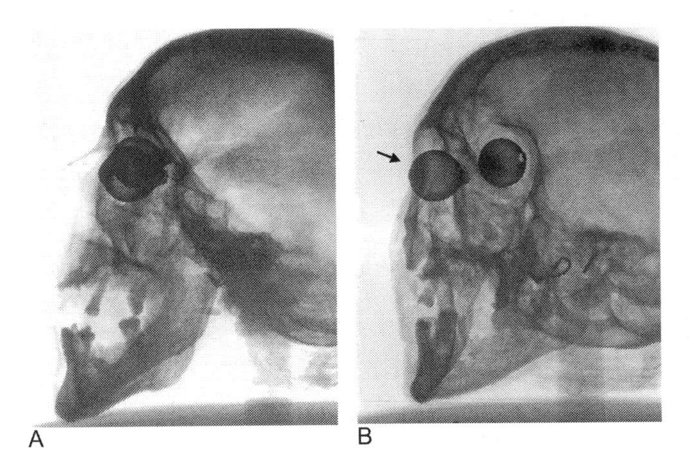

Figure 8.31. (A) Lateral Polaroid radiograph of the anterior portion of the skull revealed the glass eyes within the orbits. However, due to superimposition the eyes were not discernable. (B) An oblique projection of the skull provided a more unobstructed view of the right eye (arrow).

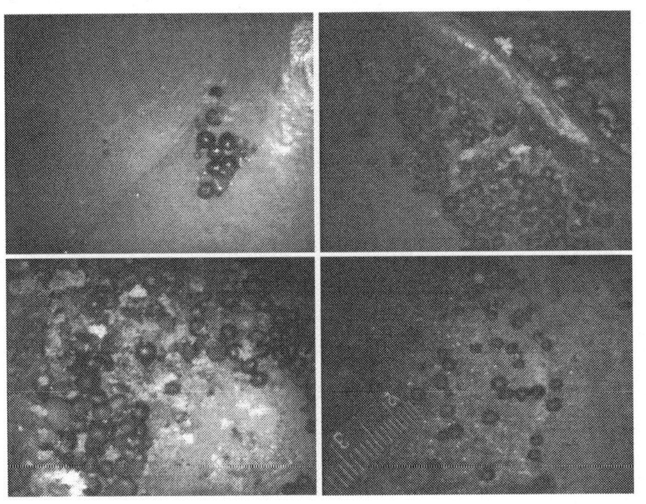

Figure 8.32. Endoscopic images showing wide distribution and relative size of mustard seeds within the endocranial vault of Jeremy Bentham's mummified head.

used in the mummified head's cheeks to maintain a full, healthful appearance. When the endoscope was introduced into the interior of the cranial vault, we were surprised to find what appeared to be seeds adhering to the inside of the skull (Figure 8.32). Several seeds were removed under endoscopic guidance and sent for analysis. The seeds were identified as mustard seeds. In the era that Bentham died, cranial volume was thought to be a measure of intellectual capacity. Bentham's cranial capacity was measured by pouring mustard seeds into the cranial vault, then quantifying that volume by pouring the seeds from the cranium into a volumetric container. Bentham surely must have approved, or even suggested such a measure be taken to further demonstrate the value of scientific study of deceased bodies and to further advance the cause of Utilitarianism.

Significance

This case is an excellent example of how paleoimaging can inform curators regarding conservation assessment. Yet using the exploratory approach, additional information appears from the data. In this case the glass eyes as well as the mustard seeds within the cranial vault. Researchers have to be willing to go beyond the stated objectives at times and realize that the time we have to study objects or individuals is precious and gathering as much data as possible often leads to interesting and informative features. The combination, in this case, of field radiography and endoscopy not only accomplished the study objects, but also added information to Jeremy Bentham's story and allowed him to once again make a case for the study of human remains.

Case 8.6: The Buddhist Monk

This case also represents the importance of maximizing the time allowed to study subjects by assuring that all aspects of the subject are examined with the available tools. This case is that of unusual artifacts associated with a self-mummified Buddhist monk, Luang Pho Dang Piyasilo. Luang Pho Dang passed away in the 1970s at the age of 79 and his mummified body is at the Wat Khunaram temple on Ko Samui Island of Thailand (Beckett and Conlogue 2015).

Self-mummification was a practice among devote Buddhists and involved a years-long process of fasting and ingesting only specific items. There are known self-mummified Buddhist monks in several countries including Cambodia, Vietnam, Japan, and, as in this case, Thailand. There are three stages in the self-mummification process. Described here are the stages to self-mummification practiced by Shingon monks of Japan. The first is a change of diet to nothing but nuts, seeds, fruits, and berries accompanied by rigorous physical activity. Body fat is markedly reduced during this stage which lasts about 1000 days. The next stage requires the monk to ingest only tree bark and roots and over time replacing physical activity with meditation. This reduces even more body fat and now even muscles begin to atrophy. In the final stage, the monk drinks a tea made from the sap of the urushi tree (this sap is often used as a varnish) which is a powerful emetic. The associated vomiting, perspiring, and urinating, dehydrates

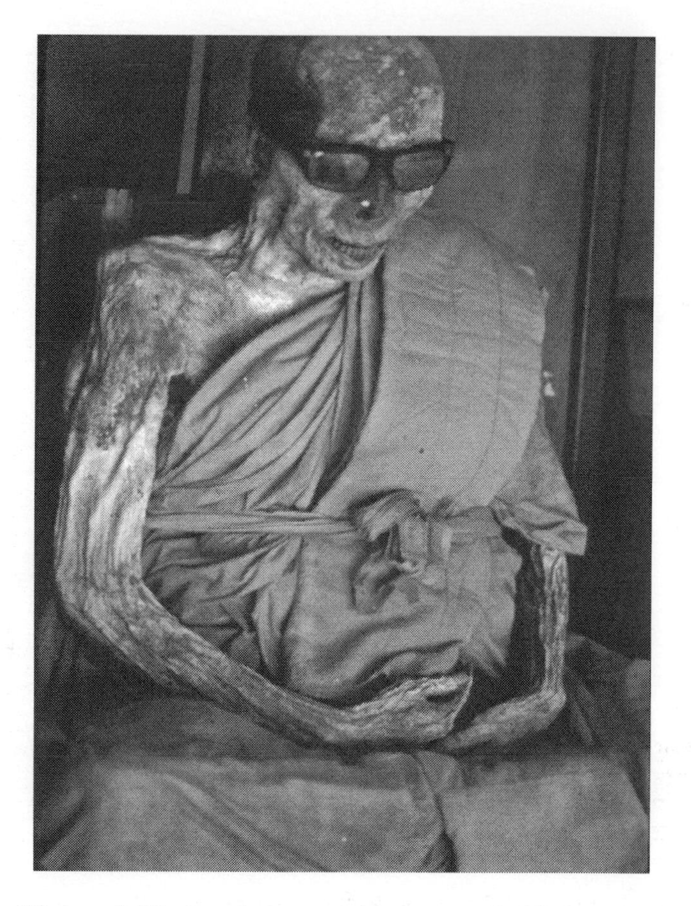

Figure 8.33. Sunglasses on the mummified remains of Luang Pho Dang Piyasilo.

the monk while still alive. Late in the second stage the monk descends into a stone tomb where he meditates with only a bamboo tube for air and a bell to indicate that he is still living. When the bell is no longer heard, the tube is removed and the tomb is sealed for 1000 days while the body proceeds toward mummification. This process is not always successful.

In our research of Luang Pho Dang we used field radiography as well as endoscopy to learn what we could about the efficacy of the self-mummification practice. In our research we discovered a few unexpected findings in the form of artifacts and interesting associations. The first unusual artifact is apparent to the unaided eye in that the mummy, seated in a lotus meditation position, is wearing sunglasses (Figure 8.33). The monks placed the sunglasses on Luang Pho Dang to hide the "sunken" eyes from the view of children who, along with others, came to pay their respects and pray to the mummified monk. The initial radiographs not only demonstrated the sunglasses but also revealed another unusual artifact. Luang Pho Dang wore dentures (Figure 8.34). Endoscopy was conducted entering the oral pharynx through the mouth, the nasal cavity from the nares, and the endocranial cavity through the supraorbital fissure of the right eye. In each of these cavities, additional

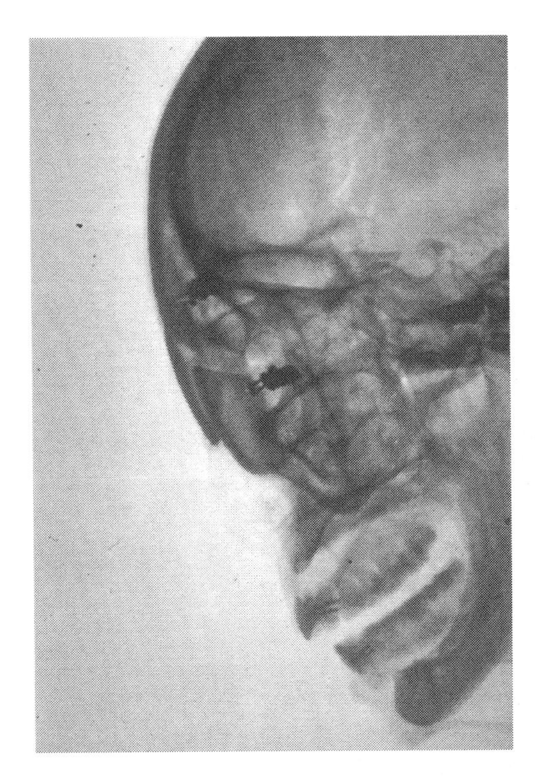

Figure 8.34. Lateral radiograph of Luang Pho Dang Piyasilo showing sunglasses and dentures.

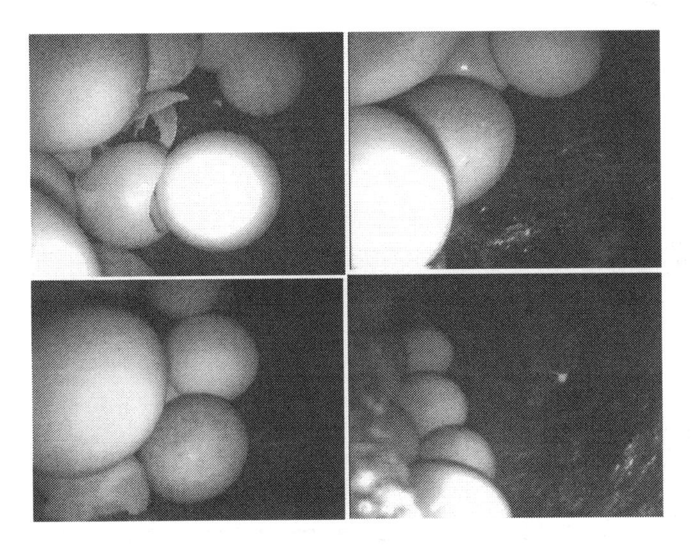

Figure 8.35. Endoscopic images of gecko eggs in the various cavities of Luang Pho Dang Piyasilo.

unusual artifacts were discovered. It appears that in death, true to the Buddhist belief of revering all living things, Luang Pho Dang had become a hatchery for a native gecko species (Figure 8.35). Whole eggs as well as eggs that had appeared to have hatched were found within these body cavities. Additional paleoimaging also revealed that Luang Pho Dang was remarkably well mummified with brain tissue and organs systems still intact although smaller in size due to dehydration (Figure 8.36).

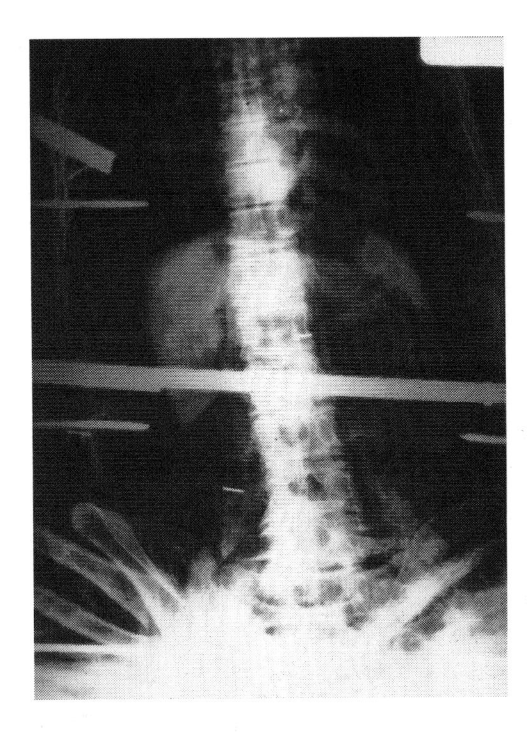

Figure 8.36. AP radiograph of Luang Pho Dang Piyasilo showing a clear liver shadow.

Significance

The case of Luang Pho Dang demonstrates again the value of using more than a single modality while also expanding preconceived objectives to include exploration of the subject within the limitations of the modalities. For the monks at the Wat Khunaram temple, the finding of the gecko eggs within the mummified remains of Luang Pho Dang became a lesson of the positive potentials of the practice of Buddhism.

Case 8.7: Lesion Biopsy in Philippi WV

Background

We present a case of a successful biopsy of a lesion within an artificially produced mummy from the late nineteenth century in Philippi, Barbour County, West Virginia. In 1888 Graham Hamrick developed a new method for embalming in an attempt to devise a safer method than using arsenic solutions. Hamrick experimented with his method by first applying it to the preservation of various samples of foods and mice. Hamrick then applied to the local courts for permission to perform his procedure on human corpses, and by court order the first two unclaimed bodies from the Trans-Allegheny Lunatic Asylum, now known as the Weston State Hospital, were given to him for this purpose. The bodies were treated with an arterial flush of a saltpeter solution, and were then exposed to sulfur fumes within a wooden box. In

1892, Hamrick received a patent for his procedure. The mummified remains are held in the Barbour County Historical Museum, located in the former railway station, in Philippi, where they remain to this day.

Based on the observed external genitalia, both mummies were female. In 2003 we examined both mummies using radiography, endoscopy, and CT scanning. We differentiated the two mummies on the basis of their current stature determined by physical measurement. The "short mummy" was approximately 62 inches (157.24 cms) in height and the "tall mummy" was approximately 68 inches (172.72 cms). Based on dental condition, lack of arthritic changes, and bone fusing patterns, it was determined that the taller mummy was approximately 30 to 40 years old, with the short mummy being in her mid-20s to early 30s at the time of death. CT scans revealed that the short mummy had more internal organ structures preserved when compared to the tall mummy. The short mummy also had a density in her left lung region that potentially represented pathology. Thus, the one known simply as "the short mummy" was selected as the subject of this case study.

The subject was well preserved with desiccated integument of a deep brown color. Neither mummy had hair, and it was reported to us that the mummies, after traveling with Barnum and Bailey and being on display at the Philippi Street Fair and the Barbour County Fair, were being stored in a local barn when a flood floated them down the street. The mummies were covered with mud and mold, and during cleaning their hair came off. Each had an anterior mid-abdominal cranial-caudal incision approximately 6 inches (15.24 cms) in length, which was a part of the mummification procedure as documented in the Patent for the method (United States Patent Number 466,524 [US466524A] January 5, 1892).

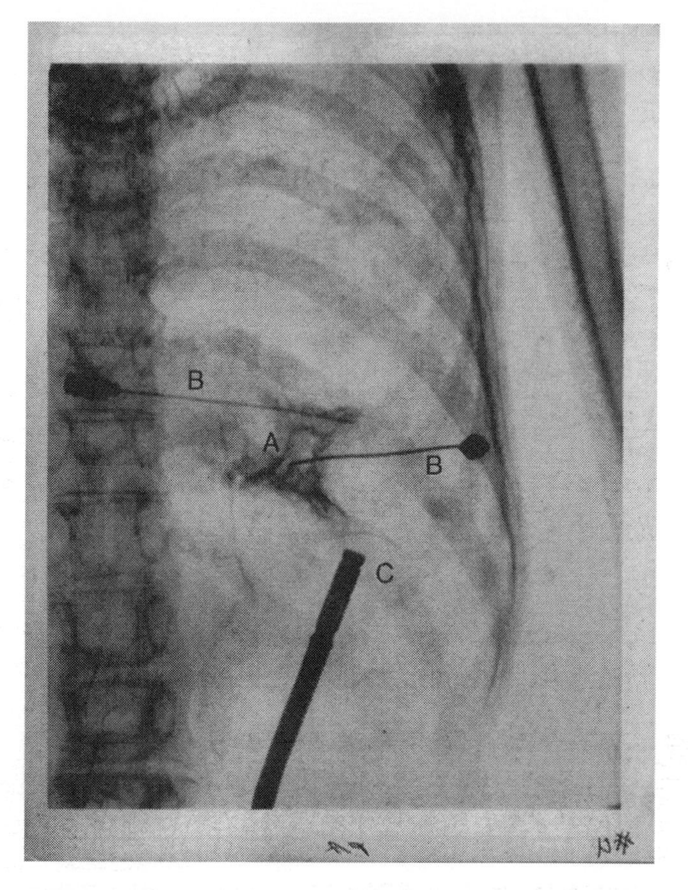

Figure 8.37. Posterior-anterior radiograph showing lesion in left lung (A). Spinal needles used for location and endoscopic guidance (B), and proximal end of endoscope in place (C).

Procedure and Diagnosis

The pathological diagnosis in this case was first presented by Woodward et al (2010) at the Paleopathology Association annual meeting in Albuquerque, New Mexico, and revisited by Woodward et al. (2011) at the 7th World Congress on Mummy Studies in San Diego, California. This case was also presented in Beckett and Conlogue (2018) describing the importance of understanding pathophysiology as it relates to the lived experience of individuals. Direct observation and radiography were employed in examining the mummies. A lesion was seen within the left lung on the posterior-anterior projection of the thorax (Figure 8.37). Spinal needles were place at a 90-degree angle from one another to assist the endoscope in accurately locating the lesion to assure successful biopsy. Once the lesion was visualized by endoscopy, a biopsy of the lesion was conducted under the endoscopic guidance (Figure 8.38). To access the lesion, a 0.5 cm (0.19 inch) "flap" was created and resealed following biopsy. The collected sample was sent to the University of Colorado Denver School of Medicine for pathological analysis.

Diagnosis by consensus was used to make the pathological determination. The interpreting team included a radiographer, an endoscopist, a radiologist skilled in interpreting images from mummified remains who offered opinion regarding the radiographic appearance, a bioanthropologist contributing the historical and regional context, and a paleopathologist who conducted the histological analysis at the University of Colorado Denver School of Medicine. Histology revealed enlarged terminal air spaces indicating a diagnosis of severe emphysema Further, the presence of stained coal macules and their distribution indicated that moderate to marked anthracosis was also present (Figure 8.39) based on the morphologic presentation and staining characteristics. Both emphysema and anthracosis were likely related to a life lived in close proximity to coal fuel, which was used in this context for heating and cooking.

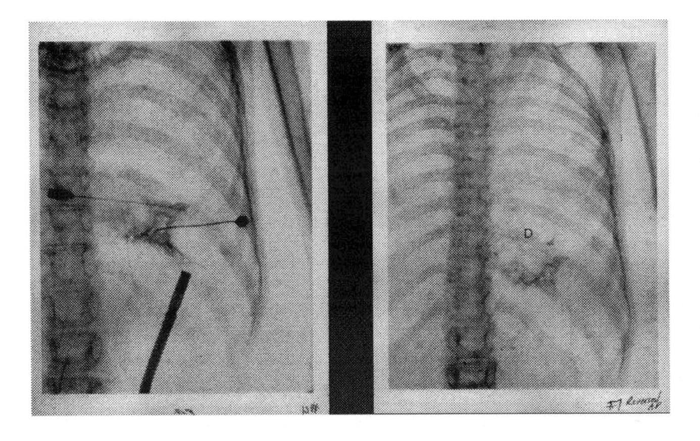

Figure 8.38. Posterior-anterior radiograph demonstrating successful biopsy of lesion on right image (D).

Furthermore, coal mining was the major industry of the region at that time.

Significance

It is important to note that the ability to determine a diagnosis was made possible by having preserved soft tissue available rather than merely the skeletal material alone. While it is clear that multiple modalities aided in the successful biopsy procedure, this case also brings in the concept of diagnosis by consensus and the utility of the bioarchaeology approach to understanding past lives. The case demonstrates the importance of using "many eyes" on the data to not only make a determination of the presence of disease but also to understand the impact of the context associated with the individual while living and the potential impact on the determined diagnosis.

Case 8.8: Ceramics

Characteristics of a culture can be derived from a variety of sources. Ceramics in particular can describe a culture in terms of the sophistication of its technologies,

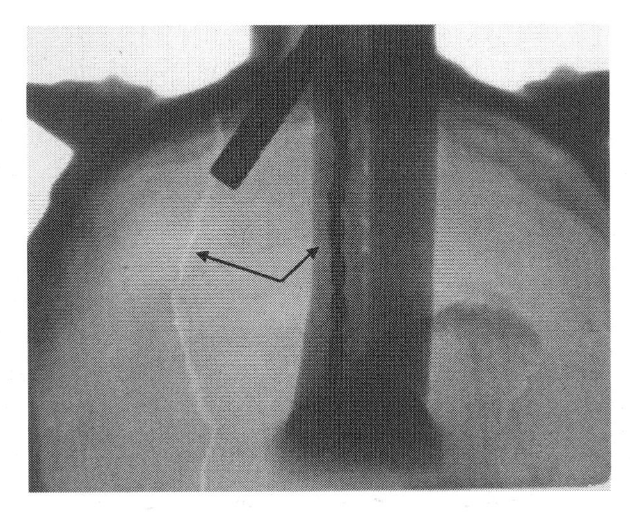

Figure 8.40. Radiograph documenting the location of the endoscope as it explores the internal features of a ceramic. The radiograph revealed repair efforts as well as a crack (arrows).

evidence of trade between and among ancient cultures, and insights derived from designs or associated iconography. It is logical then that ceramic artifacts be given critical scrutiny if researchers hope to divine all the information possible about their makers. Radiography, endoscopy, and advanced imaging modalities can all bring unique data regarding ceramics to bear on the understanding of ancient cultures.

Radiography and endoscopy can both provide complementary information regarding the condition of ceramics. The specific detailed procedural aspects of imaging ceramics can be found in *Paleoimaging: Field Applications for Cultural Remains and Artifacts* (Beckett and Conlogue 2010 CRC Press). As an example of the utility of ceramic analysis using paleoimaging methods, we describe a South American ceramic at the Yale Peabody museum in New Haven, Connecticut. A radiograph demonstrated that repair work had been done sometime in the past (Figure 8.40). A crack in the ceramic was also seen on the radiograph. The endoscope was able to examine the crack and record an

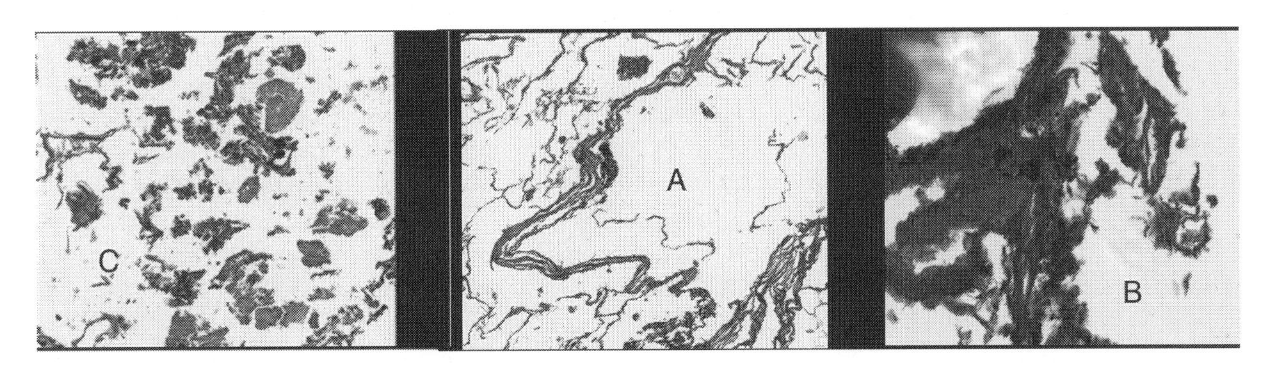

Figure 8.39. Histological analysis of tissue from the short mummy showing emphysema (A), anthracosis (B), and unidentified fungal matter (C).

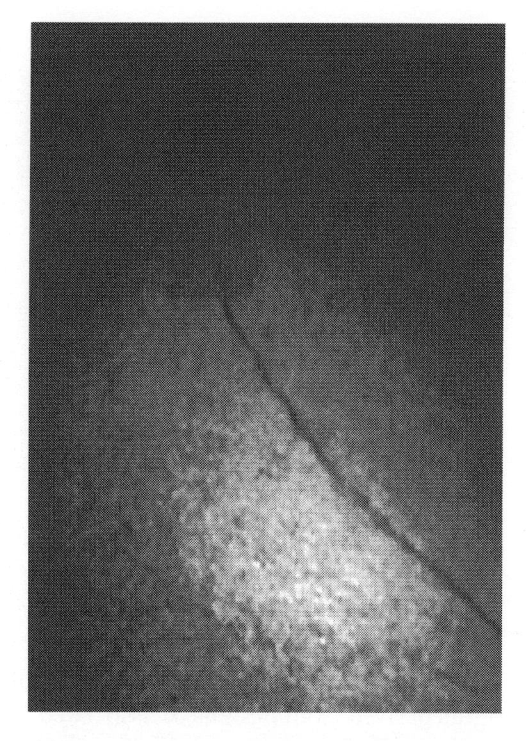

Figure 8.41. Endoscopic image of crack in the internal wall of the ceramic seen initially on X-ray.

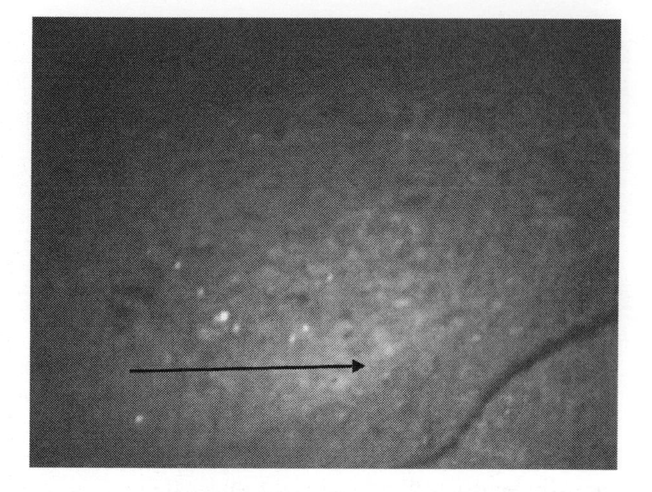

Figure 8.42. Endoscopic image of linear discoloration left by a fluid level (arrow). The ceramic was likely to have held a form of Chicha.

image for the museum (Figure 8.41). Another example of the importance of ceramic analysis is demonstrated in the study of a small Chiribaya ceramic associated with a child mummy from El Agarrobal, Peru. The endoscopic image (Figure 8.42) demonstrates the fluid level at the time of burial as well as the residual material of that fluid. The fluid was identified by examination of the residual material as being corn typically used to make Chicha, a fermented drink similar to modern beer.

The Whistle Pot

To demonstrate the field application of paleoimaging related to the imaging of complex ceramic objects, we present the following case.

An Inca whistle pot was found within the ruins of Tucume, near Chiclayo, Peru. Radiographs from various projections demonstrate the overall construction features of this specialized ceramic. The endoscope was passed into the ceramic and manipulated into position allowing visualization of the whistle mechanism within the ceramic, the structure within the structure (Figure 8.43). A radiograph documented the position of the endoscope within the pot. The data can now be incorporated into our understanding of how these specific function ceramics where made and inferences regarding the sophistication of the technology can be deduced (*Mummy Road Show—*Incas Unwrapped 2001).

If substances or objects are to be removed from within a ceramic under endoscopic guidance, it must be done in strict in accordance with the specific research goals and protocols. Samples of contents and scrapings can also be conducted under direct endoscopic visualization, documenting that the researcher is actually collecting what they believe they are collecting for further analysis.

Significance

This case demonstrates the utility of paleoimaging applications to not only ceramics but to ancient artifacts in general. The complementary data collected from as many imaging modalities as possible assures that the data collected is maximal in an attempt to better inform researchers about the cultural practices and the sophistication of technologies among peoples of the past.

Case 8.9: Preexcavation Tomb Analysis

Paleoimaging has also been applied in a variety of settings related to field archaeology. A critical issue surrounding the discovery of enclosed spaces such as ancient tombs is that of preexcavation knowledge regarding tomb structure and integrity. The tomb construction is considered an artifact of the external context, that is, the tomb is clearly in association with the mummified remains but not within them or their wrappings. In this purely field application we describe the utility of paleoimaging in preexcavation tomb analysis scenarios. Standard

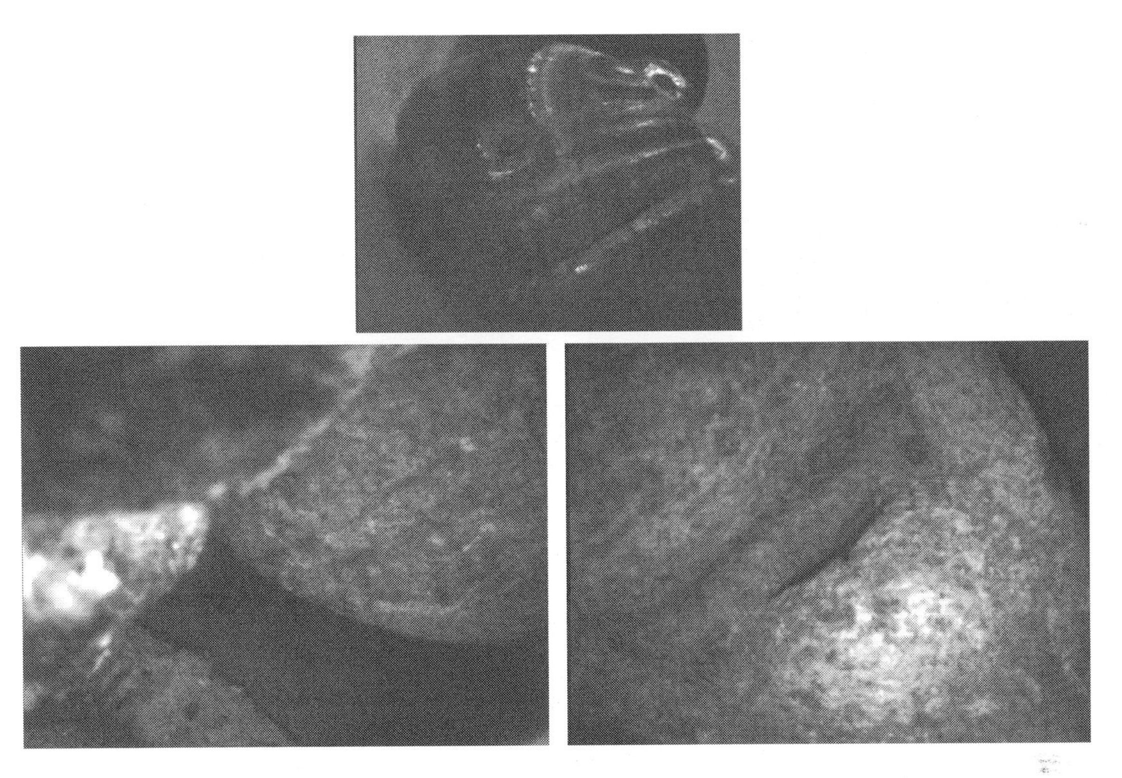

Figure 8.43. Endoscopic images of the whistle mechanism within the whistle pot pictured at top.

X-ray may not be able to be applied in this setting due to the need to place the image receptor on the opposite side of the subject, in this case a tomb wall or covering. However, if a small opening exists, endoscopy can "enter" the tomb and provide valuable data regarding the contents of the tomb, tomb construction features, and offer a cursory assessment of the tomb's integrity. These data give the archaeologist an opportunity to plan the excavation effort and prepare the research team for conservation of the artifacts or human remains from within the tomb.

Instrumentation selection is critical based on the objectives at hand. If it is a large room or vault being examined, four key features of the instrumentation need to be considered. The first is the length of the instrument. The presumed depth of the room or vault under investigation will dictate the length of the endoscope. Recall that industrial endoscopes can be 60 feet (18.28 m) in length.

The second consideration is that of illumination. Standard endoscope illumination abilities are generally exceeded when used in procedures involving even small, shallow tombs. It is therefore recommended that a "slave" scope or several fiberoptic light guides be used to enhance the illumination of enclosed tombs. This of course requires additional access route(s), fiberoptics, and light sources. Additional methods of illumination may require creative thinking at the site. Something as simple as a powerful flashlight or flashlights affixed to a ridged pole may suffice provided an access route of that size exists. Figure 8.44 presents a method of providing additional illumination for tomb analysis with a special light guide that bifurcates into two separate light guides.

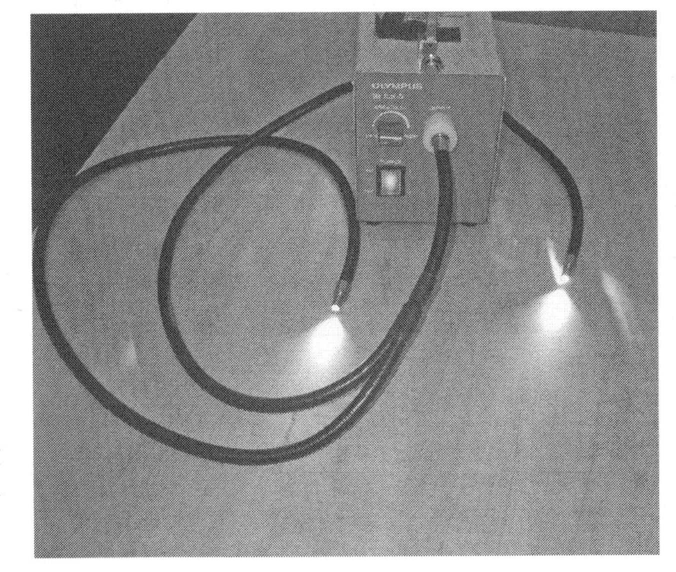

Figure 8.44. Special bifurcating light guide, which produces additional illumination in enclosed spaces such as tombs.

The third consideration is that of the selection of the proper lens. A near focus lens would not be able to bring distant objects into clear view. A far focus lens is required to view the distant reaches of the tomb, room

Figure 8.45. Distal tip of an endoscope protruding from the end of a pipe used to support the insertion tube over the length of the instrument. Note that the distal tip is still able to maneuver maintaining field of view flexibility.

Figure 8.46. Additional illumination and endoscope attached to a remote operated vehicle.

or vault. An ideal lens would be a stereo lens with one being a far focus and the other a near focus.

The final major consideration is that of insertion tube support. The fiberoptic instruments, whether industrial or medical, will follow the dependent nature of the open space. It would be important to consider a support system for the advancing scope such as a PVC or other type of pipe with just the tip of the endoscope extruding from the distal end. This method will still allow for a flexible viewing field (Figure 8.45) as the endoscope tip can still be manipulated. External illumination too may be affixed to the same support system. If the opening to the tomb, room, or vault is at the top of the space, this adaptation may not be necessary. Small remote controlled vehicles can be adapted to carry and therefore direct the advancement of a longer endoscope along the floor on a room under investigation. Additional illumination can be affixed to the remote vehicle (Figure 8.46). Additionally, remote video transmitters have also been employed for tomb analysis with reasonable success.

We present two case studies demonstrating the utility of endoscopic application to archaeological contexts. The first is a study of two ancient tombs of the Chiribaya culture. The second is the application in a modern setting where endoscopy was used to determine how many individuals were interred in a family burial tomb in Connecticut, USA.

Case Study 8.9.1: Postearthquake Tomb Analysis

In 2001, a powerful 8.0 magnitude earthquake struck southern Peru. The quake devastated the city of Moquegua. The tombs of the Chiribaya culture in the Osmore river valley of the Atacama Desert near El Agarrobal, near ILO, Peru, were impacted by the seismic event. This pre-Columbian culture dates from 900 to 1350 CE, spanning the middle horizon and the late intermediate time periods. There are literally thousands of such tombs in this remote river valley. The walls of the valley are essentially huge sandy dunes, which make up the foothills of the Andes. The Chiribaya tombs are located from 1 to 2 m (3.28 to 6.56 feet) below the desert surface among these sandy slopes. Each tomb typically holds an individual set of remains and associated grave goods. The tomb walls are often constructed of stone with dimensions of about 2 to 3 feet (0.66 to 1.0 m) wide and 3 to 5 feet (1.0 to 1.66 m) in length. The floor is generally packed earth. The depth of the tomb varies from 3 to 4 feet (1.0 to 1.33 m). The tomb may be covered with a mat constructed from reeds, with mud packing on top, then covered with sand. Alternate material used as a tomb cover may be a large capstone covered with sand. The surrounding sand is medium to fine grit and shifts with the changing winds. Preearthquake excavations have demonstrated that the Chiribaya tomb design effectively held any shifting sands outside of the tomb space. The earthquake shook the earth so violently in this region that the desert hills of the valley were pocked with depressions in the sand in the location of the subterranean tombs of the Chiribaya indicating that the surface sands had shifted into the tomb space. This was documented in the Mummy Road Show episode *Mummy Rescue* (2001b).

Even prior to the earthquake, huaqueros, or grave robbers, would routinely find Chiribaya tombs, unwrap the entombed mummies, and take the grave goods and textiles to be sold on the black market. Now, with the tombs marked by depressions in the sand, each tomb was in jeopardy of being ransacked and looted. We devised a plan to employ paleoimaging methodology to determine what impact, if any, the earthquake had on enclosed individual Chiribaya tombs and to assist in the development of plans for rescue excavation and conservation efforts.

Two tombs were examined prior to excavation using and industrial endoscope with a far focus lens. Since the earthquake occurred unexpectedly, modifications to the endoscopic instrumentation present needed to be considered. There was no time to acquire battery-powered instrumentation. The endoscopic instrumentation needed to be protected from the blowing sand and an electric power source needed to be procured. The endoscopic system was reduced to its smallest components with the instrument light source and camera control unit being fit into a backpack for protection from the environment. Tombs were selected that were near an access road. A passing taxi was flagged down, complete with a family inside. Researchers first attempted to use a power converter by accessing the taxi's battery through the cigarette lighter. The voltage output proved to be inadequate and a faint electric overheating smell filled the air. With the failure of this attempt at getting power, assistants drove back to Centro Mallqui, the research facility associated with the Chiribaya project, and retrieved a gasoline powered generator which did provide the power necessary once the output voltage was reduced by half.

Prior to endoscopic examination, sand was removed down to the level of the tomb roof exposing only an edge of the roof structure. Two tombs were examined, one having a large flat capstone roof and the other, a roof made of a mud covered woven reed mat. At the edge of the roof of the tomb with the capstone, a small opening was detected. With the instrumentation protected from the blowing sand, the endoscope was passed through the opening into the tomb. The endoscope image revealed that the tomb had partially filled with sand, burying the mummy inside. Additionally, the endoscope provided an image of a fissure in the tomb, likely produced by the earthquake, running diagonally the full length of the visible wall. This information allowed the project director to devise a plan for excavation which included precautions against cave in which would further damage the mummy and associated grave goods, as well as pose a physical risk to the workers.

While the excavation team began work on the initial tomb, the endoscopic operation was moved to the second tomb. Again a small opening was discovered along the edge of the roof. Internal construction features of the tomb were identified from the endoscope images. The walls were of piled stone and the roof was a sturdy mat of woven reeds (Figure 8.47) likely obtained from the nearby river valley. The wall construction features suggested that a mud-type mortar had been used to secure the stones of the wall in place (Figure 8.48). The endoscope revealed

Figure 8.47. Endoscopic image using a far focus lens showing the internal construction features of this Chiribaya tomb. Note the stone wall and its junction with the reed mat tomb ceiling.

Figure 8.48. Endoscopic image using a far focus lens of wall construction details. Note apparent mud-type mortar between the stones holding the rocks in place as well as keeping shifting sands out of the tomb.

Figure 8.49. Endoscopic image using a far focus lens showing a view of the sand that had entered the tomb following the seismic activity.

Figure 8.50. Endoscopic image using a far focus lens looking upward providing a view of the construction details of the reed mat used as a tomb cap.

that sand had indeed sifted into the tomb as a result of the earthquake (Figure 8.49). Using the endoscope to look upwards, the construction details of the reed mat roof could be seen clearly (Figure 8.50). Examining the area of the sand slide with the endoscope a glimpse of buried textile came into the field of view (Figure 8.51) suggesting that a mummy may be present under the sand. After additional survey of the tomb, the endoscope revealed a partially buried mummy whose head was just visible above the encroaching sand. The mummy wore a hat that was identified from the endoscopic image (Figure 8.52) by the project director as being of the Tiahuanacu culture. Using the endoscopic information, excavation and conservation plans were devised.

Since access into the tombs was from the top, support for the fiberoptic instrument was not required in this application. A far focus lens was utilized, which on this particular industrial scope, allowed ample light

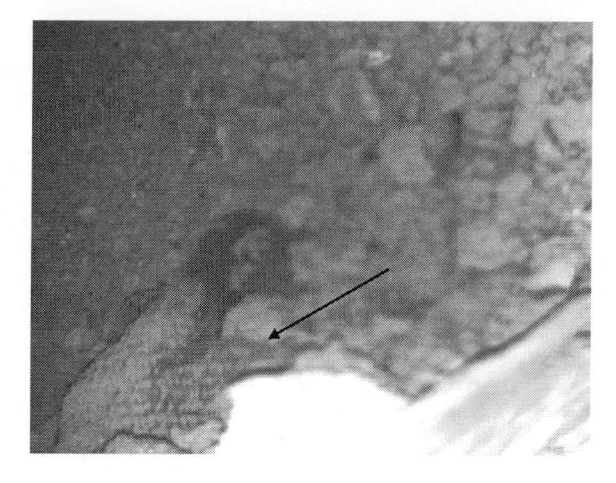

Figure 8.51. Endoscopic image showing the first evidence of remains within the tomb, a small section of textile (arrow).

to provide a well illuminated field of view. The 4-foot length of this endoscope proved to be sufficient for its application to these two Chiribaya tombs.

Case Study 8.9.2: The Starr Burial Vault—Who's in the tomb?

We were contacted in 2013 by Nick Bellantoni, Connecticut state archaeologist, to help with two projects. One was to help analyze an unearthed time capsule (described earlier in this volume) and the other request was to help determine how many people were interred in a family burial vault located in a central Connecticut cemetery. The vault, dated from 1804 (Figure 8.53) belonged to the Starr family, and both the cemetery and family records had been lost over time.

The vault was sealed and had a stone door at the entrance (Figure 8.54). There was a small natural opening at an upper margin of the vault which served as the initial entry point for endoscopy. A battery-operated articulating industrial 7 mm (0.078 inch) diameter, 4 foot (1.22 m) long endoscope was used for the project (Figure 8.55). The endoscope was introduced at the vault margin (Figure 8.56) and was able to collect only minimal images. The vault was deep and wide and it became clear that some sort slave illumination would be needed. After a quick visit to nearby hardware store, a slave illumination system was constructed. A refrigerator light bulb was selected as it was narrow in diameter and we hoped to make only the smallest opening into the vault for the additional illumination. An electric extension cord was purchased and one end was cut off. The wires were stripped and affixed directly to the refrigerator bulb using electrician's tape. Once completed and tested

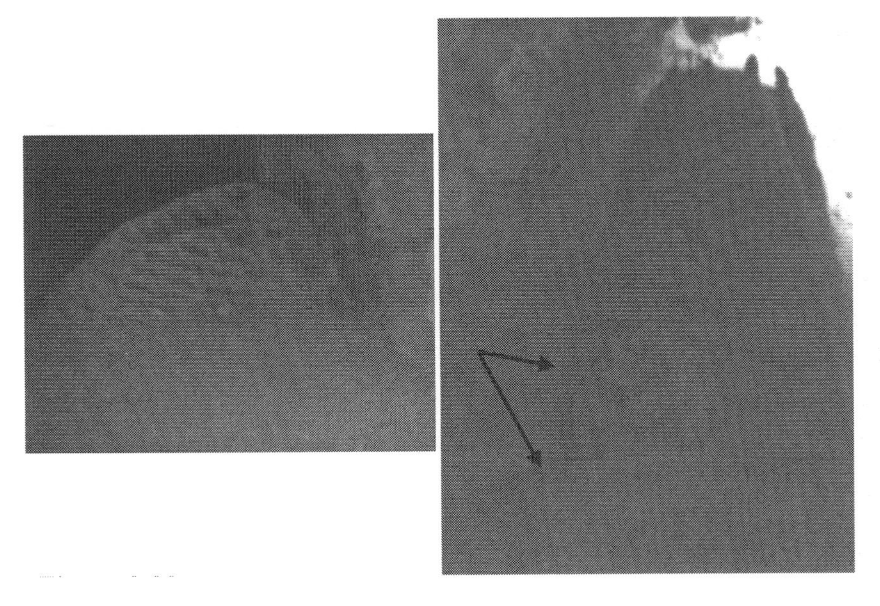

Figure 8.52. Two endoscopic views of the mummified remains wearing a hat. Image on the right shows the location of the face of the individual and the sand level that had sifted into the tomb from the seismic activity (arrows).

Figure 8.53. Engraving on the Starr family burial vault indicating the date 1804.

Figure 8.55. Portable articulating industrial endoscope used for the study.

Figure 8.54. Front view of the Starr burial vault showing stone entrance.

Figure 8.56. Endoscope introduce through vault door margin.

Figure 8.57. (A) & (B) Slave illumination constructed from a refrigerator bulb and modified extension cord (left image). Successful test of slave illumination (right image).

Figure 8.58. Access point being drilled through the roof of the burial vault.

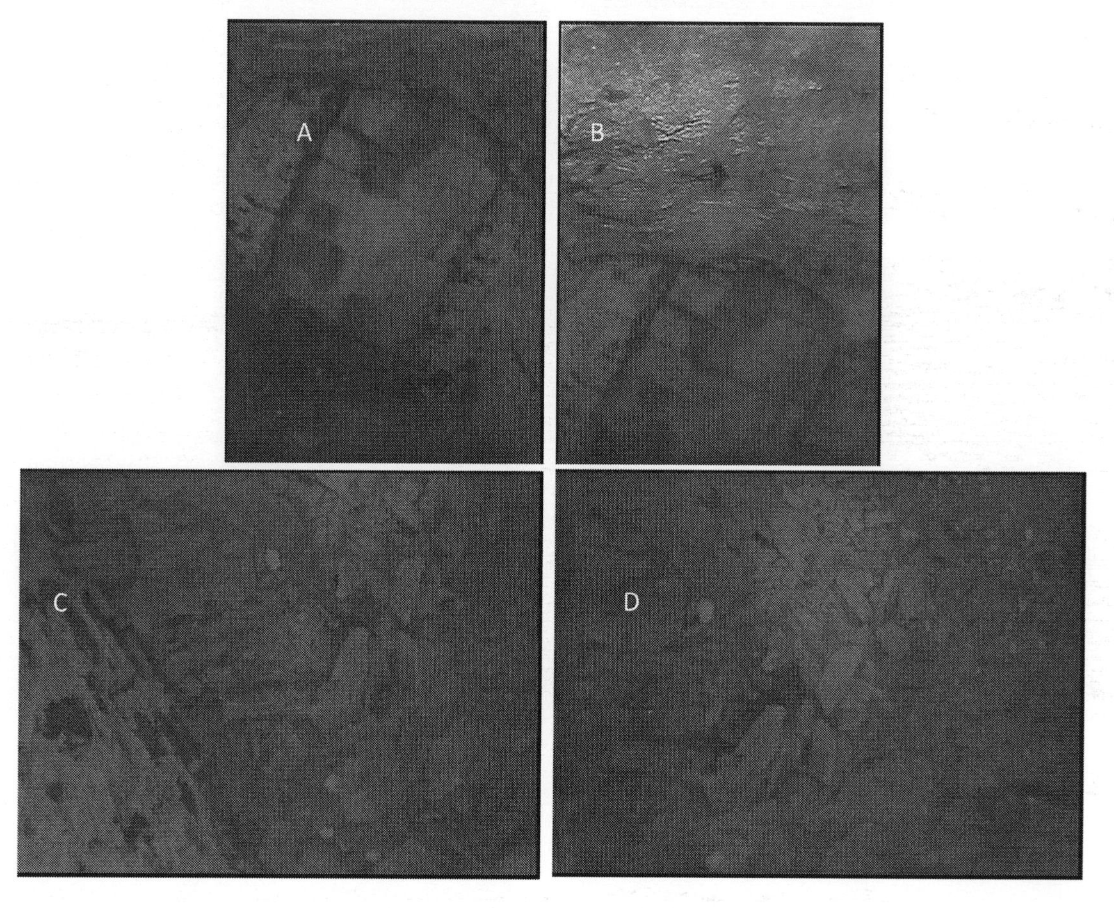

Figure 8.59. Initial endoscopic images from within burial vault showing interior of vault door (A), ceiling at front of vault (B), Coffin fragments within vault along the east and north walls (C and D).

(Figure 8.57), we were able to proceed with our burial vault analysis.

Because the entry route at the vault door margin provided only limited visualization of the entire tomb, Nick suggested that we create an opening in the tomb roof. This would allow the endoscope and slave illumination to be introduced into a single opening that would be resealed once the study was completed. The other advantage of using a roof access point is that the endoscope would have complete visual field of the entire vault interior. Also, there would be no need to construct a support device for the endoscope as gravity would keep the instrument in a relatively central location. Given that the instrument was articulating, we would be able to collect images from every aspect of the internal tomb space. An auger drill was used to make the entry point (Figure 8.58) in the rook of the tomb.

Once the endoscope and slave illumination system were introduced into the opening in the vault roof, several images were captured (Figure 8.59). At this point

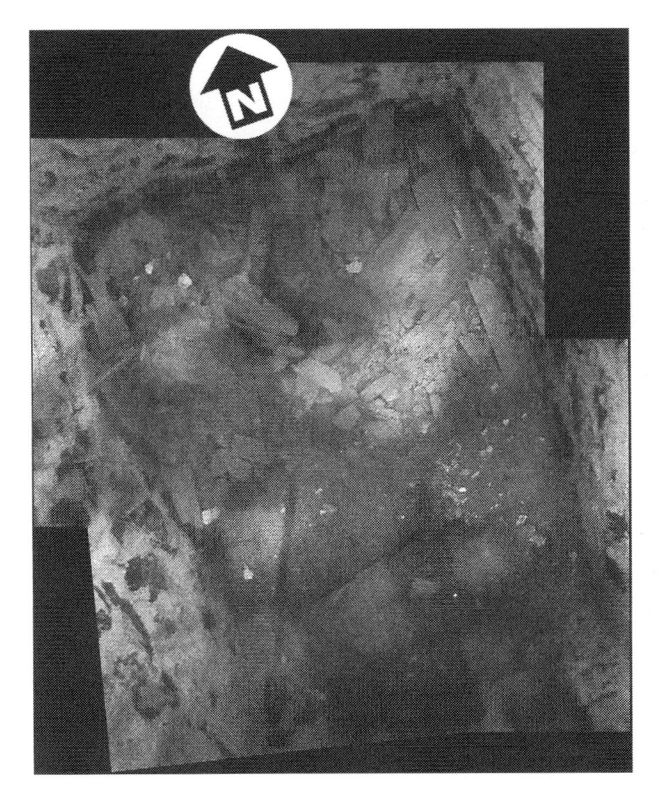

Figure 8.60. Composite image constructed from various endoscopic images of the interior of the Starr burial vault showing four burials.

it was still difficult to determine how many individuals were interred in the vault. The endoscopic images were taken to the Office of the Connecticut State Archaeologist where the puzzle of images was made into a composite image of the entire interior of the burial vault (Figure 8.60). Nick Bellantoni was able to satisfy the objective of the study and determined that there were four burials within the Starr Vault. Once the images were collected, the access port in the roof was resealed (Figure 8.61) and the sod replaced over the top of the vault.

Significance

The field endoscopy applications described in these cases demonstrates the utility of paleoimaging in the broader construct of archaeological applications. Additionally, the endoscopic application can contribute to answering more contemporary research questions as well as those from ancient peoples. Endoscopy has also been used to answer current research questions. As an example, a study was conducted to better understand the process of mummification in a Chiribaya style tomb using swine analogs (Garcia et al 2014). This research was carried out in the desert of South Central Arizona. Although not

Figure 8.61. Starr vault roof being resealed.

the Atacama desert, the dry sands and soil added to the validity of this study. Endoscopy, along with data loggers were employed to monitor changes within the tomb environment while making observations of the subject at specific intervals.

Although only endoscopy was employed in these cases, all paleoimaging modalities must be considered. In one case, plane radiography was able to be used on an individual mummy still within its tomb. The key is to have multiple modalities at the ready as each contributes unique sets of data to the research questions at hand.

Case 8.10: XRF: Varied Applications

Case 8.10.1: Homogeneity of Clay

In 2008 and again in 2010 we organized expeditions into the fringe highlands in the Aseki region of the Morobe province in Papua New Guinea. The objectives of the expeditions included determining the Smoked Body Mummification method of the Anga culture. One of the final steps in the mummification process is to rub local ochre clay onto the mummified remains. Smoked body mummification was widespread throughout the region and we hoped to determine if there were regional variations in the elemental makeup of the ochre clay used for this purpose with the idea of determining where a mummy or groups of mummies originated. We used a Bruker Tracer III XRF handheld analyzer to examine clays from a broad region of Aseki (Figure 8.62) including several sites known to hold mummies. XRF was also used on the clay that was on the mummy itself (Figure 8.63). Our findings indicated that the clays from all the regions

Figure 8.62. XRF in use examining various clay samples from the Aseki region of the Morobe Province in Papua New Guinea.

Figure 8.63. XRF of clay used in cultural practices of the Anga. Clay is being analyzed on the surface of an Anga mummy, which was compared to regional clay samples.

were in fact quite homogeneous. The next step would be to broaden the geographical reach of our study to beyond the Aseki region. A more complete description of the Smoked Body mummification method can be found in Beckett and Nelson (2015), Beckett (2015), and Beckett et al (2011).

Case 8.10.2: The Wax Masks of Gangi

In 2015, with funding from a National Geographic/Waitts Foundation grant (#W345-14), we examined a group of mummies in Gangi, Sicily. The goals of our research were to explored the bioarchaeological characteristics of the Gangi mummies. These mummies are a unique group of preserved human remains from the burial crypts in Gangi, Sicily. The 60 mummies date from the early 18th through the 19th centuries and are located in the mother church of Saint Nicolo of Bari.

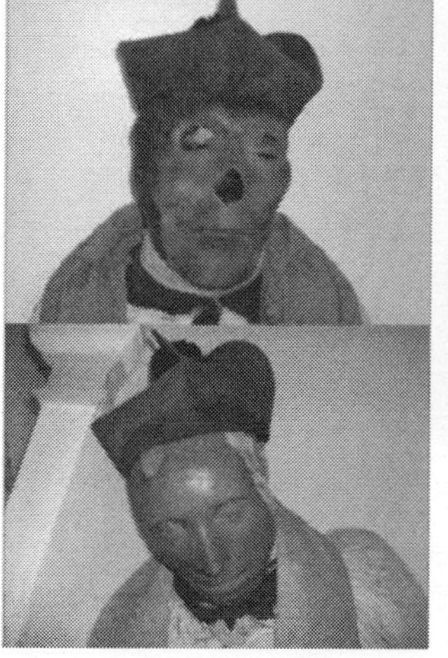

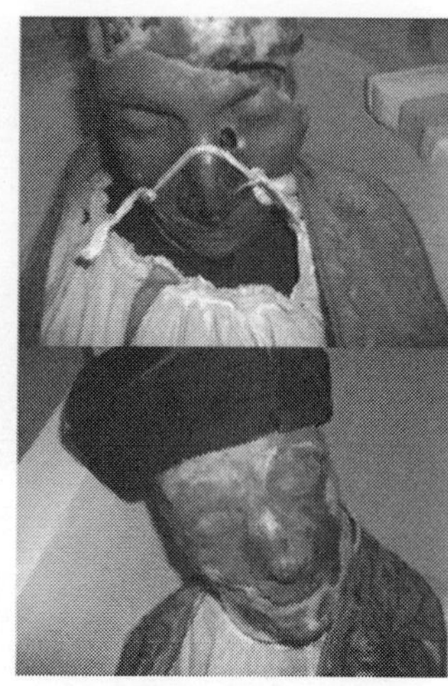

Figure 8.64. Overmodeled faces/heads with wax in Gangi, Sicily. Note the varied stages of preservation.

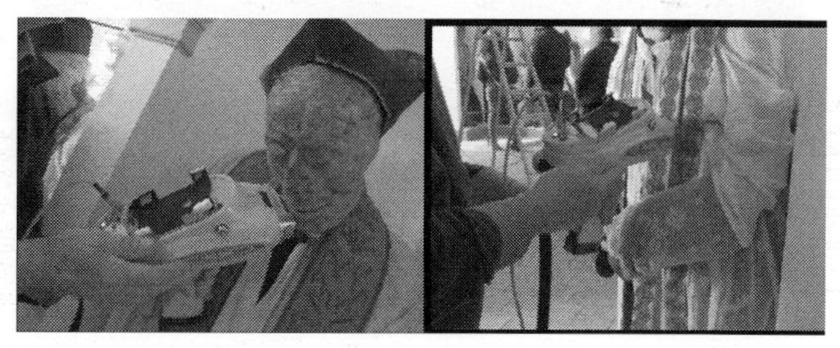

Figure 8.65. Bruker Tracer III Handheld XRF analyzer in use in Gangi, Sicily. Targeted here is a wax mask (left) and metallic thread in the vestments (right).

Often referred to as the "waxed mummies," these individuals have waxlike masks covering most of the face, likely used to give a more lifelike appearance. The intent of this expedition was to conduct paleoimaging and bioarchaeological analysis of the entire Gangi group within the crypts and within the time constraints of this study.

Interestingly, at least 41 of these mummies show a peculiar treatment consisting of an overmodeling of the face with wax (Figure 8.64). This was at times roughly made in the form of a partial reconstruction of the features. However, some specimens showed a proper wax mask, at times colored to obtain a more realistic appearance (Piombino-Mascali and Zink 2012).

X-ray fluorescence analysis was conducted with a portable Bruker Tracer III hand held unit with S1PXRF software provided by the manufacturer (Figure 8.65). Elemental analysis was used to determine the make-up and homogeneity of the wax masks as well as to determine the nature of vestments with apparent metallic thread.

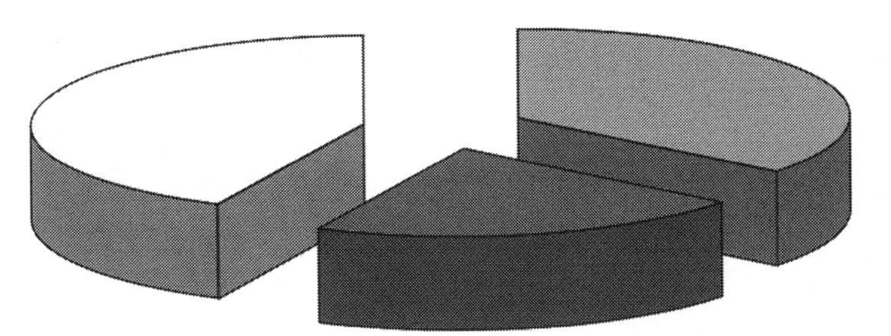

Figure 8.66. Wax mask distribution by type among the Gangi mummies.

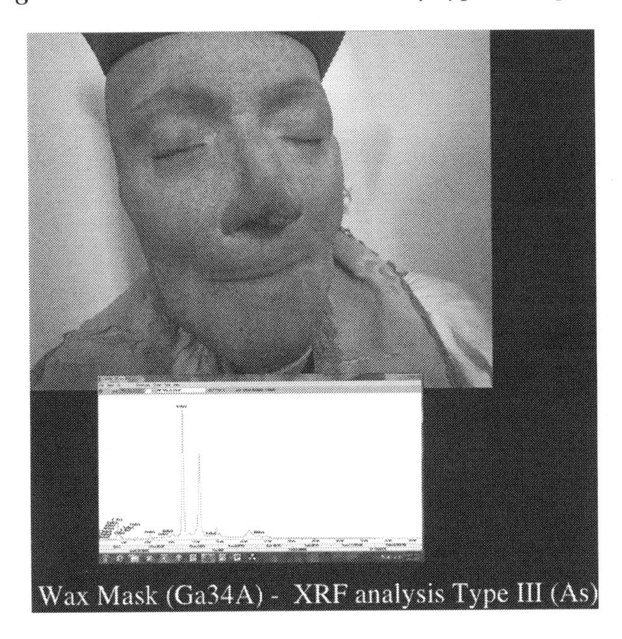

Figure 8.67. XRF tracing showing arsenic at the highest peak on a wax mask.

XRF analysis was conducted on 41 wax masks as well as several vestments worn by the mummies. Additional mummies showed evidence of wax modeling with only a few wax remnants available for analysis. Using XRF analysis we discovered that the chemistry of the wax masks varied and fell into three broad categories; type I (N=15) has elevated Calcium, type II (N=9) has lower calcium with higher chloride and nickel, and type III (N=16) has elevated arsenic. Type distribution can be found in Figure 8.66. The representative appearance and XRF analysis of type III is displayed in Figure 8.67. XRF examination of the vestments demonstrated that the metallic threads seen on radiograph were primarily made of copper and silver.

Case 8.10.3: Sylvester: Ye Olde Curiosity Shop, Seattle, Washington (we refer the reader back to Case Study 4 of this text for background on this case)

As stated in Case Study 4 of this text, multimodal analysis was conducted on *Sylvester* on a variety of occasions.

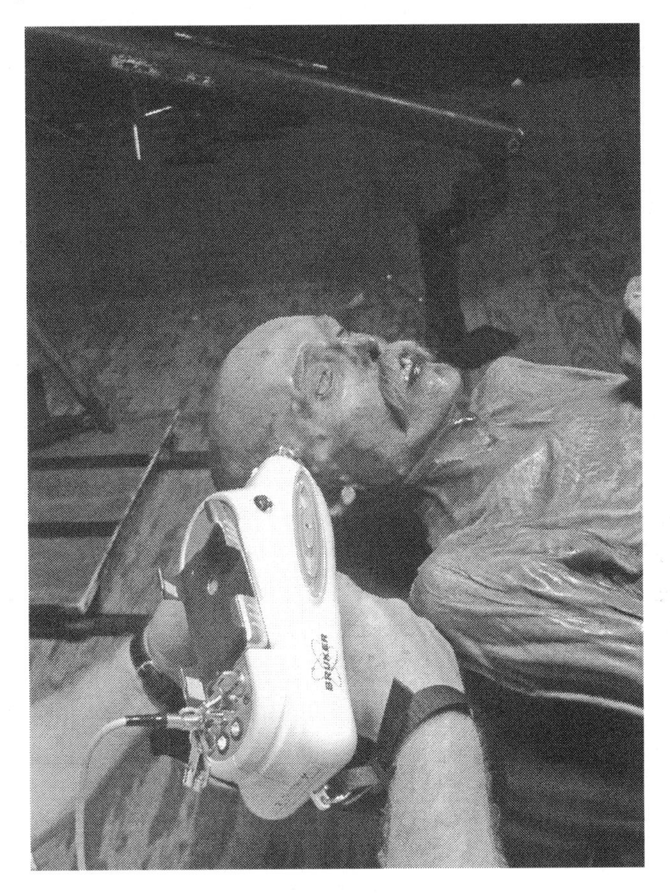

Figure 8.68. Bruker Tracer III handheld XRF instrument collecting data from "pellet" on the lateral side of *Sylvester*'s head.

In 2015, while examining *Sylvester* for the documentary *The Gunslinger Mummy* for the Mummies Alive Series on the Smithsonian Channel, XRF analysis was conducted in an attempt to determine the elemental mmake-up of the pellets and to verify the presence of arsenic in the surface tissues of the mummy.

Elemental analysis was conducted with a portable Bruker Tracer III hand-held unit with S1PXRF software provided by the manufacturer (Figure 8.68). The XRF device was focused on one of the raised areas on the side of the mummy's face where a pellet was known to be lodged as determined by X-ray

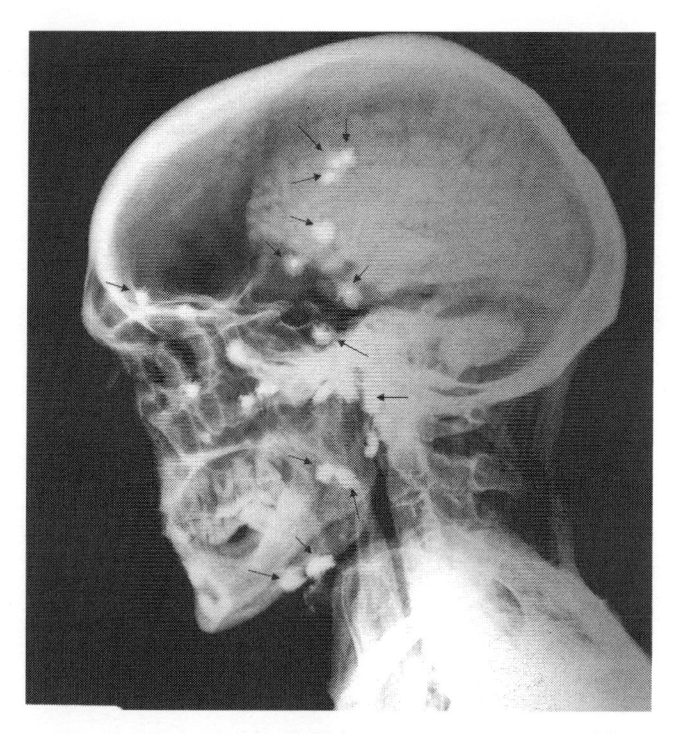

Figure 8.69. Lateral Radiograph showing multiple hyper densities on *Sylvester*'s head.

(Figure 8.69). The tracing indicated that the pellet was made predominately of lead in its elemental makeup (Figure 8.70). For comparison, a civil war bullet curated at Ye Olde Curiosity Shoppe was also examined for elemental makeup. The XRF tracing was similar to that of the pellets associated with Sylvester (Figure 8.71) also showing a spike in the lead tracing. Although this does not suggest that the mummy was in the Civil War, it rules out any other metal types associated with *Sylvester*'s pellets.

XRF analysis was also conducted on the surface of the mummy in several locations (Figure 8.72) with each tracing indicating high concentrations of arsenic. As previously described (see Case Study 4), arsenic was used as an embalming method starting toward the end of the Civil War in the United States, with continued use into the early twentieth century.

In this case XRF proved useful in identifying the elemental makeup of a metallic anomaly as well as help to verify the presence of arsenic used to embalm *Sylvester*. The fact that there is so much arsenic associated with the tissues of this mummy, the Ye Old Curiosity Shoppe was advised to assure that visitors did not come in contact with the mummy.

Case 8.10.4: Mütter Museum: Library Books

In 2018 we are asked to study various items at the Mütter Museum in Philadelphia, Pennsylvania. Discussion regarding other XRF aspects of this study can be found in Case Studies 5 and 7 of this volume. Here we present the results of XRF analysis used to determine the elemental make-up of pigments used in old fifteenth-century books from the library at the museum. Different paint pigmentation practices were used in varied geographic locations, thus, the elements used to create pigments could help determine where the particular text originated.

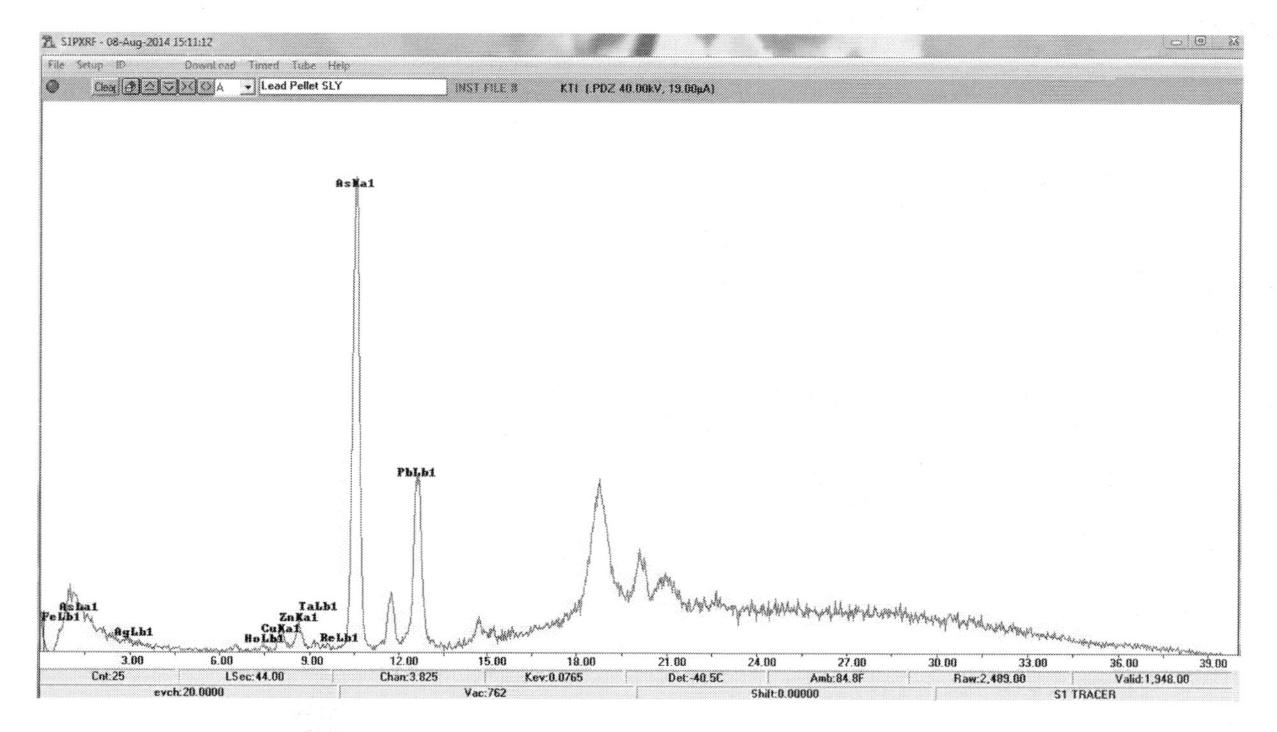

Figure 8.70. XRF tracing showing lead as a major component of the pellet on *Sylvester*. Note the arsenic level as well.

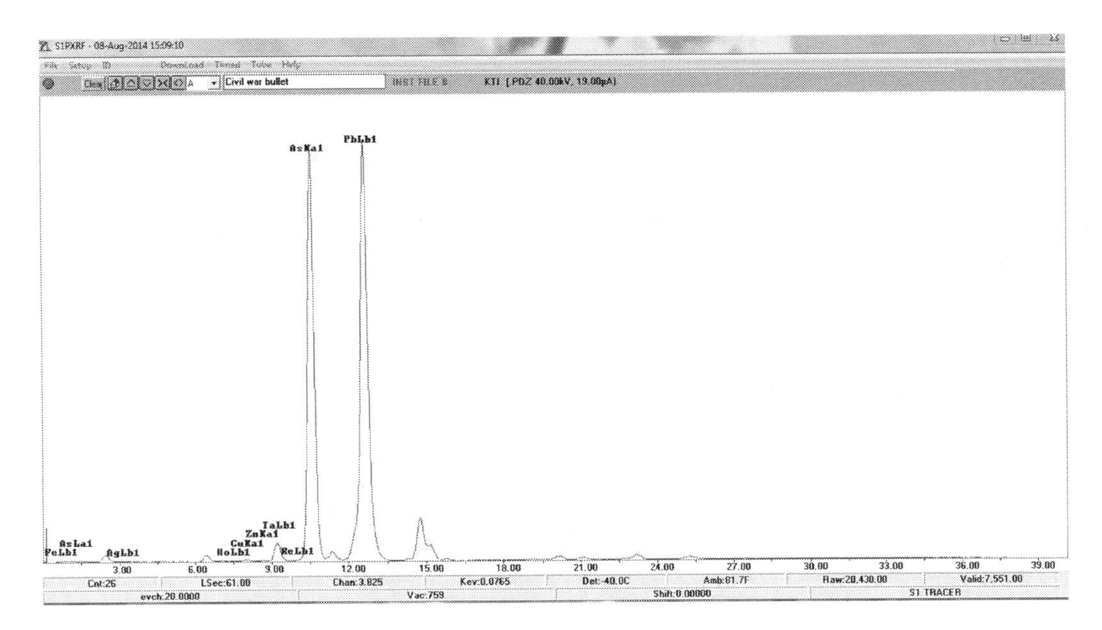

Figure 8.71. XRF tracing showing lead as major component of a civil war era bullet. Interestingly, the arsenic level was also quite high.

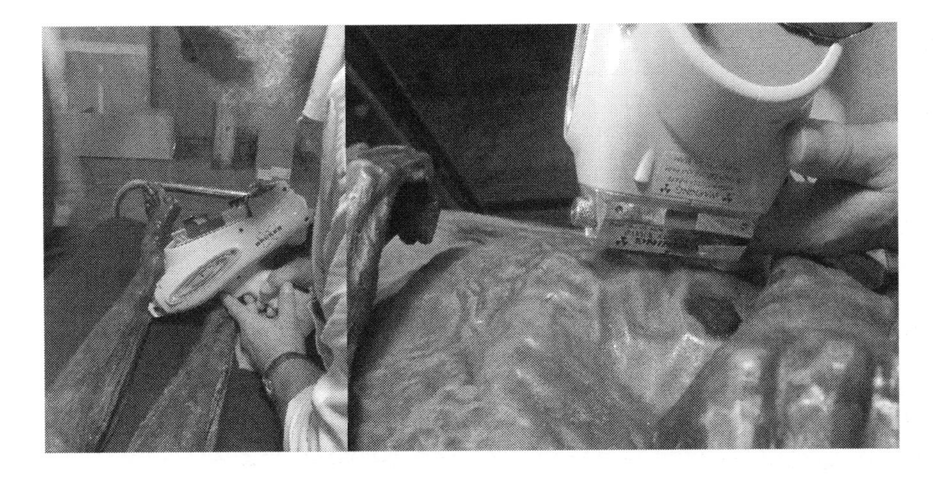

Figure 8.72. XRF in use on *Sylvester*'s inner left leg and torso.

One of the books analyzed was from circa 1471 CE (Figure 8.73). The green and red appearing colors were targeted. The results indicated that the major element in the green pigment was copper while the main elements found in the red pigment were iron and zinc (Figure 8.74).

The pigments used in an older text from the early fourteenth century were analyzed. Blue, orange, and red were analyzed and compared to other texts having similar colors. The variation among the texts indicated that there were distinct differences among the pigments used in the coloration of these ancient texts.

Figure 8.73. Pigmented art in circa 1471 AD book. Several colors were the target of XRF analysis.

Significance

These four mini cases demonstrate the utility of XRF analysis as a complementary method to the paleoimaging arsenal. Analysis of soils, clays, and stones can

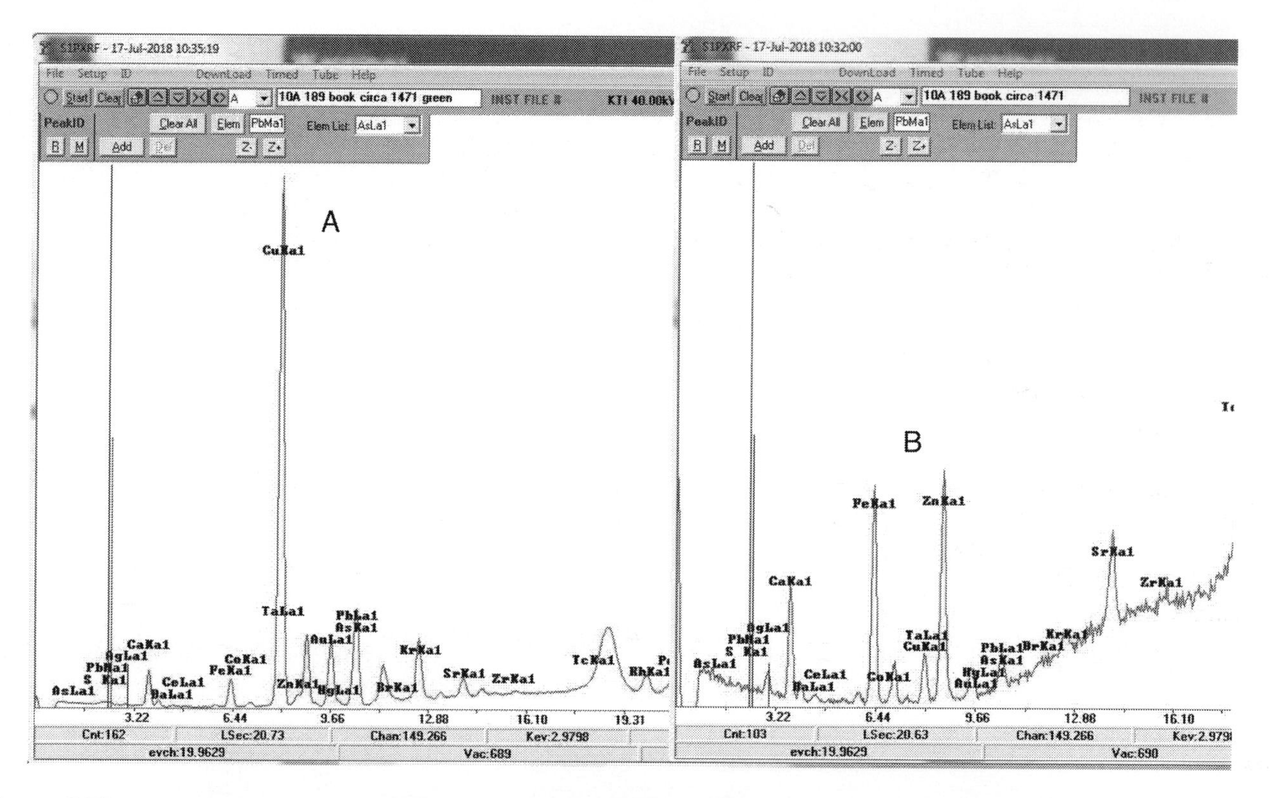

Figure 8.74. Two XRF scans showing (A) copper as the main element associated with the green pigment with iron and zinc being the major components of the red pigment (B).

help determine were associated items in a given study originated informing researchers about the migration of remains or objects. Funerary and conservation practices can be assessed by employing XRF to determine the elemental makeup of materials used in such efforts as was the case of the wax masks of Gangi. The chemical components of mummification and/or embalming solutions can be identified in a nondestructive manner using XRF analysis. Associated artifacts of interest too can be analyzed, as can discolorations left by degraded metals on the surface of a set of remains be identified effectively. The use of XRF on the pigments of the ancient books attest to the breadth of application of this modality.

All of the data collected enhances our understanding of both specific and general research questions. While the instrumentation is on the expensive side, the information derived can be invaluable to a given study and we encourage readers to explore XRF applications in any and all settings.

References

Beckett, R.G. National Geographic Society/Waitt Grants Program. *A Bioarchaeologic and Paleoimaging Exploration of the Gangi and Capuchin Mummies of Sicily, Italy—Rescuing the Past (W345-14)* (January 2015).

Beckett, R.G. Smoked Bodies of Papua New Guinea. In *Mummies Around the World: An Encyclopedia of Mummies in History, Religion, and Popular Culture*, pp. 389–393, Matt Cardin, Ed. ABC-CLIO, LLC, Santa Barbara, CA (2015). ISBN 978-1-61069-419-3

Beckett, R.G., and Conlogue, G. Buddhist Self Mummification. In *Mummies Around the World: An Encyclopedia of Mummies in History, Religion, and Popular Culture*, pp. 47–50, Matt Cardin, Ed. ABC-CLIO, LLC, Santa Barbara, CA (2015). ISBN 978-1-61069-419-3

Beckett, R.G., and Conlogue, G.J. (eds). *Paleoimaging: Field Applications for Cultural Remains and Artifacts.* CRC Press (Taylor & Francis) (September 2010). ISBN 10:1420090712, ISBN 13:978-1420090710

Beckett, R.G., and Conlogue, G.J. The Importance of Pathophysiology to the Understanding of Functional Limitations in the Bioarchaeology of Care Approach. *International Journal of Paleopathology* (July 2018). doi:10.1016/j/ijpp.2018.06.006

Beckett, R.G., and Guillen, S. Field Videoendoscopy—A Pilot Project at Centro Mallqui, El Algarrobal, Peru. Papers on Paleopathology presented at the 27th Annual Meeting, April 11–12, 2000. Supplement to Paleopathology Newsletter, No. 110 (June 2000).

Beckett, R.G., and Nelson, A.J. Mummy Restoration Project Among the Anga of Papua New Guinea. *The Anatomical Record* 298(6):1013–1025 (2015).

Beckett, R.G., Lohmann, U., and Bernstein, J. A Field Report on the Mummification Practices of the Anga of Koke Village, Central Highlands, Papua New Guinea. In

Yearbook of Mummy Studies, Volume 1, pp. 11–17, Dario Piombino-Mascali, Guest Editor. Accademia Eurpea di Bolzano, Bolzano, Italy (2011). ISBN 978-3-89937-137-6. EURAC, Bolzano, Italy, June 2011.

Bellantoni, N. personal communication (2005), personal interview.

Conlogue, G.R, Beckett, J., Posh, Y., Bailey, D., Henderson, G., and Double, T.K. Paleoimaging: The Use of Radiography, Magnetic Resonance and Endoscopy to Examine Mummified Remains. *Journal of Radiology Nursing* 27(1):5–13 (2008).

Garcia, A.M.B., Beckett, R.G., and Watson, J. Internal Environmental Characteristics of a Chiribaya Style Tomb Holding Swine Remains and Their Taphonomic Impact on Decomposition Delay, a Requisite for Mummification. Papers on Anthropology, Special Edition (July 2014).

Mummy Road Show. Incas Unwrapped. Engle Brothers Media (2001).

Mummy Road Show. A Head for Science. Engle Brothers Media (2003).

Piombino-Mascali, D., and Zink, A.R. Überlegungen zu den Mumien von Gangi und ihren Wachsmasken. *Mannheimer Geschichtblätter, Bd* 53: 65–69 (2012).

Ventura, L., Leocata, P., Beckett, R., Conlogue, G., Sindici, G., Calabrese, A., Di Giandomenico, V., and Fornaciari, G. The Natural Mummies of Popoli. A New Site in the Inner Abruzzo Region (Central Italy). *Anthropologia Portuguese* 19: 1–2 (2002). ISSN 0870-0990 Pub. Spring 2004.

Woodward, J., Gonzalez, R., Beckett, R., Conlogue, G., Cool, C., and Groshong, S. Lung Lesion Biopsy of 19th Century West Virginia Mummy. Paleopathology Association 37th Annual Meeting (North America), Albuquerque, NM (April 13th–14th 2010).

Woodward, J., Gaither, C., Gonzalez, R., Beckett, R.G., Conlogue, G.J., Cool, C., and Groshong, S. Rethinking Anthracosis: A Critical Re-examination of a Diagnostic Trend (Case Study from a 19th Century West Virginian Mummy). 7th World Congress on Mummy Studies, San Diego, California (June 12–16 2011). Poster presentation..

Index

Note: Page numbers followed by "*f*" refer to figures.